Computer Graphics and Visualisation

Computer Graphics and Visualisation

Editor:

Ivan Stanimirović, Ph.D.

ArclerPress

www.arclerpress.com

Computer Graphics and Visualisation

Editor: Ivan Stanimirović, Ph.D.

708 3rd Avenue, 6th Floor
New York
NY 10017
United States of America
www.arclerpress.com

ISBN: 978-1-68094-444-0

Library of Congress Control Number: 2016951369

About the Editor

Ivan Stanimirović, Ph.D.

Ivan Stanimirović gained his PhD from University of Niš, Serbia in 2013. His work spans from multi-objective optimization methods to applications of generalized matrix inverses in areas such as image processing and computer graphics and visualisations. He is currently working as an Assistant professor at Faculty of Sciences and Mathematics at University of Niš on computing generalized matrix inverses and its applications.

Contents

List of Contributors

Martin Lambers
University of Siegen, Germany

Andrew Glassner
The Imaginary Institute

Takahito Tejima
Pixar Animation Studios

Masahiro Fujita
Light Transport Entertainment

Toru Matsuoka
DeNA Inc

Bimal Kumar Ray
School of Information Technology & Engineering VIT University, Vellore – 632014, India

Marcos Vinicius Mussel Cirne
Institute of Computing, University of Campinas, Campinas, SP13083-852, Brazil

Hélio Pedrini
Institute of Computing, University of Campinas, Campinas, SP13083-852, Brazil

Yuen-Shan Leung
School of Computer Engineering, Nanyang Technological University, Singapore

Xiaoning Wang
School of Computer Engineering, Nanyang Technological University, Singapore

Ying He
School of Computer Engineering, Nanyang Technological University, Singapore

Yong-Jin Liu
Department of Computer Science and Technology, Tsinghua University, China

Charlie C. L. Wang
Department of Mechanical and Automation Engineering, The Chinese University of Hong Kong, Hong Kong, China

Kang Chen
Tsinghua University, Beijing 100084, China

Yu-Kun Lai
Cardiff University, Cardiff, CF24 3AA, Wales, UK

Shi-Min Hu
Tsinghua University, Beijing 100084, China

Chen Gong
School of Energy and Power Engineering, Jiangsu University, Zhenjiang 212013, China

Minguan Yang
School of Energy and Power Engineering, Jiangsu University, Zhenjiang 212013, China

Can Kang
School of Energy and Power Engineering, Jiangsu University, Zhenjiang 212013, China

Yuli Wang
School of Energy and Power Engineering, Jiangsu University, Zhenjiang 212013, China
Department of Mechanics, KTH-Royal Institute of Technology, 10044 Stockholm, Sweden

M. Anyoji
Institute of Space and Astronautical Science, Japan Aerospace Exploration Agency, 6-1-1 Yoshinodai, Chuo-Ku, Sagamihara 252-5210, Japan

D. Numata
Department of Aerospace Engineering, Tohoku University, 6-6-1 Aoba, Aoba-Ku, Sendai, Japan

H. Nagai
Department of Aerospace Engineering, Tohoku University, 6-6-1 Aoba, Aoba-Ku, Sendai, Japan

K. Asai
Department of Aerospace Engineering, Tohoku University, 6-6-1 Aoba, Aoba-Ku, Sendai, Japan

Noriaki Ichijo
IHI Corporation, 1 Shin-nakahara-cho, Isogo-ku, Yokohama 235-8501, Japan

Shinsuke Matsuno
IHI Corporation, 1 Shin-nakahara-cho, Isogo-ku, Yokohama 235-8501, Japan

Taiji Sakai
IHI Corporation, 1 Shin-nakahara-cho, Isogo-ku, Yokohama 235-8501, Japan

Yoshikatsu Tochigi
IHI Corporation, 1 Shin-nakahara-cho, Isogo-ku, Yokohama 235-8501, Japan

Meguru Kaminoyama
Division of Materials Science and Chemical Engineering, Faculty of Engineering, Yokohama National University, 79-5 Tokiwa-dai, Hodogaya-ku, Yokohama 240-8501, Japan

Kazuhiko Nishi
Division of Materials Science and Chemical Engineering, Faculty of Engineering, Yokohama National University, 79-5 Tokiwa-dai, Hodogaya-ku, Yokohama 240-8501, Japan

Ryuta Misumi
Division of Materials Science and Chemical Engineering, Faculty of Engineering, Yokohama National University, 79-5 Tokiwa-dai, Hodogaya-ku, Yokohama 240-8501, Japan

So Nishiyama
Division of Materials Science and Chemical Engineering, Faculty of Engineering, Yokohama National University, 79-5 Tokiwa-dai, Hodogaya-ku, Yokohama 240-8501, Japan

Zhe Zhu
TNList, Tsinghua University, Beijing 100084, China.

Ralph R. Martin
School of Computer Science & Informatics, Cardiff University, UK

Robert Pepperell
Cardiff School of Art & Design, Cardiff Metropolitan University, UK

Alistair Burleigh
Cardiff School of Art & Design, Cardiff Metropolitan University, UK

Hao Zhu
School of Computer Science, Northwestern Polytechnic University, Xi'an 710072, China

Qing Wang
School of Computer Science, Northwestern Polytechnic University, Xi'an 710072, China

Kunihiro Hasegawa
Keio University, Yokohama, 223-8522, Japan. E-mail: K. Hasegawa

Hideo Saito
Keio University, Yokohama, 223-8522, Japan. E-mail: K. Hasegawa

Xiaodong Tang
Machine Intelligence Lab, Sichuan University, Chengdu 610065, China

Jixiang Guo
Machine Intelligence Lab, Sichuan University, Chengdu 610065, China

Peng Li
West China College of Stomatology, Sichuan University, Chengdu 610065, China

Jiancheng Lv
Machine Intelligence Lab, Sichuan University, Chengdu 610065, China

Magnus Wrenninge
Pixar Animation Studios

Er. Avneet Kaur
Student, Computer Science Department, Guru Nanak Dev University, Regional Campus, Jalandhar, India

Er. Harman Preet Singh
Student, Electronics Department, Guru Nanak Dev University, Amritsar, India

Preface

The appliances of methods in computer graphics span from simulations, computer aided education to digital photography and entertainment. Some fundamental problems of computer graphics and visualisations are investigated, such as the complexities of illumination in virtual scenes, different aspects of modeling and animating virtual environments and processing the main aspects which differ various imaging formats. Particular methods and technologies related to computer graphics and visualization are developed. The insight is given to how graphics can be generated and manipulated, and computed based to some specific applications. A large number of novel visualisation techniques are summarized.

Geometric primitives are a staple of computer graphics. They provide artists with shapes that are easy to understand and create, yet they can be easily combined and modified into more complex structures. A new 2D geometric primitive is derived representing a smooth curved shape that blends two circles of any radii, and is controlled with a few parameters which have immediate geometric interpretations. The applications of shapes, surfaces and curves in computer graphics are introduced in the initial six chapters of the book. Also, the concept of curve segment is introduced after relaxing the definition of digital straight segment and it is used to decompose a digital curve into a sequence of curve segments

3D scene modeling has long been a fundamental problem in computer graphics. With the popularity of consumer-level RGB-D cameras, there is a growing interest in digitizing real-world indoor 3D scenes. However, modeling indoor 3D scenes remains a challenging problem because of the complex structure of interior objects and poor quality of RGB-D data acquired by consumer-level sensors. Various methods have been proposed to tackle these challenges. An overview of recent advances in indoor scene modeling techniques is presented in Chapter 7 of the book, as well as public datasets and code libraries which can facilitate experiments and evaluation.

The following eight chapters of the book present various visualization techniques to improve practical appliances of computer graphics, such as surface waves of the jet, electrical resistance tomography, videoconferencing and cranio-maxillofacial (CMF) surgery. An overview of image enhancement techniques based on the use of Particle Swarm Optimization is presented in the final chapter of the book.

A variety of mappings between a sphere and a disc and between a disc and a square, as well as combinations of both, are used in computer graphics applications, resulting in mappings between spheres and squares. Many options exist for each type of mapping; to pick the right methods for a given application requires knowledge about the nature and magnitude of mapping distortions.

An overview of forward and inverse mappings between a unit sphere, a unit disc, and a unit square is provided. Quality measurements relevant for computer graphics applications are derived from tools used in the field of map projection, and a comparative analysis of the mapping methods is given.

A novel, direct ray-tracing method for rendering Catmull-Clark subdivision surfaces is presented. This method resolves an intersection with Bezier patches without performing of polygon tessellation as done in most traditional renderers.

The instability analysis of the liquid jet issuing into ambient air was conducted with an emphasis placed upon the evolution of surface waves of the jet. An experiment was designed to visualize the microscopic morphology on the surface of a liquid jet. A spectral method was proposed to measure wavelength from the obtained jet images.

An iterative back projection method (i-BP) has been developed to improve the resolution of reconstructed images produced by electrical resistance tomography (ERT). This solution is based on an iterative calculation of the electrical fields and it is possible to reconstruct clearer images than those reconstructed by the conventional back projection method without divergence. Numerical simulations and experiments using a simple model are performed in this study. The numerical simulations show that clear images are reconstructed both near the wall and at the center by i-BP.

Face-to-face videoconferencing system is considered that uses a Kinect camera at each end of the link for 3D modeling and an ordinary 2D display for output. The Kinect camera allows a 3D model of each participant to be transmitted; the (assumed static) background is sent separately. Furthermore, the Kinect tracks the receiver's head, allowing our system to render a view of the sender depending on the receiver's viewpoint. The resulting motion parallax gives the receivers a strong impression of 3D viewing as they move, yet the system only needs an ordinary 2D display.

The recent development of light field cameras has received growing interest, as their rich angular information has potential benefits for many computer vision tasks. A novel method is introduced to obtain a dense disparity map by use of ground control points (GCPs) in the light field. Previous work optimizes the disparity map by local estimation which includes both reliable points and unreliable points. To reduce the negative effect of the unreliable points, the disparity at non-GCPs from GCPs is predicted. The method performs more robustly in shadow areas than previous methods based on GCP work, since color information and local disparity is combined.

A method for synthesizing a stroboscopic image of a moving sports player from a hand-held camera sequence is developed. This method has three steps: synthesis of background image, synthesis of stroboscopic image, and removal of player's shadow. In synthesis of background image step, all input frames masked a bounding box of the player are stitched together to generate a background image. In synthesis of stroboscopic image step, the background image, the input frame, and a mask of the player synthesize a stroboscopic image.

Volume visualization has numerous applications that benefit different knowledge domains, such as biology, medicine, meteorology, oceanography, geology, among others. With the continuous advances of technology, it has been possible to achieve considerable rendering rates and a high degree of realism. Visualization tools have currently assisted users with the visual analysis of complex and large datasets. Marching cubes is one of the most widely used real-time volume rendering methods. A methodology is developed for speeding up the marching cubes algorithm on a graphics processing unit and discusses a number of ways to improve its performance by means of auxiliary spatial data structures.

In the field of cranio-maxillofacial (CMF) surgery, surgical simulation is becoming a very powerful tool to plan surgery and simulate surgical results before actually performing a CMF surgical procedure. Reliable prediction of facial soft tissue changes is in particular essential for better preparation and to shorten the time taken for the operation. A surgical simulation system is provided to predict facial soft tissue changes caused by the movement of bone segments during CMF surgery.

A simple-yet-effective method for isotropic meshing relying on Euclidean distance transformation based centroidal Voronoi tessellation (CVT) is presented. This approach improves the performance and robustness of computing CVT on curved domains while simultaneously providing high-quality output meshes.

Editor
Ivan Stanimirović, Ph.D.

CHAPTER 1

MAPPINGS BETWEEN SPHERE, DISC, AND SQUARE

Martin Lambers

University of Siegen, Germany

ABSTRACT

A variety of mappings between a sphere and a disc and between a disc and a square, as well as combinations of both, are used in computer graphics applications, resulting in mappings between spheres and squares. Many options exist for each type of mapping; to pick the right methods for a given application requires knowledge about the nature and magnitude of mapping distortions.

This paper provides an overview of forward and inverse mappings between a unit sphere, a unit disc, and a unit square. Quality measurements relevant for computer graphics applications are derived from tools used in the field of map projection, and a comparative analysis of the mapping methods is given.

INTRODUCTION AND BACKGROUND

Mappings between spheres, discs, and squares are useful tools in many areas of computer graphics. Examples include panoramic imaging [German et al. 2007; Fong 2014], environment mapping [Greene 1986; Heidrich and Seidel 1998], and generating points on a disc or sphere for sampling purposes [Shirley and Chiu 1997; Sloan et al. 2005].

Important properties of such mappings include the angle and area distortions that they introduce [Floater and Hormann 2005]. Some applications require equal-area mappings that preserve area ratios, and others require conformal mappings that preserve angles locally. No mapping can be both equal-area and conformal at the same time, and preserving one quality often results in strong distortions in the other. Many applications, in particular in computer graphics, require mappings that allow efficient sampling of maps [Snyder and Mitchell 2001] without introducing artifacts. A balanced mapping for this purpose provides both small area distortions and small angle distortions, although neither distortion has to be zero.

This paper gives an overview of mappings between a unit sphere, a unit disc, and a unit square, with formulas for forward and inverse transformation. Furthermore, we derive two quality measurements relevant for computer graphics applications based on established tools from the field of map projection, and we compare the mappings based on these measurements.

Section 2 starts with mappings between discs and squares, Section 3 describes map projections between spheres (or hemispheres) and discs, and Section 4 details methods to combine methods from both categories to produce mappings between spheres and squares. Section 5 provides numerical

Citation: Martin Lambers, Mappings between Sphere, Disc, and Square, Journal of Computer Graphics Techniques Vol. 5, No. 2, 2016. http://jcgt.org/published/0005/02/01/

analysis results for all mappings based on the derived quality measurements. The supplementary material consists of C++ source code that implements all mapping and analysis methods as well as all tools necessary to recreate the figures and results presented in this paper.

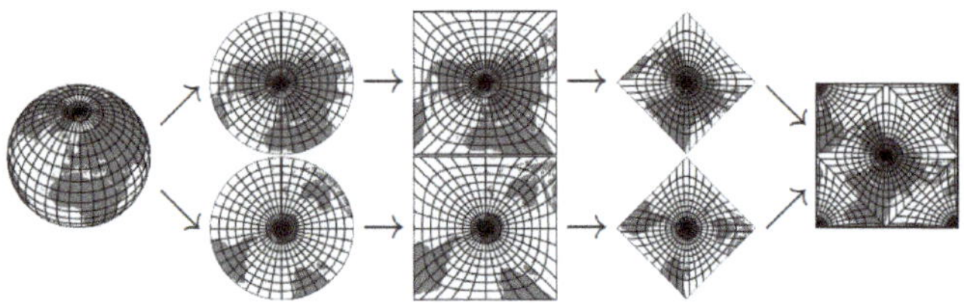

Figure 1: A mapping between a sphere and a square, composed of a mapping between a hemisphere and a disc, a mapping between a disc and a square, and an arrangement of two squares in a new square.

MAPPINGS BETWEEN DISC AND SQUARE

This section provides an overview of mappings between the closed unit disc D and the closed unit square R. We identify points on D using either polar coordinates, with radius r and angle φ, $0 \leq r \leq 1$, $-\pi < \varphi \leq \pi$, or Cartesian coordinates, u and v with $r = \sqrt{u^2 + v^2}$ and φ = atan2(v, u). Points on R are identified using Cartesian coordinates x and y, $-1 \leq x \leq +1$, $-1 \leq y \leq +1$. The mappings are summarized and compared in Table 1.

Radial Stretching

Perhaps, the most direct method of mapping a disc to a square is to adjust the radius of a point on the disc according to its angle

For (x, y) ∈ R, we have a distance of $t = \sqrt{x^2 + y^2}$ to the origin and a polar angle of φ = atan2(y, x). The polar radius of (r, φ) ∈ D can then be set to r = t cos φ for φ ∈ [−π/4, +π/4] (and accordingly for the remaining ranges of φ). Using cos φ = x/t, sin φ = y/t, tan φ = v/u, and a method applied by Cline to Shirley's equal-area mapping [Shirley and Cline 2011] to reduce the number of cases, this leads to the following simple equations (see the derivation by Fong for details [Fong 2015]):

Table 1: Overview of mappings between a disc and a square

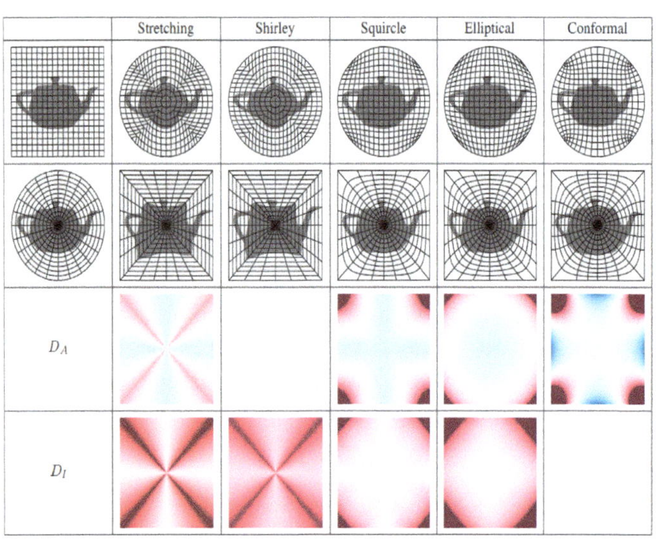

Disc to square mapping:

$$r = \sqrt{u^2 + v^2}$$

$$(x, y) = \begin{cases} (0,0) & \text{if } r = 0 \\ (\text{sgn}(u) \cdot r, \text{sgn}(v) \cdot rv/u) & \text{if } r > 0 \text{ and } u^2 \geq v^2 \\ (\text{sgn}(u) \cdot ru/v, \text{sgn}(v) \cdot r) & \text{if } r > 0 \text{ and } u^2 < v^2 \end{cases}$$

Square to disc mapping:

$$t = \sqrt{x^2 + y^2}$$

$$(u, v) = \begin{cases} (0,0) & \text{if } t = 0 \\ (\text{sgn}(x) \cdot x^2/t, \text{sgn}(y) \cdot xy/t) & \text{if } t > 0 \text{ and } x^2 \geq y^2 \\ (\text{sgn}(x) \cdot xy/t, \text{sgn}(y) \cdot y^2/t) & \text{if } t > 0 \text{ and } x^2 < y^2 \end{cases}$$

This mapping is neither conformal nor equal-area. It suffers from strong angular and area distortions.

Shirley's Equal-Area Mapping

Shirley constructs an equal-area map between a disc and a square by mapping concentric disc strings to concentric square strips [Shirley and Chiu 1997]. Note that Ros¸ca derived an equivalent mapping (except for a scale factor) using a different approach [Ros¸ca 2010]. Both prove the equal-area property by showing that the Jacobian is constant. The following formulas for the disc-to-square mapping are based on Shirley's code samples. The formulas for the inverse mapping are based on Cline's method for reducing the number of cases [Shirley and Cline 2011].

Disc to square mapping:

$$r = \sqrt{u^2 + v^2}$$

$$\varphi = \begin{cases} \text{atan2}(v, u) & \text{if atan2}(v, u) \geq -\pi/4 \\ \text{atan2}(v, u) + 2\pi, & \text{otherwise} \end{cases}$$

$$(x, y) = \begin{cases} (r, \frac{4}{\pi} r\varphi) & \text{if } \varphi < \pi/4 \\ (-\frac{4}{\pi} r(\varphi - \pi/2), r) & \text{if } \varphi < 3\pi/4 \\ (-r, -\frac{4}{\pi} r(\varphi - \pi)) & \text{if } \varphi < 5\pi/4 \\ (\frac{4}{\pi} r(\varphi - 3\pi/2), -r), & \text{otherwise} \end{cases}$$

Square to disc mapping:

$$(r, \varphi) = \begin{cases} (x, \frac{\pi}{4} y/x) & \text{if } x^2 > y^2 \\ (y, \frac{\pi}{2} - \frac{\pi}{4} x/y) & \text{if } x^2 \leq y^2 \text{ and } y^2 > 0 \\ (0, 0), & \text{otherwise} \end{cases}$$

Note that by writing the square to disc mapping of the radial stretching method in terms of r, φ, using cos φ = x/t and sin φ = y/t, one can see that Shirley's mapping uses the same stretching of the radius but modifies the angle, φ.

This mapping is equal-area. It suffers from strong angular distortions, especially around the discontinuities at the diagonals of the square.

Fernandez-Guasti's Squircle Mapping

Fernandez-Guasti introduced a geometric form that can be varied between square and ′ circle using a "squareness" parameter

[Fernandez-Guasti 1992 ´]; he later called this form squircle. Note that the term squircle is sometimes used to refer to a special case of a superellipse. To avoid ambiguities, we therefore use the term "Fernandez- ´ Guasti's squircle".

In terms of Cartesian coordinates, the equation that describes Fernandez-Guasti's ´ squircle is $\frac{s^2}{k^4}x^2y^2 - \frac{x^2+y^2}{k^2} + 1 = 0$, where s is the squareness parameter and k is the radius of the circle (for s = 0) or half the side length of the square (for s = 1). For values of s between 0 and 1, the geometry resembles both square and circle.

Fong proposes to map concentric circles to concentric squircles to construct a mapping between a unit disc and a unit square [Fong 2014]. For this purpose, he sets s = k and varies s from 0 to 1, taking $r = s = \sqrt{x^2 + y^2 - x^2y^2}$ as disc radius.

Disc to square mapping:

$$w = \frac{\operatorname{sgn}(uv)}{\sqrt{2}}\sqrt{u^2 + v^2 - \sqrt{(u^2+v^2)(u^2+v^2-4u^2v^2)}}$$

$$(x, y) = \begin{cases} (w/v, w/u) & \text{if } |w| > 0 \\ (u, v), & \text{otherwise} \end{cases}$$

Square to disc mapping:

$$u = x\frac{\sqrt{x^2 + y^2 - x^2y^2}}{\sqrt{x^2+y^2}}$$

$$v = y\frac{\sqrt{x^2 + y^2 - x^2y^2}}{\sqrt{x^2+y^2}}$$

Note that (0, 0) must be mapped to (0, 0) as a special case.

This mapping is neither equal-area nor conformal.

Elliptical Arc Mapping

Nowell derived a method to map a square to a disc by mapping lines of constant x and lines of constant y in the square to ellipses in the disc [Nowell 2005]. Cigolle et al. mention an elliptical mapping between a disc and a square [Cigolle et al. 2014]. Their paper omits details, but their implementation in the supplementary material shows that they derived equivalent formulas for the mapping from square to disc and additional formulas for the inverse mapping. The simpler formulas for the inverse mapping given below were derived by Fong [Fong 2015].

Disc to square mapping:

$$x = \frac{1}{2}\sqrt{2 + u^2 - v^2 + 2\sqrt{2}u} - \frac{1}{2}\sqrt{2 + u^2 - v^2 - 2\sqrt{2}u}$$

$$y = \frac{1}{2}\sqrt{2 - u^2 + v^2 + 2\sqrt{2}v} - \frac{1}{2}\sqrt{2 - u^2 + v^2 - 2\sqrt{2}v}$$

Square to disc mapping:

$$u = x\sqrt{1 - \frac{y^2}{2}}$$

$$v = y\sqrt{1 - \frac{x^2}{2}}$$

This mapping is neither equal-area nor conformal.

Conformal Mapping

In complex analysis, the Schwarz-Christoffel transformation provides a way to construct conformal transformations between simple polygons and the upper half of the complex plane. Since there exists a conformal transformation between the upper half of the complex plane and the open unit disc, one can construct a conformal mapping between a square and a disc. Indeed, this special case was used as illustration and motivation in Schwarz' original publication on the topic. However, formulas for forward and inverse mappings suitable for implementation on computers were not available for some time.

Conformal mapping of a disc onto a rotated square using the Schwarz-Christoffel transformation is a core element of the Peirce quincuncial map projection [Peirce 1879]; see also Section 4. The formulas given below are based on Lee's analysis of Peirce's projection [Lee 1976].

The mapping from disc to square first rotates the disc by 45◦ . This step is not necessary, but it makes this mapping consistent with the others with regard to the orientation of the square content. Then, the rotated disc is conformally mapped to a rotated square with corners (1, 0), (0, 1), (−1, 0), (0, −1). This square is then rotated and scaled to fit the unit square. The conformal mapping is based on the incomplete elliptic Legendre integral, F, with a modulus of k = 1/ √ 2. This integral must be computed using iterative methods. Numerical libraries usually provide the necessary methods; our supplementary material includes an implementation based on the Landen transformation.

The mapping from square to disc first rotates and scales the unit square back into the square with corners (1, 0), (0, 1), (−1, 0), (0, −1). It then uses the complexvalued Jacobian elliptic function cn with modulus k = 1/ √ 2 to conformally map that square to the unit circle. Afterwards, the inverse of the optional rotation is applied. This mapping requires the value K = F(π/2) ≈ 1.854, which is the complete elliptic integral of the first kind with modulus k = 1/ √ 2. The function cn must again be computed using iterative methods. Numerical libraries often provide realvalued implementations that compute the related functions cn, sn, and dn at the same time; our supplementary material includes an implementation based on the arithmeticgeometric mean. For the special case of k = 1/ √ 2, the complementary elliptic modulus $k' = \sqrt{1 - k^2}$ is identical to k, and the complex cn function can be computed from real-valued cn, sn, and dn as follows:

$$\operatorname{cn}(x + iy) = \frac{\operatorname{cn}(x)\operatorname{cn}(y)}{1 - \operatorname{dn}^2(x)\operatorname{sn}^2(y)} - i\frac{\operatorname{sn}(x)\operatorname{dn}(x)\operatorname{sn}(y)\operatorname{dn}(y)}{1 - \operatorname{dn}^2(x)\operatorname{sn}^2(y)}$$

Note that Stark derives optimized numerical methods for the special case of conformal mappings between unit sphere and unit disc [Stark 2009].

Disc to square mapping:

$$u' = (u - v)/\sqrt{2}$$
$$v' = (u + v)/\sqrt{2}$$
$$A = u'^2 + v'^2$$
$$B = u'^2 - v'^2$$
$$T = \sqrt{(1 + A^2)^2 - 4B^2}$$
$$U = 1 + 2B - A^2$$
$$\alpha = \operatorname{acos}((2A - T)/U)$$
$$\beta = \operatorname{acos}(U/(2A + T))$$
$$x' = \operatorname{sgn}(u')(1 - F(\alpha)/2K)$$
$$y' = \operatorname{sgn}(v')(F(\beta)/2K)$$
$$x = x' + y'$$
$$y = y' - x'$$

Square to disc mapping:

$$x' = x/2 - y/2$$
$$y' = x/2 + y/2$$
$$w = \operatorname{cn}(K(1 - x') - iKy')$$
$$u = (\Re(w) + \Im(w))/\sqrt{2}$$
$$v = (\Im(w) - \Re(w))/\sqrt{2}$$

This mapping is conformal, except for the four singular points located on the corners of the square. Area deformation is substantial, especially near the singular points.

MAPPINGS BETWEEN SPHERE AND DISC

This section covers mappings between the unit sphere, S, and the unit disc, D. We identify points on S using the longitude λ and the colatitude θ, $-\pi < \lambda \leq \pi$, $0 \leq \theta \leq \pi$. The colatitude measures the angle to the north pole (by convention (0, 0, 1) in Cartesian coordinates). We use colatitude instead of latitude (which measures the angle to the equatorial plane), because the resulting formulas are shorter. The longitude measures the angle in the xy-plane. Points on D are again identified using polar coordinates with radius r and angle φ, $0 \leq r \leq 1$, $-\pi < \varphi \leq \pi$.

The problem of mapping the sphere onto the disc is one of the classical areas of map projection, and the methods discussed in this section are well known in that field. In the following sections, all methods map the north pole to the center of the unit disc, set the polar angle $\varphi = \lambda - \pi/2$, and compute radius r as a function of the colatitude θ. We will discuss only this radius function for each method.

Only a subset of the mappings covered here can map the whole sphere to the unit disc; others are restricted to a hemisphere. By shifting the north pole of the sphere to another point and suitably recomputing longitude and colatitude, other projection centers can be chosen. In Section 4, we will use the south pole as an additional projection center to cover both north and south hemispheres. For this case, the new colatitude is simply $\pi - \theta$, and the longitude remains unchanged.

The mappings are summarized and compared in Table 2.

Equal-Area Projection (Lambert Azimuthal)

Lambert designed several important map projections [Snyder 1987], among them the azimuthal equal-area map projection.

Sphere to disc mapping:

$$r = \sin(\theta/2)$$

Disc to sphere mapping:

$$\theta = 2\operatorname{asin}(r)$$

When projecting just one hemisphere instead of the whole sphere, an additional scale factor of $\sqrt{2}$ is applied to the radius so that the unit disc is filled.

This mapping can map the whole sphere in a disc. It is an equal-area mapping. Angular distortions increase with distance to the pole.

Conformal Projection (Stereographic)

The stereographic map projection is a conformal projection that was already known in ancient Greece [Snyder 1987].

Table 2: Overview of mappings between a sphere and a disc

	Equal-Area	Conformal	Harmonic Mean	Mixture	Equidistant
Sphere to disc	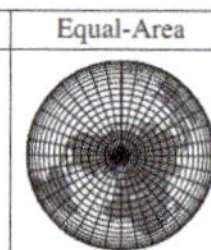		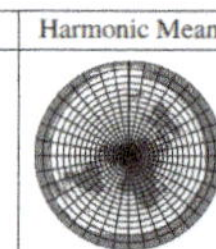		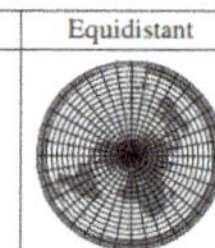
Hemisphere to disc	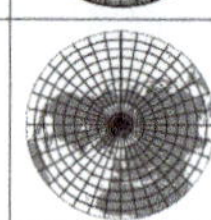	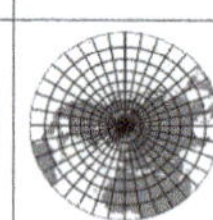	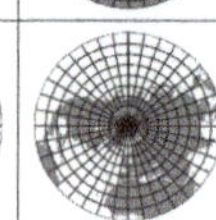	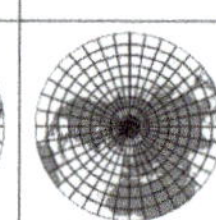	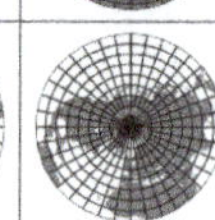
D_A (hemisphere)		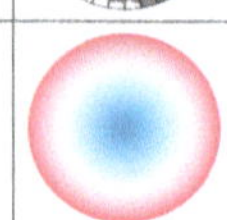	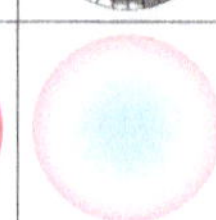	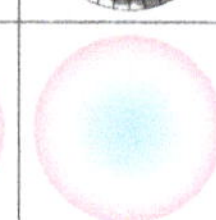	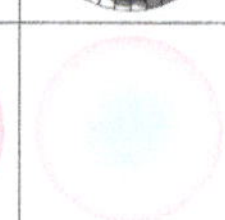
D_I (hemisphere)	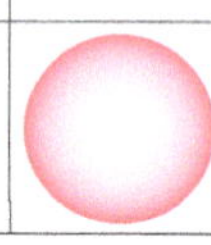				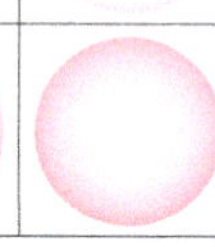

Hemisphere to disc mapping:

$$r = \tan(\theta/2)$$

Disc to hemisphere mapping:

$$\theta = 2\operatorname{atan}(r)$$

This mapping cannot be used to map a complete sphere in a disc. It is a conformal mapping. Scale increases with distance from the pole.

Harmonic Mean of Equal-Area and Conformal Projection (Breusing)

Many attempts have been made to balance the area-preserving qualities of the Lambert azimuthal equal-area projection with the angle-preserving qualities of the stereographic projection, with the goal of arriving at a map projection with only moderate area and angle distortions throughout. Breusing is credited with the idea of using the geometric mean of both projections; Young preferred the harmonic mean over the geometric and arithmetic means and stated that it leads to simpler formulas than the alternatives while being an error-minimizing projection in some sense [Young 1920].

Sphere to disc mapping:

$$r = \tan(\theta/4)$$

Disc to sphere mapping:

$$\theta = 4\,\mathrm{atan}(r)$$

When projecting just one hemisphere instead of the whole sphere, an additional scale factor of $\frac{1}{\sqrt{2}-1}$ is applied to the radius so that the unit disc is filled.

This mapping can map the whole sphere in a disc. It is neither equal-area nor conformal, but both area and angular distortions are moderate.

Mixture of Equal-Area and Conformal Projection

Instead of using a fixed relation between equal-area and conformal projection, Fong proposes to use a parameterized mixture of both [Fong 2014]. The tradeoff between area and angular distortions can be chosen using a parameter $\beta \in [0, 1]$, with $\beta = 0$ choosing the stereographic projection and $\beta = 1$ choosing the Lambert azimuthal equal-area projection. Fong applied this idea to the whole sphere, which lead to difficulties since the stereographic projection requires an infinite plane to map the complete sphere; in his version, the parameter β can only approach zero, but not become zero. We restrict the mixed projection to the hemisphere instead and can, therefore, use simpler formulas that furthermore do not impose a restriction on β.

Hemisphere to disc mapping:

$$r = \frac{\sqrt{1+\beta}\tan(\theta/2)}{\sqrt{1+\beta\tan^2(\theta/2)}}$$

Disc to hemisphere mapping:

$$\theta = 2\,\mathrm{atan}\left(\frac{r}{\sqrt{1+\beta(1-r^2)}}\right)$$

For $\beta = 0$, $r = \tan(\theta/2)$ and $\theta = 2\ \mathrm{atan}(r)$, thus this mapping becomes the stereographic mapping. For $\beta = 1$, $r = \frac{\sqrt{2}\tan(\theta/2)}{\sqrt{1+\tan^2(\theta/2)}} = \sqrt{2}\sin(\theta/2)$ and $\theta = 2\,\mathrm{atan}(r/\sqrt{2-r^2}) = 2\,\mathrm{asin}(r/\sqrt{2})$, thus this mapping becomes the Lambert azimuthal equal-area mapping in its hemisphere variant.

This mapping cannot map the whole sphere in a disc. It can be equal-area (for $\beta = 1$) or conformal (for $\beta = 0$) and balances area against angular distortions for $0 < \beta < 1$.

Equidistant Projection

The equidistant map projection has been known for many centuries; its origin cannot be clearly identified [Snyder 1987]. Its main features are its simplicity and the preservation of distances measured from the center of the projection. Its area and angular distortions fall between those of the equal-area and conformal projections, thus making this projection another candidate for a compromise between both.

Sphere to disc mapping:

$$r = \theta/\pi$$

Disc to sphere mapping:

$$\theta = r\pi$$

When projecting just one hemisphere, instead of the whole sphere, an additional scale factor of 2 is applied to the radius so that the unit disc is filled.

This projection can map the whole sphere in a disc. It is neither conformal nor equal-area, but balances area and angular distortions. Distances to the center are preserved.

MAPPINGS BETWEEN SPHERE AND SQUARE

For projecting a sphere onto a square, there are essentially two layout options, described in the following sections.

Table 3: Selected mappings between a sphere and a square in quincuncial layout

Hemisphere to disc mapping	Lambert	Stereographic	Harmonic Mean	Mixture	Equidistant
Disc to square mapping	Shirley	Conformal	Elliptical	Squircle	Elliptical
Example map	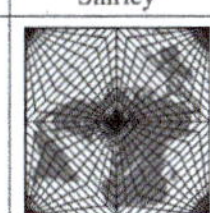	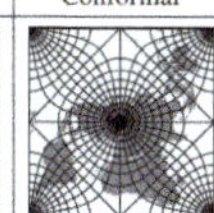			
D_A		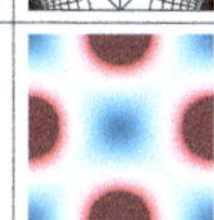		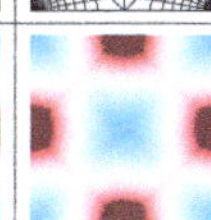	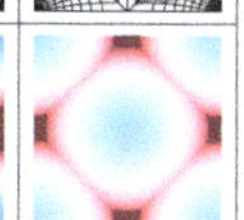
D_I	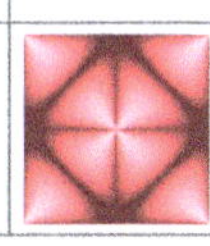		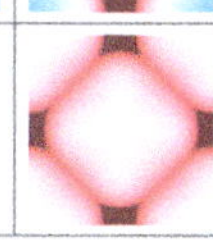	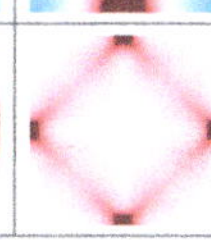	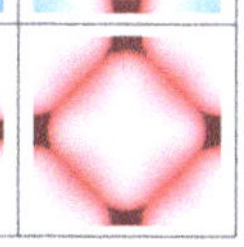

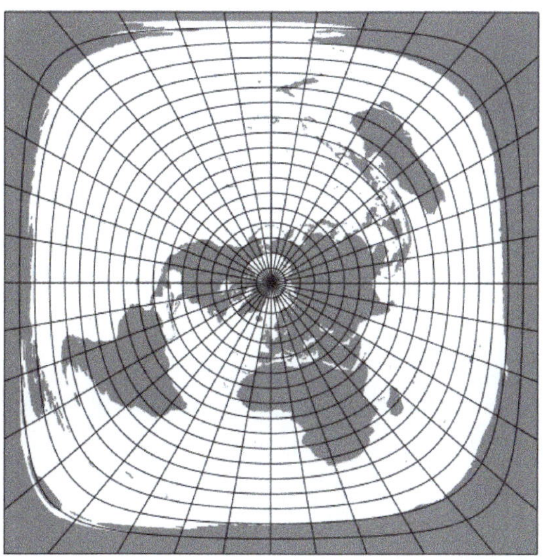

Figure 2: Example map with the south pole of the sphere mapped to the square border. Here the equidistant azimuthal projection was combined with the disc-to-square mapping based on Fernandez-Guasti's squircle.

Pole-at-border Layout

The first layout option projects the whole sphere onto a disc using one of the methods from Section 3 that is capable of this, and then applies one of the methods from Section 2 to map that disc to a square.

In this layout, the sphere point opposite the projection center is mapped to the border of the square. In our examples, the projection center is the north pole, and the south pole is spread across the border. Figure 2 shows an example map.

Obviously, this layout leads to very strong distortions in the region around the point opposite the projection center. This limits its usefulness in applications that require acceptable sampling quality throughout the map, but there are still use cases for this layout, for example in panoramic imaging [Fong 2014].

Quincuncial Layout

Peirce's quincuncial map projection [Peirce 1879] shown in Figure 3 introduced this layout. It projects each hemisphere onto its own disc, maps these discs to two squares, and then arranges the squares into a single square as depicted in Figure 4. The center part and the four corner parts form a quincunx.

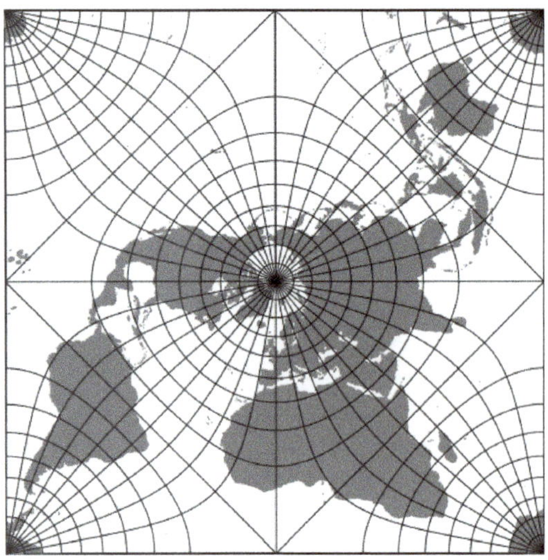

Figure 3: The original quincuncial map by Peirce combines stereographic conformal projection from each hemisphere to a disc, conformal mapping of these discs to two squares, and arrangement of the squares in a quincuncial layout.

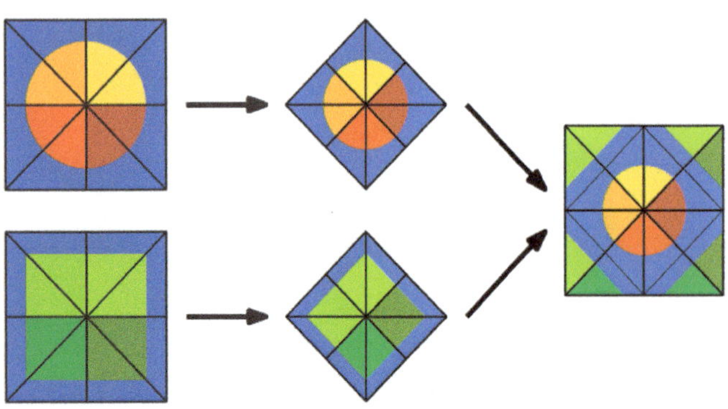

Figure 4: Arrangement of two squares into a new square in quincuncial layout. The second square is mirrored along its borders to fit into the new square.

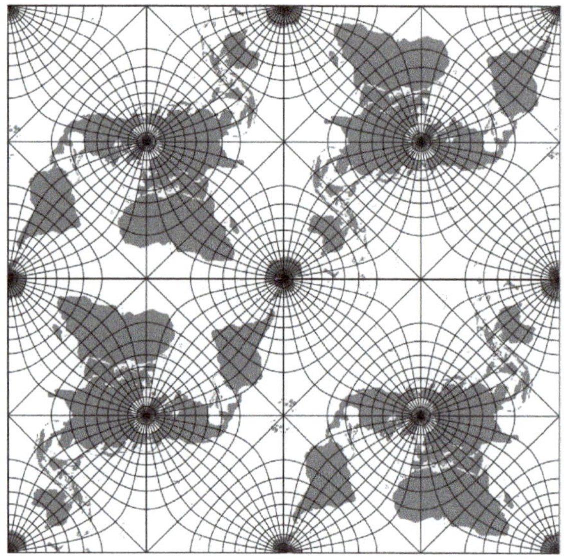

Figure 5: Tiling of the quincuncial layout. The upper-left and lower-right quarters are the original map, the upper-right and lower-left quarters are rotated by 180°.

The sphere point opposite the projection center is mapped to the four corners of the square. Distortions are much smaller than in the opposite-point-at-border layout. Additionally, the quincuncial layout has the nice property that maps can be tiled, as shown in Figure 5: when leaving the map at any border point except the four corners, in any direction, there is a continuation point where we can re-enter the map without disruption.

The quincuncial layout has been used in computer graphics to represent an octahedron inside a square for the purpose of vector representation [Meyer et al. 2010; Cigolle et al. 2014] or sphere parametrization [Praun and Hoppe 2003] and for the display of panoramic images [German et al. 2007].

To arrange two unit squares into a unit square in quincuncial layout, both must first be rotated by −45° and scaled by $1/\sqrt{2}$. Each quadrant of the second input square R_2 is then mirrored along its border in that quadrant; see Figure 4.

Selected mappings in quincuncial layout are summarized and compared in Table 3. Note that there are methods that map directly between sphere and octahedron or square, without using the disc as an intermediate step. These include Snyder's equalarea map projection for polyhedral globes [Snyder 1992] and Gringorten's square equal-area world map [Gringorten 1972]. Furthermore, Clarberg describes an optimized SIMD implementation of a mapping between sphere and square using Shirley's equal-area mapping and an octahedral layout [Clarberg 2008]. These methods are not discussed in this paper.

ANALYSIS

In this section, we derive quality measurements and provide numerical analysis results for all mappings. Note that all results were obtained using IEEE double precision floating-point numbers and computations.

Distortion Measurements

To evaluate the mapping methods discussed in the preceding sections, we use a standard tool from the field of map projection: Tissot's indicatrix [Snyder 1987].

The idea of the indicatrix is that any map projection maps an infinitesimal circle on the sphere onto an infinitesimal ellipse on the map. This ellipse describes the local characteristics of the map projection. For example, a conformal map projection preserves angles, and the local ellipse will therefore be a circle, but generally not of the same size as the original circle. An equal-area map projection preserves area, and the size ratio of the local ellipse to the original circle will be constant throughout the map, but the axes of the ellipse will have varying orientation and length.

In general, for any pair of lines that intersect at a given point on the sphere, the angle at which they intersect on the map will not be identical (unless the map projection is conformal). The greatest deviation from the correct angle at a given point is called the maximum angular deformation ω.

Both the original circle and the mapped ellipse are infinitesimal, but Tissot's indicatrix allows to compute the ratio between corresponding properties. The most important ellipse properties are the semi-major axis a and the semi-minor axis b. Both are measured relative to the original circle: the identity mapping will result in $a = b = 1$.

For applications in computer graphics, two values derived from a and b are of special interest, since they determine the sampling quality of a map projection:

The Local Area Distortion D_A

The determinant of the Jacobian matrix of a mapping gives the local scale factor s, which can also be determined numerically as $s = ab$. In a strict sense, s must be 1 everywhere on the map for the mapping to be truly area-preserving, but usually source and destination have different areas, and an equal-area mapping will have a constant scale factor representing the ratio R of destination and source areas, e.g. $s \equiv 4/\pi$ for equal-area mappings from disc to square. We therefore use $D_A = ab/R$ as a measurement of local area distortion.

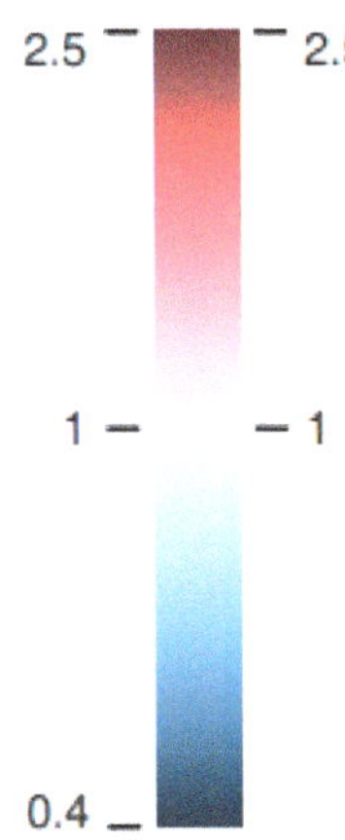

Figure 6: Color map for D_A and D_I in Tables 1, 2, 3 and Figure 7. D_A (left scale) can deviate upward or downward from the ideal value 1, with direction of the deviation encoded in hue. D_I (right scale) can only deviate upward from 1, where it uses the same color encoding as D_A.

The Local Isotropy Distortion D_I

The ratio of a and b is a measurement for the isotropy distortion: $D_I = a/b$. The ideal value is 1. Larger anisotropy typically leads to degraded sampling quality in computer graphics applications. Note that conformal maps have $D_I \equiv 1$, but $D_I \equiv 1$ does not imply that a map is conformal: ω might still be larger than zero locally.

These two distortion measurements are color-coded using a color map generated with the methods described by Wijffelaars et al. [Wijffelaars et al. 2008] as shown in Figure 6; they are displayed for all relevant mappings in Tables 1, 2, and 3.

Table 1 shows that for mappings between disc and square, D_A tends to increase strongly in the corners of the square, except for the radial stretching method and, of course, Shirley's equal-area mapping. In fact, D_A grows indefinitely in the corners for Fernandez-Guasti's squircle method, elliptical arc mapping, and conformal mapping, ´ with conformal mapping showing the largest errors and affected areas. D_I is strongest at the square diagonals for the radial stretching mapping and Shirley's equal-area mapping, but it does not grow indefinitely for these methods. Fernandez-Guasti's ´ squircle method and elliptical arc mapping show indefinitely growing D_I values in the corners of the square. For conformal mapping, $D_I \equiv 0$ as expected.

Interestingly, Shirley's equal-area mapping exhibits the lowest D_I measurements of the non-conformal mappings. It is therefore a good candidate if its discontinuity at the square diagonals is acceptable for the application. On the other hand, Fernandez- ´ Guasti's squircle method and elliptical arc mapping provide small D_A and D_I values for the largest part of the square, as can also be seen by looking at the mapped teapot shapes; if an application is mainly interested in the interior of the square and not its corners, these methods are good candidates.

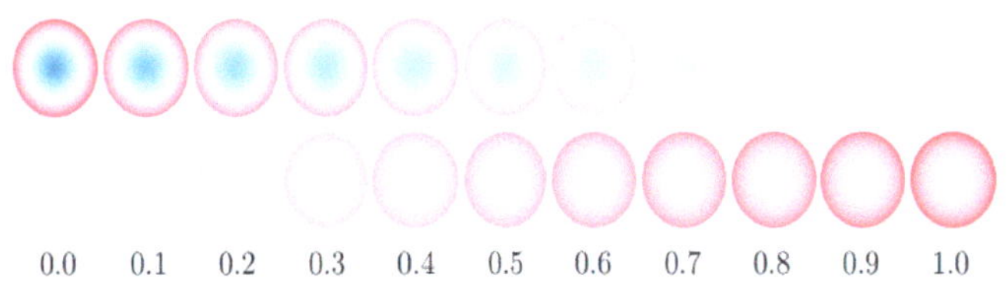

Figure 7: D_A (top) and D_I (bottom) of the method described in Section 3.4, for varying β.

Table 2 shows that the harmonic mean, mixture, and equidistant mappings all provide good compromises in terms of D_A and D_I when compared to the equalarea and conformal mappings. We used $\beta = 0.4$ for the mixture method since it delivers the best compromise; see Figure 7. Still, the harmonic mean method might be preferable if an adjustable error tradeoff is not required.

Table 3 shows only a small subset of the many possible quincuncial combinations of methods. The distortions introduced by sphere/disc and disc/square mappings combine. Compromises between equal-area and conformal mappings still exhibit relatively large values for D_A and D_I at the corners of the inner square, mainly caused by the disc/square mapping. For some applications, it is possible to position these four points in regions of low interest, e.g. oceans for applications that visualize Earth landmass data.

Precision Measurements

We tested the numerical precision of our implementation by placing a uniform grid on the square map, applying inverse mapping to each grid point to obtain coordinates in the original domain (disc or sphere), and then mapping these coordinates first to the map and then back again. For each obtained point in the original domain, we then have a distance to the point resulting from forward and inverse transformation. The maximum distance is the error measurement.

The mappings between disc and square all have very low errors. Measured on Earth's equatorial disc, the distances are in the micrometer range or below, with two exceptions: Fernandez-Guasti's squircle mapping has an error in the millimeter range, ´ and conformal mapping has an error in the meter range. Of course, these are implementation dependent, but we did not arrive at lower distances for the conformal mapping when using different numerical libraries for the computation of F and cn. The errors of mappings between sphere and square are dominated by the errors of the disc/square mappings used. On an Earth-sized sphere, they are again mostly in the micrometer range, except when Fernandez-Guasti's squircle mapping or conformal ´ mapping are used, in which case errors in the millimeter (squircle) or meter range (conformal) occur.

CONCLUSION

This paper gives an overview of mappings between a disc and a square, between a sphere and a disc, and (by composition) between a sphere and a square. It provides ready-to-implement formulas for both the forward and inverse mappings, and it analyzes all mappings using distortion measurements that are relevant for applications in computer graphics.

Since requirements in terms of mapping properties strongly depend on the application area, general recommendations cannot be made. Instead, this paper provides analysis results intended to help pick the right mapping for a given application.

ACKNOWLEDGEMENTS

The polygonal world map data used in maps throughout this paper is provided by Bjorn Sandvik, http://thematicmapping.org/downloads/world borders.php, license CC BY-SA 3.0.

REFERENCES

1. CIGOLLE, Z. H., DONOW, S., EVANGELAKOS, D., MARA, M., MCGUIRE, M., AND MEYER, Q. 2014. A survey of efficient representations for independent unit vectors. Journal of Computer Graphics Techniques 3, 2 (April), 1–30. URL: http: //jcgt.org/published/0003/02/01/. 5, 15
2. CLARBERG, P. 2008. Fast equal-area mapping of the (hemi)sphere using SIMD. Journal of Graphics, GPU, and Game Tools 13, 3, 53–68. URL: http://dx.doi.org/10.1080/2151237X.2008.10129263. 16
3. FERNANDEZ ´ -GUASTI, M. 1992. Classroom notes: Analytic geometry of some rectilinear figures. Int. J. Mathematical Education in Science and Technology 23, 6, 895–913. URL: http://dx.doi.org/10.1080/0020739920230607. 5
4. FLOATER, M. S., AND HORMANN, K. 2005. Surface parameterization: a tutorial and survey. In Advances in Multiresolution for Geometric Modelling, Mathematics and Visualization. Springer, New York, 157–186. URL: http://dx.doi.org/10.1007/3- 540-26808-1_9. 2
5. FONG, C. 2014. An indoor alternative to stereographic spherical panoramas. In Proc. Bridges 2014: Mathematics, Music, Art, Architecture, Culture, 103–110. URL: http: //archive.bridgesmathart.org/2014/bridges2014-103.html. 1, 5, 10, 13
6. FONG, C., 2015. Analytical methods for squaring the disc. http://arxiv.org/abs/ 1509.06344. Accessed: 2015-10-06. 2, 6
7. GERMAN, D. M., D'ANGELO, P., GROSS, M., AND POSTLE, B. 2007. New methods to project panoramas for practical and aesthetic purposes. In Proc. Computational Aesthetics in Graphics, Visualization, and Imaging, Eurographics Association, Aire-la-Ville, Switzerland. URL: http://dx.doi.org/10.2312/COMPAESTH/COMPAESTH07/015- 022. 1, 15
8. GREENE, N. 1986. Environment mapping and other applications of world projections. IEEE Computer Graphics and Applications 6, 11 (Nov.), 21–29. URL: http://dx.doi. org/10.1109/MCG.1986.276658. 1
9. GRINGORTEN, I. I. 1972. A square equal-area map of the world. Journal of Applied Meteorology 11, 5, 763–767. URL: http://dx.doi.org/10.1175/1520-0450(1972)011<0763:ASEAMO>2.0.CO;2. 16
10. HEIDRICH, W., AND SEIDEL, H.-P. 1998. View-independent environment maps. In Proc. ACM SIGGRAPH/EUROGRAPHICS Workshop on Graphics Hardware, ACM, New York, 39–ff. URL: http://dx.doi.org/10.1145/285305.285310. 1
11. LEE, L. 1976. Conformal projections based on jacobian elliptic functions. Cartographica 13, 1, 67–101. URL: http://dx.doi.org/10.3138/X687-1574-4325-WM62. 6
12. MEYER, Q., SUSSMUTH ¨ , J., SUSSNER, G., STAMMINGER, M., AND GREINER, G. 2010. On floating-point normal vectors. Computer Graphics Forum 29, 4, 1405–1409. URL: http://dx.doi.org/10.1111/j.1467-8659.2010.01737.x. 15
13. NOWELL, P., 2005. Mapping a square to a circle. http://mathproofs.blogspot. com/2005/07/mapping-square-to-circle.html. Accessed: 2015-10-06. 5
14. PEIRCE, C. 1879. A quincuncial projection of the sphere. American Journal of Mathematics 2, 4, 394–396. URL: http://dx.doi.org/10.2307/2369491. 6, 13
15. PRAUN, E., AND HOPPE, H. 2003. Spherical parametrization and remeshing. ACM Trans. Graph. 22, 3 (July), 340–349. URL: http://dx.doi.org/10.1145/882262.882274. 15
16. ROS¸CA, D. 2010. New uniform grids on the sphere. Astronomy & Astrophysics 520, A63. URL: http://dx.doi.org/10.1051/0004-6361/201015278. 4
17. SHIRLEY, P., AND CHIU, K. 1997. A low distortion map between disk and square. Journal of graphics tools 2, 3, 45–52. URL: http://dx.doi.org/10.1080/10867651.1997.10487479. 1, 4

18. SHIRLEY, P., AND CLINE, D., 2011. Improved code for concentric map. http://psgraphics.blogspot.de/2011/01/improved-code-forconcentric-map.html. Accessed: 2016-03-18. 2, 4

19. SLOAN, P.-P., LUNA, B., AND SNYDER, J. 2005. Local, deformable precomputed radiance transfer. ACM Trans. Graph. 24, 3 (July), 1216–1224. URL: http://dx.doi.org/ 10.1145/1073204.1073335. 1

20. SNYDER, J., AND MITCHELL, D., 2001. Sampling-efficient mapping of spherical images. http://research.microsoft.com/en-us/um/people/johnsny/ papers/spheremap_tr.pdf. Microsoft Research Technical Report. 2

21. SNYDER, J. 1987. Map projections—a working manual, vol. 1395 of Professional Paper. US Geological Survey. 8, 11, 16

22. SNYDER, J. 1992. An equal-area map projection for polyhedral globes. Cartographica 29, 1, 10–21. URL: http://dx.doi.org/10.3138/27H7-8K88-4882-1752. 16

23. STARK, M. M. 2009. Fast and stable conformal mapping between a disc and a square. Journal of Graphics, GPU, and Game Tools 14, 2, 1–23. URL: http://dx.doi.org/10.1080/2151237X.2009.10129277. 7

24. WIJFFELAARS, M., VLIEGEN, R., VAN WIJK, J. J., AND VAN DER LINDEN, E.-J. 2008. Generating color palettes using intuitive parameters. Computer Graphics Forum 27, 3, 743–750. doi:10.1111/j.1467-8659.2008.01203.x. 17

25. YOUNG, A. E. 1920. Some Investigations in the Theory of Map Projections. Royal Geographical Society, London. URL: http://www.archive.org/details/cu31924029951401. 10

CHAPTER 2

GLOBS: A PRIMITIVE SHAPE FOR GRACEFUL BLENDS BETWEEN CIRCLES

Andrew Glassner

The Imaginary Institute

ABSTRACT

Geometric primitives are a staple of illustration systems. They provide artists with shapes that are easy to understand and create, yet they can be easily combined and modified into more complex structures. Here we introduce a new 2D geometric primitive called a glob. It is a smooth curved shape that blends two circles of any radii. Globs are controlled with a few parameters which have immediate geometric interpretations.

INTRODUCTION

Almost every illustration system offers a mix of free-form and predefined shapes that can be used as starting points for more complicated shapes. These shapes can be broken down into three categories: geometrically primitive shapes (e.g., circles and polygons), compound shapes (e.g., rectangles with circles on the ends), and procedural shapes (e.g., swept shapes and algorithmically-generated blends).

Part of the design of an illustration system involves choosing the right collection of these primitives. A list that's too small can be constraining, while a list that's too big can be unwieldy and bewildering.

In this paper, we take our inspiration for a new 2D shape from a popular class of 3D primitives which combine two spheres with a connector.

One such sphere-and-connector shape is the cone-sphere introduced by Max [1990]. This primitive smoothly joins two non-overlapping spheres with a right circular cone. Another sphere-and-connector shape emerges from an implicit surface technique popularized by Blinn [1982]. This approach models each sphere as a spherically symmetric Gaussian density field called a blob and then extracts an isosurface from the combined field of all the blobs. This naturally produces a smooth join between each pair of spheres that are close enough together.

Figure 1: A gallery of globs.

Citation: Andrew Glassner, Globs: A Primitive Shape for Graceful Blends Between Circles, Journal of Computer Graphics Techniques Vol. 4, No. 3, 2015. http://jcgt.org/published/0004/03/01/

Both of these primitives have a lot going for them: The cone-spheres require no parameters or controls, and blobs produce lovely stretching and clumping effects as the blob centers move with respect to one another. They are both easily adapted to a 2D drawing system.

These primitives each have drawbacks, though. Because cone-spheres have no shape parameters, they offer no variation or control, and the silhouette is always a straight line joining two circles. Blobs have more parameters, but these offer little control over the fundamental nature of the shapes they produce. For example, as two blobs pull apart, the neck between them gets thinner and thinner until the two shapes disconnect, but one cannot control the length or shape of this neck. To compensate, some modeling systems allow the designer to use other shapes to generate density fields [Wyvill et al. 1999]. This approach is very flexible and offers an exciting breadth of control, but that very flexibility introduces a significant increase in complexity and effort from the designer.

We have designed a 2D family of shapes that generalizes some of the best features of cone-spheres and blobby spheres, offering a wide range of shapes from a relatively small set of parameters. Some examples are shown in Figure 2. Our shapes provide an explicit curved neck between any two circles. The circles may overlap, and the neck can bulge inward or outward and move flexibly in the space between the circles. We can recreate classic cone-sphere and blobby shapes, but we can also easily create new kinds of shapes that would otherwise be difficult to produce, such as necks that start abruptly at one end but grow gracefully at the other, and asymmetric, bulging necks.

Figure 2: A gallery of globs.

THE GEOMETRY

The heart of the idea is that we build a pair of Bezier curves between the two circles. ´ We construct the curves so that they have at least first-derivative continuity with both circles. The designer can adjust many visual aspects of this connective neck.

Figure 3 shows the basic idea. We call the two circles C_0 and C_1, with respective centers C_0 and C_1, and radii r_0 and r_1. It is tempting to simplify the geometry by placing C_0 at the origin and C_1 directly to its right along the positive X-axis, and indeed one can do this with no loss of generality. As a practical matter, though, we have found that it's more convenient to solve the general case using coordinate-free vector techniques. This lets us produce results that can be immediately translated into code, without the need to write additional steps for scaling, rotation, and translation after the construction is done.

The first step is to introduce a local coordinate system. We create the normalized vector $\widehat{\mathbf{U}}$ on the axis from C_0 to C_1:

$$\mathbf{U} = C_1 - C_0,$$

$$\widehat{\mathbf{U}} = \frac{\mathbf{U}}{|\mathbf{U}|}.$$

We can then find the perpendicular $\widehat{\mathbf{V}}$ by requiring that it satisfies

$$\widehat{\mathbf{V}} \cdot \widehat{\mathbf{U}} = 0.$$

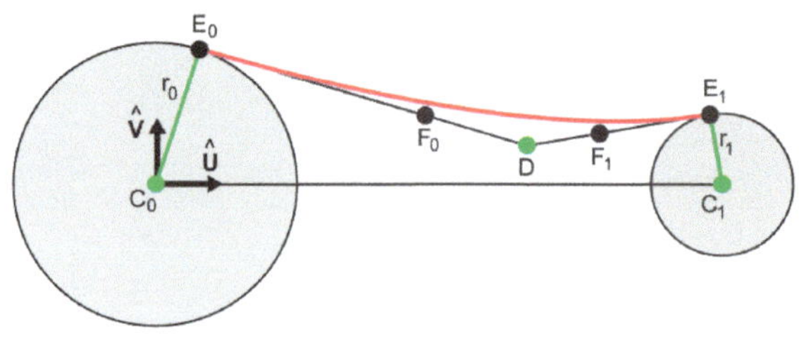

Figure 3: The geometry of a glob. C_0 and C_1 are the centers of circles with radii r_0 and r_1. To build a coordinate system, we find vector $\widehat{\mathbf{U}}$ by normalizing the vector from C_0 to C_1, and then form its perpendicular $\widehat{\mathbf{V}}$. The designer specifies the circle centers and the radii, along with the point D. The system computes points E_0 and E_1 which are the points of contact of a line through D and tangent to each circle. The points F_0 and F_1 are placed along the lines (E_0, D) and (E_1, D). From these points, we draw the Bezier curve ´ (E_0, F_0, F_1, E_1).

This is particularly easy in 2D if we allow ourselves to momentarily refer to coordinate values:

$$\widehat{\mathbf{V}} = (\widehat{U}_y, -\widehat{U}_x).$$

The narrowest (or widest) part of the neck is given by a point D that the designer can place anywhere outside of the circles. To create our Bezier curve, we draw lines from ´ D to each circle so that they are tangent to the circle. In the figure, these points are labeled E_0 and E_1. They serve as the endpoints for the Bezier curve.

To build a cubic Bezier curve we need two control points. We locate these on the ´ lines (E_0, D) and (E_1, D); they are marked F_0 and F_1 in the figure. The locations of F_0 and F_1 are found using two designer-specified scalars that tell us where they should be placed along their respective lines.

The curve we want is then given by (E_0, F_0, F_1, E_1). By construction, this has first-derivative continuity with the circles at both ends.

Note that D can be literally anywhere that is not within either of the two circles. It can be below the line (C_0, C_1) or far outside the convex hull of the circles.

It is fun (and instructive) to find the E and F points using plane geometry, creating a web of right triangles and solving for their lengths and angles. However, a coordinate-free vector approach is much simpler and robust.

We start with finding point E_0. Figure 4 shows the geometry for this step. We can think of Figure 4 as a subroutine: given a circle with center A and radius r, and a second point B that is outside the circle, find a point P_0 on the circle such that the line (P_0, B) is tangent to the circle. As the figure shows, there are two points that fulfill that condition. We indicate which one we want using one more argument to our routine (discussed in a moment). When we use this diagram to find point P0, then points P_0, A, and B in Figure 4 correspond to E_0, C_0, and D in Figure 3.

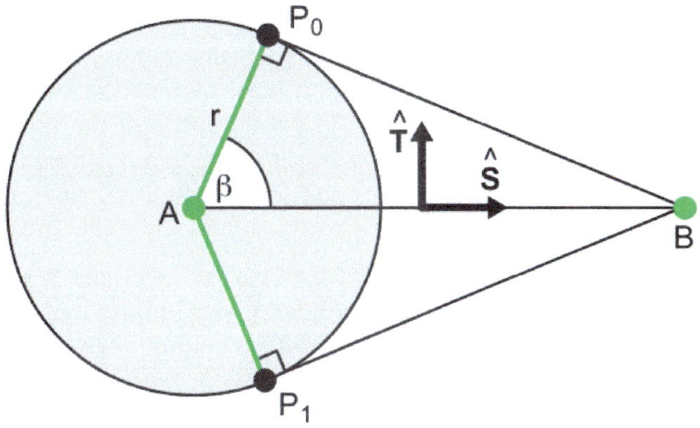

Figure 4: We are given the circle defined by center A and radius r, along with point B. We seek the points P_0 and P_1 that are on lines tangent to the circle and through point B. We find β and use that to add scaled versions of the coordinate system $(\widehat{\mathbf{S}}, \widehat{\mathbf{T}})$ to point A.

We begin by constructing a frame of perpendicular unit vectors $\widehat{\mathbf{S}}$ and $\widehat{\mathbf{T}}$, where $\widehat{\mathbf{S}}$ points from A to B. To find P0, we only need to find angle β. We know one leg and the hypotenuse of right triangle APOB. The length of the remaining leg is provided by Pythagoras:

$$|P_0B| = \sqrt{|AB|^2 - r^2}.$$

Now we can find β using arc-tangent:

$$\beta = \tan^{-1}(|P_0B| / r).$$

From this, we can create the two points P_0 and P_1, one on each side of $\widehat{\mathbf{S}}$. The expressions are identical except that we add a scaled version of $\widehat{\mathbf{T}}$ when forming P_0 and subtract it for P_1:

$$P_0 = A + (r\cos(\beta)\,\widehat{\mathbf{S}}) + (r\sin(\beta)\,\widehat{\mathbf{T}}),$$
$$P_1 = A + (r\cos(\beta)\,\widehat{\mathbf{S}}) - (r\sin(\beta)\,\widehat{\mathbf{T}}).$$

Essentially we're placing the radius vector at A, pointing at B, then rotating it by β, and finding the components of the new vector in the $\widehat{\mathbf{S}}$ and $\widehat{\mathbf{T}}$ directions.

Both P_0 and P_1 satisfy our initial criteria. We mentioned above that we have one additional argument that lets us pick the one we want. This argument specifies whether we want the one that is on our left or right as we stand at A and look towards B. To find which point lies on which side, we find two cross products and take the sign of their z-component:

$$\mathbf{K_0} = (P_0 - A) \times \widehat{\mathbf{S}},$$
$$\mathbf{K_1} = (P_1 - A) \times \widehat{\mathbf{S}},$$
$$s_0 = \text{sgn}(\mathbf{K_0}_z),$$
$$s_1 = \text{sgn}(\mathbf{K_1}_z).$$

By construction, one of these values will always be positive (on our left) and the other will always be negative (on our right). So, if we want the left-hand point, we return P_0 if $s_0 > 0$; otherwise, we return P_1. For the right-hand point, we return P0 if $s_0 < 0$, else P_1.

When applied to both circles, this method provides us with points E_0 and E_1 that are the endpoints of our Bezier curve. The next step is to find the internal control ′ points F_0 and F_1.

To find F_0, the designer specifies a scalar value a. This gives us a point on the line from E_0 (when a = 0) to D (when a = 1). This is something of a tightness or tension parameter, since it pulls the curve more or less forcefully towards the point D. We find F_1 in the same way, using tension parameter b:

$$F_0 = E_0 + a(D - E_0),$$
$$F_1 = E_1 + b(D - E_1).$$

We can now draw the cubic Bezier curve ′ (E_0, F_0, F_1, E_1). By construction, this has first-derivative continuity with the circles at both ends.

Since point D can be anywhere outside of the two circles, we can produce a wide range of squeezes and bulges. Because the tightness parameters a and b are independent, we can individually adjust how quickly the neck forms at each end, as shown in Figure 5.

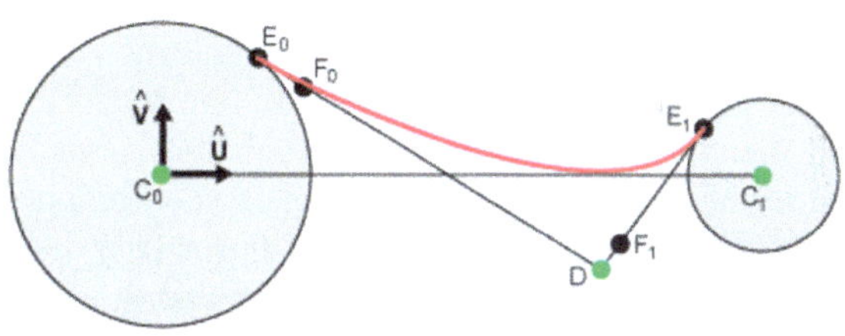

Figure 5: Parameter a controls the location of point F0 on the line (E_0, D), and simliarly parameter b controls the location of point F_1 on the line (E_1, D). These parameters are independent, allowing us to create neck shapes that blend asymmetrically into the two circles.

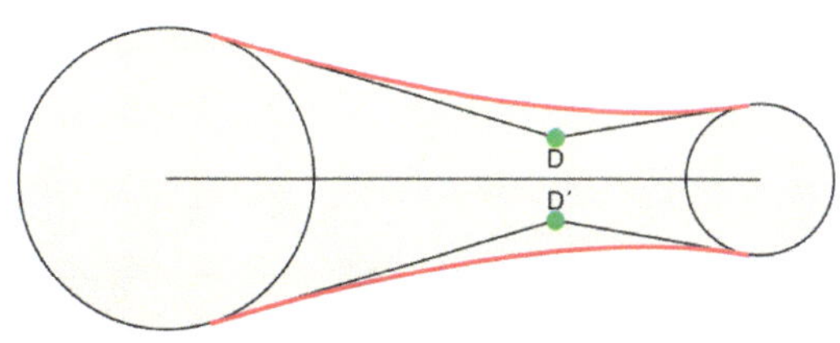

Figure 6: To create a symmetric glob, find the point D' that is the mirror reflection of D around the line (C_0, C_1) and create a new curve as before.

We can make a symmetric glob by drawing another Bezier curve that mirrors ′ the first about the line (C_0, C_1). This curve has the same basic form as the one we just looked at, so we'll use the same labels for the points but attach a prime mark to distinguish the lower points from the upper. We can find a new point D' that is the mirror image of D by breaking D into its projections along $\widehat{\mathbf{U}}$ and $\widehat{\mathbf{V}}$ and then recombining them, negating the component along $\widehat{\mathbf{V}}$:

$$D_u = (D - C_0) \cdot \widehat{\mathbf{U}},$$
$$D_v = (D - C_0) \cdot \widehat{\mathbf{V}},$$
$$D' = C_0 + D_u\widehat{\mathbf{U}} - D_v\widehat{\mathbf{V}}.$$

A typical result is shown in Figure 6.

We can construct much more interesting globs by creating the lower Bezier curve ′ independently of the upper one, as shown in Figure 7. Thus, the user can place the point D' anywhere outside the two circles, and from that we will find points E_0' and E_1'. Using tension parameters a' and b' , we find control points F_0' and F_1' , giving us a new Bezier curve. These two curves can interact in many ways, producing a generous ′ variety of shapes, as shown in Figure 2.

DISCUSSION

Cusps and Loops

The construction variables discussed above may be chosen so that the resulting Bezier ′ curve forms a cusp, or even a loop. It is possible to detect both of these cases [Stone and DeRose 1989], and one could then place limits on some or all of the design parameters to prevent such shapes from forming. We prefer to leave the values unconstrained, so designers are free to explore and use the entire design space.

Unexpected Corners

Our geometry for finding the tangent points is robust and fast, but it can produce a sharp corner where one might expect a smooth blend. This is because, although the curve will be tangent to the circle at the point of type E, depending on the tension parameters and the location of D (or D'), the curve may be shaped so that it does not wrap around the circle, but instead passes through it. The result is what appears to be a corner where the neck emerges from the circle, as shown in Figure 8.

One could detect this condition (perhaps by moving very slightly along the curve and testing to see if that point is inside the circle), and then enforce constraints to avoid it. But just as with cusps and loops, we don't try to prevent designers from creating such globs, because they can be useful.

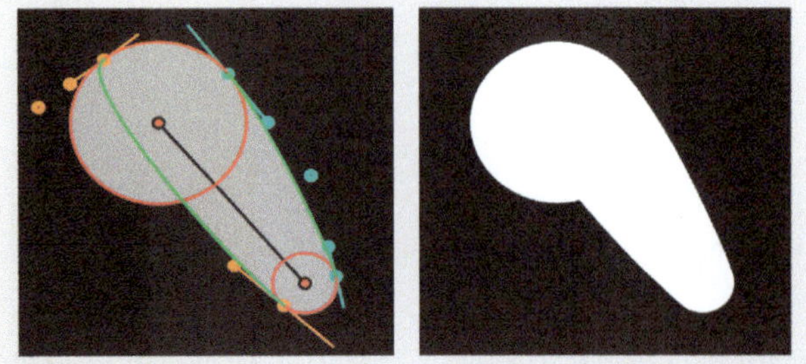

Figure 8: A sharp corner produced in our interactive tool. Left: Here we've drawn the two Bezier curves in green. Right: The glob without the interactive controls.

Tangents, Normals, Offset Curves, and Motion Paths

A nice feature of globs is that they have easy-to-compute tangent and normal vectors. For points on the circular ends, finding tangents and normals is trivial: the normal is merely the unit vector from the center of the circle to the point on the perimeter, and the tangent is its perpendicular. It's also easy to find these vectors along the Bezier ′ curves. The tangent is given by the standard equation for the tangent to a Bezier curve ′ at a given point, and the normal is its perpendicular [Shirley et al.].

We can use these normals to approximate an offset curve. It is well known that one cannot explicitly construct a Bezier curve that is the offset of another [′ Kamermans 2015], but there are many approximate algorithms. One of the simplest is to evaluate the curve at many points and find the normal at each point. An approximate offset curve can be producing simply by scaling the normals and joining them together as a spline.

The inner and outer glob offset curves in Figure 9 were constructed in this way. We sampled many points, found the normals, scaled them, and connected the endpoints together in a single closed Catmull-Rom curve.

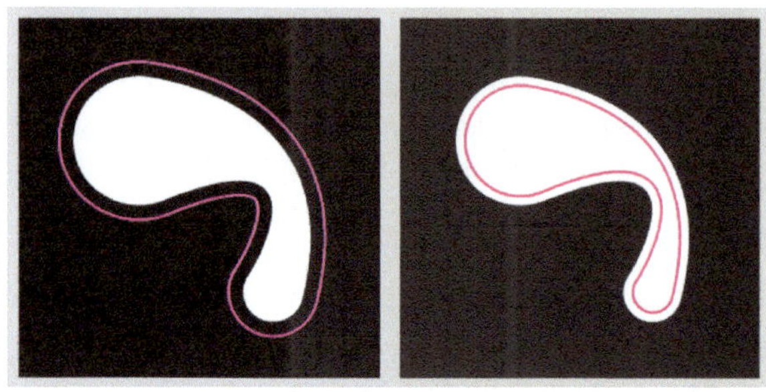

Figure 9: An outer and inner offset curve.

Figure 10 shows the same glob but with the normal vectors included. In this image, we have reduced the number of points evaluated along the curve from the number used in Figure 9 so the normal vectors are easier to see. The inner curve is constructed in the same way, only the normals are scaled by a negative amount.

One note of caution when working with this approach, though, is that one must remember that Bezier curves are not uniformly parameterized. That is, taking equal ′ steps of the input parameter (say t going from 0 to 1 in steps of .1) will usually not result in equally-spaced points along the curve. This phenomenon is visible in the more highly curved portion of the shape in Figure 10.

When the sampling density of points along the curve is low, this non-uniform spacing has the risk of creating artifacts in the resulting offset curve. Probably the easiest way to resolve the problem is to simply use more points. Another option is to explicitly adjust the evaluation parameter for the Bezier curve so that it corresponds ′ to arclength along the curve. This can be done efficiently by pre-computing the approximate arclength at many points along the curve and then looking up each input value in that table, returning a replacement evaluation parameter that produces a point that is at the desired distance along the curve. That is, we hand the table a value of t in the range [0, 1], and we get back a value t' in the same range such that when we evaluate the curve using t', the point we get back is t percent of the way along the curve.

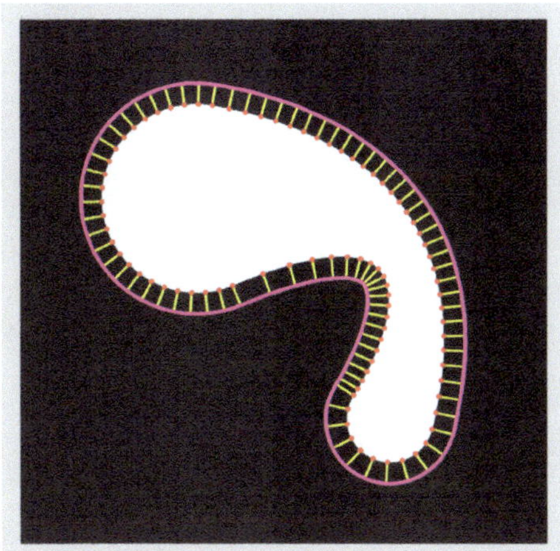

Figure 10: Creating the outer offset curve in Figure 9. The glob is evaluated at many points (red), the normals are found (yellow) and scaled, then joined together as a Catmull-Rom curve to form the offset curve.

Depending on the particular curve shape and offset amount, offset Bezier curves ´ can exhibit loops, swallowtails, and other non-smooth features. In particular, tight turns and large offsets reliably lead to cusps. The upper-left of Figure 11 shows one such example. Notice that the inner offset for this same glob, shown in the upperright, does not share the swallowtail in the outer offset. These phenomena are a natural property of approximated offset Bezier curves and are not specific to globs. ´ In general, as with the cusps and loops mentioned above, it's a judgment call by the designer to determine whether to accept these features, or to eliminate them by changing the distance of the offset (lower-left of Figure 11) or changing the shape (lower-right of Figure 11).

Because it's so straightforward to find points along the perimeter of the glob, the shape may also be conveniently used as a motion path. Using the arclength-based point spacing discussed above will give uniform speed along the glob's perimeter.

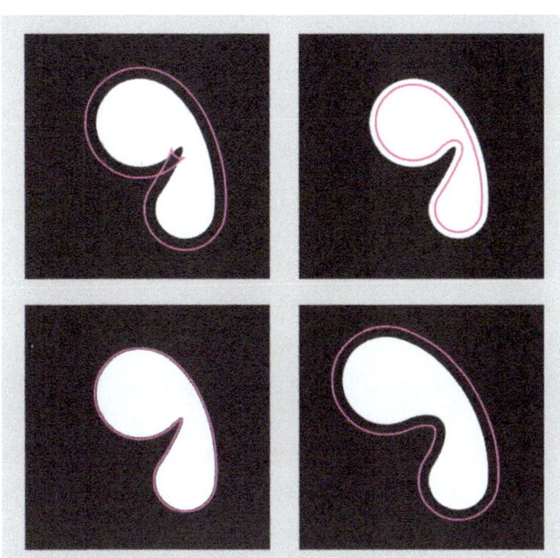

Figure 11: Upper-left: A glob's outer offset with a swallowtail cusp. Upper-right: The inner offset has no cusp. Lower-left: Reducing the distance of the offset removes the cusp. Lowerright: Modifying the shape to remove the cusp.

Smoothing Multiple Globs

An interesting issue arises when two globs share a common circle at one end. In some cases, they can produce a sharp corner where they overlap, as shown in the left of Figure 12. This is no different than when any two primitives overlap: there is no natural or automatic blending. And in many situations this contrast between smooth curves and sharp corners can be attractive. But because globs normally have a very smooth nature, there are times when we would like them to blend together smoothly as well.

One can design variations on the glob geometry to explicitly produce smooth surfaces when two globs overlap at a common endpoint. That would handle the case of two globs, but then one would need to design new special case geometry for three globs, another special case for four, and so on. We haven't found an explicit geometric construction that will always provide smooth joins for any number of shared globs.

Figure 12: Left: A deformed hexagonal net of globs, showing corners where they happen to overlap. Right: Smoothing the result by thresholding an implicit surface derived from the globs. All the sharp corners are now nicely rounded.

Happily, we can solve this problem by using implicit surfaces, like those used by traditional Gaussian blobs [Gourmel et al. 2013]. In 2D, treat each white pixel on the left of Figure 12 as the center of a small radially symmetric blob. For each pixel outside of a glob, sum the field contributions from all in-glob pixels (in practice, only consider pixels that are within the blob's radius, since the contribution from all other pixels will be 0). Normalize the field and then threshold it, creating a smooth isosurface as shown on the right in Figure 12. In this figure, there is some thickening of the shapes due to the spread of the blob fields. To compensate, one can draw slightly thinner shapes in the first place, or use a higher density threshold when extracting the isosurface. This technique can be thought of as using globs as the primitives for building an implicit surface [Bloomenthal 1997]. Indeed, we think the match is a natural one. Globs offer us the ability to control the shape of the blend between spherical functions when we want that control, and an isosurface naturally creates other blends when we don't need to explicitly shape them.

Specifying Globs

We have built a small stand-alone design program for making globs. Using this program, the designer can specify all the glob parameters interactively.

As shown in Figure 13, the interface closely matches the design structure in Figure 7. We draw small disks to represent each construction point. The points associated with the unprimed points are in teal, while the primed points are in orange. Circle centers are in red.

The points D and D0 are highlighted with a black dot in their center. These may be dragged anywhere in the window (though as we'll discuss below, dragging them into the circles will produce non-smooth results). The E family of points are constrained to move on the circles themselves, but pulling them towards or away from their corresponding circle center allows one to adjust the radius of that circle. Finally, the F family of points may be dragged anywhere on the line joining their corresponding D and E points, including regions outside the interval defined by those points. The glob is recalculated and redrawn every time a point is moved. Because the calculation is so fast, the design is fluid and interactive in real time, even when running inside a browser [Glassner 2015b].

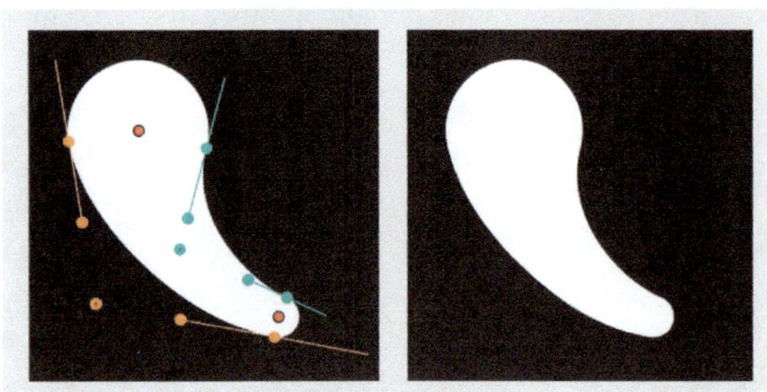

Figure 13: Left: Our design interface in action. The red dots are the centers of the circles. One set of curve points are in teal, the other points are in orange. Points D and D0 have a darker center. Right: This glob without the interface elements.

If the user adjusts a circle's radius by moving one of its corresponding E points towards or away from the circle center, that point will also move slightly around the circumference of the circle, in order to maintain tangency. In practice, we have found that this effect causes no confusion or surprise, since the point follows the designer's intended location as best it can given the constraints.

To construct the glob, the system infers the parameters a, b, a' and b' . For example, a is given by $a = |F_0 - E_0|/|D - E_0|$, where we use signed lengths, since point F0 may be dragged outside the interval (E_0, D).

Pressing a key allows the designer to turn these interfaces elements on and off, so the glob can be viewed without distraction.

API

We have implemented globs in our open-source library [Glassner 2015a] for the Processing system. We provide two slightly different constructors. The first is based directly on Figure 7: the user provides the circle centers and radii, the locations of points D and D', and the four control parameters a, b, a' and b' .

Requiring the explicit locations of D and D' can be inconvenient when the circle centers are moving over time, but we want to preserve the overall shape of the glob. To make this easy, a second API replaces the explicit location of D with a pair of scalars that describe the location of D in terms related to its components in the ($\hat{U}$, $\hat{V}$) system in Figure 7.

Let's focus on point D. Because D may not be placed inside either of the circles, the $\hat{U}$ -coordinate is expressed as a percentage of the length of the line segment formed by joining the circle centers, and then selecting only the region between them. This line is marked (P_0, P_1) in Figure 14. As d_c runs from 0 to 1, we locate a point along the line segment from P_0 to P_1. The perpendicular displacement of the point is given by parameter d_c, which is again a percentage of the distance $|P_0, P_1|$. Positive values of d_p move the point D away from the line (P_0, P_1) towards the curve's control points, as shown in the figure. Negative values push it in the opposite direction. The point D' is specified in the same way, with its own two scalars, d'_c and d'_p.

As with all our other design parameters, we place no restrictions on these controls, so designers are free to use any values they like in order to fully explore the space of shapes the algorithm can create.

Globs are easily animated. A particularly interesting case is when the two circles overlap. The construction method works fine in this situation, only requiring (as usual) that we keep the points D and D' outside of both circles. Thus, we can start with one circle completely within the other, and let it emerge, as shown in Figure 15. We can draw the neck as soon as at least some of both circles becomes visible.

EXAMPLES

Globs can create curved, organic shapes. They can also be chained, with one glob sharing an endpoint with another, leading to articulated multi-joint models that can exhibit subtly changing shapes over time without requiring external mechanisms like spatial deformations.

For example, Figure 16 shows a bug with multiple legs. Each leg is defined by a simple data structure that holds each joint radius and position. The legs can be positioned with direct or inverse kinematics, just like any chain structure. And the shapes of the globs can change in response to their motion over time, simulating a dynamics effect.

Figure 17 shows frames from three different animations that use globs to create moving, abstract designs. Over time the globs move and change shape in complex and subtle ways.

RELATED WORK

Globs have roots in common with other shapes beyond cone-spheres [Max 1990] and blobs [Blinn 1982]. The approach of Ma et al. [Ma et al. 2012] offers an analytic blending function for cone-spheres, with special-case geometry for creating smooth joins where two cone-spheres share a common end. Similarly, Bastl et al. [Bastl et al. 2015] offers a system for combining many cone-spheres together, but their blends are limited to cones that produce strictly convex shapes. Finally, one can consider globs to be special cases of a general swept sphere surface, as described by van Wijk [van Wijk 1985]. A swept sphere requires a path and a radius profile. We have found that globs offer a simpler alternative to the sometimes challenging design problem of crafting these two curves to achieve a desired shape, particularly when it comes to getting a smooth transition from the end spheres to a curved neck. We feel that a large part of the appeal of the glob primitive comes from the variety of shapes that can be produced with just a few controls, each of which has a specific geometric action.

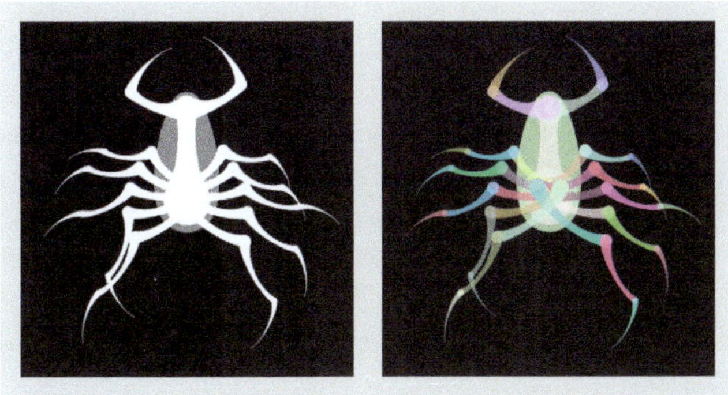

Figure 16: Globs can form organic shapes, particularly when they're chained together by sharing common endpoints. Left: A bug made completely out of globs. Right: The individual globs.

Figure 17: Frames from animations made with globs. The top two frames are from different moments in the same animation; the bottom two are from different animations.

FUTURE WORK

It would be appealing to construct globs with continuity in the second derivative or higher. To get C^2 -continuity with this geometry, we'd have to give up the freedom of placing the F points where we like, which we feel would sacrifice too much of the variety and control that makes globs attractive in the first place. We are currently investigating other geometries and spline types, seeking the same simple and direct interface controls but providing C^2 -continuity (or, better yet from a visual standpoint, G^2 geometric continuity). In the meantime, we note that being limited to C^1 parametric continuity isn't always such a bad thing: Max's cone-spheres are only C^1 -continuous and they have proven to be a popular and useful primitive. We also observe that even without a constructive guarantee of C^2 -continuity, most of the globs we have made are visually smooth. The examples in all the figures here are typical in this respect.

It's natural to think about promoting globs into 3D surfaces. It would be easy enough to create a surface of revolution by rotating any glob around a line, such as the line joining the circle centers. But this is a very limited technique, as it would produce rotationally symmetric shapes that lose much of the asymmetry that makes globs interesting. We are investigating a variety of 3D constructions for promoting a given glob into 3D while maintaining C^1 -continuity, and for creating 3D globs directly with a minimal and direct set of design controls.

CONCLUSION

We've shown that with just two points and four scalars, a designer can create a graceful and highly controllable neck between two circles of different radii. The neck can curve asymmetrically, and the designer can control both the location of the thinnest (or thickest) part of the neck, and how sharply the neck rises to join the circle at each end.

ACKNOWLEDGEMENTS

Thank you to Steven Drucker and Eric Haines for their help in clarifying the presentation, and to John Hughes for enlightening conversations about patches.

IMPLEMENTATION

A basic implementation of this technique is offered by the Glob class in Listings 1, 2, and 3. The code is in Processing (a Java-like language). The full implementation in our open-source library, with both constructors discussed above, is part of the library's complete source code included in the library download [Glassner 2015a].

```
class Glob {

  // The input geometry of a Glob
  PVector C0, C1;       // circle centers
  float r0, r1;         // circle radii
  PVector D, Dp;        // target points D and Dprime
  float a, b, ap, bp;   // control scalars a, b, aprime, bprime

  // the points we derive from the input geometry
  PVector U, V;
  PVector E0, E0p, E1, E1p, F0, F0p, F1, F1p;

  // these are for picking which tangent point we want
  final int SIDE_LEFT = -1;
  final int SIDE_RIGHT = 1;

  // make a new Glob with these parameters.  Save them,
  // then build the geometry.
  Glob(PVector _C0, float _r0, PVector _C1, float _r1,
       PVector _D,  float _a,  float _b,
       PVector _Dp, float _ap, float _bp) {
    C0 = _C0.copy();
    C1 = _C1.copy();
    r0 = _r0;
    r1 = _r1;
    D = _D.copy();
    a = _a;
    b = _b;
    Dp = _Dp.copy();
    ap = _ap;
    bp = _bp;
    buildGeometry();
  }
```

Listing 1: An implemention of a Glob class in Processing, Part 1.

```
// This is the heart of the class.  Using the definition of Glob
// geometry, // find the coordinate system (U, V), then the
// tangent points E, and from them the Bezier control points F.
void buildGeometry() {
  U = PVector.sub(C1, C0);
  U.normalize();
  V = new PVector(U.y, -U.x);

  E0 = getTangentPoint(C0, D, r0, SIDE_RIGHT);
  E1 = getTangentPoint(C1, D, r1, SIDE_LEFT);
  E0p = getTangentPoint(C0, Dp, r0, SIDE_LEFT);
  E1p = getTangentPoint(C1, Dp, r1, SIDE_RIGHT);

  F0 = PVector.lerp(E0, D, a);
  F1 = PVector.lerp(E1, D, b);
  F0p = PVector.lerp(E0p, Dp, ap);
  F1p = PVector.lerp(E1p, Dp, bp);
}

// The P-finding routine.  Given a circle of center A
// and radius r, a point B outside the circle, and a
// choice of "side", return a point on the circle that
// forms a tangent line to the circle with point B.
PVector getTangentPoint(PVector A, PVector B, float r, int side) {
  PVector S = PVector.sub(B, A);
  S.normalize();
  PVector T = new PVector(S.y, -S.x);

  float ab = A.dist(B);
  float pb = sqrt(sq(ab)-sq(r));
  float beta = atan2(pb, r);
  float uscl = r * cos(beta);
  float vscl = r * sin(beta);
  PVector P0 = new PVector(A.x + (uscl*S.x) + (vscl*T.x),
                           A.y + (uscl*S.y) + (vscl*T.y));
  PVector P1 = new PVector(A.x + (uscl*S.x) - (vscl*T.x),
                           A.y + (uscl*S.y) - (vscl*T.y));
```

Listing 2: An implemention of a Glob class in Processing, Part 2.

```
  // now pick one or the other, using the sign of
  // cross products from each P to A with S
  PVector dP0 = PVector.sub(P0, A);
  PVector dP1 = PVector.sub(P1, A);
  float p0sgn = S.cross(dP0).z;
  float p1sgn = S.cross(dP1).z;
  // this next test should never succeed if r>0
  if (p0sgn * p1sgn > 0) { // both are negative or positive
    println("getTangentPoint:␣both␣points␣on␣same␣side␣of␣line!");
    return P0;
  }
  if (side == SIDE_RIGHT) { // the positive side is on the right
    if (p0sgn > 0) return P0;
    return P1;
  }
  if (p0sgn < 0) return P0;
  return P1;
}

// a utility method to draw the Glob in a straightforward way
void render(boolean drawNeck, boolean drawCaps) {
  if (drawCaps) {
    ellipse(C0.x, C0.y, 2*r0, 2*r0);
    ellipse(C1.x, C1.y, 2*r1, 2*r1);
  }
  if (drawNeck) { // this shape is what it's is all about!
    beginShape();
      vertex(E0.x, E0.y);
      bezierVertex(F0.x, F0.y, F1.x, F1.y, E1.x, E1.y);
      vertex(E1p.x, E1p.y);
      bezierVertex(F1p.x, F1p.y, F0p.x, F0p.y, E0p.x, E0p.y);
    endShape(CLOSE);
  }
}
}
```

Listing 3: An implemention of a Glob class in Processing, Part 3.

REFERENCES

1. BASTL, B., KOSINKA, J., AND LAVI ´ CKA ˇ , M. 2015. Simple and branched skins of systemsof circles and convex shape. Graphical Models 78 (March), 1–9. 15
2. BLINN, J. F. 1982. A generalization of algebraic surface drawing. ACM Transactions onGraphics 1, 3 (July), 235–256. 2, 15
3. BLOOMENTHAL, J., Ed. 1997. Introduction to Implicit Surfaces. Morgan Kaufmann, LosAlamitos, CA. 12
4. GLASSNER, A. 2015. The AU library. Open-source library for the Processing graphicssystem. URL: http://www.imaginary-institute.com/resources/AULibrary/AULibrary.php. 13, 17
5. GLASSNER, A. 2015. Globs. Imaginary Institute Technical Note #11, April.URL: http://imaginary-institute.com/resources/TechNote11/TechNote11.html. 13, 21
6. GOURMEL, O., BARTHE, L., CANI, M.-P., WYVILL, B., BERNHARDT, A., PAULIN, M.,AND GRASBERGER, H. 2013. A gradient-based implicit blend. ACM Transactions onGraphics 32, 2. 12
7. KAMERMANS, M. P. 2015. A Primer on Bezier Curves. Online tutorial. URL: ´ http://pomax.github.io/bezierinfo. 9
8. MA, Y., TU, C., AND WANG, W. 2012. Distance computation for canal surfaces using conespherebounding volumes. Computer Aided Geometric Design 29, 5 (June), 255–264. 15
9. MAX,N.1990.Cone-spheres.ProceedingsofSIGGRAPH '90, 59–62. 2, 15SHIRLEY, P., ASHIKHMIN, M., AND MARSCHNER, S. Fundamentals of Computer Graphics.A K Peters, Natick, MA. 9
10. STONE, M., AND DEROSE, T. 1989. A geometric characterization of parametric cubiccurves. ACM Transactions on Graphics 8, 3 (July), 157–163. 8
11. VAN WIJK, J. 1985. Ray Tracing Objects Defined By Sweeping A Sphere. PhD thesis, DelftUniversity of Technology. 15
12. WYVILL, B., GALIN, E., AND GUY, A. 1999. Extending The CSG Tree. Warping, Blendingand Boolean Operations in an Implicit Surface Modeling System. Computer GraphicsForum 18, 2 (June), 149–158. 2

CHAPTER 3 DIRECT RAY TRACING OF FULL-FEATURED SUBDIVISION SURFACES WITH BEZIER CLIPPING

3

Takahito Tejima[1], Masahiro Fujita[2], and Toru Matsuoka

[1]Pixar Animation Studios

[2]Light Transport Entertainment

[3]DeNA Inc

ABSTRACT

We present a novel, direct ray-tracing method for rendering Catmull-Clark subdivision surfaces. Our method resolves an intersection with Bezier patches without performing of polygon tessellation as done in most traditional renderers. It supports the full set of RenderMan and OpenSubdiv subdivision surface features, including hierarchical edits, creases, semi-sharp creases, corners, the chaikin rule, and holes.

Our method is fast (compared to traditional CPU ray tracers), robust and crack-free, has very low memory requirements, and minimizes BVH construction and traversal overhead for high subdivision levels. It computes ray-surface intersection using Bezier clipping on patches obtained from the full-featured subdivision surfaces.

In this paper, we explain our implementation and evaluate its performance and memory characteristics for primary ray casting. We further show examples of indirect illumination using secondary ray casting and note that because the method does not require view-dependent pre-tessellation, may offer further advantages in that case.

Citation: Takahito Tejima, Masahiro Fujita, and Toru Matsuoka, Direct Ray Tracing of Full-Featured Subdivision Surfaces with Bezier Clipping, Journal of Computer Graphics Techniques Vol. 4, No. 1, 2015. http://jcgt.org/published/0004/01/04/

(a) Direct ray trace rendering

(b) Close view of (a)

(c) Memory usage (GB)

Figure 1: (a) A result of ray casting using our algorithm. 1.1M patches at 1K x 1K resolution, rendered in 0.218s with 305.2MB of memory. (b) Close view of the same model in 1.226 s. (c) Memory usage of PreTess:pre-tessellation, BC2:Bezier clipping method with 2 patches in ´ leaf nodes and BC16:Bezier clipping method with 16 patches in leaf nodes.

(a) Rendering example of the bike model

(b) Rendering example of a car model. Isolation level 5, 2.2M patches, 597MB

Figure 2: Global illumination renderings by tracing secondary rays using our method.

INTRODUCTION

Subdivision surfaces are smooth surfaces obtained by recursively subdividing a control mesh. Modern subdivision surfaces contain many features necessary for authoring complex shapes. It is essential that any production renderer support the full set of such features, as defined by the RenderMan [Pixar Animation Studios 2005] specification and its open equivalent, OpenSubdiv [OpenSubdiv]. These features include the semi-sharp crease introduced by Derose et al. [1998] and the ForseyBartels [1988] hierarchical representation. A full list of these features is found in the OpenSubdiv online manual Subdivision Surfaces page, http://graphics.pixar. com/ opensubdiv/docs/subdivision_surfaces.html.

We propose an efficient direct ray tracing method for feature adaptive CatmullClark subdivision surfaces using fast and robust Bezier patch intersection. Our method ´ gives the intersection on the limit position of the subdivision surface, without having densely tessellated quads or triangles. It significantly reduces the memory footprint for both BVH nodes and geometry. Also, we address the crack issues on the patch boundaries which arise from non-uniform patch conformation and floating point computation accuracy.

An intersection algorithm is not only for rendering. It can also be used for global illumination (shadow and secondary ray) effect, collision detection, cloth simulation, texture painting tools, etc.

The Catmull-Clark subdivision method is the most common one employed in modeling and rendering software packages, so we focus on it in this paper.

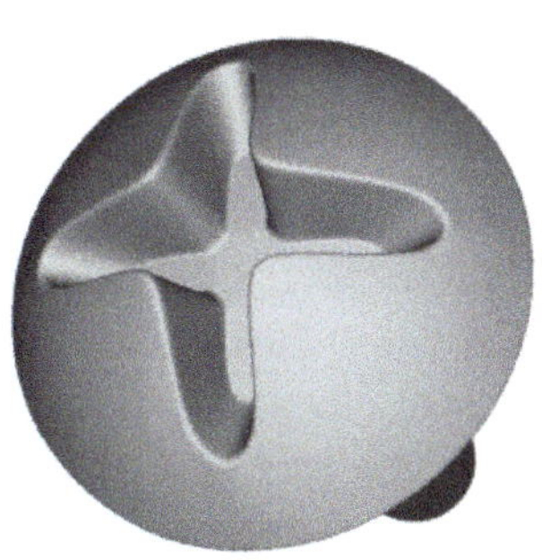

(a) Rendering example

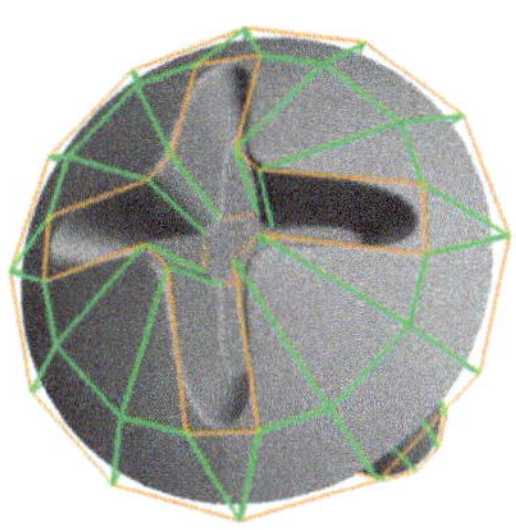

(b) GL rendering by OpenSubdiv

Figure 3: (a) A screw modeled by 84 faces with creases. (b) The control cage of the screw and GL rendering by OpenSubdiv [OpenSubdiv].

RELATED WORK

We classify ray tracing methods for subdivision surfaces into two categories, a) Pre tessellation and b) Direct intersection, following Muller et al. [2003]. Pre-tessellation techniques are usually preferred, because they are simple and fast. Christensen et al. [2003] proposed using ray differentials to construct multiresolution caches for tessellated faces.

Kobbelt et al.'s [1998] direct intersection method introduced a bounding envelope technique for intersecting a ray with a subdivision surface. Benthin et al. [2007] proposed the efficient direct rendering of subdivision surfaces using packet ray tracing. Their method recursively subdivides a patch for a ray packet and the final intersection is computed by approximating patches with polygons.

More recently, full-featured subdivision surface rendering using GPU has been proposed [Nießner et al. 2012a; Nießner et al. 2012b]. They introduced feature adaptive analysis, which selectively refines around creases, corners, hierarchical edits and extraordinary vertices, and then represents a subdivision surface as a set of bicubic B-spline patches. We notice that this analysis is also useful for ray-tracing, since B-spline patch can be easily converted into Bezier patch, and direct B ´ ezier patch ´ intersection methods for ray tracing have already been studied, using the Newton method [Martin et al. 2000] and Bezier clipping [´ Efremov et al. 2005].

OUR APPROACH

Our algorithm is composed of the following four stages: 1) Generate B-spline patches by feature adaptive subdivision. 2) Convert B-spline patches to Bezier patches. 3) ´ Construct BVH using the bound of generated Bezier patch. 4) Compute B ´ ezier - ray ´ patch intersection using robust and crack-free Bezier clipping.

Algorithm 1: Our Bezier - ray intersection algorithm.

```
function BEZIERPATCHCLIP(patch, level, clipDir)
    rotPatch ← XYROTATE(patch, clipDir)
    if MAXEXTENT(rotPatch) ≤ ε or level ≥ kMaxLevel then
        return BILINEARPATCHINTERSECT(patch)
    else
        (r_min, r_max) ← BEZIERCLIPRANGE(rotPatch, clipDir)
        nextClipDir ← clipDir == U ? V : U
        nextLv ← clipDir == V ? level + 1 : level
        if (r_max − r_min) ≥ 0.5 then
            patch0 ←BEZIERPATCHCROP(patch, clipDir, 0, 1/2)
            patch1 ←BEZIERPATCHCROP(patch, clipDir, 1/2, 1)
            hit0 ←BEZIERPATCHCLIP(patch0, nextLv, nextClipDir)
            hit1 ←BEZIERPATCHCLIP(patch1, nextLv, nextClipDir)
            return NEAREST(hit0, hit1)
        else
            patch ← BEZIERPATCHCROP(patch, clipDir, r_min, r_max)
            return BEZIERPATCHCLIP(patch, nextLv, nextClipDir)

function BEZIERISECT(patch, ray)
    patch ← ZALIGN(patch, ray)
    return BEZIERPATCHCLIP(patch, 0, U)
```

Generate B-spline Patches by Feature-Adaptive Subdivision

We follow Nießner et al. [2012a] for feature adaptive tessellation of Catmull-Clark subdivision surfaces. Firstly, the method builds adjacency structure and a feature adaptive mesh representation using half-edge algorithm. A face is classified as an irregular patch if it contains extraordinary vertices with degree other than four, if its edges or vertices have creases, or if it contains hierarchical edits. Irregular patches are further subdivided until a user-specified subdivision level has been reached or they become regular (Fig. 5 left). We also ensure that patches contain a single crease. We do this by applying direct semi-smooth crease evaluation on the patch instead of iteratively subdividing to its sharpness level [Nießner et al. 2012b]. Single-crease patches suppress the total number of patches to be generated (Fig. 4). All of this work is done during a CPU preprocessing phase. It does not require re-computation unless the underlying topology changes.

As a result of the feature adaptive analysis, B-spline patches are generated for regular patches, and Gregory patches are generated for the remaining irregular patches. We translated them into Bezier patches for intersection calculations. Single-crease ´ patches can be split into two or three Bezier patches depending on whether the sharp- ´ ness is integer or fractional, as described in Nießner et al. [2012b]. We average inner control points of Gregory patches to replace with Bezier patches, assuming irregu- ´ lar patches are sufficiently isolated. Their surface derivatives can be evaluated with Gregory basis, once a surface parameter of the intersection has been determined.

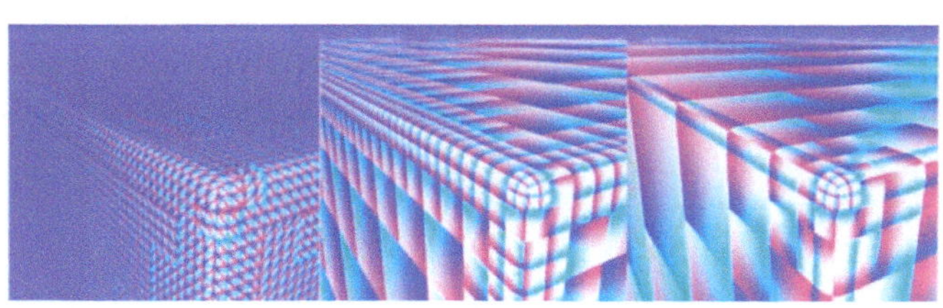

Figure 4: Comparison of the patch conformation around the edge with sharpness 8.0. Left: Dense quads from uniform subdivision at level 8. Center: Patches from feature adaptive subdivision. Right: Patches from feature adaptive subdivision with single crease patch enabled.

Convert B-spline Patches to Bezier Patches

When converting B-spline control points into Bezier control points, we use bireversal- ´ invariant evaluation in a similar way as shown in Nießner et al. [2012a]. It produces bitwise identical results regardless of the uv direction of the base patches, which we confirmed by an exhaustive search of all representable floating point values on [0, 1). Nießner et al. [2012a] also showed that for the patches generated by different subdivision levels that also share a boundary, the parent control points should be used to ensure watertight evaluation.

We set a flag on the patch generated to classify it as a transition patch (a patch that shares a boundary with patches of different subdivision level [Nießner et al. 2012a]). This flag is used in conservative intersection algorithm to prevent cracks (holes), which will be described in detail in Section 3.4.3.

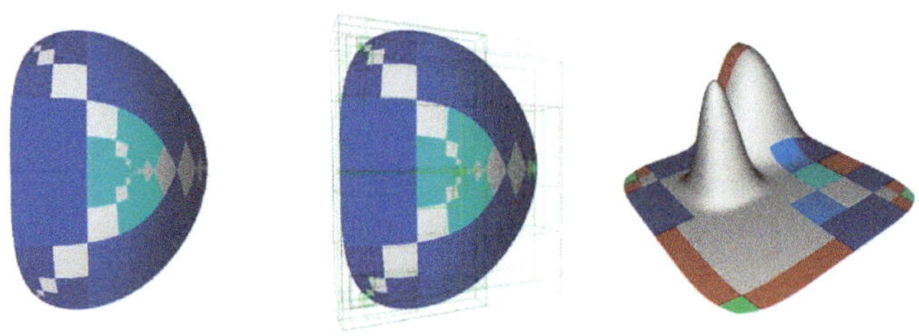

Figure 5: Left: Feature adaptive subdivision. Each patch has different colors. Middle: Its corresponding BVH visualization. Right: Hierarchical edits are also supported (From an OpenSubdiv example).

Construct the BVH from Generated Bezier Patch Bounds

Next, we construct an axis-aligned BVH (Bounding Volume Hierarchy) [Rubin and Whitted 1980] for the Bezier patches generated in Section ´ 3.1. Thanks to the convex property of a Bezier surface, we only need to compute the bounding box enclosing ´ the control points of Bezier patches. See Fig. ´ 5 middle.

Compute Bezier Patch Intersection

Because we are intersecting rays against bicubic Bezier patches, many new challenges ´ arise that are not typically addressed in traditional bilinear triangle intersection methods.

We use Bezier clipping, since Newton iteration has an initialization problem known ´ as the initial guess. Firstly, we transform the patch to align the local Z-axis to the ray direction in order to gain the numerical efficiency and stability. Then we rotate the patch on the XY -plane at each clipping iteration to determine the clipping range more efficiently [Efremov et al. 2005]. Note that the rotated patch is used only for range determination. Bezier clipping is always applied to the ray aligned patch to avoid ´ floating point errors. Once the clipping iteration converged, our method approximates the remaining small patch with a bilinear patch. The intersection of the bilinear patch can be numerically found in a robust way [Ramsey et al. 2004]. See Algorithm 1 for details.

We further added the following extension to ensure crack-free intersections across patch boundaries.

Bezier Cropping

Our method crops a patch from domain ([0, 1], [0, 1]) to ([u0, u1], [v0, v1]) for each iteration of Bezier clipping. Since feature adaptive analysis of subdivision surfaces ´ produces arbitrarily oriented Bezier patches, and IEEE 754 floating point addition ´ and multiplication are neither associative nor distributive, we also need to modify the cropping operation for reversal-invariance (Fig. 6).

Although exhaustive stress-testing of this code is impossible due to the combinatorial explosion, we still confirmed that it computes bitwise identical control points between adjacent patches for some of our test data and OpenSubdiv examples.

Optimal Epsilon Selection

Our method terminates clipping iterations when the maximum extent of a cropped patch becomes less than a threshold ϵ, or when the clipping iteration reaches kM axLevel iterations. We then find an intersection with a ray by approximating the surface with a bilinear patch. The optimal size of the bilinear patch is ideally smaller than 1 pixel of the screen for the eye ray.

To compute an optimal ϵ for the bilinear patch, we use ray differentials [Igehy 1999]. We approximate the distance from the ray origin to the patch by the hit distance to the axis-aligned bounding box of the patch, and conservatively estimate optimal epsilon.

```
// p0 p1 p2 p3
// 0----s--------t---1
// 1----T--------S---0
BezierCrop(vec r[], vec p[], int stride, float s, float t) {
  vec p0 = p[0*stride],
      p1 = p[1*stride];
      p2 = p[2*stride];
      p3 = p[3*stride];
  float T = 1-s, S = 1-t;
  s = 1-T; t = 1-S;

  r[0*stride] =
    (p0*T*T*T + p3*s*s*s) + (p1*3*s*T*T  + p2*3*s*s*T);
  r[1*stride] =
    (p0*T*T*S + p3*s*s*t) + (p1*T*(2*S*s + T*t) + p2*s*(2*t*T + s*S));
  r[2*stride] =
    (p3*t*t*s + p0*S*S*T) + (p2*t*(2*s*S + t*T) + p1*S*(2*T*t + S*s));
  r[3*stride] =
    (p3*t*t*t + p0*S*S*S) + (p2*3*S*t*t  + p1*3*S*S*t);
}

BezierPatchCrop(vec cp[16], dir clipDir,
                float u0, float u1, float v0, float v1) {
  if (clipDir == U) {
    for (int i = 0; i < 4; ++i) BezierCrop(cp[i*4], cp[i*4], 1, u0, u1);
  } else {
    for (int i = 0; i < 4; ++i) BezierCrop(cp[i], cp[i], 4, v0, v1);
  }
}
```

Figure 6: Reversal-invariant Bezier cropping.

For the eye ray, the optimal epsilon ϵ is computed as follows,

$$\epsilon = \frac{1}{2} \cdot \min\left(\left|\frac{\partial P}{\partial x}\right|, \left|\frac{\partial P}{\partial y}\right|\right) \tag{1}$$

where $\frac{\partial P}{\partial x}$ and $\frac{\partial P}{\partial y}$ are the partial derivatives of an approximate hit position P, which is estimated according to the pixel plane (see Fig. 7 right).

The optimal epsilon for secondary ray or others are computed similarly by tracing ray differentials.

Conservative Intersection Algorithm

The refinement of the surface to bicubic patches may result in adjacent patches that meet at the split between two patches at the next level of subdivision. These patches are identified as transition patches during feature adaptive analysis. Each of these transition patches has one to four transitioning edges which split at the midpoint of the edge. For GPU rasterizer-based rendering, a transition patch will be split into several sub-patches to avoid cracks where the tessellation interval mismatches [Nießner et al. 2012a]. Though there is no tessellation in our method, cracks may still appear as a result of the floating point computation if each side of a transitioning boundary edge is computed from control points at different levels of refinement.

We introduce a conservative intersection algorithm to address this problem. When the ray fails to intersect a transitioning edge, the method further subdivides the patch into four sub-Bezier patches at the middle of the parameter domain, $(u, v) = (\frac{1}{2}, \frac{1}{2})$. We then search for an intersection within these sub patches (Fig. 7 left and middle). See Fig. 8 for results. This conservative intersection algorithm is only needed when the expected intersection point is along one of the transitioning boundary edges of a transition patch. To guarantee the watertightness between these four sub-patches and adjacent patches, we override the border control points of the adjacent patches with control points from the subdivided four sub-patches during B-spline-to-Bezier ′ conversion process. This guarantees that they are bitwise identical.

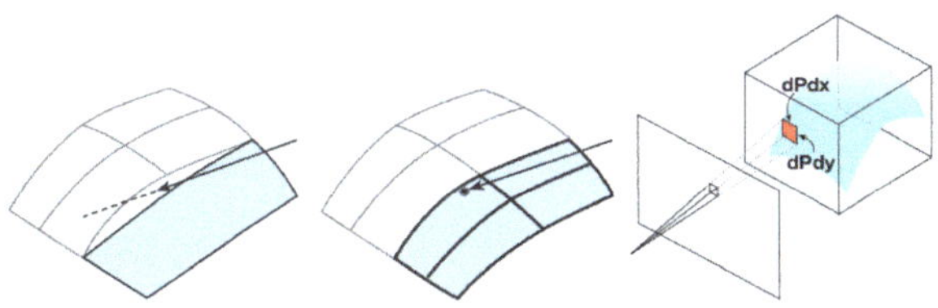

Figure 7: Left: Ray misses the surface because of a crack. Middle: Our conservative intersection algorithm generates four sub-patches on demand to fill a crack. Right: Ray differentials for the optimal ϵ selection.

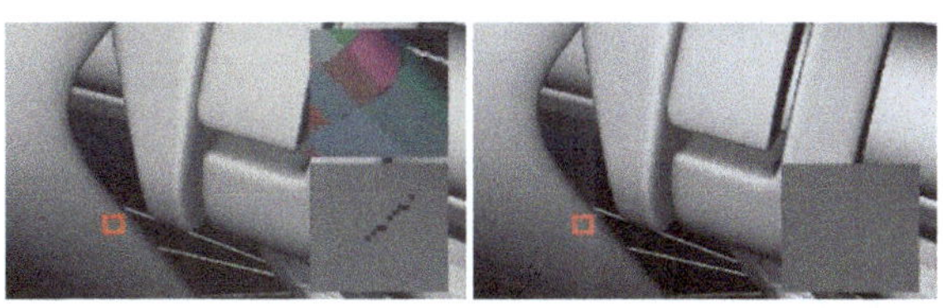

Figure 8: A rendering from the Bike model. Left: A crack appears without the conservative intersection algorithm near transition patch. Right: Crack-free rendering with the conservative intersection algorithm.

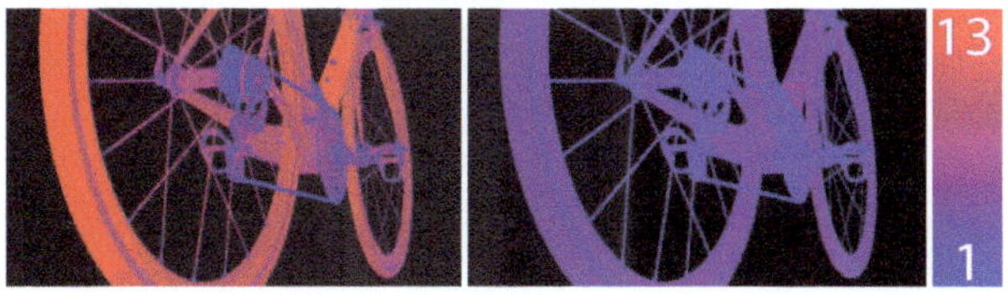

Figure 9: Visualization of the recursion level for Bezier intersection. Left: B ′ ezier clipping ′ disabled (Na′ıve midpoint subdivision). Right: Bezier clipping enabled.

IMPLEMENTATION AND RESULTS

Our implementation uses the OpenSubdiv [OpenSubdiv] library and custom C++ ray tracer. The input mesh is first processed by OpenSubdiv in order to build a feature adaptive hierarchical bicubic patch representation.

For the BVH, we have implemented a BVH builder with binned SAH partition [Shevtsov et al. 2007]. We compared two configurations for the maximum number of primitives (Bezier patches) in the leaf node, which are 2 and 16. Multi-threading is ′ implemented using Intel Thread Building Blocks [Intel Threading Building Blocks].

Bezier Clipping Efficiency

Fig. 9 shows the efficiency that our clipping algorithm gains by exploiting the convex hull property of Bezier patches. Most pixels converge in less than five levels of recur- ′ sion (Fig. 9 right). By comparison, they would need up to 13 levels of recursion to converge if we always split the patch at the midpoint (na′ıve intersection method for Bezier patch. Fig. ′ 9 left).

Memory and Performance

We measured the performance of our renderer for the Bike model against the following methods: Pre-tessellation (PreTess), our Bezier clipping method (BC) and our ′ method with conservative intersection algorithm (BCC). The maximum number of Bezier clipping iteration (kM axLevel) is set to 16, which is enough high for most view configurations in our experiment. All methods use single precision.

The Bike model is composed of 51k faces of initial control cage, with 30k semisharp creased edges. Feature adaptive isolation produces 1.1M patches at isolation level 5. Applying uniform pre-tessellation up to the same level of subdivision generates 104M triangles. Fig. 1c and Fig. 10 show the memory footprint of both PreTess and BC/BCC methods. While the number of triangles of the uniform tessellation increases by 4x for each level, the number of Bezier patches stays moderate. Note that the level has different meaning in PreTess and BCC/BC. PreTess level is a subdivision level, whereas BCC/BC level is a feature isolation level. In PreTess, the surface smoothness depends on the level. On the other hand, the surface is always smooth in BCC/BC since there is no tessellation, and the level controls the accuracy around extraordinary vertices and creases instead.

Method	# of Leaf Primitives	Lvl 1 (in MB)	Lvl 2	Lvl 3	Lvl 4	Lvl 5
PreTess	16	18.3	67.7	241.6	854.5	3164.0
BC16/BCC16	16	32.2	78.6	135.5	181.5	225.9
BC2/BCC2	2	43.2	106.1	182.8	245.3	305.2
# of triangles		0.4M	1.6M	6.5M	26M	104M
# of Bézier patches		164K	402K	694K	931K	1.1M

Figure 10: Memory footprints (geometry + BVH) of PreTess and BC/BCC in different levels. Triangle vertices are indexed.

Fig. 11 and Fig. 12 show the performance in two view configurations. The rendering time of BCC16 is between Lvl 4 and Lvl 5 of PreTess. BCC2 requires more memory for

BVH but it is much faster, since Bezier intersection is more expensive ´ than BVH traversal. BCC crack-free rendering is similar to BC, which shows the efficiency of conservative intersection algorithm.

CONCLUSION AND FUTURE WORK

We present an efficient and practical method for ray tracing of Catmull-Clark subdivision surfaces with semi-sharp creases and hierarchical edits. Our method uses Bezier ´ patches for the efficient and precise computation of the intersection.

We propose robust, crack-free and automatic precision selection independent of geometric scale for Bezier-ray intersection. These properties are attractive for pro- ´ duction rendering, as well as other applications including collision detection.

Our method is competitive with pre-tessellation methods in speed, while signifi- cantly reducing memory requirements. In this paper, we mainly focused on memory reduction and we evaluate results against uniformly tessellated triangles. We wish to pursue a more comprehensive performance comparison against other optimized renderers as future work.

Although some renderers use adaptive tessellation for efficiency, they often generate comparable numbers of triangles to those used in our tests. We also see many additional benefits from using a higher-order representation, including faster BVH updating for real-time animation and less bandwidth usage.

Our technique is computationally intensive and works on a large data set with a small working-set memory footprint. It is thus a good candidate for seeking realtime rendering and deformation of subdivision surfaces through a massively parallel implementation on a GPU.

View	Method	Level	Traverse (sec)	Intersect (sec)	Total time (sec)
	PreTess	3	0.053	0.051	0.138
	PreTess	4	0.072	0.081	0.192
	PreTess	5	0.124	0.181	0.368
Distant	BCC16	3	0.037	0.186	0.252
(Fig. 1a)	BCC16	4	0.040	0.191	0.260
	BCC16	5	0.042	0.198	0.271
	BCC2	3	0.047	0.136	0.212
	BCC2	4	0.050	0.142	0.217
	BCC2	5	0.053	0.137	0.218
	BC2	5	0.055	0.120	0.205
	PreTess	3	0.447	0.689	1.391
	PreTess	4	0.770	1.286	2.512
	PreTess	5	1.517	2.593	4.961
Close	BCC16	3	0.265	2.233	2.689
(Fig. 1b)	BCC16	4	0.284	2.520	3.022
	BCC16	5	0.325	2.940	3.519
	BCC2	3	0.362	0.584	1.033
	BCC2	4	0.398	0.610	1.106
	BCC2	5	0.456	0.673	1.226
	BC2	5	0.452	0.558	1.116

BCC16 : Bézier Clipping & conservative intersection, leaf primitives = 16
BCC2 : Bézier Clipping & conservative intersection, leaf primitives = 2
BC2 : Bézier Clipping, leaf primitives = 2

Figure 11: Rendering time comparison at 1k x 1k resolution. Measured on Intel Xeon E5- 2680 2.7 GHz (8 cores, 16 threads). Traverse + Intersect does not equal to Total time because of shading and threading management cost, etc. Intersect of BC and BCC includes the normal vector evaluation.

We also plan to add support for displacement mapping using a Ptex-like data structure [Lee et al. 2000; Nießner and Loop 2013] for detailed geometric representation, which will make our method more practical for use in production rendering.

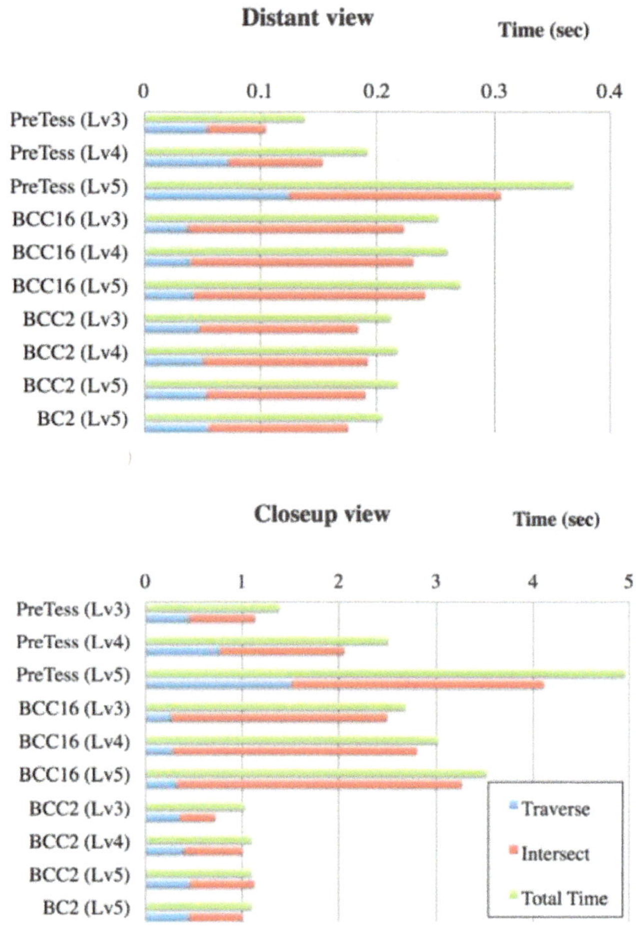

Figure 12: Plot of the Bike model rendering time.

ACKNOWLEDGEMENTS

We thank Yasutoshi Mori for the courtesy of the Bike model and the car modell. We also thank Manuel Kraemer, Mark Meyer, Tony DeRose, David G. Yu and the reviewers for their insightful comments and reviews and Amanda Turner of Williams College for proofreading.

REFERENCES

1. BENTHIN, C., BOULOS, S., LACEWELL, D., AND WALD, I. 2007. Packet-based ray tracingof catmull-clark subdivision surfaces. SCI Institute Technical Report UUSCI-2007-011, University of Utah. URL: http://www.sci.utah.edu/publications/SCITechReports/UUSCI-2007-011.pdf. 71
2. CHRISTENSEN, P. H., LAUR, D. M., FONG, J., WOOTEN, W. L., AND BATALI, D. 2003.Ray differentials and multiresolution geometry caching for distribution ray tracing in complexscenes. In Computer Graphics Forum, vol. 22, Wiley Online Library, 543–552. URL:http://dx.doi.org/10.1111/1467-8659.t01-1-00702. 71

3. DEROSE, T., KASS, M., AND TRUONG, T. 1998. Subdivision surfaces in character animation. In Proceedings of the 25th Annual Conference on Computer Graphics and InteractiveTechniques, SIGGRAPH '98, ACM, 85–94. URL: http://doi.acm.org/10.1145/280814.280826. 70

4. EFREMOV, A., HAVRAN, V., AND SEIDEL, H.-P. 2005. Robust and numerically stablebezier clipping method for ray tracing nurbs surfaces. In ´ Proceedings of the 21stspring conference on Computer graphics, ACM, 127–135. URL: http://dl.acm.org/citation.cfm?id=1090144. 71, 74

5. FORSEY, D. R., AND BARTELS, R. H. 1988. Hierarchical b-spline refinement. In Proceedingsof the 15th Annual Conference on Computer Graphics and Interactive Techniques,SIGGRAPH '88, ACM, 205–212. URL: http://doi.acm.org/10.1145/54852.378512. 70

6. IGEHY, H. 1999. Tracing ray differentials. In Proceedings of the 26th annual conferenceon Computer graphics and interactive techniques, ACM Press/ Addison-Wesley PublishingCo., 179–186. URL: http://dx.doi.org/10.1145/311535.311555. 75

7. INTEL THREADING BUILDING BLOCKS. URL: https://www.threadingbuildingblocks.org/. 77

8. KOBBELT, L. P., DAUBERT, K., AND SEIDEL, H.-P. 1998. Ray tracing of subdivisionsurfaces. In Rendering Techniques 98. Springer, 69–80. URL: http://dx.doi.org/10.1007/978-3-7091-6453-2_7. 71

9. LEE, A., MORETON, H., AND HOPPE, H. 2000. Displaced subdivision surfaces. In Proceedingsofthe 27th annual conference on Computer graphics and interactive techniques,ACM Press/Addison-Wesley Publishing Co., 85–94. URL: http://dx.doi.org/10.1145/344779.344829. 79

10. MARTIN, W., COHEN, E., FISH, R., AND SHIRLEY, P. 2000. Practical ray tracing oftrimmed nurbs surfaces. J. Graph. Tools 5, 1 (Jan.), 27–52. URL: http://dx.doi.org/10.1080/10867651.2000.10487519. 71

11. MULLER ¨ , K., TECHMANN, T., AND FELLNER, D. 2003. Adaptive ray tracing of subdivisionsurfaces. In Computer Graphics Forum, vol. 22, Wiley Online Library, 553–562. URL:http://dx.doi.org/10.1111/1467-8659.t01-2-00703. 71

12. NIESSNER, M., AND LOOP, C. 2013. Analytic displacement mapping using hardware tessellation.ACM Trans. Graph. 32, 3 (July), 26:1–26:9. URL: http://doi.acm.org/10.1145/2487228.2487234. 79

13. NIESSNER, M., LOOP, C., MEYER, M., AND DEROSE, T. 2012. Feature-adaptive gpurendering of catmull-clark subdivision surfaces. ACM Trans. Graph. 31, 1 (Feb.), 6:1–6:11. URL: http://doi.acm.org/10.1145/2077341.2077347. 71, 72, 73,76

14. NIESSNER, M., LOOP, C. T., AND GREINER, G. 2012. Efficient evaluation of semi-smoothcreases in catmull-clark subdivision surfaces. In Eurographics (Short Papers), 41–44.URL: http://dx.doi.org/10.2312/conf/EG2012/short/041-044. 71, 72

15. OPENSUBDIV. OpenSubdiv 3.0.0 alpha. URL: http://graphics.pixar.com/opensubdiv/. 70, 71, 77

16. PIXAR ANIMATION STUDIOS, 2005. The RenderMan interface version 3.2.1. URL: http://renderman.pixar.com/view/rispec/. 70

17. RAMSEY, S. D., POTTER, K., AND HANSEN, C. 2004. Ray bilinear patch intersections.Journal of Graphics Tools 9, 3, 41–47. URL: http://dx.doi.org/10.1080/10867651.2004.10504896. 74

18. RUBIN, S. M., AND WHITTED, T. 1980. A3-dimensional representation for fast renderingof complex scenes. In Proceedings of the 7th Annual Conference on Computer Graphicsand Interactive Techniques, ACM, New York, NY, USA, SIGGRAPH '80, ACM, 110–116.URL: http://doi.acm.org/10.1145/800250.807479. 74

19. SHEVTSOV, M., SOUPIKOV, A., AND KAPUSTIN, A. 2007. Highly Parallel Fast KDtreeConstruction for Interactive Ray Tracing of Dynamic Scenes. Computer GraphicsForum 26, 3, 395–404. URL: http://dx.doi.org/10.1111/1467-8659.t01-2-00703. 77

CHAPTER 4

A TECHNIQUE FOR PIECEWISE LINEAR APPROXIMATION OF 2D DIGITAL CURVE

Bimal Kumar Ray

School of Information Technology & Engineering VIT University, Vellore – 632014, India

ABSTRACT

This paper introduces the concept of curve segment after relaxing the definition of digital straight segment and uses this concept to decompose a digital curve into a sequence of curve segments. For each curve segment, the maximum deviation of it from its approximating line segment is computed and the segment with the highest maximum deviation is split into two at a point most distant from the line segment, if the deviation exceeds a threshold. Only one vertex is added to the existing set of vertices in iteration until no more vertices can be added to the approximation. Experiments show improvement over a similar work.

INTRODUCTION

In computer vision it is necessary to extract features from the description of digital curve of objects present in a scene so as to recognize the objects. For feature extraction various types of approximations are made of a digital curve and one such approximation is piecewise linear approximation that represents a digital curve by a sequence of piece straight line segments. If the approximation is open at both ends then it is called a poly line approximation otherwise, it is called a polygonal approximation. A large amount of research that address poly line / polygonal approximation of digital curve have been reported. These algorithms are categorized as optimal / sub-optimal and approaches are sequential / iterative in nature. The optimal algorithms (e.g., [1, 2, 3, 4]) either look for minimum number of line segments with a pre specified error value or minimize approximation error for a fixed number of line segments. Dynamic programming and concept of evolutionary computing (e.g., [5, 6]) have been used as optimization technique. On the other hand, suboptimal algorithms look for a reasonably good approximation based on a criterion function – usually departure (measured by perpendicular distance) of curve points from the approximating line segment. The sequential algorithms (e.g., [7, 8, 9]) make a single pass through data whereas iterative procedures process data repeatedly (e.g., iterative split-and-merge [10], iterative split [11]). A variant of merging technique that iteratively eliminates collinear or quasi linear points from a curve by comparing its departure from the candidate line segment joining the nearest pseudo vertices, is iterative point elimination introduced by Visvalingam and Whytt [12], Zhu and Chirlian [13] and Pikaz and Denstein [14]. Bhowmick and Bhattacharya [15] relaxed some of the properties and dropped some other properties of digital straight segment (DSS) introduced in [16] to make a fine piecewise linear approximation and then merged consecutive segments using area deviation (used by Wall and Danielsson [9]) and maximum distance as metric (used in e.g., [14]) to obtain a final coarse poly line / polygonal approximation. This paper

Citation: Bimal Kumar Ray, A Technique for Piecewise Linear Approximation of 2D Digital Curve, doi.org/10.14257/ijcg.2016.7.1.01.

relaxes the definition of digital straight segment (DSS) to obtain a coarse approximation and then performs incremental splitting to produce a finer approximation.

A DSS is identified by the following properties [16].

- A DSS can have at most two directions that can differ by unity modulo eight and one of the directions must occur singly.
- The non-singular runs can differ in length by unity.
- Singular runs are as uniformly distributed as possible.

The criterion (iii) being fuzzy in nature, a more precise definition of DSS conjectured in [17] is reproduced here for the convenience of the reader.

- A DSS can have at most two directions that can differ by unity modulo eight and one of the directions must occur singly.
- The length of non-singular runs must be consecutive integers.
- One of the non-singular runs must occur singly and the runs of other non-singular runs must also be consecutive integers.
- The rule (iii) should be applicable iteratively on non-singular runs.

Bhowmick and Bhattacharya [15] introduced the concept of approximate digital straight segment (ADSS) retaining rule (i), modifying rule (ii) and dropping rules (iii) and (iv). Consequently, it is not necessary for non-singular run lengths to be of consecutive integers. Rather, designating these run lengths by p and q with the constraint q > p , they impose a restriction on the value of q stating that $q = p + floor\left(\frac{p+1}{2}\right)$ floor . In order that the end sections of an ADSS are not too long, denoting the run length of the left and right end section (non-singular) of an ADSS by l and r respectively, they impose a constraint on its value stating that the maximum value of l and r can be $p + floor\left(\frac{p+1}{2}\right)$ floor . The bound on q is specified so that the middle portion, though not strictly (mathematically) straight but appears to be (perceptually) straight, whereas the bound on l and r are specified so that an ADSS is perceptually (though not mathematically) straight on its either ends. As stated in [15], instead of using $floor\left(\frac{p+1}{2}\right)$ floor for q, l and r, some other values e.g. $floor\left(\frac{p+3}{4}\right)$ floor for q and $floor\left(\frac{p+1}{2}\right)$ floor for l and r could be used. The ADSS extraction algorithm, in contrast to DSS, does not require iteration and produces less number of segments than DSS extraction algorithm does, but the choice of parameters namely, $floor\left(\frac{p+1}{2}\right)$ or $floor\left(\frac{p+3}{4}\right)$ floor is ad hoc in nature.

Since some of the consecutive ADSS may be quasi linear hence they use a sequential merging technique in the line of Wall and Danielsson [9] to reduce the number of ADSS and make a poly line / polygonal approximation of the curve. Since they use area deviation and maximum distance as criterion function without using a 'peak test' (as it was by Wall and Danielsson [9]) hence the approximation does not retain sharp turning which is required for defect detection on object boundary and to retain its sharp features, depending on the application. A sequential merging technique, if not designed carefully, rounds off sharp turnings. To compensate for the same, Wall and Danielson [9] use 'peak test' and Dunham [2], in his optimal algorithm, uses distance to a line segment instead of conventional perpendicular distance.

A digital curve $\mathcal{D}$ can be described by Freeman chain code [18] and can be approximated either by a poly line, if it is an open curve or by a polygon, if it is closed, to any desired degree of accuracy. One can use the definition of DSS for this approximation but it results in a considerably large number of piece straight line segments. This is why Bhowmick and Bhattacharya [15] introduce the concept of ADSS relaxing some of the properties of DSS and dropping others. An ADSS reduces the number of piece straight line segments and subsequent merging produces the final approximation.

In this paper a digital curve is segmented into curve segments relaxing the definition of DSS and then using an incremental splitting additional vertices are added to curve segments to produce a piecewise linear approximation. Bhowmick and Bhattacharya [15] look to a digital curve at a fine level and then merge the consecutive segments so as to reduce the number of vertices. This paper creates a relatively coarser representation by initially representing a digital curve as a consecutive collection of curve segments and then inserting additional vertices into a curve segment one at a time (incremental splitting) and thereby producing a finer representation of the curve using piece straight line segments. Bhowmick and Bhattacharya [15] rely on merging scheme whereas this paper uses splitting. The initial splitting into curve segments uses a sequential scan of the input curve and the next phase for decomposition of curve segments uses incremental splitting.

The rest of the paper is organized as follows. In the next section, the concept of curve segment is introduced and the decomposition process of a curve into curve segments is described. In Section 3, a splitting technique called incremental splitting is introduced and is used to decompose curve segments so as to add additional vertices to a curve. In Section 4, experimental results are presented along with a discussion of the same and conclusion is drawn in Section 5.

CURVE SEGMENT

This paper makes an initial coarse segmentation of a digital curve by dropping all the rules in the definition of DSS except the first one. Instead of using the first rule as it is, this paper modifies it and uses the modified rule to break a chain coded digital curve into a number of curve segments. The first rule of DSS, as already stated, states that

A DSS can have at most two directions that can differ by at most unity modulo eight and one of the directions must occur singly.

A curve segment is defined as consisting of consecutive points on a chain coded curve such that the successive points can differ in direction by at most unity modulo eight and the two directions can have arbitrary run lengths. The Figure 1 (redrawn from [15]) shows a number of open digital curves. Every DSS is a curve segment (Figure 1(a)) and so also every ADSS (Figure 1(b)) but not vice versa. The Figures 1(c) and 1(d) are curve segments but are not DSS/ADSS. According to the definition of curve segment introduced here a digital curve may consist of one or more curve segments each which may appear to be visually straight. It may be noted here that in a curve segment it is not necessary for one of the directions to occur singly (in contrast to the definition of DSS and ADSS).

(a)

(b)

(c)

(d)

Figure 1: DSS, ADSS and Curve Segments (a) a DSS which is also a Curve Segment, (b) an ADSS which is also a Curve Segment, (c) a Curve Segment which is not a DSS/ADSS (d) another Curve Segment which is not a DSS/ADSS and has a Large Maximum Deviation.

A digital curve can be decomposed into a number of curve segments. Since the ultimate objective in this paper is to make a poly line / polygonal approximation of a chain coded 2D digital curve hence it may be necessary to decompose a curve segment into visually perceived straight line segments. The segment in Figure 1(c) may require decomposition but the segment in Figure 1(d) needs to be decomposed into smaller segments (may be at the most two) because of its large deviation from a line segment joining its end points. The digital curve in Figure 2 starting from the top left corner ending at the bottom right corner of its bounded rectangle consists of five curve segments, namely $S_1(6, 7)$, $S_2(0, 7)$, $S_3(0, 1)$, $S_4(0, 7)$, $S_5(7, 6)$, the segment S_1 is the left most and S_5 is the right most curve segments of the curve and the pair of digits adjacent to a curve segment Si indicates the two directions on it. Though in each of the segments, in this figure, one of the two directions occurs singly (the second digit of the pair indicated against a segment) but it is not a constraint in the definition of a curve segment.

Figure 2: An Open Digital Curve with Four Curve Segments.

Definition: A curve segment consists of at most two directions (of eight direction chain code) differing by unity modulo eight.

At most two directions differing by unity modulo eight are considered to recognize a curve segment and in contrast to the definition of DSS, one of the directions need not occur singly. According to the definition of curve segment stated above, Figure 3(a) has only one curve segment and the chain directions in the curve segment are 0 and 1 only which differ by unity. If two directions do not differ by unity modulo eight then a new curve segment is recognized. The Figure 3(b) has five curve segments – each of these segments has only one direction – either 1 or 7 – appearing in alternate segments and these directions, using modulo eight differ by 2.

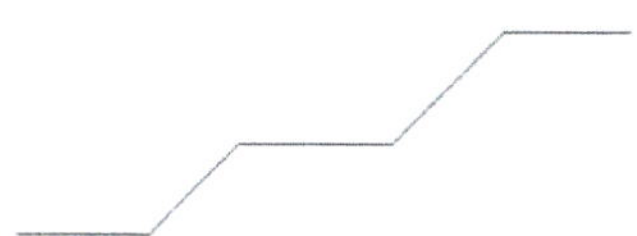

(a)

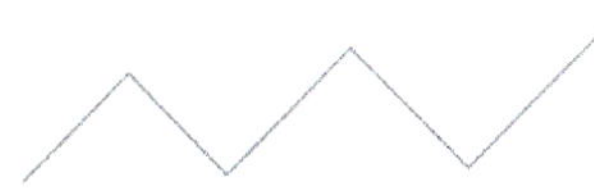

(b)

Figure 3: (a) A Curve Segment with Directions of Chain Code Differing by Unity but Neither of the Two Directions Occur Singly. (b) A Digital Curve consisting of Multiple Curve Segments (as many as five).

The definition of curve segment is used to decompose a digital curve $\mathcal{D}$ into a number of curve segments $\mathcal{C}_1, \mathcal{C}_2, \ldots, \mathcal{C}_k$ (say) each of which is an open curve though the input curve D could be a closed one. The list ($\mathcal{C}_1, \mathcal{C}_2, \ldots, \mathcal{C}_k$) forms a chain – the end point of the curve segment $\mathcal{C}_j$ is the starting point of the curve segment $\mathcal{C}_{j+1}$ and if $\mathcal{D}$ is a closed curve then the end point of the last curve segment $\mathcal{C}_k$ coincides with the starting point of the first curve segment $\mathcal{C}_1$. If $\mathcal{D}$ is an open curve then the decomposition of it into curve segments $\mathcal{C}_j$ ` s is initiated from one of the end points of $\mathcal{D}$; on the other hand, if $\mathcal{D}$ is closed then starting from an arbitrary point on the curve the definition of curve segment is applied on it to recognize the same. The decomposition process is performed and continued along the entire curve beyond the starting point. The starting point may be an end point of a curve segment after the curve had been traversed in its entirety and in this case the process of curve segment recognition terminates, if not, the processing is carried on beyond the starting point until the end point of a curve segment coincides with the starting point of one the segments already generated. The decomposition is independent of the starting point on the input curve. The end points of the curve segments constitute the initial set of vertices of the approximating poly line / polygon. In contrast to ADSS recognition, this decomposition does not require a control parameter.

It may be observed here that the decomposition of a curve into curve segments requires comparisons only and the number of comparisons is equal to n – 1 for an open curve and exactly n, for a closed curve; n being the size (number of points) of the curve. The computational complexity of the decomposition process of a curve into curve segments is therefore O (n) .

A leaf shaped curve along with three other curves namely, an infinity curve, a chromosome shaped curve and a curve consisting of multiple semicircular arcs, that are used extensively in the literature are decomposed using the decomposition scheme described above and the output overlaid on the digital curve are shown in Figures 4(a) through 4(d), in this order. The curves are described in the clockwise direction and the starting point is arbitrary. The end points of curve segments are depicted on the figures with solid circles.

(a)

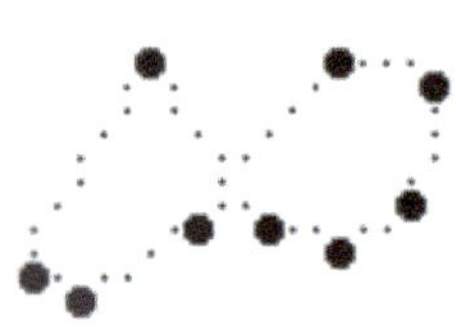

(b)

(c)

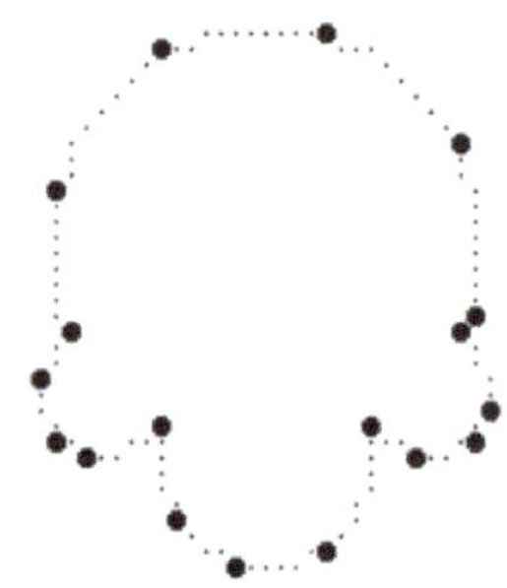

(d)

Figure 4: Decomposition of a Digital into Curve Segments. The End Points of Segments are indicated with Solid Circles.

INCREMENTAL SPLITTING

Since the deviation of a curve segment from the line segment joining the end points of the curve segment may be high (see Figure 1(d) and various curve segments on the curves in Figure 4), so an incremental approach is proposed to insert additional vertices between the end points of a curve segment and thereby to obtain a better approximation within a pre specified threshold. The maximum of the perpendicular distance of the points of a curve segment from its approximating line segment is computed for each curve segment and the segment with the highest deviation is split at a point most distant from the approximating line segment, if the deviation is beyond a threshold. Consider a curve segment C with its end points p_i and p_j and the intermediate points $p_k \; (i < k < j)$. The maximum of the perpendicular distance of the points p_k `s from the line segment $p_i p_j$ is the maximum of

$$\frac{|(x_k - x_i)(y_j - y_i) - (y_k - y_i)(x_j - x_i)|}{\sqrt{(y_j - y_i)^2 + (x_j - x_i)^2}},$$

the maximum is over k satisfying $i < k < j$.

Let us denote this maximum deviation of a curve segment C from its approximating line segment by maxDevC. The maximum of maxDevC over all the curve segments determines the curve segment that needs to be split at a point most distant from its approximating line segment provided that the distance is beyond a threshold. A curve segment is split only once during an iteration. One iteration results in addition of at most one vertex to the current set of vertices. Hence this splitting is incremental in nature and so it is called incremental splitting. The Figure 5 shows the output of incremental splitting on the leaf shaped curve as vertices are added to it one by one in iteration. The Figure 4(a) obtained after decomposition of the leaf shaped curve into curve segments has eighteen curve segments. For incremental splitting of the curve segments a threshold of unity is used and Figures 5(a) through 5(e) show the output of incremental splitting as vertices are added to the curve segments one by one in iteration. The new vertex added in iteration is shown in orange. The total number of vertices in Figures 5(a) through 5(e) is 19 through 23, in this order. The number of vertices increases as iteration progresses until no more vertices need to be added within the specified tolerance determined by the threshold.

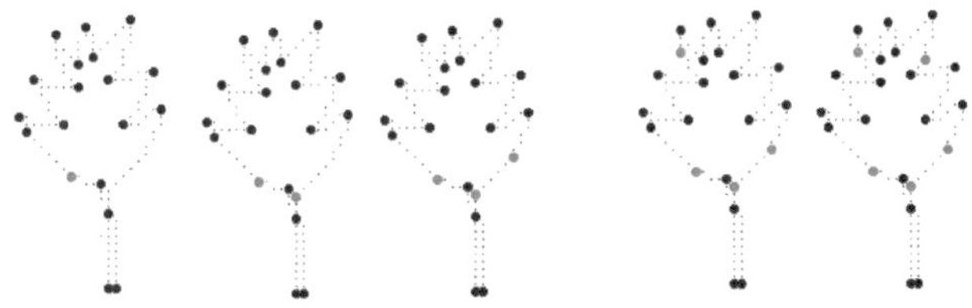

Figure 5: Vertices are Added Incrementally One in an Iteration after Initial Segmentation of the Leaf Shaped Curve into Curve Segments.

In iteration it is necessary to compute perpendicular distance of (almost) all points of the entire digital curve. If the number of iterations required to achieve a desirable approximation as determined by the threshold is t then the computational complexity of this phase of the procedure is O (tn). It is also observed earlier in Section 2 that the computational complexity of decomposition process of a digital curve into curve segments is O (n) and so the computational complexity of the entire approximation process is O (tn). An overview of the procedure consisting of initial segmentation followed by incremental splitting is presented below in the form of an algorithm.

Algorithm Piecewise Linear ApproximationInput: A chain coded curve.

Output: A poly line / polygonal approximation

Begin

Step 1. Divide the chain coded curve into segments using the definition of curve segment.

Repeat

Step 2. For each curve segment, compute the maximum deviation of the segment from its approximating line segment.

Step 3. Find out the curve segment with the highest maximum deviation and if the highest maximum deviation exceeds a threshold then split it into two sub segments at a point most distant from the approximating line segment.

Until no such segment exists

Step 4. The consecutive vertices are joined to form the desired approximation.

End.

It may be observed here that instead of deriving an approximation with a threshold on maximum deviation, the proposed method can also be used to derive an approximation with a pre specified number of line segments. The modification of the above algorithm to achieve the same is trivial and so is omitted here.

EXPERIMENTS AND DISCUSSION

The accuracy of a piecewise linear approximation is measured by the approximation error defined by maximum error and integral square error. An approximation wherein all piece straight line segments are close to the input curve has less maximum error as well as integral square error and an approximation which is a slack one produces higher error value. There exists a tradeoff between the number of vertices and the approximation error. The higher the number of vertices (a tight approximation) is, the less is the error and the lower the number of vertices is, the higher is the error, provided that vertices are selected carefully. In order to compare approximation produced by two different techniques, figure of merit [19] defined by the ratio of compression ratio (CR) to integral square error, is used. If integral square error is found to be zero then the figure of merit is redefined to be of very high value and the approximation is regarded as the best approximation but a trivial one. This approximation has the highest number of vertices among all other possible linear approximations of the curve. The higher the value of figure of merit is the better is the approximation. The compression ratio is defined by the ratio of the number of points on the input digital curve to the number of vertices in the approximation. If n is the number of points on the input digital curve and m is the number vertices in its approximation then the compression ratio is defined by

$$CR = \frac{n}{m}.$$

The maximum error is defined by the maximum absolute deviation of the points of a digital curve from the sides of the approximating polygon and integral square error is the sum of squares of deviation of the points of the digital curve from the sides of the approximating polygon. The deviation of a curve point from a side of the approximating polygon is measured by its perpendicular distance from the side. If $A(p_i)$ and $B(p_j)$ be the two end points of a side of an approximation then the perpendicular distance of the points p_k $(i < k < j)$ of the curve is defined by

$$e_k = \frac{|(x_j - x_i)(y_k - y_i) - (y_j - y_i)(x_k - x_i)|}{\sqrt{(x_j - x_i)^2 + (y_j - y_i)^2}}.$$

The maximum value of e_k is the maximum deviation of the points of the curve segment between A and B and is defined by

$$\max E_{AB} = \max\{ e_k : i < k < j\}.$$

The overall maximum deviation of the curve from its approximation is the maximum error and is defined by

$$E_\infty = \max E_{XY},$$

where XY is any side of the approximation.

The integral square error of the approximation is the sum of squares of perpendicular distance e_k and is defined by

$$E_2 = \sum_{k=1}^{n} e_k^2.$$

The figure of merit (FoM), expressed in percentage is defined by

$$FoM = \frac{CR}{E_2} \times 100$$

The technique developed in this paper has been tested on a number of digital curves and compared with those obtained by using the technique in [15]. A sample of the test results is presented here. The figures 6 through 15 show the polygonal approximation of ten digital curves (overlaid on the input curve) obtained using the proposed method and those obtained using [15]. The four curves in figures 6 through 9 are the ones used in Figure 4 and these curves have been used extensively in a large number of research papers; the remaining curves are from MPEG 7 dataset [20]. In each of the figures 6 through 15, the top most row shows the approximations obtained by the proposed method – decomposition into curve segments followed by final outcome of incremental splitting, the middle row shows the ones obtained by decomposing the curve using ADSS and then merging ADSS using maximum error as criterion metric and the third row shows the same using cumulative error as criterion metric. Each row shows the polygonal approximations for three different values of threshold parameter $\tau = 1, 2, 3$; from left to right. The approximation is overlaid on its input digital curve and the vertices of the approximation are shown with solid circles on the curve.

The fidelity of the approximations namely, the number of vertices (m), maximum error (E_∞), integral square error (E_2), compression ratio (CR) and figure of merit – FoM, expressed in percentage – for different values of threshold (τ) and for different digital curves are shown in Table I.

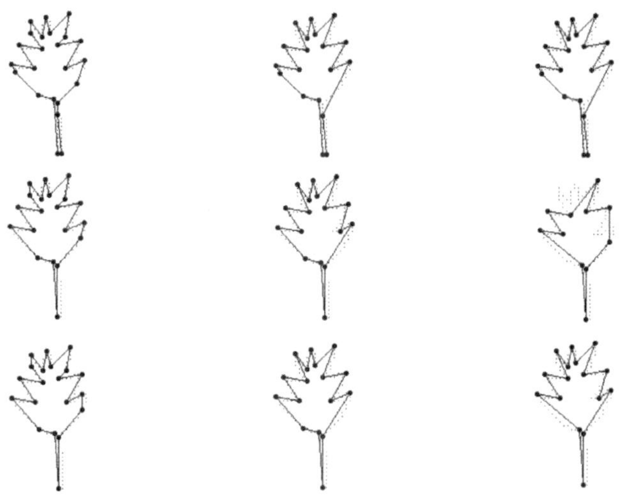

Figure 6: A Leaf Shaped Curve and it Polygonal Approximation.

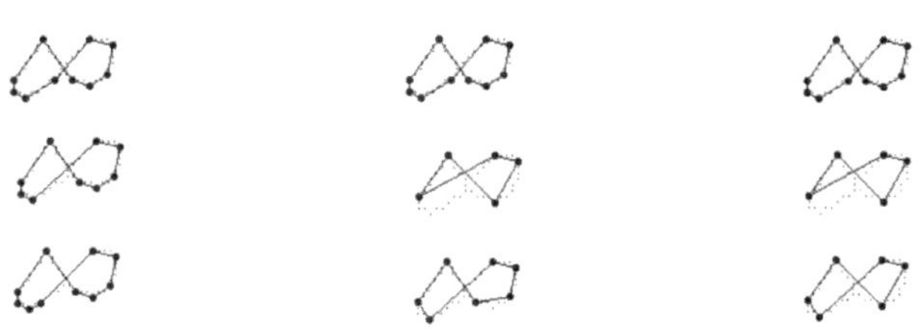

Figure 7: An Infinity Curve and its Polygonal Approximation.

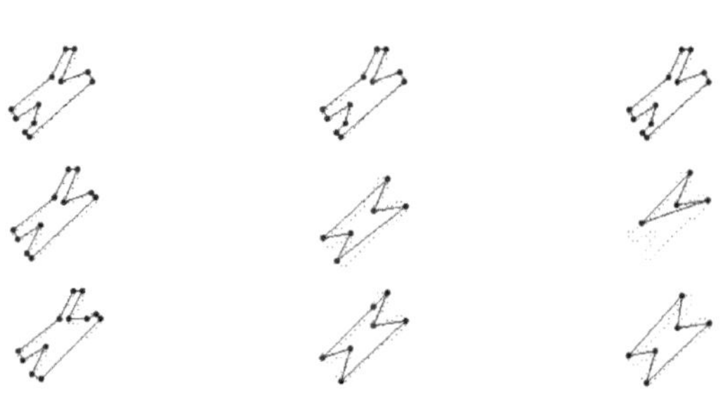

Figure 8: A Chromosome Shaped Curve and its Polygonal Approximation.

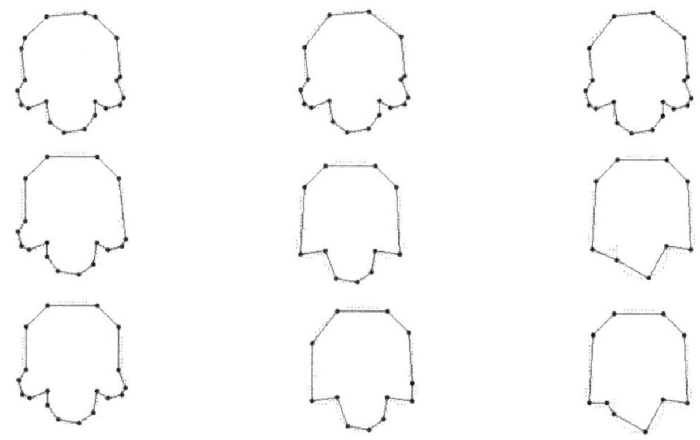

Figure 9: A Digital Curve with Four Semicircular Arc and its Polygonal Approximation.

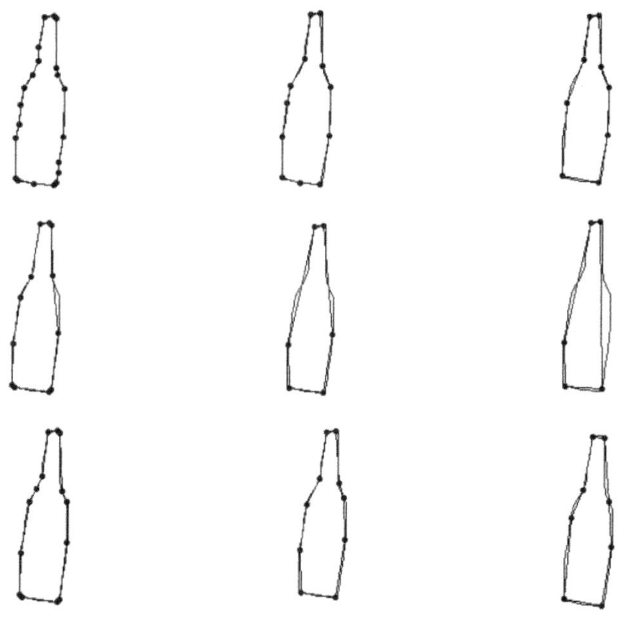

Figure 10: A Bottle and its Polygonal Approximation.

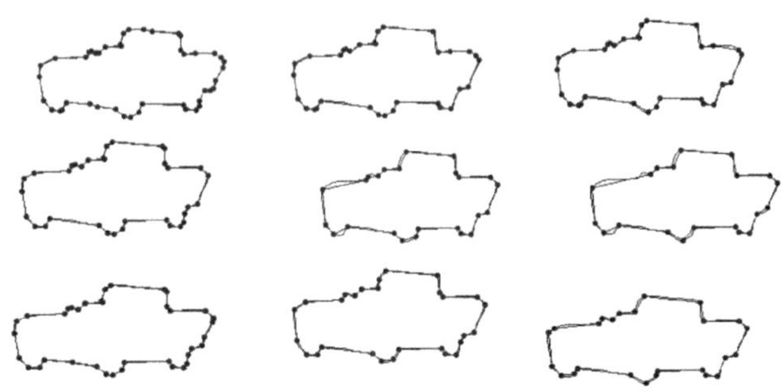

Figure 11: A Car and its Polygonal Approximation.

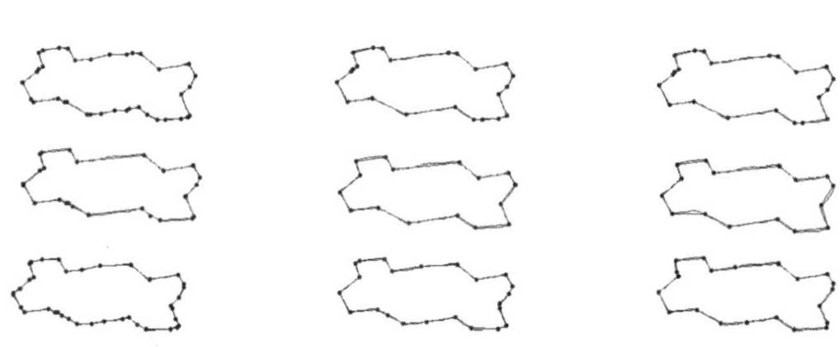

Figure 12: A Brick and its Polygonal Approximation.

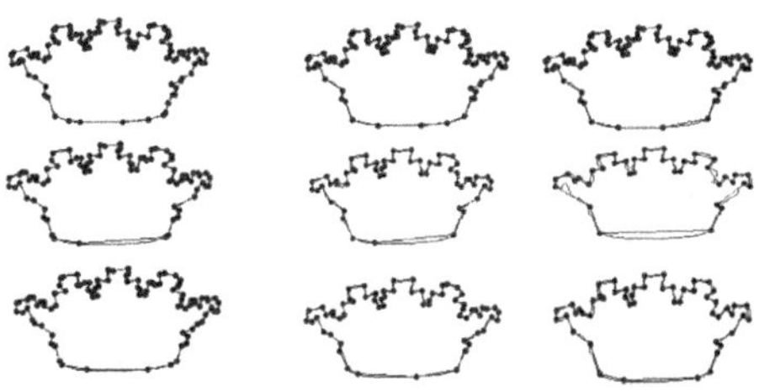

Figure 13: A Crown and its Polygonal Approximation.

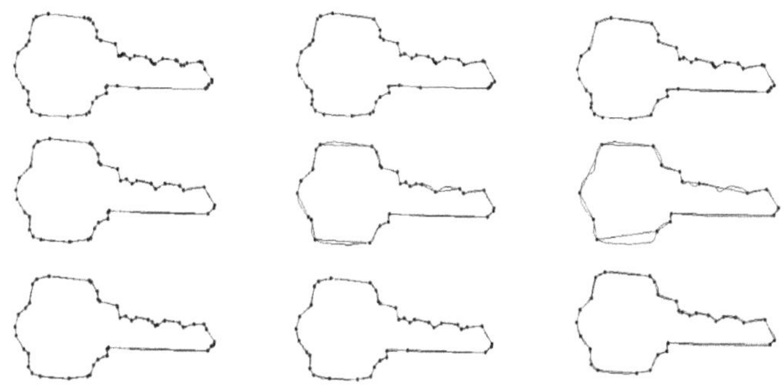

Figure 15: A Key and its Polygonal Approximation.

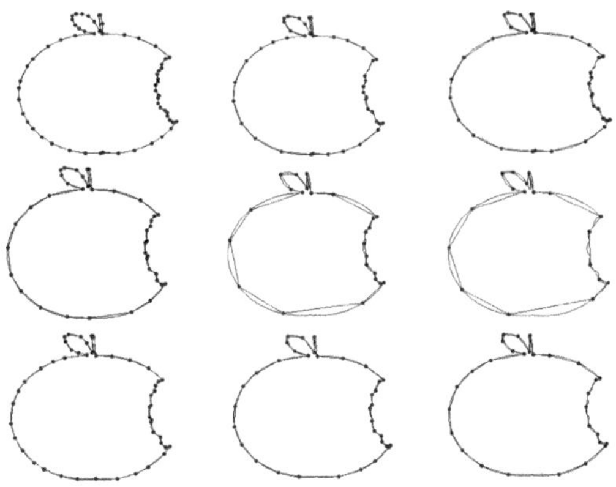

Figure 14: A Bitten Apple and its Polygonal Approximation.

Table I: Number of Vertices, Maximum Error, Integral Square Error, Compression Ratio and Figure of Merit of Polygonal Approximations of Different Digital Curves for Values of τ = 1, 2, 3

Digital curve	Number of points	τ	Fidelity measures of polygonal approximation														
			Incremental splitting					ADSS & Merging									
								Maximum error criterion					Cumulative error criterion				
			m	E_∞	E_2	CR	FoM	m	E_∞	E_2	CR	FoM	m	E_∞	E_2	CR	FoM
Leaf (Figure 6)	120	1	23	0.90	14.26	5.21	37	20	1	22.37	6	27	20	1	25.4	6.0	24
		2	19	1.34	28.21	6.32	22	17	1.92	44.84	7.1	16	17	1.53	38.8	7.1	18
		3	19	1.34	28.21	6.32	22	11	6.67	391.3	10.91	3	16	1.92	60.0	7.5	12
Infinity curve (Figure 7)	45	1	10	0.73	4.30	4.5	105	9	1.14	6.8	5	74	10	0.73	4.4	4.5	102
		2	10	0.73	4.30	4.5	105	5	3.66	110.8	9	8	7	1.48	11.0	6.4	58
		3	10	0.73	4.30	4.5	105	5	3.66	110.8	9	8	6	1.6	23.5	7.5	32
Chromosome (Figure 8)	60	1	12	0.88	8.11	5.0	62	11	0.89	13.21	5.45	41	12	1.00	13.8	5.0	36
		2	12	0.88	8.11	5.0	62	6	2.30	61.42	10.00	16	7	1.58	26.0	8.6	33
		3	12	0.88	8.11	5.0	62	4	8.22	620.25	15	2	6	2.30	71.7	10.0	14
A figure with multiple circular arcs (Figure 9)	102	1	21	0.88	12.55	4.86	39	17	1.40	26.49	6.00	23	18	1.00	32.6	5.7	17
		2	19	1.05	17.60	5.37	31	11	1.56	48.25	9.27	19	12	1.56	44.9	8.5	19
		3	19	1.05	17.60	5.37	31	9	3.68	104.70	11.33	11	10	2.22	82.1	10.2	12
Bottle (Figure 10)	327	1	21	0.90	36.43	15.57	43	12	4.28	410.6	27.2	7	14	1.72	168.3	23.4	14
		2	12	1.91	162.97	27.25	17	6	3.74	850.7	54.5	6	10	2.25	344.8	32.7	9
		3	9	2.72	328.01	36.33	11	5	8.13	4014.3	65.4	2	8	3.12	740.2	40.9	6
Car (Figure 11)	443	1	45	0.97	65.35	9.84	15	34	1.85	135.8	13.03	10	37	1.48	114.2	12.0	10
		2	33	1.94	147.34	13.42	9	24	4.96	846.15	18.46	2	28	2.06	240.9	15.8	7
		3	31	2.95	239.17	14.29	6	20	4.57	854.91	21.15	3	25	2.79	488.5	17.7	4
Brick (Figure 12)	500	1	37	0.97	74.57	13.51	18	25	2.73	407.6	20.0	5	39	1.27	117.4	12.8	11
		2	23	1.80	182.19	21.74	12	16	2.99	629.30	31.25	5	28	2.06	240.9	15.8	7
		3	22	2.74	216.74	22.73	10	16	4	1069.74	31.25	3	21	2.26	415.9	23.8	6
Crown (Figure 13)	570	1	103	0.95	80.63	5.53	7	83	3.59	569.9	6.9	1.2	93	1.68	154.8	6.1	4

		2	95	1.66	122.37	6.00	5	55	4.74	1158.65	10.36	0.9	64	2.13	325.0	8.9	3
		3	94	2.69	204.41	6.06	3	39	7.45	3883.54	14.62	0.4	52	3.16	545.9	11.0	2
Bitten apple (Figure 14)	697	1	61	1.00	78.52	11.43	15	40	3.54	874.74	17.43	2	50	1.70	254.5	13.9	5
		2	43	1.94	330.87	16.21	5	24	10.62	12739.6	29.0	2	35	2.15	586.4	19.9	3
		3	36	2.75	758.94	19.36	3	18	12.52	16463.8	38.7	0.2	29	2.68	1051.7	24.0	2
Key (Figure 15)	791	1	58	0.95	98.30	13.64	14	39	1.93	314.0	20.28	6.46	46	1.71	255.2	17.2	7
		2	45	1.85	255.96	17.58	7	29	5.41	3029.66	27.3	0.9	38	2.32	464.93	20.8	4
		3	38	2.78	661.31	20.82	3	16	14.08	15866.6	49.4	0.3	30	2.85	1513.6	26.4	2

A qualitative as well as quantitative analysis of experiments is made using visual perception and the fidelity measures (CR, $E_{¥}$, E_2 and FoM). It is observed that the shape of the leaf curve is distorted badly when the approximation is generated using maximum error criterion of [15] and with $\tau = 3$ (Figure 6, second row, extreme right). The approximations produced by the proposed scheme are found to be better than those of [15]. The shape of the infinity curve (Figure 7) too is distorted for $\tau = 2$ and $\tau = 3$ when approximated by [15], especially with maximum error criterion. But the approximations produced by the proposed scheme are found to remain close to the input curve. Out of the four digital curves (figures 6 through 9) that have been used extensively in the literature for testing, the most affected one by the scheme of [15] is the chromosome shaped curve (Figure 8). The approximation is highly distorted loosing its entire shape when maximum error is used as criterion metric with a threshold of $\tau = 3$. On the contrary, the approximations produced by the proposed scheme are found to be better than those of [15] using either of the criterion metrics, for all the three values of the threshold as well. The approximation produced by the proposed scheme for the curve with multiple semi circular arcs (Figure 9) is found to be better than those produced by [15] which are distorted badly specially for $\tau = 3$, loosing corner points of the curve from the expected set of vertices of the approximation. The approximation scheme of [15] straightens curved regions for the bottle image (Figure 10), producing a high departure in the approximation from the input curve with $\tau = 3$ using maximum error criterion. On the contrary, the approximations produced by the proposed scheme are found to be better than those of [15]. The method of [15] straightens curved regions for $\tau = 2$ and $\tau = 3$ with maximum error as well as cumulative error criterion, producing large deviation of the approximation from the input curve; but the approximations generated by the proposed scheme do not smooth out curved regions. The approximations produced by the proposed scheme are better than those of [15] for the brick image (Figure 12) too and the deviation in the quality of approximations in [15] is more with maximum error criterion than with the cumulative error criterion. The approximation of the crown image (Figure 13) as obtained using maximum error criterion of [15] is found to loose the shape of the lower portion of the input curve with all the three values of the threshold parameter τ and the loss of shape is most vivid with $\tau = 3$ and with maximum error as criterion metric. Though the approximations produced with cumulative error as criterion metric is better in this respect but the ones produced by the proposed scheme is found to be better than the approximations produced by either criterion of [15] for all the three values of the threshold parameter. The proposed scheme picks up more vertices at region with high curvature highlighting all the details of the image. For the bitten apple (Figure 14) too, the proposed scheme detects more vertices at regions that contain changes at fine level (bitten portion of the apple). The scheme of [15] with $\tau = 3$ is found to smooth out sharp features present in the bitten portion of the apple and it is more so with maximum error criterion than cumulative error criterion. The approximation produced by the cumulative error criterion is better than that with maximum error criterion but the approximation produced by the proposed scheme is better than either of the two. The key image (Figure 15) too is approximated better by the proposed scheme than by [15] especially with $\tau = 3$ using maximum error criterion.

As a general observation it is found that the technique proposed in [15] rounds off sharp turnings and locate vertices away from where it should be. Moreover, this technique fails to approximate curvilinear regions appropriately (see figure 14 and lower portion of figure 13 specifically and others too), specially with maximum error as criterion metric, and similar deficiencies are observed in the approximations produced by [15] using cumulative error criterion, though these approximations are better than those produced by maximum error criterion but are not better than those produced by the proposed scheme. The approximations produced by the proposed scheme are found to be better than those produced by [15] using either of the two criteria – maximum error and cumulative error. The proposed method succeeds to locate vertices at the location where it should be and succeeds to retain sharp turnings. It also detects a sufficient number of vertices in the curvilinear regions and thereby maintains an approximation close to the input curve. So it may be concluded that as far as visual perception goes, the approximations produced by the proposed scheme are better than those produced by [15].

It is observed from Table I that the approximation error (maximum error and integral square error) produced by the proposed scheme is lower than that produced by applying ADSS followed by merging [15] and this difference is found to be more significant at higher values of the threshold (τ). Picking up some sample data from the Table I, it is found that with threshold $\tau = 3$, the maximum error for the leaf shaped curve (Figure 6) in the approximation produced by [15] with maximum error as criterion metric is 6.67 and cumulative error as criterion it is 1.92 whereas the same in the proposed scheme is 1.34. The integral square error in the former (i.e. [15]) is 391.3 with maximum error criterion and 60.0 with cumulative error criterion whereas in the later it is 28.21. For the infinity curve (Figure 7) it is observed that even with a threshold of $\tau = 2$, the maximum error in the approximation produced by [15] with maximum error as criterion metric is 3.66 and with cumulative error as criterion it is 1.48 whereas the same in the proposed scheme is 0.73. The integral square error in the former is 110.8 with maximum error criterion and 11.0 with cumulative error criterion whereas in the later it is 4.30. These measures are higher for [15] with cumulative error criterion with threshold $\tau = 3$ whereas it remain the same for $\tau = 2$ in the proposed scheme. For the chromosome shaped curve (Figure 8) the approximations produced by the proposed scheme remain the same for three values of threshold whereas it is not so for the approximations produced by [15]. The maximum error and integral square error in the proposed scheme are 0.88 and 8.11 respectively whereas in the approximation produced by [15] the maximum error and integral square error are respectively 2.30 and 61.42 for $\tau = 2$ and 8.22 and 620.25 for $\tau = 3$ using maximum error as the metric and these values are considerably high as compared to those of the proposed scheme. With cumulative error as the metric the maximum error and integral square error of the approximations produced by [15] are respectively 1.58 and 26.0 with $\tau = 2$ and 2.30 and 71.7 with $\tau = 3$. Though these values are lower than those for maximum error criterion of [15] but are still higher than the respective values in the proposed scheme. Similar observations can be made for other curves too. It is also observed that the figure of merit of the approximations generated by the proposed scheme is higher than that produced by using [15] establishing that the proposed method is better than [15].

CONCLUSION

The concept of curve segment and a technique for curve splitting called incremental splitting have been introduced and the same have been applied to approximate digital curves by piece straight line segments. The initial segmentation scheme using the concept of curve segment is simpler in concept and in implementation as compared to the concept of ADSS and its implementation [15]. The ADSS extraction scheme is complicated with too many tests and is also difficult to comprehend and implement. The extraction algorithm also needs to call another routine repeatedly, as many times as the number of ADSS presents on a curve. In contrast, the curve segment extraction scheme proposed here is simple and so also its implementation. In [15], the ADSS are merged to make a linear approximation, whereas in this paper the curve segments are split incrementally. In [15], the authors started with a fine approximation and obtained a coarser one through subsequent merging, whereas in this paper a coarse approximation is initiated and then it is split incrementally to produce a finer one. Experiments show improvement in the quality of approximation over [15].

REFERENCES

1. Y. Kurozumi and W. A. Davis, "Polygonal approximation by the minimax method", Computer Graphics and Image Processing, vol. 19, (1982), pp. 248-264.
2. J. G. Dunham, "Optimum piecewise linear approximation of planar curves", IEEE Transactions on Pattern Analysis and Machine Intelligence, vol. PAMI-8, (1986), pp. 67-75.
3. J. C. Perez and E. Vidal, "Optimum polygonal approximation of digitized curves", Pattern Recognition Letters, vol. 15, (1994), pp. 743-750.
4. M. Salotti, "Optimal polygonal approximation of digitized curves using the sum of square deviations criterion", Pattern Recognition, vol. 35, (2002), pp. 435-443.
5. P. Y. Yin, "Genetic particle swarm optimization for polygonal approximation of digital curves", Pattern Recognition and Image Analysis, vol. 16, (2006), pp. 223-233.
6. B. Wang, H. Shu and L. Luo, "A genetic algorithm with chromosome-repairing for min - # and min - ε polygonal approximation of digital curves", Journal of Visual Communication and Image Representation, vol. 20, (2009), pp. 45-56.
7. C. Williams, "An efficient algorithm for piecewise linear approximation of planar curves", Computer Graphics and Image Processing, vol. 8, (1978), pp. 286-293.
8. J. Sklansky and V. Gonzalez, "Fast Polygonal Approximation of Digitized Curves", Pattern Recognition, vol. 12, (1980), pp. 327-331.
9. K. Wall and P.-E. Danielsson, "A fast sequential method for polygonal approximation of digitized curves", Computer Vision, Graphics and Image Processing, vol. 28, (1984), pp. 220-227.
10. T. Pavlidis and S. L. Horowitz, "Segmentation of plane curves", IEEE Transactions on Computer, vol. 23, (1974), pp. 860-870.
11. U. E. Ramer, "An iterative procedure for polygonal approximation of plane curves", Computer Graphics and Image Processing, vol. 1, (1972), pp. 244-256.
12. M. Visvalingam and J. D. Whyatt, "Line generalization by repeated elimination of points", Cartographic Journal, vol. 30, (1993), pp. 46-51.
13. P. Zhu and P. M. Chirlian, "On critical point detection of digital shapes", IEEE Transactions on Pattern Analysis and Machine Intelligence, vol. PAMI – 17, (1995), pp. 737-748.
14. A. Pikaz and I. Dinstein, "An algorithm for polygonal approximation based on iterative point elimination", Pattern Recognition Letters, vol. 16, (1995), pp. 557-563.
15. P. Bhowmick and B. Bhattacharya, "Fast Polygonal Approximation of Digital Curves Using Relaxed Straightness Properties", IEEE Transactions on Pattern Analysis and Machine Intelligence, vol. PAMI – 29, (2007), pp. 1590-1602.
16. H. Freeman, "Techniques for the Digital Computer Analysis of Chain-Encoded Arbitrary Plane Curves", Proceedings of the National Electronics Conference, vol. 7, (1961), pp. 421-432.
17. A. Rosenfeld, "Digital Straight Line Segments", IEEE Transactions on Computers, vol. 23, (1974), pp. 1264-1268.
18. H. Freeman, "On the Encoding of Arbitrary Geometric Configurations", IRE Transactions on Electronic Computers, vol. 10, (1961), pp. 260-268.
19. D. Sarkar, "A simple algorithm for detection of significant vertices for polygonal approximation of chain-coded curves", Pattern Recognition Letters, vol. 14, (1993), pp. 959-964.
20. http://www.dabi.temple.edu/~shape/MPEG7/dataset.html.

CHAPTER 5

MARCHING CUBES TECHNIQUE FOR VOLUMETRIC VISUALIZATION ACCELERATED WITH GRAPHICS PROCESSING UNITS

Marcos Vinicius Mussel Cirne, Hélio Pedrini

Institute of Computing, University of Campinas, Campinas, SP13083-852, Brazil

ABSTRACT

Volume visualization has numerous applications that benefit different knowledge domains, such as biology, medicine, meteorology, oceanography, geology, among others. With the continuous advances of technology, it has been possible to achieve considerable rendering rates and a high degree of realism. Visualization tools have currently assisted users with the visual analysis of complex and large datasets. Marching cubes is one of the most widely used real-time volume rendering methods. This paper describes a methodology for speeding up the marching cubes algorithm on a graphics processing unit and discusses a number of ways to improve its performance by means of auxiliary spatial data structures. Experiments conducted with use of several volumetric datasets demonstrate the effectiveness of the developed method.

INTRODUCTION

Volume visualization techniques have allowed users to explore and analyze complex data in several domains of knowledge, such as medicine, geology, oceanography, meteorology, biology, among others. Visualization tools provide functionalities for manipulating and rendering volumetric datasets, improving the visual comprehension of their structures or patterns.

The development of efficient algorithms for representing, manipulating and rendering complex and large datasets is a challenge of volume visualization. Despite the substantial advances in the field, the use of a central processing unit (CPU) to perform general purpose graphics processing tasks has not been enough to provide effective interactivity or real-time rendering, especially when employed in very large datasets. The constant technological progress enabled the emergence of powerful graphics processing units (GPUs), capable of rendering complex three-dimensional models at a high degree of realism.

The capability of GPUs have been impelled by their high level of parallelism and their ability to perform geometric primitive and floating point operations in a fast and efficient way. GPUs have been recently used for acceleration of various applications, such as fluid dynamics simulation, seismic analysis, medical image reconstruction, and weather forecasting, resulting in an expressive gain over the CPUs. This has been possible due to the development of the general-purpose computing on graphics processing units (GPGPU), making them even more flexible through their high parallelism and adaptable application programming.

As a result of these technological advances, volume visualization techniques have also evolved considerably over the last years. Real-time volume rendering accelerated

Citation: Marcos Vinicius Mussel Cirne and Hélio Pedrini, Marching cubes technique for volumetric visualization accelerated with graphics processing units. doi:10.1007/s13173-012-0097-z.

through GPUs has become an effective tool for volumetric data visualization and analysis.

This work presents a methodology for accelerating on GPUs a volume visualization technique for isosurface extraction, called marching cubes. The performance of the method is improved by means of auxiliary spatial data structures. Experimental results obtained on several volumetric datasets demonstrate the effectiveness of the proposed method.

The contributions of this work are a comparative performance analysis of the marching cubes technique with different spatial data structures, and a development of an application capable of manipulating datasets from several fields of knowledge, which permits its use as a framework to be integrated in visualization environments, obtaining high real-time rendering rates as well.

This paper is organized as follows. Section 2 briefly reviews some relevant concepts of volume visualization and isosurface extraction, as well as the marching cubes algorithm and some spatial data structures used to improve the performance of the algorithm. Section 3 presents a methodology for speeding up the marching cubes technique on GPU. Section 4 describes and discusses the experimental results obtained by applying the proposed method to a number of volumetric datasets. Section 5 concludes the paper with some final remarks.

RELATED CONCEPTS AND WORK

This section describes an overview of the volumetric visualization, followed by concepts of isosurface extraction, marching cubes algorithm, and a description of some data structures used to improve the performance of this algorithm.

Volumetric Visualization

Volumetric visualization [11, 19, 30] consists of a set of techniques used to study objects and natural phenomena from various fields of knowledge, such as biology, medicine, meteorology, oceanography, microscopy, geology, astronomy. The basic idea of these techniques is to perform a two-dimensional projection (usually on a computer screen) from these volumes.

The volumetric data is usually represented by a set of volume elements, called voxels, where each one contains a specific value in a regular grid contained in the three-dimensional space. A voxel can be defined by a tuple $\langle x, y, z, S \rangle$, , which represents the value SS associated to some property of a volume data, located at a 3D grid position (x,y,z)(x,y,z).

Volumetric visualization algorithms can be classified into two categories [11]: direct volume rendering (DVR) and surface-fitting (SF). The first one is characterized by the direct element mapping onto the screen space, without the use of geometric primitives as an intermediary representation, whereas the second consists of stages of feature extraction and representation of isosurfaces (surfaces that represent a set of points with the same scalar value), which are later rendered for visualization. These isosurfaces can be defined from surface primitives (such as polygons) or by a certain threshold.

Examples of DVR techniques include raycasting [25, 27], splatting [42, 47], cell-projection [48,49] and shear-warp [22, 26]. Examples of SF techniques are contour connection [20, 34] and marching cubes [14, 24, 29, 39, 46].

Isosurface Extraction

An isosurface can be defined as a set of points that have the same value (called *isovalue*) in a volume data, that is, $\{(x, y, z) \in \Re^3 : f(x, y, z) = h\}$, for a grid position (x,y,z) (x,y,z) and some isovalue $h \in \Re$.. The isosurface extraction process involves the generation of meshes (usually triangular) that approximately represents a certain surface. In the medical field, for instance, this procedure is commonly used in the visualization of organs, tissues and anatomic structures.

A very known isosurface extraction technique is the marching cubes algorithm [9, 14, 29, 33,46], which was originally developed to improve the study of 3D medical images. Later, many researches were conducted to optimize this technique through the use of spatial data structures to improve the processing of volume data. However, with the advent of modern graphics cards, techniques that take most advantages from the graphics hardware have been explored due to the high degree of parallelism present in these cards.

In relation to isosurface extraction approaches in GPU, Reck et al. [40] and Buatois et al. [3] proposed methods for extraction from unstructured tetrahedral meshes. Tatarchuk et al. [44] showed an implementation of a hybrid method that employs both marching cubes and marching tetrahedra [4, 15] techniques, using geometry shaders in GPU. Martin et al. [31] developed a technique to efficiently distribute all the work load of the isosurface extraction procedure among GPU resources in a cluster.

Pascucci [38] proposed a pipeline for the isosurface extraction procedure in which most of the stages is done in GPU, assigning only to the CPU the tasks of accessing the volume data and sending a set of vertices (corresponding to the volume cells) for the GPU. In his proposal, the GPU does not have access to the volume dataset. Therefore, the CPU is responsible for transmitting all kind of relevant information about the vertices.

Ciznicki et al. [6] presented an isosurface extraction approach for CT and MRI images that combines the marching tetrahedra algorithm with histogram pyramids [10, 50] using multiple GPUs. Using a single GPU, their application provided a speedup of 107 times comparing to a standard CPU version. With four GPUs, it achieved a speedup of 3.3 times, in relation to the single GPU version.

Schindler et al. [41] proposed an adaptation of the marching cubes algorithm called marching correctors, which extracts isosurface from smoothed particle hydrodynamics (SPH) datasets. The GPU is responsible for computing the selection of seed cells of the datasets, which is the most expensive part of the proposed algorithm, achieving a performance gain of two orders of magnitude, comparing to other approaches that handle SPH datasets.

Marching Cubes

The marching cubes technique uses a divide-and-conquer approach in which the volume data is processed through their cells (voxels), that are equivalent to cubes. In each cell, the intersection between its respective edges and the isosurface is verified. The values of each vertex cells are then compared to a given isovalue h and these vertices are classified as "inside" or "outside" the isosurface. The first case is applied when the value of the vertex is greater than or equal to h and the second one when it is less than h. Once defined the type of intersection, an approximation of the isosurface contained in the cell is done by constructing triangles.

As each of the 8 vertex cells has only two possible states, there is a total of 2^8=25628=256 cases of intersection between isosurface and cell edge, which are listed in a lookup-table. However, some pairs of these cases are symmetric or complementary to each other, which restrains the problem to 15 cases, as illustrated in Fig. 1. A demonstration of the marching cubes algorithm using different isovalues is shown in Fig. 2.

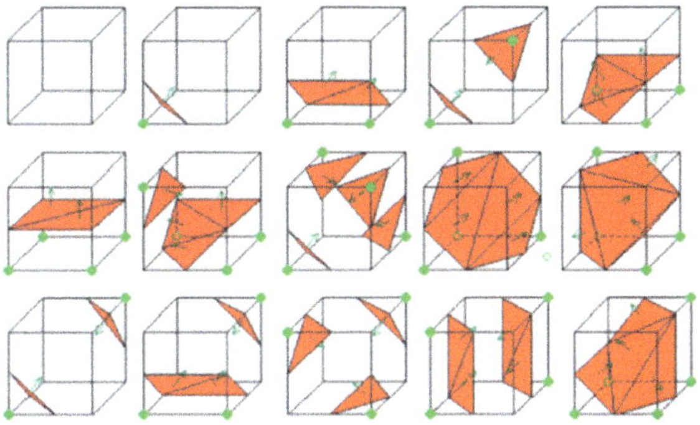

Figure 1: Illustration of the 15 basic cases of the marching cubes technique. The *green vertices* are the ones classified as "inside" the isosurfaces, whereas the remaining as "outside" them. Image extracted from [29].

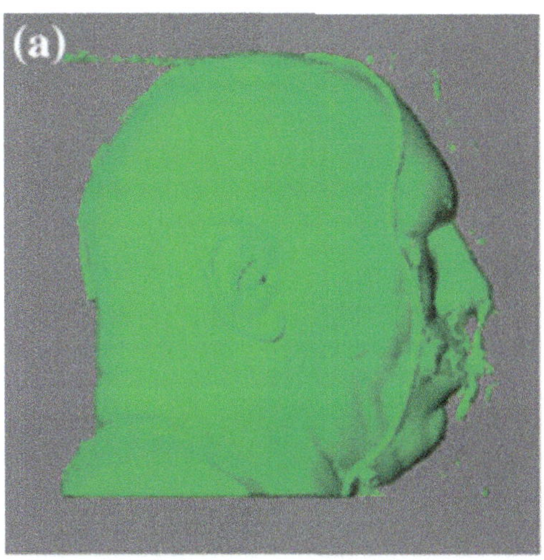

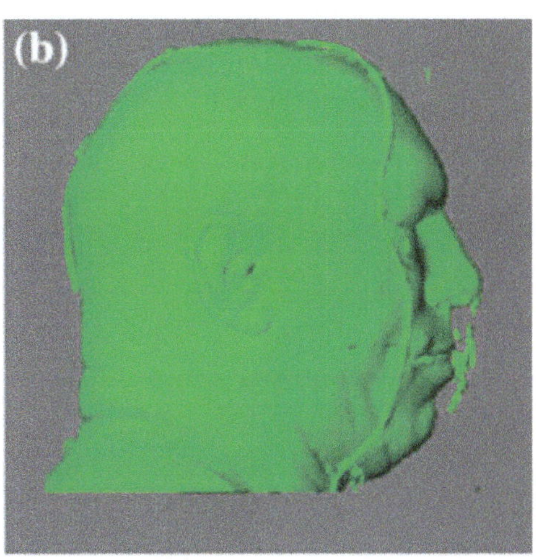

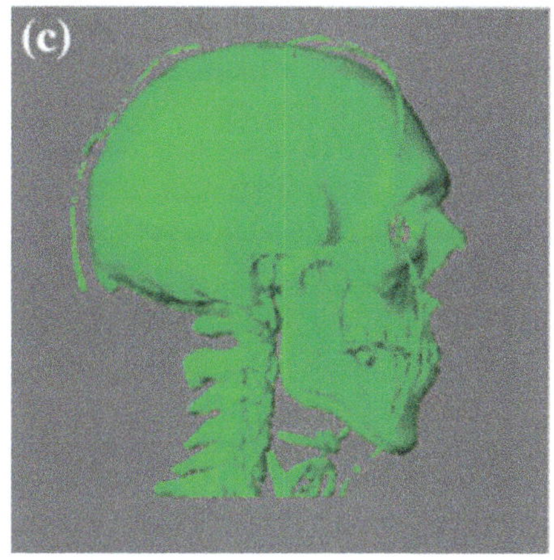

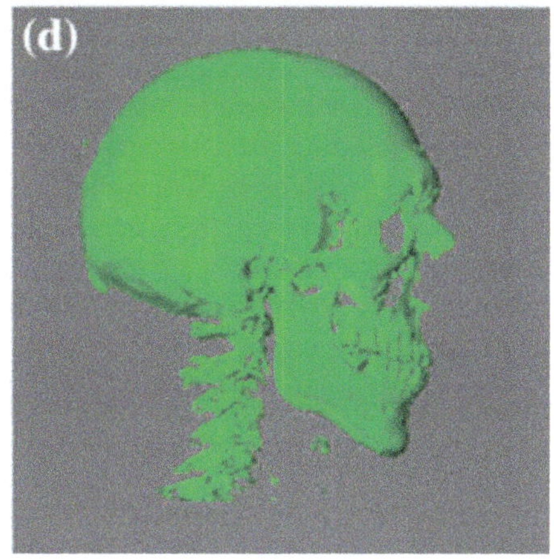

Figure. 2: Volume rendering of a male head dataset using marching cubes with different isovalues:a 30, b 50, c 75, d 100.

The pseudocode of the marching cubes technique can be briefly described according to the Algorithm 1. The advantage of this algorithm is that the processing of a cell is independent of the other ones, which allows its parallelization. However, as a disadvantage, it may generate holes in the isosurfaces, due to topological ambiguities of the cases.

Algorithm 1 runs in time O(n)O(n), where n is the total number of processed cells. On the other hand, many of these cells are empty, incurring an unnecessary waste of time. To minimize this waste, some spatial data structures are used to only process the active cells, that is, the ones that are intercepted by an isosurface, reducing the complexity of the algorithm.

Algorithm 1 Marching Cubes(V, h)

Input: Volume data V and an isovalue h.

Output: List of vertices to be rendered, together with their respective normals.

for each voxel (cube) v of V **do**
  Calculate an index to the cube, comparing the 8 density values of the cube vertices with the isovalue h.
  Using the calculated index, verify the edge list from a lookup-table.
  Using the scalar values in each vertex of the edge, find the surface-edge intersections by linear interpolation.
  Calculate a unitary normal in each cube vertex by the method of central differences [16]. Interpolate the normal to each triangle vertex.
  Return the triangle vertices and the vertex normals.
end for

In the context of the acceleration of marching cubes algorithm on the GPU, Johansson and Carr [18] conducted a comparative analysis of its execution using data structures, such as k-d trees [2] and interval trees [5], reporting the rendering rate speedups obtained in relation to the CPU.

Their approach is based on a caching cell topology technique, which stores the 15 cases of marching cubes in GPU (once it can cache geometry in a very efficient way) and improves the performance of the case classification stage by means of an optimization of the pre-computation step on the CPU, making use of the span-space properties. The method achieves a maximum speedup (between the GPU acceleration with an interval tree and its CPU counterpart) of 4.3 times. However, the authors do not make experiments with larger datasets due to hardware limitations.

Goetz et al. [13] optimized the marching cubes algorithm using a vertex shader, achieving an interactive isosurface reconstruction, but their approach does not use any accelerating data structures to improve the overall performance of the algorithm, obtaining a maximum speedup of approximately 2.0 times.

Newman and Yi [32] developed an in-depth research about the possibilities of developing the marching cubes technique, describing their respective properties, extensions and attempts to solve its limitations. However, the paper only shows the differences between these possibilities in terms of algorithm complexity as well as visualization results, and does not make an analysis with volume datasets.

Smistad et al. [43] presented an implementation of the marching cubes algorithm written in OpenCL [37] that runs entirely in the GPU. Like [6], it uses the idea of histogram pyramids to generate the output stream of vertices to be rendered and runs as fast as CUDA and shader implementations, providing a very efficient storage scheme as well. However, the drawback of their implementation lies on the interoperability between OpenCL and OpenGL.

Concerning recent applications that make use of the marching cubes algorithm in GPU, Dembogurski et al. [7] used a marching cubes histogram pyramid implementation for a procedural terrain generation; Donlon et al. [8] accelerated the visualization and quantification of MRI datasets to help in the treatment of patients that suffer from rheumatoid and psoriatic arthritis; Kim et al. [21] presented a method for computing the surfaces of a protein molecule in interactive time; Lang et al. [23] developed an environment for fast and automated analysis of large SBFSEM (serial block-face scanning electron microscopy) datasets to extract neuron morphologies.

Accelerating Data Structures

There are several classes of data structures that are very useful to avoid the processing of empty cells. One of them consists of interval-based representations, which uses cell intervals to group cells [32]. The advantage of this type of representation is in its flexibility, being applied not only on regular grids, but also on non-regular grids, once it works from an interval space, instead of using the mesh space itself.

The main methods of this class are based on a representation called span-space [28], where each cell of the volume data is mapped to a two-dimensional point, whose coordinates xx and y correspond, respectively, to the minimum and maximum values among the eight vertices that constitute a cell. From a given isovalue *h*, the points of the span-space that represent the active cells are the ones where $x \leq h$ and $y \geq h$.

A general scheme of the span-space is shown in Fig. 3. The blue area corresponds to the active cells of a volume data and the yellow areas to the cells that are not rendered, due to the fact that x>hx>h (yellow area located right of the blue area) or y<hy<h (yellow area located below the blue area). No cell can be mapped to the red area, once *x* is never greater than *y*.

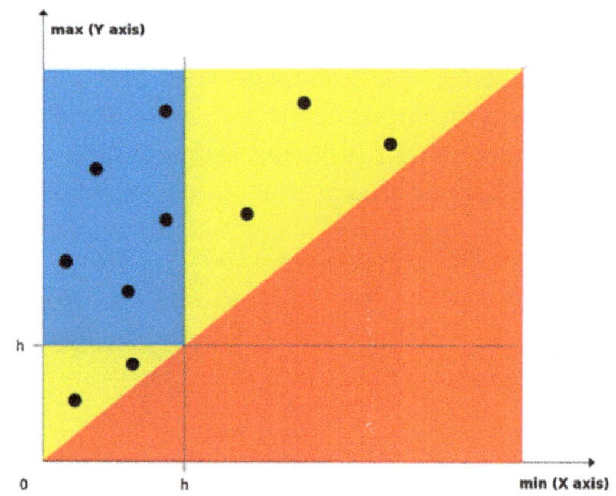

Figure 3: Representation of the span-space proposed by Livnat et al. [28].

This section describes some spatial data structures and how they can be used to improve the performance of the marching cubes algorithm.

k-d Tree

The k-d tree [2] is a special case of the binary search tree, used to organize points located in a k-dimensional space. Each non-leaf node represents a splitting hyperplane that divides the space into two parts in a specific direction, which is defined according to the depth of this node in the tree. The left subtree contains all the points located at the left of the hyperplane and the right subtree contains the ones to the right. The leaf nodes store one point each.

In the marching cubes algorithm, the volume data is mapped onto a span-space before constructing the tree, once the queries in the k-d tree are faster when working with points in a 2D plane rather than in a 3D space. Furthermore, every node stores a point in the span-space, instead of storing the points only in the leaves. The construction takes O(n log n) time, where *n* is the total number of cells in the volume data, and demands a storage space of O(n)O(n).

When searching in the tree, given an isovalue h, it will traverse only the nodes that correspond to the active cells of the volume data. Thus, the query takes $O(\sqrt{n} + p)$ time, where *p* is the number of active cells.

Interval Tree

The interval tree [5] is an ordered tree used to store intervals of values in 1D. Similarly to the k-d tree, it is an extension of the binary search tree, and allows an efficient search of all intervals that overlap with a given interval or point.

The root of the tree stores a value that corresponds to the median of the endpoints of all intervals and a list of intervals that contain this value. The left subtree stores the intervals that are completely below the median and the right subtree stores the ones completely above the median. Then, the process is repeated recursively for each subtree. It takes a construction time of $O(n \log n)$ and, like the k-d tree, a storage space of O(n)O(n).

The span-space is suitable for constructing an interval tree. In this case, the intervals correspond to the volume cells, and the endpoints are the minimum and maximum values of the cell, which stands for its coordinates in the span-space.

Searching in an interval tree takes O(logn+p) time, where *p* is the number of active cells, which makes it more efficient than the k-d tree. On the other hand, it demands higher memory space.

Quadtree and Octree

A quadtree [12] is a tree data structure where every non-leaf node has exactly four children. It is used to partition a region in a 2D space into four equal regions (or quadrants). These regions are then partitioned into other four subregions, and so on, until the subregion is empty, which characterizes a leaf node. The 3D analogous structure of a quadtree is called octree, which partitions a 3D space region into eight subregions (or octants).

Once the span-space is a 2D space, it can be represented by a quadtree. Let l be the number of bits used to store the volume data values, which means that there are 2^l possible values (ranging between 0 and 2^l-1) for a vertex cell. Thus, the span-space is a $2^l \times 2^l$ region, and the points correspond to the mapped cells. Every node in the tree stores the information of a point in the span-space.

However, more than one cell can be mapped to a same point in the span-space. To overcome this problem, each node in the quadtree also stores a pointer to a list of the volume data cells that were mapped to this point. Then, the queries can be made as usual, traversing the nodes corresponding to the active cells.

In the octree case, the tree is built directly from the volume data. However, in case of non-regular grids (i.e., when volume dimension is not a power of two), the subregions have different sizes, once we are partitioning cell regions.

METHODOLOGY

The significant evolution of the programmability of the graphics hardware has allowed the isosurface extraction procedure to be accelerated by the GPU, taking advantage of its parallel architecture. However, the bus used to establish a communication between the CPU and the GPU is a bottleneck for this acceleration, which means that transferring all the tasks to the GPU may not be the best solution. Thus, in order to maximize the performance of this procedure, an adequate planning of the graphics pipeline is needed, picking up the tasks that can be run on the CPU and the ones that can be transferred to the GPU, as well as a proper use of all the memory hierarchy. Some proposals of graphics pipeline for isosurface extraction were made by Buatois et al. [3], Johansson [17], Martin et al. [31], Pascucci [38], Reck et al. [40], and Tatarchuk et al. [44].

The methodology proposed in this work is restricted to the marching cubes technique, rather than generalizing to the isosurface extraction process. Figure 4 shows a general scheme, composed of six stages. At the Stage 1, the CPU reads a volume dataset of dimensions $N_x \times N_y \times N_z$, which is then allocated both in the main memory (RAM, used by the CPU) and in the video memory (VRAM, used by the GPU). Except for the octree, an extra memory space is allocated for the span-space related to the volume data.

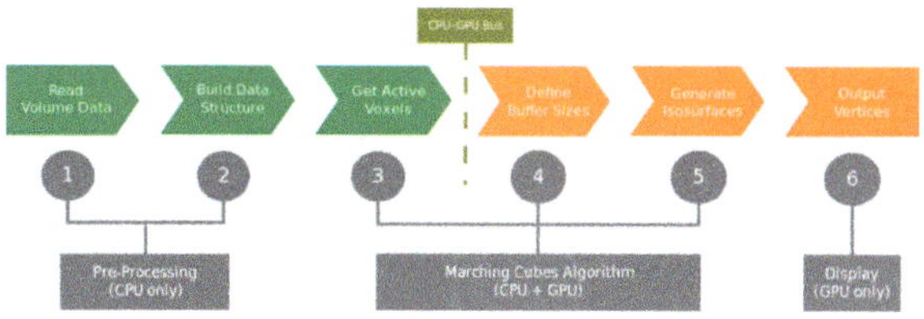

Figure 4: Our method for acceleration of the marching cubes algorithm. Stages 1 and 2 are responsible for the preprocessing stage; stages 3 to 5 correspond to the execution of marching cubes and stage 6 makes the display of vertices on the screen. *Green boxes* stand for the actions executed on CPU, whereas the orange boxes the ones on GPU.

Later, one of the spatial data structures described in Sect. 2.4 is constructed from the volume data and stored only in the main memory (stage 2). Then, the volume data is freed from the main memory, but it remains allocated in the video memory.

Algorithm 2 details the two aforementioned stages of the scheme. Once the preprocessing stage is done, the marching cubes algorithm is started (stage 3). From an isovalue h specified by the user, the CPU performs a search in the data structure, traversing only the nodes that correspond to the active volume cells, and creating a list of these cells, which is then transferred to the GPU via communication bus.

Algorithm 2 PreProcessVolumeData(V, d)

Input: Volume dataset V of dimensions $N_x \times N_y \times N_z$ and an integer d associated to an auxiliary data structure (-1 for no structure)

Allocate both in RAM and VRAM a space of size $N_x \times N_y \times N_z \times$ number of bytes that represent each 3-D position (x, y, z) of V
if $d \neq$ -1 **then**
    if $d \neq$ "OCTREE" **then**
        Create the span-space S related to V
        Free V from RAM
        From S, build and allocate in RAM the data structure related to d
        Free S from RAM
    else
        From V, build and allocate an octree in RAM
        Free V from RAM
    end if
end if

With the list of active cells and the isovalue h, the marching cubes algorithm then proceeds on the GPU. Each cell is classified into one of the 15 cases of marching cubes (shown in Fig. 1) by comparing hh to the eight cell vertices. From this comparison, a cell index is created and then used to define the number of vertices needed to render the isosurface contained in the cell. After this procedure is done for all active cells, the total number of vertices to be output can be determined, which will define the exact size of video memory needed to allocate two vertex buffers: one for storing these vertices and other for their respective normals (stage 4).

After that, the list of active cells is traversed by the GPU once more to generate the triangles that comprise the isosurfaces (stage 5). For each active cell of the list, the GPU calculates the isosurface intersections with the 12 edges of the cell by interpolating the vertices and the normals calculated by the GPU from the volume data. Once the cell index and the intersections are found, the GPU obtains the list of vertices and normals related to the isosurface, writing them in the respective vertex buffers. Finally, the volume data is rendered from these buffers (stage 6).

All the procedures executed by the GPU are parallelized, once the results obtained from a cell are independent of the others. However, the speedup achieved with the acceleration of the marching cubes relies on the way this parallelization occurs. When a task is assigned to the GPU, it creates a specific amount of blocks.[1] All of these blocks contain a specific number of threads (which is the same for all blocks), responsible for running a part of this task.

The amount of blocks to be created depends on the number of active cells and the number of threads per block, also known as block size. The block size is chosen in such a way that it is neither too low, assigning much work for all threads and not maximizing the task performance at all, nor too high, causing an overhead of starting and terminating threads.

The parallel processing of the list of active cells is made from a specific program, called GPU kernel. In our work, the GPU kernel was implemented using the CUDA architecture. In addition to the algorithms that are responsible for the execution of the marching cubes technique, some of the GPU inherent resources were employed in order to improve the rendering rate of the volume data. Among these resources are the use of texture memory, which is faster for handling read-only data, to store the lookup-tables employed by the marching cubes algorithm and the volume data itself, and the use of shared memory, which permits the data sharing among threads contained in a same block, besides being faster than the standard video memory. In the GPU marching cubes algorithm, the shared memory is used to compute, for each active cell, the intersections between an isosurface contained in the cell and the cell edges.

The pseudocodes of the following algorithms were adapted from [36]. Before the execution of these algorithms, the respective number of blocks (as well as their sizes) used to help on the parallelization of their procedures are determined.

Algorithm 3 represents the first step of the execution of marching cubes in GPU (stage 4 of Fig. 4). The goal of this algorithm is to calculate the exact amount of video memory that will be used to store the vertices and the normals related to the volume data. Once this amount is obtained, the GPU allocates the appropriate space in the vertex buffers, which will then store the vertices to be output and their respective normals.

Once this procedure is done, the Algorithm 4 is started. It is important to point out the repetition of the calculation of the cell indexes (line four of the Algorithms 3 and 4), which in GPU is faster than storing the results provided by Algorithm 3 in an array and retrieving them in the subsequent algorithm. Later, the vertex and normal buffers (called *P* and *N*, respectively) are filled and the volume data is visualized, thus finishing the steps of the marching cubes technique.

Algorithm 3 GetNumVertices(V, N, h)

Input: List V of active voxels, list N of the number of vertices that compose the isosurfaces of each voxel of V and isovalue h

1: **for** each voxel v of V in parallel **do**
2: Determine the positions of the 8 vertices of v.
3: For each position, fetch the volume data texture memory to retrieve the respective scalar values of the vertices.
4: Calculate the index of v, comparing its scalar values to the isovalue h.
5: Determine the number of vertices of the isosurface contained in v from the calculated index (fetching the 15-case lookup-table texture memory) and add this value in N.
6: **end for**

Algorithm 4 GenerateIsosurfaces(P, N, V, h)

Input: Buffers P and N of positions and normals of the vertices to be rendered, list V of active voxels and isovalue h

```
for each voxel v of V in parallel do
    Determine the positions of the 8 vertices of v.
    For each position, fetch the texture memory of the volume data to retrieve the re-
    spective scalar values of the vertices.
    Calculate the index of v, comparing its scalar values to the isovalue h.
    Calculate, by interpolation, the intersections in each edge of v using shared memory
    and store in an array I.
    Determine the number of vertices of the isosurface contained in v from the calculated
    index (fetching the texture of the 15-case lookup-table).
    for each triangle t of v do
        Find the edges of v intercepted by the vertices of t fetching the intersections
        table texture memory.
        Calculate the normal of t (which will be the same for the 3 vertices of t).
        From I, add the positions of the vertices of t in P.
        Add the normals of t in N.
    end for
end for
```

EXPERIMENTAL RESULTS

The tests were executed on an AMD Phenom II X6 1090T 3.2 GHz processor with 8 GB of RAM, and an NVIDIA GeForce GTS 450 with 1 GB of VRAM (together with its most recent drivers), using a C-like programming language, OpenGL 4.2 and CUDA 4.1 APIs.

The experiments were made using 8-bit datasets from [1] and [45], where each scalar value ranges from 0 to 255. Table 1 shows a list of volume datasets used in the tests, together with their respective dimensions (in voxels), isovalues (input to the marching cubes algorithm), number of triangles rendered in the screen (which depends on the isovalue), and memory space allocated during the execution of the marching cubes algorithm, which corresponds to the size of the volume datasets (1 byte per voxel) plus the amount of the vertex and normal buffers (4 bytes per vertex and normal, which leads to a total of 24 bytes per triangle, once there are two buffers). The isovalues for "Fuel", "Hydrogen atom" and "Engine" datasets were the same as those used by [18], so that a more accurate comparison can be made. The results of the rendering of each dataset, made from the application described in this work, are shown in Fig. 5.

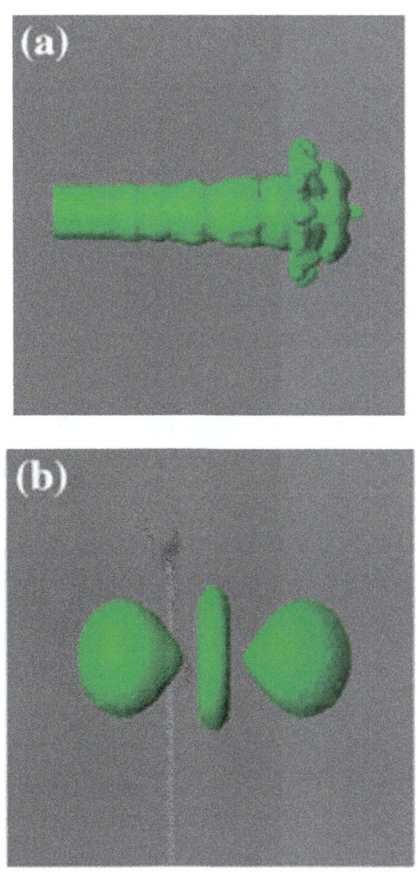

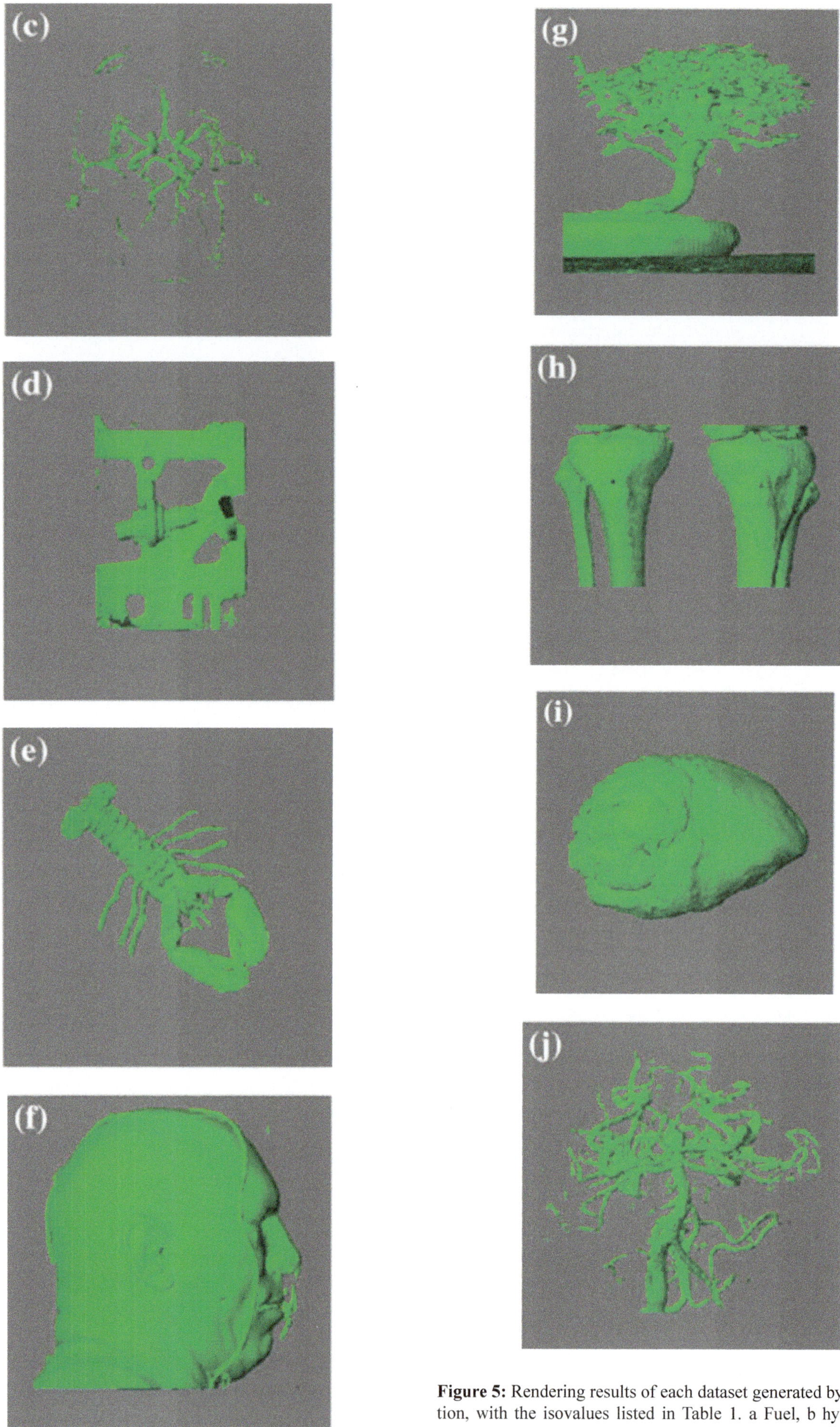

Figure 5: Rendering results of each dataset generated by the application, with the isovalues listed in Table 1. a Fuel, b hydrogen atom , c angiography, d engine, e lobster, f head, g bonsai,h knee, i sheep heart, j aneurism.

Table 1: List of volume datasets with their respective sizes in voxels, isovalues, number of triangles and memory space allocated during execution of marching cubes algorithm (in megabytes)

Volume name	**Dimensions**	**Isovalue**	**# Triangles**	**Space (MB)**
Fuel	64×64×6464×64×64	10	11,534	0.51
Hydrogen atom	128×128×128128×128×128	20	47,864	3.09
Angiography	256×320×128256×320×128	80	84,974	11.94
Engine	256×256×128256×256×128	155	207,592	12.75
Lobster	301×324×56301×324×56	45	317,024	12.46
Head	128×256×256128×256×256	50	544,588	20.46
Bonsai	256×256×256256×256×256	45	858,118	35.64
Knee	379×229×205379×229×205	60	1,027,838	40.49
Sheep heart	352×352×256352×352×256	80	1,397,064	61.87
Aneurism	512×512×512512×512×512	45	835,068	147.11

Figure 6 shows two plots that illustrate the average time (in milliseconds) of 50 executions of the marching cubes implementation on the GPU for different block size values, using each of the volume datasets and their respective isovalues listed in Table 1. The plot (a) stands for the executions of a brute force implementation of the marching cubes algorithm that runs without the aid of accelerating data structures and sequentially traverses all voxels of a volume dataset (including the empty ones), and (b) the executions using an interval tree to store the voxels from the datasets. From both plots, it can be noticed that for block sizes of 64 and higher, the running time of the marching cubes increases very slightly, and it does not rely on whether a data structure is used or not for acceleration. In other words, for any data structure used in the marching cubes algorithm, the behavior of the curves in the plot will be the same. As mentioned in Sect. 3, although a higher number of threads means higher parallelization, the time spent to create the threads also gets higher, hence stabilizing the performance. Thus, all the tests were run with a block size value of 64.

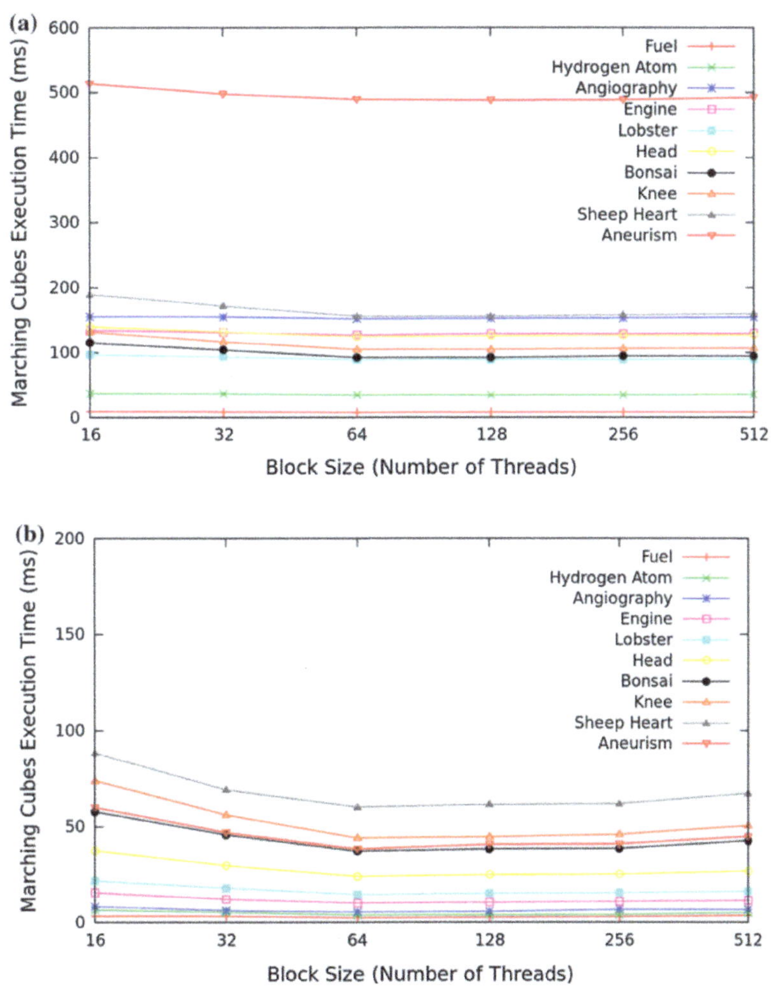

Figure 6: Average times of executions of the marching cubes algorithm on GPU for different block sizes. Graph a shows the results for the brute force version and b for the interval tree.

Table 2 shows the average frame rate of the execution of marching cubes algorithm in CPU and GPU, for all data structures described in Sect. 2.4, and comparing to their respective CPU versions of the algorithm. These results do not consider the time spent on the pre-processing stages (volume data reading and data structure construction), regarding only the events that occur between the search in the data structure and the volume display on the screen (Stages 3–6 of Fig. 4).

Table 2: Average frame rate (in frames per second) of the execution of marching cubes algorithm in CPU and GPU, with different data structures, comparing against the brute force version

Volume name	Brute force	k-d tree	Interval tree	Quadtree	Octree
CPU					
Fuel	83.3	105.6	**114.4**	108.0	98.3
Hydrogen atom	17.5	23.4	**25.6**	24.0	19.2
Angiography	7.5	12.9	**14.1**	13.6	10.7
Engine	4.6	5.2	**5.7**	5.5	4.8
Lobster	3.2	3.7	**4.1**	3.9	3.6
Head	1.8	2.0	**2.3**	2.1	1.9
Bonsai	1.2	1.3	**1.6**	1.4	1.3
Knee	1.1	1.2	**1.4**	1.3	1.1
Sheep heart	0.8	0.9	**1.0**	0.9	0.8
Aneurism	0.6	0.9	**1.3**	1.2	0.7
GPU					
Fuel	195.4 (2.3)	220.7 (2.1)	**246.4 (2.2)**	229.9 (2.1)	205.7 (2.1)
Hydrogen Atom	77.0 (4.4)	142.8 (6.1)	**165.0 (6.4)**	149.5 (6.2)	96.5 (5.0)
Angiography	24.7 (3.3)	109.6 (8.5)	**133.7 (9.5)**	89.2 (6.6)	58.7 (5.5)
Engine	26.6 (5.8)	61.0 (11.7)	**81.1 (14.2)**	56.8 (10.3)	38.4 (8.0)
Lobster	30.1 (9.4)	42.8 (11.6)	**58.5 (14.3)**	29.8 (7.6)	27.4 (7.6)
Head	17.9 (9.9)	22.7 (11.4)	**35.8 (15.6)**	28.9 (13.8)	20.9 (11.0)
Bonsai	10.7 (8.9)	13.2 (10.2)	**25.9 (16.2)**	18.7 (13.4)	11.5 (8.8)
Knee	8.2 (7.4)	9.7 (8.1)	**22.4 (16.0)**	10.7 (8.2)	9.1 (8.2)
Sheep Heart	6.3 (7.9)	7.4 (8.2)	**16.3 (16.3)**	8.9 (9.9)	6.6 (8.3)
Aneurism	2.1 (3.5)	10.2 (11.3)	**23.7 (18.2)**	11.9 (9.9)	9.5 (13.5)

Values between *parenthesis* correspond to the acceleration factor related to their respective data structure versions of marching cubes in CPU for each volume dataset

As it is possible to observe, the interval tree provided the best results (highlighted in bold in Table 2), not only among all the data structures used in the tests, but also in the acceleration factor compared to the CPU marching cubes, achieving a maximum speedup of 18.2 times for the "Aneurism" dataset. This result was expected because the interval tree has asymptotically a better query time than the other structures. Furthermore, the obtained speedups are superior than those of Johansson and Carr's approach [18], which achieves a maximum speedup of 4.3 times (for the "Hydrogen Atom" dataset and the interval tree) using pre-calculated normals, while the method proposed in this paper calculates them on-the-fly.

Another important fact to be pointed out is the performance of quadtree, which obtained a better frame rate than the k-d tree and the octree, standing only behind the interval tree. It achieved a maximum speedup of 13.8 times for the "Head" dataset. For the other datasets, excluding the "Fuel", the speedup was between 6.2 and 10.3.

Concerning the building time of the data structures, quadtree had a much higher performance than the other ones, as shown in Fig. 7. For all datasets used in the tests, the building time of the quadtree was very much smaller than the other data structures, not having a significant gain of time as the volume datasets get larger, which is very efficient for real applications that process great amounts of volume data. For the rest of the data structures, the building time increases considerably among the datasets.

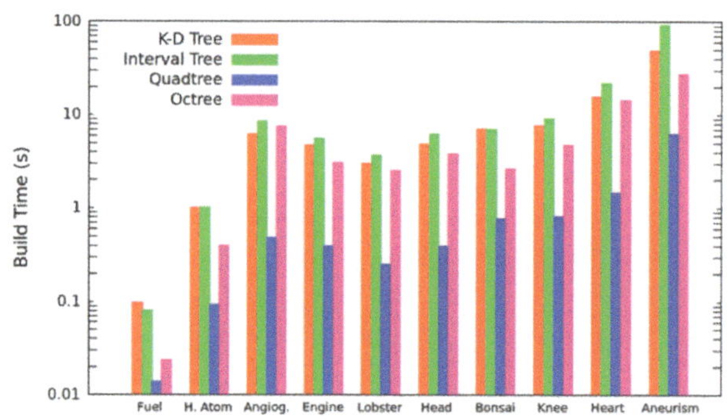

Figure 7: Average building times of the data structures for each volume dataset.

Octree provided the second best building times. Even though its building algorithm is similar to the one of quadtree, the fact that it is applied in the 3D space brings on a higher waste of time, once the total number of subdivisions is higher. In third place, comes the k-d tree, which has a worse building time than the octree because of the successive executions of the algorithm that finds the median of the points located in the span-space. Finally, interval tree achieved the worst building times among the tested data structures. It happened due to the time spent in sorting the cell lists, which has a higher time complexity than finding a median.

The bottleneck of this approach resides on the fact that the searches in the data structures are done on the CPU. It is feasible to implement all of the data structure algorithms on the GPU, as well as storing the data structure itself in the video memory, but since most of the tree search algorithms are recursive and CUDA does not support recursions, if non-recursive versions of these algorithms were implemented on the GPU, there would have a large waste of time and space to create stacks and loops used to simulate the eventual recursive calls.

CONCLUSIONS AND FUTURE WORK

Volume visualization techniques allow users to explore and analyze tridimensional data, which benefit several knowledge domains, such as biology, medicine, meteorology, oceanography, geology. A challenging task of volume visualization is the development of efficient algorithms for representing, manipulating and rendering complex and large datasets.

This paper described a comparative analysis among four different spatial data structures for speeding up the marching cubes algorithm through graphics processing units, together with an approach using CUDA framework. Time complexity of the algorithm depends on the volume data cells that contain an isosurface, instead of the total number of cells, avoiding the processing of empty cells.

Experimental results obtained from several volumetric datasets demonstrate that it was possible to accelerate the marching cubes algorithm by a factor of approximately 18 times when compared to the CPU approach.

Among the four data structures described in this paper, interval tree provided the best rendering rates, but the time spent in building the structure was relatively high. On the other hand, quadtree achieved very satisfactory building times, even for large volume datasets, besides slightly lower rendering rates compared to those of the acceleration with an interval tree. However, since the building of a data structure is done only once, while the search is performed whenever the volume needs to be rendered, it is more worthwhile to use the interval tree rather than the quadtree in this case.

Directions for future work include the implementation of the data structures mentioned in this paper on the GPU, together with their respective building and searching operations so that they can be done in parallel, and an extension of the proposed method to open frameworks, such as OpenCL [37], once that CUDA framework is restricted to NVIDIA [35] graphic cards. Furthermore, a case study with more powerful graphic cards (such as those from NVIDIA Kepler architecture) is desired as well.

ACKNOWLEDGMENTS

The authors are grateful to FAPESP, CNPq, and National Institute of Science and Technology in Medicine Assisted by Scientific Computing (INCT/MACC) for the financial support.

REFERENCES

1. The volume library. http://lgdv.cs.fau.de/External/vollib
2. Bentley J (1975) Multidimensional binary search trees used for associative searching. Commun ACM 18(9):509–517
3. Buatois L, Caumon G, Lévy B (2006) GPU accelerated isosurface extraction on tetrahedral grids. In: Advances in visual computing. Lecture notes in computer science, vol 4291, Springer, Berlin, pp 383–392
4. Chan S, Purisima E (1998) A new tetrahedral tesselation scheme for isosurface generation. Comput Graph 22(1):83–90
5. Cignoni P, Marino P, Montani C, Scopigno R (1997) Speeding up isosurface extraction using interval trees. IEEE Trans Visual Comput Graph 3:158–170
6. Ciznicki M, Kierzynka M, Kurowski K, Ludwiczak B, Napierala K, Palczynski J (2011) Efficient isosurface extraction using marching tetrahedra and histogram pyramids on multiple GPUs. In: Proceedings of the 9th international conference on parallel processing and applied mathematics, Torun, Poland, pp 343–352
7. Dembogurski B, Clua E, Vieira M, Leta F (2008) Procedural terrain generation at GPU level with marching cubes. In: Proceedings of the VII Brazilian symposium of games and digital entertainment—computing track, Belo Horizonte, MG, Brazil, pp 37–40
8. Donlon B, Veale D, Brennan P, Gibney R, Carr H, Rainford L, Ng C, Pontifex E, McNulty J, FitzGerald O, Ryan J (2012) MRI-based visualisation and quantification of rheumatoid and psoriatic arthritis of the knee. In: Visualization in medicine and life sciences II, mathematics and visualization, Springer, pp 45–59
9. Dürst M (1988) Letters: additional reference to marching cubes. ACM Comput Graph 22(4):72–73
10. Dyken C, Ziegler G, Theobalt C, Seidel H (2008) High-speed marching cubes using histopyramids. Comput Graph 27(8):2028–2039
11. Elvins T (1992) A survey of algorithms for volume visualization. SIGGRAPH Comput Graph 26(3):194–201
12. Finkel R, Bentley J (1974) Quad trees: a data structure for retrieval on composite keys. Acta Inf 4(1):1–9
13. Goetz F, Junklewitz T, Domik G (2005) Real-time marching cubes on the vertex shader. In: Eurographics. Dublin, Ireland
14. Gong F, Zhao X (2010) Three-dimensional reconstruction of medical image based on improved marching cubes algorithm. In: Proceedings of the international conference on machine vision and human-machine interface, Kaifeng, China, pp 608–611
15. Guéziec A, Hummel R (1995) Exploiting triangulated surface extraction using tetrahedral decomposition.

IEEE Trans Visual Comput Graph 1(4):328–342

16. Jeffreys H, Jeffreys B (1988) Central differences formula. In: Methods of mathematical physics, Cambridge University Press, Cambridge, pp 284–286
17. Johansson G (2005) Accelerating isosurface extraction by caching cell topology with graphics hardware. Master's thesis, University College Dublin, Ireland
18. Johansson G, Carr H (2006) Accelerating marching cubes with graphics hardware. In: Proceedings of the conference of the center for advanced studies on collaborative research. Toronto, ON, Canada
19. Kaufman A (1991) Volume visualization. IEEE Computer Society Press, Los Alamitos
20. Keppel E (1975) Approximating complex surfaces by triangulation of contour lines. IBM J Res Dev 19(1):2–11
21. Kim B, Kim K, Seong J (2012) GPU accelerated molecular surface computing. Appl Math Inf Sci 6(1S):185S–194S
22. Lacroute P (1996) Fast volume rendering using a shear-warp factorization of the viewing transformation. PhD thesis, Stanford University, Stanford, CA, USA
23. Lang S, Drouvelis P, Tafaj E, Bastian P, Sakmann B (2011) Fast extraction of neuron morphologies from large-scale SBFSEM image stacks. J Comput Neurosci 31(3):533–545
24. Lengyel E (2010) Transition cells for dynamic multiresolution marching cubes. J Graph GPU Game Tools 15(2):99–122
25. Levoy M (1990) Efficient ray tracing of volume data. ACM Trans Graph 9(3):245–261
26. Li T, Xie M, Zhao W, Wei Y (2010) Shear-warp rendering algorithm based on radial basis functions interpolation. In: Proceedings of the 2nd international conference on computer modeling and simulation, Sanya, China, pp 425–429
27. Liu B, Clapworthy G, Dong F (2009) Accelerating volume raycasting using proxy spheres. Comput Graph Forum 28(3):839–846
28. Livnat Y, Shen HW, Johnson R (1996) A near optimal isosurface extraction algorithm using the span space. IEEE Trans Visual Comput Graph 2(1):73–84
29. Lorensen W, Cline H (1987) Marching cubes: a high resolution 3D surface construction algorithm. Comput Graph 21(4):163–169
30. Lum EB, Wilson B, liu Ma K (2004) High-quality lighting and efficient pre-integration for volume rendering. In: Proceedings of the joint Eurographics—IEEE TVCG symposium on visualization, pp 25–34
31. Martin S, Shen HW, McCormick P (2010) Load-balanced isosurfacing on multi-GPU clusters. In: Proceedings of the Eurographics symposium on parallel graphics and visualization, Norrküping, Sweden, pp 91–100
32. Newman T, Yi H (2006) A survey of the marching cubes algorithm. Comput Graph 30(5):854–879CrossRef
33. Nielson GM, Hamann B (1991) The asymptotic decider: resolving the ambiguity in marching cubes. In: Proceedings of the 2nd conference on visualization, San Diego, CA, USA, pp 83–91
34. Nurzyńska K (2009) 3D object reconstruction from parallel cross-sections. In: Bolc L, Kulikowski J, Wojciechowski K (eds) Computer vision and graphics. Lecture notes in computer science, vol 5337, Springer, Berlin, pp 111–122
35. NVIDIA CUDA C programming guide version 3.2.http://developer.download.nvidia.com/compute/cuda/3_2_prod/toolkit/docs/CUDA_C_Programming_Guide.pdf
36. NVIDIA (2012) CUDA C/C++ SDK code examples. http://developer.nvidia.com/cuda-cc-sdk-code-samples
37. OpenCL The khronos group. http://www.khronos.org/opencl/
38. Pascucci V (2004) Isosurface computation made simple: hardware acceleration, adaptive refinement and tetrahedral stripping. In: Proceedings of the joint Eurographics—IEEE TVCG symposium on visualization, Konstanz, Germany, pp 293–300
39. Pöthkow K, Weber B, Hege HC (2011) Probabilistic marching cubes. Comput Graph Forum 30(3):931–940
40. Reck F, Dachsbacher C, Grosso R, Greiner G, Stamminger M (2004) Realtime isosurface extraction with graphics hardware. In: Proceedings of the Eurographics 2004 short presentations and interactive demos, Grenoble, France, pp 33–36
41. Schindler B, Fuchs R, Waser J, Peikert R (2011) Marching correctors—fast and precise polygonal isosurfaces of SPH data. In: Proceedings of the 6th international smoothed particle hydrodynamics European research interest community (SPHERIC) workshop, Hamburg, Germany, pp 125–132
42. Schlegel P, Pajarola R (2009) Layered volume splatting. In: Advances in visual computing, lecture notes in computer science, vol 5876, Springer, pp 1–12
43. Smistad E, Elster AC, Lindseth F (2011) Fast surface extraction and visualization of medical images using openCL and GPUs. In: Proceedings of the joint workshop on high performance and distributed computing for medical imaging, Toronto, Canada
44. Tatarchuk N, Shopf J, DeCoro C (2007) Real-time isosurface extraction using the GPU programmable geometry pipeline. In: Proceedings of the ACM SIGGRAPH 2007 courses, San Diego, CA, USA, pp 122–137
45. Volvis: volume datasets. http://www.volvis.org
46. Wang Z, Fan B, Li N, Zhang H (2009) Iso-surface extraction and optimization method based on marching cubes. In: Proceedings of the international conference on semantics, knowledge and grid, Zhuhai, China, pp 458–460
47. Westover L (1990) Footprint evaluation for volume rendering. In: Proceedings of the 17th annual conference on computer graphics and interactive techniques, Dallas, TX, USA, pp 367–376

48. Wilhelms J (1990) A coherent projection approach for direct volume rendering. Technical report of University of California, Santa Cruz, CA, USA
49. Zhu S, Gu YL (2008) Volume rendering algorithm of irregular volume based on cell projection. Comput Eng Appl 44(15):68–70
50. Ziegler G, Tevs A, Theobalt C, Seidel HP (2006) On-the-fly point clouds through histogram pyramids. In: Proceedings of the 11th international fall workshop on vision, modeling and visualization, Aachen, Germany, pp 137–144

CHAPTER 6

A UNIFIED FRAMEWORK FOR ISOTROPIC MESHING BASED ON NARROW-BAND EUCLIDEAN DISTANCE TRANSFORMATION

Yuen-Shan Leung[1], Xiaoning Wang[1], Ying He[1], Yong-Jin Liu[2], and Charlie C. L. Wang[3]

[1]School of Computer Engineering, Nanyang Technological University, Singapore

[2]Department of Computer Science and Technology, Tsinghua University, China

[3]Department of Mechanical and Automation Engineering, The Chinese University of Hong Kong, Hong Kong, China

ABSTRACT

In this paper, we propose a simple-yet-effective method for isotropic meshing relying on Euclidean distance transformation based centroidal Voronoi tessellation (CVT). Our approach improves the performance and robustness of computing CVT on curved domains while simultaneously providing high-quality output meshes. While conventional extrinsic methods compute CVTs in the entire volume bounded by the input model, we restrict the computation to a 3D shell of user-controlled thickness. Taking voxels which contain surface samples as sites, we compute the exact Euclidean distance transform on the GPU. Our algorithm is parallel and memory-efficient, and can construct the shell space for resolutions up to 2048^3 at interactive speed. The 3D centroidal Voronoi tessellation and restricted Voronoi diagrams are also computed efficiently on the GPU. Since the shell space can bridge holes and gaps smaller than a certain tolerance, and tolerate non-manifold edges and degenerate triangles, our algorithm can handle models with such defects, which typically cause conventional remeshing methods to fail. Our method can process implicit surfaces, polyhedral surfaces, and point clouds in a unified framework. Computational results show that our GPU-based isotropic meshing algorithm produces results comparable to state-of- the-art techniques, but is significantly faster than conventional CPU-based implementations.

INTRODUCTION

Triangle meshes have found widespread acceptance in computer graphics as a simple, convenient, and versatile representation of surfaces. However, raw meshes obtained from 3D scanners are often unsuitable for subsequent geometric processing, since they may contain holes, gaps, noise, degenerate triangles, and non-manifold edges. A popular approach to improve mesh quality is to use centroidal Voronoi tessellation (CVT), which can generate a highly regular distribution of sites with respect to a given density function. A typical CVT-based remeshing method iteratively updates the generator of each Voronoi cell until it coincides with its center of mass. An isotropic mesh is then obtained as the dual graph of the computed CVT. A key step in each iteration in CVT computation is to construct a Voronoi diagram (VD). Although this is fairly simple to do in Euclidean space, doing so in curved domains is expensive due to the lack of a closed-form formula for geodesic distance. To tackle this challenge, some researchers parameterize the input models in $\mathbb{R}^2$ and computed a 2D CVT whose density function compensates for the parameterization distortion. These parameterization based methods can compute intrinsic CVTs on simple meshes of good quality, but they do not

Citation: Yuen-Shan Leung, Xiaoning Wang, Ying He, Yong-Jin Liu, Charlie C. L. Wang, "A unified framework for isotropic meshing based on narrow-band Euclidean distance transformation," doi:10.1007/s41095-015-0022-4

work for point clouds, imperfect meshes, or meshes with complicated topology, where parameterization is non-trivial. A practical alternative is to compute a restricted Voronoi diagram (RVD) [1], which is the intersection of the given model and a CVT defined in $\mathbb{R}^3$. RVD methods are easy to implement and can easily handle models with complicated geometry and topology. Although efficient clipping algorithms (e.g., Ref. [2]) have been proposed, their performance is still too low for time-critical applications. Moreover, current RVD methods assume the input is a manifold mesh, and they do not work for other surface representations, such as scanned point samples.

In this paper, we propose a new RVD-based computational framework for isotropic meshing, with the goal of improving performance as well as robustness of computing RVD while simultaneously maintaining the high quality of the output meshes. Rather than computing CVTs in the entire volume bounded by the input model, our idea is to restrict the computation to a 3D shell of user-controlled thickness. Taking voxels which contain surface samples as sites, we compute the exact Euclidean distance transform on the GPU. Our algorithm is parallel and memory-efficient, and can construct a shell space with resolution 20483 at interactive speed. The 3D centroidal Voronoi tessellation and restricted Voronoi diagrams are also computed efficiently on the GPU. Computational results show that our GPU-enabled isotropic meshing algorithm produces results comparable to state-of-the-art techniques, but runs significantly faster than conventional CPU based implementations. It is also worth noting that our method can process various representations, such as implicit surfaces, polyhedral surfaces, and point clouds, in a unified framework. Moreover, since the shell space can bridge holes and gaps smaller than a certain tolerance, and also tolerate non-manifold edges and degeneracies, our algorithm works well on imperfect meshes with such defects, for which conventional remeshing methods often fail. See Fig. 1.

This paper makes the following contributions:

- We give a unified framework for constructing isotropic meshes from point clouds, polyhedral surfaces, and implicit surfaces via voxel representation. It avoids computationally expensive components often used in existing methods, such as data fitting, isosurface extraction, and geodesic distance computation.
- Our framework produces a topologically consistent shell under user control, so it can bridge holes and gaps, and tolerate noise, to some degree. It also works well for models with non-manifold edges and degenerate triangles.
- We give a fast, memory-efficient algorithm for computing narrow-band distance fields on a GPU. Our implementation on an nVidia Quadro K5000 with 4 GB RAM can compute the exact Euclidean distance transform at interactive speed. The CVT, RVD, and the dual Delaunay triangulations are also computed in parallel on the GPU.

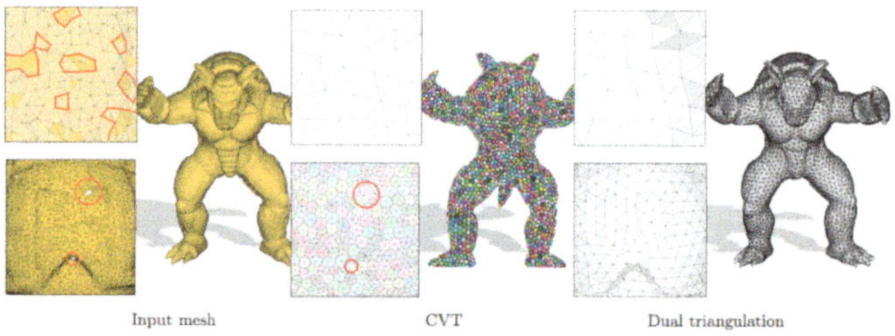

Figure 1: Isotropic meshing on an imperfect mesh with non-manifold edges, degenerate triangles and holes.

RELATED WORK

Geodesic Voronoi Diagrams

Although Voronoi diagrams in Euclidean space have been well studied, Voronoi diagrams in 2-manifold meshes (geodesic Voronoi diagrams, GVDs) have received little attention. Liu et al. [3] pointed out the fundamental difference between conventional Voronoi diagrams and GVDs, and they pioneered a practical algorithm for constructing a GVD on a triangle mesh. Given a triangle mesh M with n vertices and m (< n) sites on M, their algorithm has a theoretical time complexity $O(n^2 \log n)$ and runs empirically in linear time when m is close to n. Liu and Tang [4] proved that the combinatorial complexity of a GVD is O(m(g + n)), where g is the genus of M. Based on a local Voronoi diagram, Xu et al. [5] developed an exact algorithm for computing a polyline-sourced GVD on a triangle mesh.

Centroidal Voronoi Tessellations

A centroidal Voronoi tessellation is a Voronoi diagram whose generating points are the centers of mass of the corresponding Voronoi cells. Thanks to its many favorable geometric properties, the CVT has been used in a wide range of applications [6]. It can be defined by the critical points of the CVT energy function. A popular way to compute a CVT is Lloyd's algorithm [7], which iteratively moves each generator to the corresponding mass center until convergence. Lloyd's method is conceptually simple and easy to implement, but as a gradient-descent method, it only has linear convergence. Liu et al. [8] proved that the CVT energy function has 2nd order smoothness in most situations encountered in computer graphics, so one can achieve quadratic or super-linear convergence by use of Newton or quasi-Newton optimization methods. Rong et al. [9] developed a GPU-based method for computing a CVT in the plane and observed significant speedup over CPU methods.

To compute the CVT on a genus-0 surface, Alliez et al. [10] conformally parameterized the surface to a disk and evaluated the centroids over a weighted density function expressed in $\mathbb{R}^2$. Rong et al. [11] extended the CVT energy function to the spherical $\mathbb{S}^2$ and hyperbolic $\mathbb{H}^2$ domains, and thus can process surfaces of all topological types. Shuai et al. [12] developed a GPU-enabled algorithm for computing a periodic CVT in $\mathbb{H}^2$ and used it to construct isotropic meshes for high-genus surfaces. Recently, Wang et al. [13] proposed an intrinsic method for computing the CVT on an arbitrary manifold triangle mesh. Rather than computing the mass centers of Voronoi cells which requires area integration, their algorithm computes the Riemannian centers using exponential maps. These Riemannian centers provide a good approximation of the mass centers if there are sufficient seeds.

These parameterization-based and exponential map based CVT algorithms are intrinsic and thereby independent of the embedding space. However, they are computationally expensive and impractical for time-critical applications. Rather than computing CVT on surfaces directly, Yan et al. [1] proposed a novel indirect method based on computing a restricted Voronoi diagram, that is, the intersection between the input mesh and a 3D CVT. Using a kdtree to quickly identify and compute the intersection of each triangle face with its incident Voronoi cells, their algorithm computes the RVD in O(n log m) time, where m is the number of seed points and n is the number of triangles of the input mesh. They also adopted a quasi-Newton method to efficiently compute the 3D CVT in the volume bounded by the input mesh.

Lu et al. [14] computed a CVT using line segments and graphs as generators. CVT can also be defined using anisotropic metrics [15] and Lp distances [16].

Chen et al. [17] proposed an iterative method for generating a constrained centroidal Delaunay mesh (CCDM). With local vertex relation, their method does not require geodesic distances and can guarantee that the computed CCDM has the same topology as the input mesh. However, their method cannot handle non-manifold edges and degenerate triangles. It is also unclear whether their method can be extended to point clouds and implicit functions.

Li et al. [18] presented an elegant method for triangulating the conformal uniformization domain via planar Delaunay refinment. They gave explicit estimates for the Hausdorff distance, normal deviation, and differences in curvature measures between the surface and the mesh.

Distance Computation

A key step when intrinsically computing a CVT on a polyhedral surface is to determine geodesic distances, a fundamental problem in computer graphics and computational geometry. Classical computational geometry approaches include the MMP algorithm [19], the CH algorithm [20], and their many variants (e.g., Refs. [21, 22]). Although these methods can compute the exact solution on arbitrary manifold meshes, they are computationally expensive. Partial differential equation (PDE) approaches, such as the fast marching method [23] and the heat method [24], are efficient and can flexibly handle a wide range of geometric domains, including triangle meshes, point clouds, regular grids and volumes. They can also be easily generalized to an anisotropic setting [25]. However, they only compute a first-order approximation, and thus the results are sensitive to model tessellation and resolution. Motivated by the local structure of the discrete geodesic problem, Ying et al. [26] proposed the saddle vertex graph (SVG), a sparse graph which encodes geodesic information on a triangle mesh. Computing a geodesic distance is equivalent to finding a shortest path in this graph. However, the performance of SVG methods depends greatly on the number and distribution of saddle vertices in the input meshes, and it is unclear whether it can be extended to imperfect meshes, implicit surfaces, or point clouds, as it is difficult to determine saddle vertices in such cases.

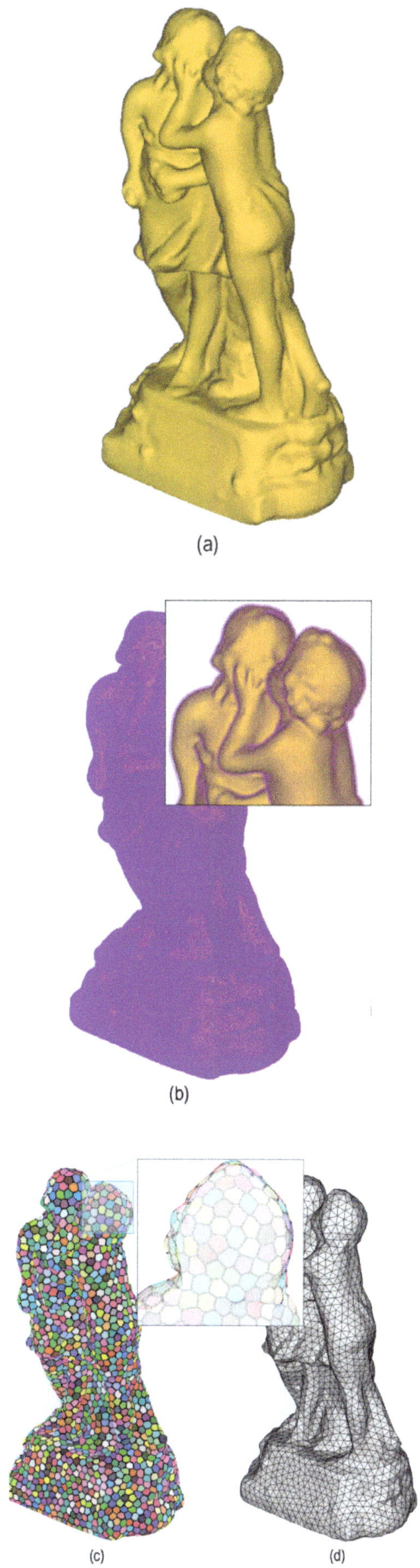

Figure 2: Overview of our approach using the Sculpture model. (a) Input mesh; (b) shell space with d = 3; (c) CVT with 3000 seeds; (d) output isotropic mesh.

Since computing geodesic distances is expensive, many applications seek practical ways to give approximate solutions with accuracy control. The most widely used approach is to use a distance field, which encodes the distance from each grid node to the surface of the model (uniformly or adaptively) [27]. An approximate distance field can be efficiently computed by a distance-transformation method, e.g., based on the chamfer distance transformation (CDT) [28] or the vector-city vector distance transform (VCVDT) [29].

Recent work has focused on the Euclidean distance transformation (EDT). Given a d-dimensional grid with N = n^d grid points, where S grid points are colored and the other N − S grid points are not colored, for each grid point, the EDT aims to compute the Euclidean distance to the closest colored grid point. However, this process is typically computationally intensive in 3 or more dimensions. GPU-based algorithms have been developed to provide an efficient solution [30]. Cao et al. [31] presented an efficient algorithm, the parallel banding algorithm (PBA), to compute the exact EDT on a GPU. Their algorithm, however, can quickly exhaust graphics memory: the highest resolution that can be achieved by PBA is 5123 on a cutting-edge graphics card, which does not provide sufficient accuracy to guarantee the correctness of the constructed CVT for many real-world models. The new algorithm proposed in this paper is more sophisticated in its memory usage and can achieve 3D EDT for resolutions up to 2048^3.

Surface Reconstruction and Meshing from Points

Constructing a high-quality mesh from unorganized point samples plays an important role in computer graphics. Although numerous techniques are available, all tackle the problem in two separate stages, that is, constructing an initial surface first, and then improving the mesh quality using the remeshing techniques. Existing surface reconstruction methods are based on either computational geometry or implicit functions.

Computational geometry approaches aim to generate a piecewise linear surface, topologically equivalent to the sampled surface and also geometrically close. Representative work includes crust [32], cocone [33], and their many variants. These algorithms provide theoretical guarantees if the input points are densely sampled. However, in practice, this condition may not hold.

In presence of noise and outliers, which is typical for samples obtained by scanning, a common approach is to fit the samples using the zero set of an implicit function. A popular method for oriented point samples is Poisson surface reconstruction [34]; an implicit surface is first generated and tessellated into a polygonal mesh later. Although tessellation step can be computed on the GPU, fitting an implicit surface uses timeconsuming global operators. Sheung and Wang [35] presented a robust mesh reconstruction method for unoriented noisy points. An approximate CVT is computed on the point set to down-sample the input point cloud to a smaller number of pointa. Then, a Voronoi diagram based mesh generation method, tight cocone [36], is employed to generate the mesh. As VD-based surface reconstruction is memory intensive, only datasets with a modest number of points can be handled. Moreover, it is hard to parallelize the computation.

Our proposed method is different from existing ones in that it performs surface reconstruction and meshing in an integrated manner. Our method is more efficient and elegant since it can completely bypass implicit fitting as well as isosurface extraction, making it an ideal tool for processing scanned point samples.

ALGORITHM

Let O denote the input 3D mesh. We first construct a voxel representation M of O at a given resolution res. Then we construct a shell space $\bar{P}$ consisting of off-surface points, where each point in $\bar{P}$ has a distance $d_p \leqslant d$ to its closest point on M (see Fig. 2). The threshold d is specified by the user and is model-dependent.

Our isotropic meshing algorithm adopts Lloyd's framework. Starting with k randomly generated seeds, it minimizes the CVT energy by iteratively updating the seed positions. In each iteration, it computes a Voronoi diagram confined to the shell space and moves the seeds toward the corresponding mass centers. The algorithm projects the seeds back to $\bar{P}$ if they move outside the shell space. After convergence, it propagates the seed information in the shell space to determine connected Voronoi cells and extracts the dual Delaunay triangulation. Our method is outlined in Algorithm 1, and described in detail in the following.

Algorithm 1: Isotropic meshing based on EDT

Input: 3D surface O, voxel resolution res, shell space thickness d, convergence threshold ϵ, and number of seeds k.

Output: Isotropic mesh with k vertices.

$S \leftarrow k$ random seeds
$M \leftarrow$ Voxelization(O, res)
$\bar{P} \leftarrow$ ShellSpaceConstruction(M, res, d)
while convergence not reached **do**
  $V_k \leftarrow$ SearchClosestSeedInShell($\bar{P}$, S)
  $C_k \leftarrow$ CenterMass(V_k)
  $\bar{C}_k \leftarrow$ UpdateSeed($\bar{P}$, C_k)
  $S \leftarrow \bar{C}$
end while
$V_k \leftarrow$ ShellFlooding($\bar{P}$, S)
return DualTriangulation(V_k)

Memory-Efficient Shell Space Construction

We introduce a memory-efficient way to construct shell spaces in real-time. We extend the parallel banding algorithm (PBA) of Cao et al. [31] to compute the Euclidean distance transform (EDT) in a narrow-band. Their algorithm partitions the input domain into small chunks of equal size, which can be processed in parallel. The results are then merged concurrently. Although their method is exact and efficient, it is impractical for large models due to its memory requirements. Our method overcomes this problem by on-the-fly computation and integrating fast bitmap indexing technology on the GPU. We explain the principle in two dimensions for simplicity; the idea easily extends to three dimensions.

The input image is divided into a virtual grid made up of occupied and unoccupied pixels; the former pixels, the sites ∈ S, are run-length encoded. Every pixel undergoes a two-step process: (i) find the nearest site S_{ij}, among all sites in row j; (ii) determine the closest site, among all the nearest sites, in the current column i. During the first step we assign a thread to process each row as it is more efficient to do more computation in a single thread than to repeatedly access global memory with multiple threads. The second step extends the divide-and-merge approach of PBA, by employing warp-vote and warp-shuffle functions in NVIDIA's CUDA to exchange information between nearest sites within a chunk. (A warp is a pool of threads that executes in parallel.) Every thread in the same warp does the same calculation, avoiding warp variations that often compromise performance.

Figure 3 shows an example. When the threads in a warp reach column i, each row computes the corresponding nearest sites S_{ij}. The nearest site of the current pixel is shown in blue. Note that only some sites (empty blue dots) satisfy the distance constraint. Therefore, sites S_{i1} of thread 1 can be safely discarded. We set a barrier to ensure that every thread obtains some sites before exchanging information. After synchronization, we sweep each S_{ij} to other threads in the same warp to update the closest site of the current pixel (i, j), based on the distance function d_{ij}. A bitmap stores a Boolean value for every pixel; 0 indicates that the corresponding nearest sites cannot be the closest sites of the current column. Then the threads repeat the same procedure for the next column i + 1, until they reach the last column. In the final step we collect the closest sites with value 1 in different chunks and merge them to find the pixels that form the shell region. As the nearest sites are computed on-the-fly and the temporary result only needs indexing by a bitmap, our algorithm requires less memory than the PBA method.

```
// For simplicity, we give a 2D version here
function ShellSpaceConstruction(M, res, d)
for all thread j = 0 to res in parallel do
  for i = 0 to res do
    S_ij ← GetNearestSite(M, j, d)
    discard S_ij if ‖ d_ij ‖> d
    set barrier // Ensure every thread gets S_ij
    // Compare with other threads in same warp
    // warp size = h, current warp id = k
    C_k ← S_ij
    for x = 0 to h do
      if IsCloser(C_k, C_x) then
        C_k ← C_x
        id ← x
      end if
    end for
    // Mark the closest site of pixel (i, j)
    Bitmap[i][id] = true
  end for
end for
Collect and merge the closest sites if Bitmap[i][j] = true
return P̄ // return pixels located inside the shell
```

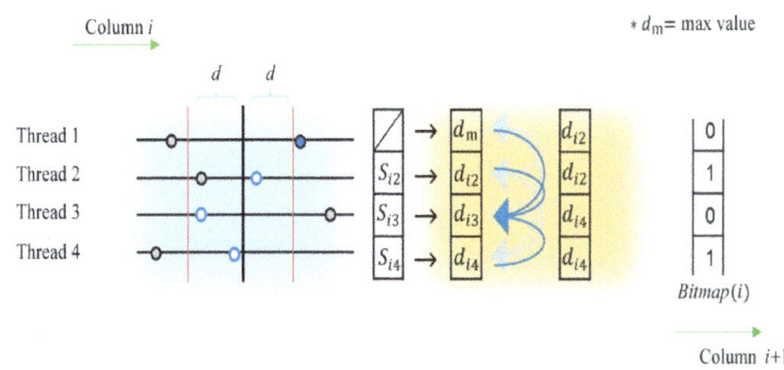

Figure 3: Illustrative example of distance field computation in a narrow band. See the text for an explanation and function ShellSpaceConstruction for the pseudo code.

Constructing 3D Voronoi Diagrams in Shell Space

The shell space represented by $\bar{P}$ is used to constrain construction of the Voronoi diagram and update the positions of seeds. Initially, the seeds $S = \{s_1, \ldots, s_k\}$ are located on the input mesh. We collect points $\in \bar{P}$ that share the same closest seeds to build the Voronoi diagram.

We perform a proximity search to find the closest seed for all query points from $\bar{P}$. To speed up the process, the seeds are projected onto a uniform grid G with smaller resolution of res (e.g., 32^3), so that, for a query point q, it just find seeds in the grid cell G_q in which q falls. If any border of the grid cell is closer to q than the seed found in G_q, query point q considers the neighboring cell of G_q.

Computing the CVT

Updating the seeds' positions towards a uniform distribution is crucial for constructing the CVT. Optimal positions can be reached by minimizing the following energy function:

$$E(S) = \sum_{i=1}^{m} \int_{V_i} \rho(p)\|p - s_i\|^2 \mathrm{d}p$$

where V_i is the Voronoi cell of seed s_i, $p \in \bar{P}$, and ρ is a non-negative user-defined density function.

In Lloyd's algorithm, a seed s_i moves iteratively toward the corresponding mass center c_i of Voronoi diagram V_i until convergence. However, the mass center could be located far from the surface, as it is constructed in the shell space. We determine the following new position to replace the mass center in each iteration:

$$\bar{c}_i = s_i + u\frac{\overrightarrow{s_i c_i}}{\|\overrightarrow{s_i c_i}\|}$$

where $u \in \mathbb{R}^+$ is the magnitude of movement of the seeds. We observe that if the seeds move with different magnitudes, the area of CVT calls will largely vary depending on surface curvature. In order to guarantee topological consistency, the new center is projected back onto M if it moves outside the shell space, as shown in Fig. 4.

Computing the Dual Triangulations

Upon convergence, all the generators are uniformly distributed. We next extract the dual Delaunay triangulation.

First, we find the direct neighbors of all seeds, where direct means two voxels from their Voronoi cells are connected. Adjacent neighbors can be found by flooding the information from all seeds to all voxels in the shell $\in \bar{P}$. Each voxel stores a hash table to hold the locations of its 26 neighbors. Each propagation step updates the current seed information to neighboring voxels until all voxels have been reached. This approach avoids producing the wrong connectivity for seeds that are geometrically close, but topologically far from each other. We then organize direct neighbors in clockwise order and finally extract the triangle mesh.

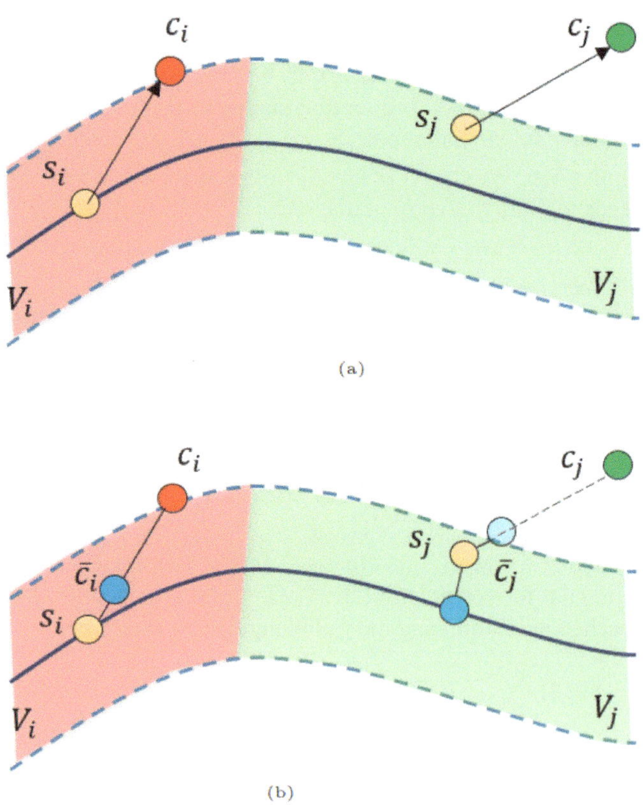

Figure 4: Illustration of the update process in an iteration for two seeds. (a) Yellow dots: seeds of Voronoi cells V_i (in red) and V_j (in green). Red and green dots: their respective mass centers. (b) The seeds move along vector $\vec{sc}$ to new centers (blue dots). We project $\bar{c}_j$ (light blue dot) to the surface since it is outside the shell region.

EXPERIMENTAL RESULTS

All tests were performed on a PC with an Intel Xeon E5 2.5 GHz CPU and an nVidia Quadro K5000 GPU with 4 GB RAM.

Narrow-Banded Distance Fields

Table 1 lists the time and peak memory requirements for varying parameter d and res (see Fig. 5). Clearly, as d increases, the time increases insignificantly compared to the increased number of nearest sites in the shell. This is due to the low cost of intra-warp communication and the reduced warp divergence in our algorithm. Also, the memory consumption is remarkably small, considering the scene is represented by a high resolution uniform grid. Previous algorithms (e.g., Ref. [31]) typically require at least 10 times more memory than ours.

Table 2 compares our algorithm with PBA on the Sculpture model at resolution 5123 . Since PBA computes a full distance map, its performance is independent of distance d. Our algorithm consumes significantly less memory and runs much faster than PBA for a reasonably small d.

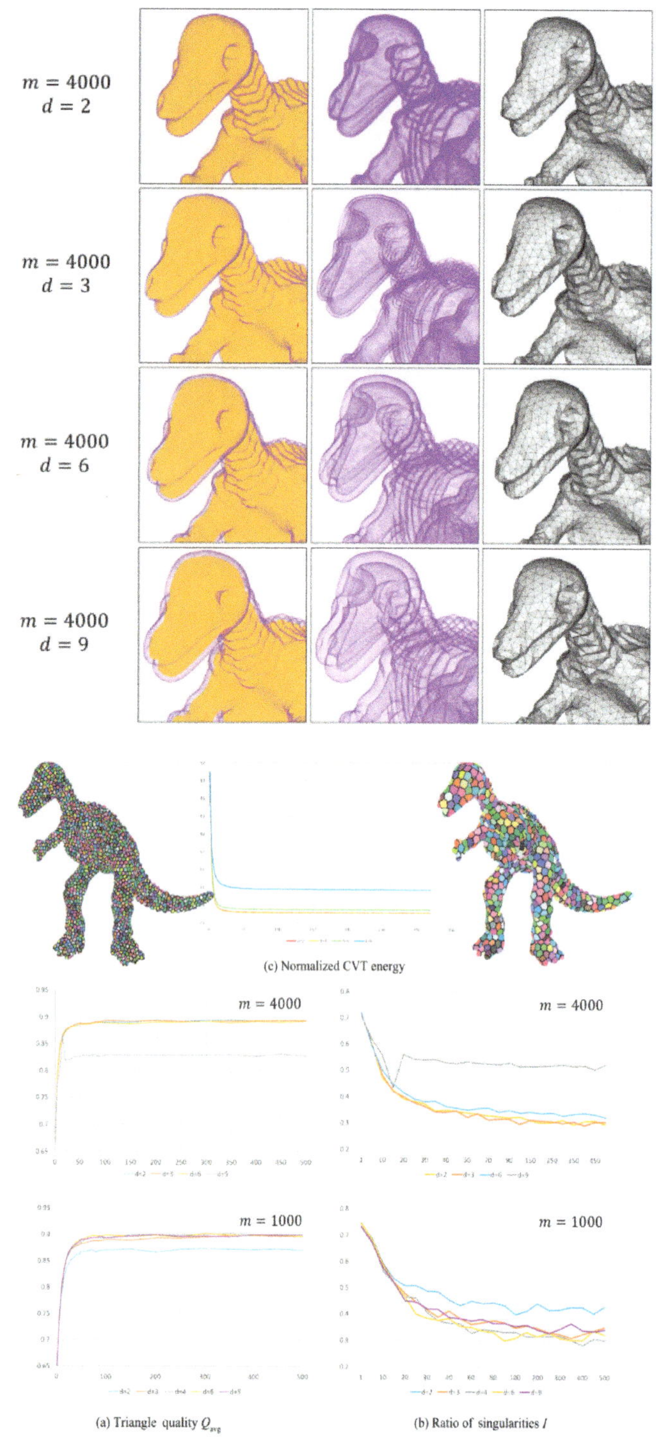

Figure 5: Mesh quality for various shell space parameter values d. (a) Triangulation quality measure. (b) Singularity ratio. (c) Our GPU-based Lloyd algorithm usually converges in 100–200 iterations; d has little impact on the convergence rate. Horizontal axis: iteration number. Vertical axis: normalized CVT energy function.

Table 1: Performance of our algorithm for different d at resolutions 1024^3 and 2048^3

Model	d	Memory (MB)	Time (s)	Memory (GB)	Time (s)
Dinosaur	1	149	1.186	1.18	12.3
	3	174	1.239	1.23	13.1
	6	206	1.313	1.30	13.3
	9	235	1.383	1.36	13.5

Table 2: Comparison of our algorithm to PBA at resolution 512^3

Model	Memory (MB)	d	Time (s)
Sculpture (PBA)	1073	—	0.310
Sculpture (ours)	26.6	1	0.147 (×2.1)
	33.7	3	0.173 (×1.8)
	49.7	6	0.200 (×1.6)
	66.1	15	0.286 (×1.1)
	76.2	20	0.339 (×0.9)

CVT Computation

Following Ref. [13], we adopted the following criteria to measure the triangle mesh quality: (i) triangle quality Q(t) defined by $6P_t / \sqrt{3}H_t$, where P_t and H_t are the inradius and the length of the longest edge of triangle t respectively, (ii) the smallest angle θ_{min} and the average θ_{avg} minimal angle for all triangles, (iii) the ratio of singularities, defined by v_s/k, where v_s is the number of non-6-valent vertices and k is the number of vertices.

Flexible Inputs: One advantage of our algorithm is that the CVT construction is independent of input topology, thus allowing a wide range of input types such as point clouds, implicit surfaces, and meshes with non-manifold surfaces. Figure 6 shows that our method can be applied to an irregular point cloud. However, the uneven density of points causes failure during triangulation, i.e., holes and a nonmanifold mesh. The shell space can help to resolve this issue because it covers the uneven space where points cannot be reached. Figure 7 investigates the influence of shell distance on irregular data sets. It shows that the geometric shape and density of the point cloud directly affect the choice of the shell distance d.

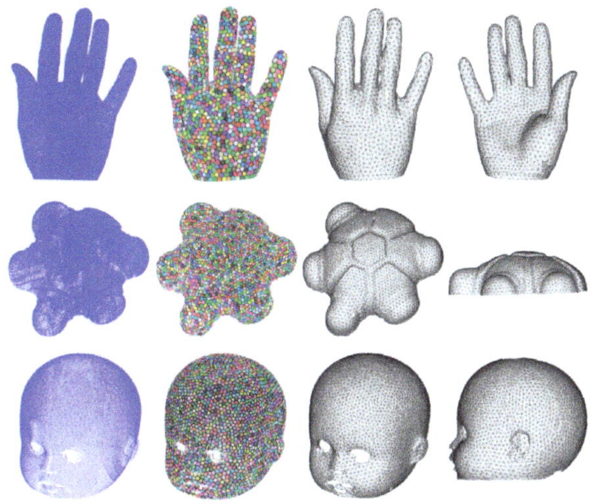

Figure 6: Experimental results on scanned point samples.

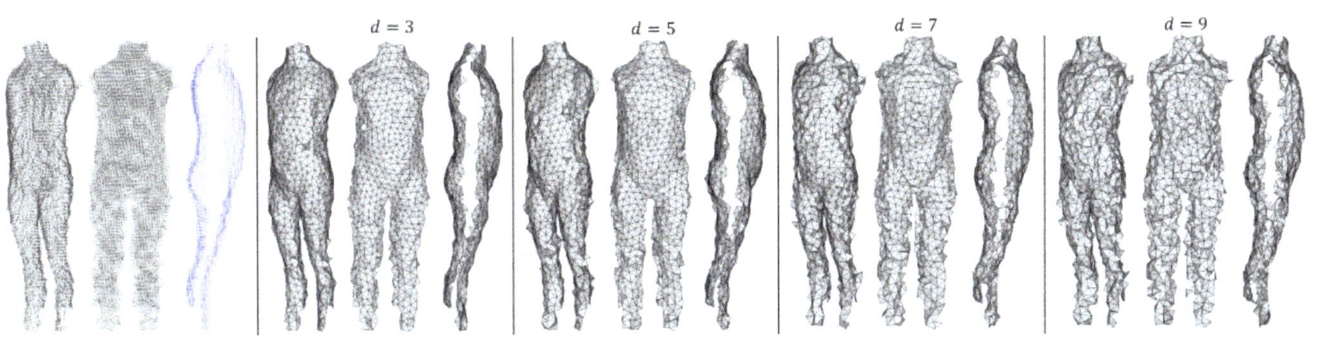

Figure 7: Isotropic meshing on noisy scanned point samples. We observe that d ∈ [3, 5] helps to bridge holes and tolerate noise, producing fairly good results. However, if d exceeds that range, there is a large error in the computed CVT, leading to poor results.

We have also successfully applied our algorithm to implicit surfaces (see Fig. 8) and other implicit representations (see Fig. 9). More examples can be found in Fig. 12.

Figure 1 shows the result from an imperfect mesh with non-manifold edges, degenerate triangles and holes. Thanks to its defect-tolerant nature, our method can handle these issues easily

Accuracy and Efficiency Control: We allow the user to balance accuracy and efficiency by choice of the offset d. Figure 5 shows the relationship between the distance d, the number of generators, and the quality of the remeshed surface. As the offset increases to 9, with 4000 generators, the mesh quality of the dinosaur model dramatically drops. This also happens when the offset decreases to 2 with 1000 generators. Figure 5(b) clearly illustrates the difference in quality for different values of d. Along with other examples in Table 3, we can see that the mesh has best quality with offset distance in the range 2–6. Figure 10 compares our method with two parameterization-free isotropic meshing methods, an intrinsic CVT method [13] and an extrinsic RVD method [1].

Thanks to its GPU-friendly structure and the computational power of modern GPUs, our method runs significantly faster than their CPU-based implementations.

Topology Consistency: The shell space also guarantees topological consistency between the input and the remeshed surface. Our algorithm constrains the seeds to lie within a shell of width 2d during the update process, so the output is topologically consistent with respect to the shell. Figure 11 illustrates the importance of this offset volume. The bottle model consists of an inner tube which is very close to the outer surface, close enough that only a shell of width 2 (d = 1) can separate these two parts when the resolution is 1024^3. However, width 2 is so thin that the seeds can barely move inside, leading to poor remeshing quality (Q_{avg} = 0.86, Q_{min} = 0.10). A possible solution would be to increase the grid size. Since our approach is scalable, this could be improved by using a graphic card with larger memory.

Table 3: Model complexity and runtime performance. SS: time (in seconds) for shell construction; m: the number of seeds; T: average time for each Lloyd iteration; n: the number of iterations; I: singularity ratio

Model	d	SS (s)	Number of sites	m	T (s)	n	I	Q_{min}	Q_{avg}	$\theta_{min}(°)$	$\theta_{avg}(°)$	Total time (s)
Sculpture	3	0.966	1.04×10^6	3000	0.064	100	0.25	0.639	0.907	36.1	52.4	7.2
Heptoroid	2	1.429	2.63×10^6	9000	0.138	120	0.24	0.624	0.902	35.3	51.9	19.5
Helix	2	1.212	4.4×10^5	4000	0.036	100	0.29	0.589	0.889	33.4	50.9	5.14
Pegaso	2	0.948	1.33×10^6	8000	0.063	150	0.26	0.600	0.894	31.5	51.3	10.6
Dinosaur	2	0.880	5.5×10^5	4000	0.025	160	0.28	0.636	0.894	30.2	51.2	4.8
	4	0.913	5.5×10^5	1000	0.046	170	0.31	0.602	0.900	30.6	51.8	9.2
Armadillo	2	0.944	1.26×10^6	4000	0.051	200	0.26	0.613	0.902	30.3	51.9	11.3
Mask	3	0.897	6.3×10^5	2000	0.042	170	0.28	0.613	0.901	33.4	51.9	8.2
Trung hand (points)	2	0.949	1.17×10^6	2000	0.042	100	0.32	0.198	0.895	12.8	51.5	5.2
Turtle toy (points)	4	0.946	8.2×10^5	2000	0.077	120	0.22	0.373	0.911	23.5	52.6	10.8
Baby head (points)	5	0.26	2.8×10^5	3000	0.069	120	0.29	0.279	0.891	16.9	51.1	9.34

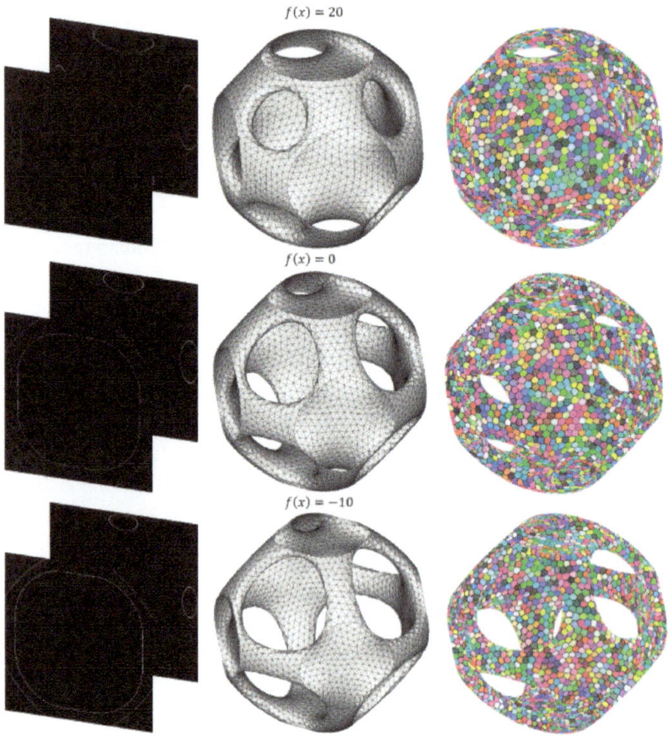

Figure 8: Generating isotropic meshes from an implicit function. There are 3000 seeds and d=3.

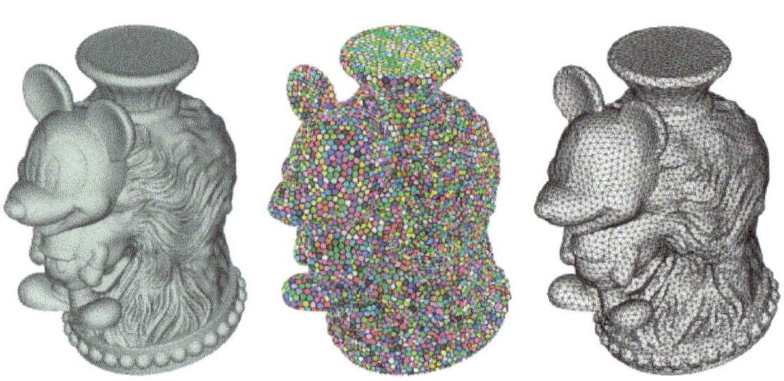

Figure 9: Generating isotropic meshes with 8000 seeds and d=2 from an implicit representation: layered depth normal image [37].

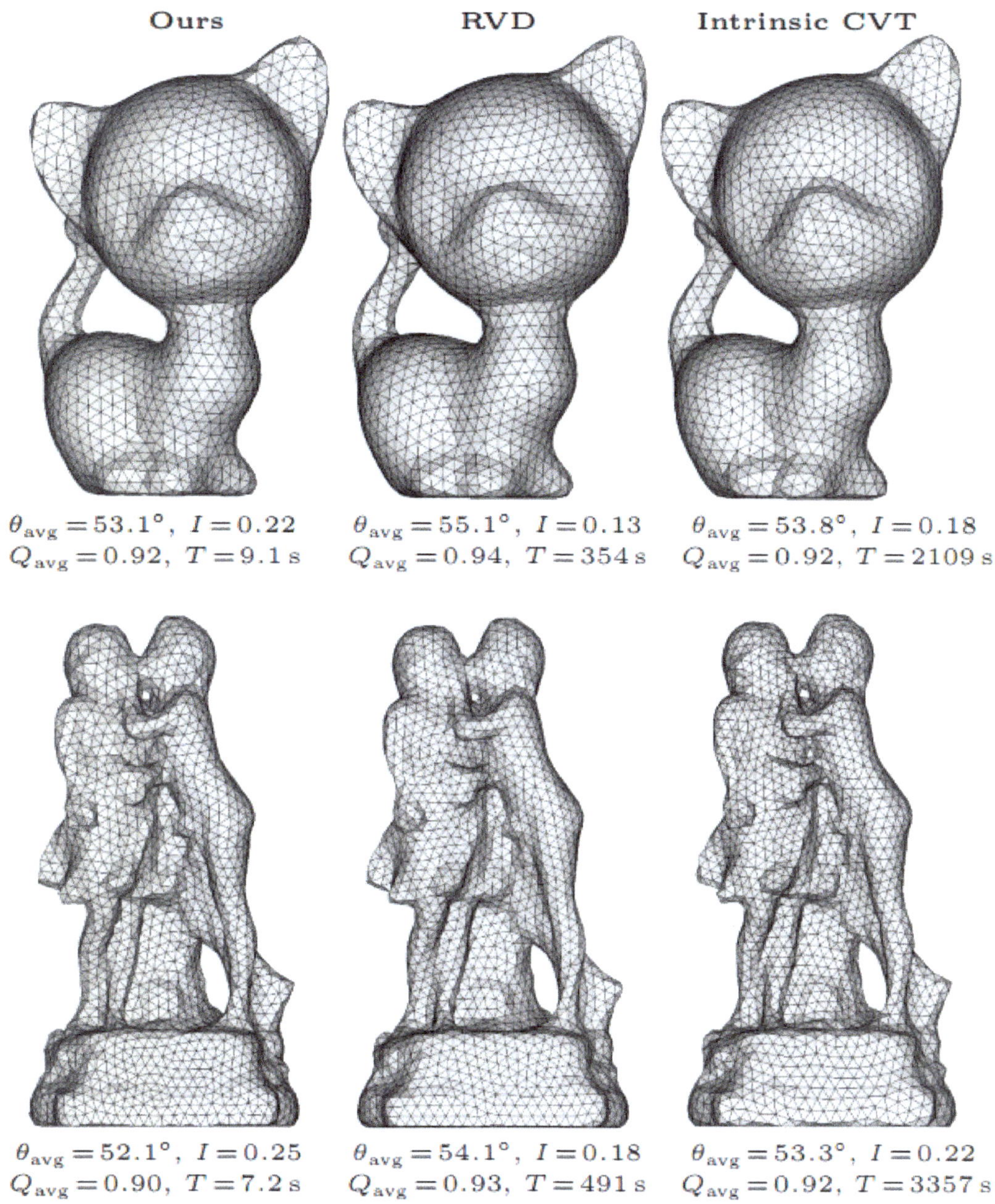

Figure 10: Comparison with the RVD method [1] and the intrinsic CVT method [13].

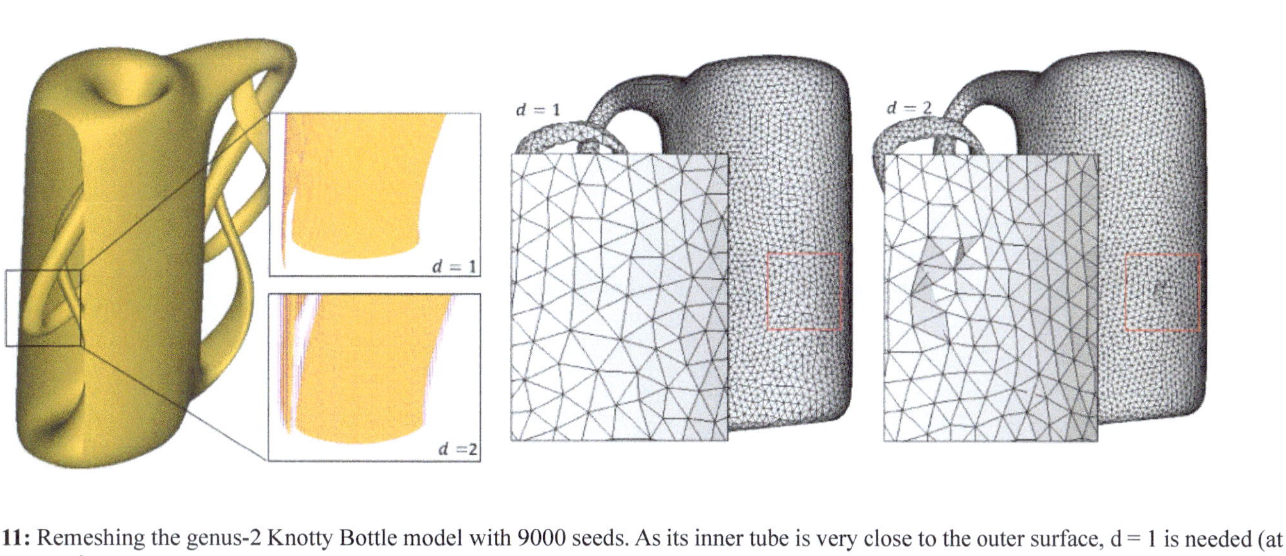

Figure 11: Remeshing the genus-2 Knotty Bottle model with 9000 seeds. As its inner tube is very close to the outer surface, d = 1 is needed (at resolution 1024^3) to produce a shell space with the same topology as the mesh, whereas d = 2 does not give such a guarantee.

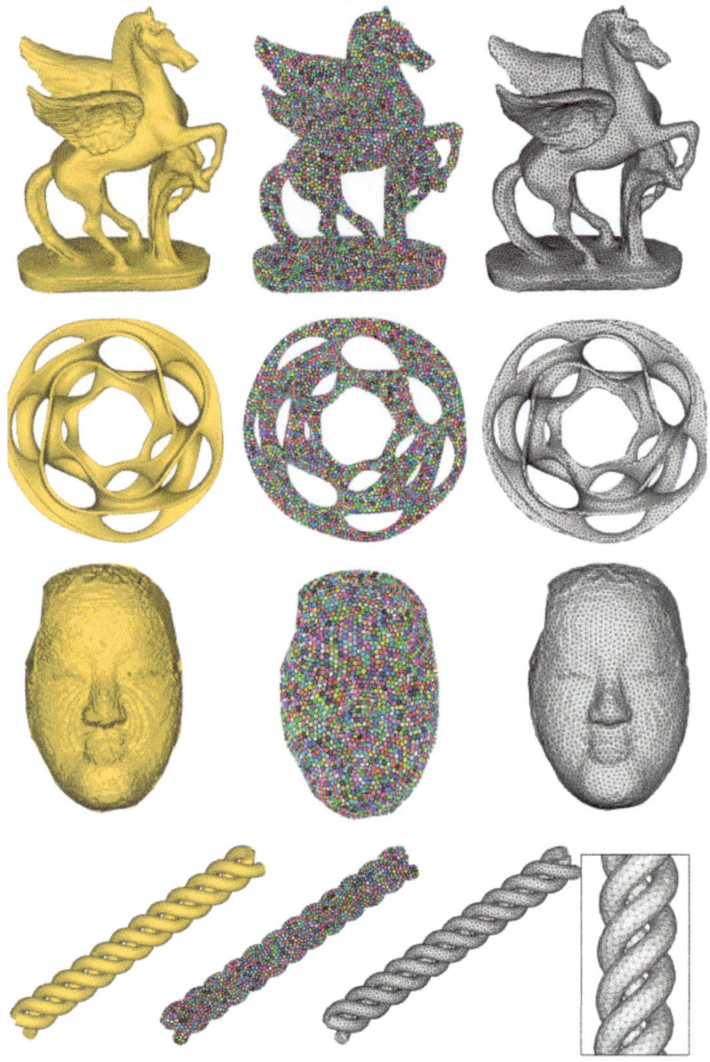

Figure 12: Experimental results. Images are rendered at highresolution, allowing zooming in for examination.

CONCLUSIONS

This paper has presented a robust, efficient method for constructing isotropic meshes using the Euclidean distance transform. Our algorithm constructs a narrow band enclosing the input surface, in which 3D centroidal Voronoi tessellations and restricted Voronoi diagrams are computed. Our algorithm is fully parallel and memoryefficient, and can construct the shell space with resolution up to 2048^3 at interactive speed. Moreover, our method can process implicit surfaces, polyhedral surfaces and point clouds in a unified framework. Computational results show that our GPU-friendly isotropic meshing algorithm produces results comparable to state-of-the-art techniques, but runs significantly faster than conventional CPUbased implementations.

Our current implementation adopts a constant resolution to construct the shell space. This, however, is not optimal, since it is pessimistic for the regions with fairly flat geometry, and it may be inadequate for the highly-curved regions. In the future, we aim to develop a geometry-aware algorithm for constructing in parallel the shell space with adaptive resolution.

ACKNOWLEDGEMENTS

The NTU authors are partially supported by AcRF RG40/12 and MOE2013-T2-2-011. Y.-J. Liu is partially supported by National Natural Science Foundation of China (Nos. 61432003 and 61322206) and the TNList Cross-discipline Foundation. C. C. L. Wang is partially supported by HKSAR Research Grants Council (RGC) General Research Fund (GRF), CUHK/14207414.

REFERENCES

1. Yan, D.-M.; Lévy, B.; Liu, Y.; Sun, F.; Wang W. Isotropic remeshing with fast and exact computation of restricted Voronoi diagram. *Computer Graphics Forum* Vol. 28, No. 5, 1445–1454, 2009.
2. Yan, D.; Wang, W.; Lévy, B.; Liu Y. Efficient computation of clipped Voronoi diagram for mesh generation. *Computer-Aided Design* Vol. 45, No. 4, 843–852, 2013.
3. Liu Y. J.; Chen, Z.; Tang K. Construction of iso-contours, bisectors, and Voronoi diagrams on triangulated

surfaces. *IEEE Transactions on Pattern Analysis and Machine Intelligence*Vol. 33, No. 8, 1502–1517, 2011.

4. Liu, Y.-J.; Tang K. The complexity of geodesic Voronoi diagrams on triangulated 2-manifold surfaces. *Information Processing Letters* Vol. 113, No. 4, 132- 136, 2013.
5. Xu, C.; Liu, Y.-J.; Sun, Q.; Li, J.; He Y. Polyline–sourced geodesic Voronoi diagrams on triangle meshes. *Computer Graphics Forum* Vol. 33, No. 7, 161–170, 2014.
6. Du, Q.; Gunzburger M. D.; Ju L. Constrained centroidal Voronoi tessellations for surfaces.*SIAM Journal on Scientific Computing* Vol. 24, No. 5, 1488–1506, 2002.
7. Lloyd S. Least squares quantization in PCM. *IEEE Transactions on Information Theory*Vol. 28, No. 2, 129–137, 1982.
8. Liu, Y.; Wang, W.; Lévy, B.; Sun, F.; Yan, D.-M.; Lu, L.; Yang C. On centroidal Voronoi tessellation Energy smoothness and fast computation. *ACM Transactions on Graphics* Vol. 28, No. 4, Article No. 101, 2009.
9. Rong, G.; Liu, Y.; Wang, W.; Yin, X.; Gu X. D.; Guo X. GPU-assisted computation of centroidal Voronoi tessellation. *IEEE Transactions on Visualization and Computer Graphics* Vol. 17, No. 3, 345–356, 2011.
10. Alliez, P.; de Verdière, É. C.; Devillers, O.; Isenburg M. Isotropic surface remeshing. In: Proceedings of the Shape Modeling International, 49, 2003.
11. Rong, G.; Jin, M.; Shuai, L.; Guo X. Centroidal Voronoi tessellation in universal covering space of manifold surfaces. *Computer Aided Geometric Design* Vol. 28, No. 8, 475–496, 2011.
12. Shuai, L.; Guo, X.; Jin M. GPU-based computation of discrete periodic centroidal Voronoi tessellation in hyperbolic space. *Computer-Aided Design* Vol. 45, No. 2, 463–472, 2013.
13. Wang, X.; Ying, X.; Liu, Y.-J.; Xin, S.-Q.; Wang, W.; Gu, X.; Mueller-Wittig, W.; He Y. Intrinsic computation of centroidal Voronoi tessellation (CVT) on meshes. *Computer-Aided Design* Vol. 58, 51–61, 2015.
14. Lu, L.; Lévy, B.; Wang W. Centroidal Voronoi tessellation of line segments and graphs.*Computer Graphics Forum* Vol. 31, No. 2, 775–784, 2012.
15. Lévy, B.; Bonneel N. Variational anisotropic surface meshing with Voronoi parallel linear enumeration. In: Proceedings of the 21st International Meshing Roundtable, 349–366, 2013.
16. Lévy, B.; Liu Y. Lp centroidal Voronoi tessellation and its applications. *ACM Transactions on Graphics* Vol. 29, No. 4, Article No. 119, 2010.
17. Chen, Z.; Cao, J.; Wang W. Isotropic surface remeshing using constrained centroidal Delaunay mesh. *Computer Graphics Forum* Vol. 31, No. 7, 2077–2085, 2012.
18. Li, H.; Zeng, W.; Morvan J. M.; Chen, L.; Gu X. Surface meshing with curvature convergence. *IEEE Transactions on Visualization and Computer Graphics* Vol. 20, No. 6, 919–934, 2014.
19. Mitchell J. S. B.; Mount D. M.; Papadimitriou C. H. The discrete geodesic problem. *SIAM Journal on Computing* Vol. 16, No. 4, 647–668, 1987.
20. Chen, J.; Han Y. Shortest paths on a polyhedron. In: Proceedings of the 6th Annual Symposium on Computational Geometry, 360–369, 1990.
21. Xu, C.; Wang, T.; Liu, Y.; Liu, L.; He Y. Fast wavefront propagation (FWP) for computing exact discrete geodesics on meshes. *IEEE Transactions on Visualization and Computer Graphics* Vol. 21, No. 7, 822–834, 2015.
22. Ying, X.; Xin, S.-Q.; He Y. Parallel chen-han (PCH) algorithm for discrete geodesics. *ACM Transactions on Graphics* Vol. 33, No. 1, Article No. 9, 2014.
23. Kimmel, R.; Sethian J. A. Computing geodesic paths on manifolds. *Proceedings of the National Academy of Sciences of the United States of America* Vol. 95, 8431–8435, 1998.
24. Crane, K.; Weischedel, C.; Wardetzky M. Geodesics in heat: A new approach to computing distance based on heat flow. *ACM Transactions on Graphics* Vol. 32, No. 5, Article No. 152, 2013.
25. Campen, M.; Heistermann, M.; Kobbelt L. Practical anisotropic geodesy. *Computer Graphics Forum* Vol. 32, No. 5, 63–71, 2013.
26. Ying, X.; Wang, X.; He Y. Saddle vertex graph (SVG): A novel solution to the discrete geodesic problem. *ACM Transactions on Graphics* Vol. 32, No. 6, Article No. 170, 2013.
27. Jones M. W.; Baerentzen J. A.; Sramek M. 3D distance fields: A survey of techniques and applications. *IEEE Transactions on Visualization and Computer Graphics* Vol. 12, No. 4, 581–599, 2006.
28. Marchand-Maillet, S.; Sharaiha Y. M. Euclidean ordering via chamfer distance calculations. *Computer Vision and Image Understanding* Vol. 73, No. 3, 404–413, 1999.
29. Satherley, R.; Jones M. W. Vector-city vector distance transform. *Computer Vision and Image Understanding* Vol. 82, No. 3, 238–254, 2001.
30. Hoff, K. E.; Keyser, J.; Lin, M.; Manocha, D.; Culver T. Fast computation of generalized Voronoi diagrams using graphics hardware. In: Proceedings of the 26th Annual Conference on Computer Graphics and Interactive Techniques, 277–286, 1999.
31. Cao, T.-T.; Tang, K.; Mohamed, A.; Tan T.-S. Parallel banding algorithm to compute exact distance transform with the GPU. In: Proceedings of the 2010 ACM SIGGRAPH Symposium on Interactive 3D Graphics and Games, 83–90, 2010.
32. Amenta, N.; Bern, M.; Kamvysselis M. A new Voronoi-based surface reconstruction algorithm. In: Proceedings of the 25th Annual Conference on Computer Graphics and Interactive Techniques, 415–421, 1998.
33. Amenta, N.; Choi, S.; Dey T. K.; Leekha N. A simple algorithm for homeomorphic surface reconstruction. In: Proceedings of the 16th Annual Symposium on Computational Geometry, 213–222, 2000.
34. Kazhdan M. M.; Bolitho, M.; Hoppe H. Poisson surface reconstruction. In: Proceedings of the 4th Eurographics Symposium on Geometry Processing, 61–70, 2006.
35. Sheung, H.; Wang C. C. L. Robust mesh reconstruction from unoriented noisy points. In: Proceedings of SIAM/

ACM Joint Conference on Geometric and Physical Modeling, 13–24, 2009.

36. Dey T. K.; Goswami S. Tight cocone: A water-tight surface reconstructor. In: Proceedings of the 8th ACM Symposium on Solid Modeling and Applications, 127–134, 2003.

37. Wang C. C. L.; Leung, Y.-S.; Chen Y. Solid modeling of polyhedral objects by layered depth-normal images on the GPU. *Computer-Aided Design* Vol. 42, No. 6, 535–544, 2010.

CHAPTER 7

3D INDOOR SCENE MODELING FROM RGB-D DATA: A SURVEY

Kang Chen[1], Yu-Kun Lai[2], and Shi-Min Hu[1]

[1]Tsinghua University, Beijing 100084, China
[2]Cardiff University, Cardiff, CF24 3AA, Wales, UK

ABSTRACT

3D scene modeling has long been a fundamental problem in computer graphics and computer vision. With the popularity of consumer-level RGB-D cameras, there is a growing interest in digitizing real-world indoor 3D scenes. However, modeling indoor 3D scenes remains a challenging problem because of the complex structure of interior objects and poor quality of RGB-D data acquired by consumer-level sensors. Various methods have been proposed to tackle these challenges. In this survey, we provide an overview of recent advances in indoor scene modeling techniques, as well as public datasets and code libraries which can facilitate experiments and evaluation.

INTRODUCTION

Consumer-level color and depth (RGB-D) cameras (e.g., Microsoft Kinect) are now widely available and are affordable to the general public. Ordinary people can now easily obtain 3D data from their real-world homes and offices. Meanwhile, other booming 3D technologies in areas such as augmented reality, stereoscopic movies, and 3D printing are also becoming closer to our daily life. We are living on a "digital Earth". Therefore, there is an ever-increasing need for ordinary people to digitize their living environments.

Despite this great need, helping ordinary people quickly and easily acquire 3D digital representations of their living surroundings is an urgent yet still challenging research problem. Over the past decades, we have witnessed an explosion of digital photos on the Internet. Benefiting from this, image-related research based on mining and analyzing the vast number of 2D images has been greatly boosted. In contrast, while the growth of 3D digital models has accelerated over the past few years, the growth remains comparatively slow, mainly because making 3D models is a demanding job which requires expertise and is time-consuming. Fortunately, the availability of low-cost RGB-D cameras along with recent advances in modeling techniques offers a great opportunity to change this situation. In the longer term, 3D big data has the potential to change the landscape of 3D visual data processing.

This survey focuses on digitizing real-world indoor scenes, which has received significant interest in recent years. It has many applications which may fundamentally change our daily life. For example, with such techniques, furniture stores can offer 3D models of their products online so that customers can better view the products and choose furniture to buy. People without interior design experience can give digital representations of their homes to experts or expert systems [1, 2] for advice on better furniture arrangement. Anyone with Internet access can virtually visit digitized museums all over

Citation: Kang Chen, Yu-Kun Lai, and Shi-Min Hu, 3D indoor scene modeling from RGB-D data: a survey, DOI 10.1007/s41095-015-0029-x.

the world [3]. Moreover, modeled indoor scenes can be used for augmented reality [4, 5] and can serve as a training basis for intelligent robots to better understand real-world environments [6].

Nevertheless, indoor scene modeling is still a challenging problem. The difficulties mainly arise from two causes [7]: Firstly, unlike outdoor building facades, interior objects often have much more complicated 3D geometry, with messy surroundings and substantial variation between parts. Secondly, depth information captured by consumer-level scanning devices is often noisy, may be distorted, and can have large gaps. To address these challenges, various methods have been proposed in the past few years and this is still an active research area in both computer graphics and computer vision communities.

The rest of the paper will be organized as follows. We first briefly introduce in Section 2 different types of RGB-D data and their properties. Publicly available RGB-D datasets as well as useful programming libraries for processing RGBD data will also be discussed. In Section 3, we systematically categorize existing methods based on their underlying design principles, overview each technique, and examine its advantages and disadvantages. Finally, in Section 4, we summarize the current state of the art and elaborate on future research directions.

RGB-D DATA

"One cannot make bricks without straw." Despite the importance of indoor scene modeling and the fact that RGB-D scanners have been available for decades, it did not become a research focus until the year 2010 when Microsoft launched its Kinect motion sensing input device. Kinect has a more far-reaching significance than as the game controller it was originally released for, because it has a built-in depth sensor with reasonable accuracy at a very affordable price. Such cheap RGB-D scanning devices make it possible for ordinary people to own one at home, enabling development and wide use of 3D modeling techniques for indoor scene modeling. Before discussing modeling algorithms in detail, we first briefly introduce RGB-D data in this section, including different types of RGB-D data and their properties.

Types and Properties

A variety of techniques have been developed to obtain RGB-D data. These include passive techniques such as stereoscopic camera pairs where the depth is derived from disparity between images captured from each camera, and active techniques where some kind of light is emitted to assist depth calculation. The latter are widely used due to their effectiveness (e.g., particularly for textureless surfaces) and accuracy. Currently, light detection and ranging (LiDAR) is the main modality for acquiring RGB-D data. Depending on their working approach, LiDAR systems can be divided into two classes: scannerless LiDAR and scanning LiDAR [8]. In scannerless LiDAR systems, the entire scene is captured with each laser or light pulse, as opposed to point-by-point capture with a laser beam in scanning LiDAR systems. A typical type of scannerless LiDAR system is the time-of-flight (ToF) camera, used in many consumer-level RGB-D cameras (including the latest Kinect v2). ToF cameras are lowcost, quick enough for real-time applications, and have moderate working ranges. These advantages make ToF cameras suitable for indoor applications. Alternatively, some RGB-D cameras, including the first generation of Kinect, are based on structured light. The depth is recovered by projecting specific patterns and analyzing the captured patterned image. Both ToF and structured light techniques are scannerless, so they can produce dynamic 3D streams, which allow more efficient and reliable 3D indoor scene modeling.

Laser pulses in a ToF camera and patterns used for structured light cameras are organized in a 2D array, so that depth information can be represented as a depth image. The depth image along with an aligned RGB image forms an RGB-D image frame which depicts a single view of the target scene, including both the color and the shape. Such RGB-D image frames can be unprojected to 3D space forming a colored 3D point cloud. RGB-D images and colored point clouds are the two most common representations of RGBD data. RGB-D images are mostly used by the computer vision community as they have the same topology as images, while in the computer graphics community, RGB-D data are more commonly viewed as point clouds. Point clouds obtained from a projective camera are organized (also called structured or ordered) point clouds because there is a one–one correspondence between points in the 3D space and pixels in the image space. This correspondence contains adjacency information between 3D points which is useful in certain applications, e.g., it can simplify algorithms or make algorithms more efficient as neighboring points can be easily determined. Knowing the camera parameters, organized colored point clouds, and the corresponding RGB-D images are equivalent. If an equivalent RGB-D image does not exist for a colored point cloud, then the point cloud is unorganized (unstructured, unordered). To fully depict a target scene, multiple RGB-D image frames captured from different views are typically needed. As scannerless cameras are usually used, scene RGB-D data captured are essentially RGBD image streams (sequences) which can later be stitched into a whole scene point cloud using 3D registration techniques.

Depending on the operational mechanism, LiDAR systems cannot capture depth information on surfaces with highly absorptive or reflective materials. However, such materials are very common in real-world indoor scenes, and are used as mirrors, window glass, TV screens, and steel surfaces etc. This is a fundamental limitation of all laser-based systems. Apart from this common limitation, consumer-level RGB-D cameras have other drawbacks caused by their low cost. Firstly, the spatial resolution of such cameras is generally low (512×484 pixels in the latest Kinect). Secondly, the depth information is noisy and often has significant camera distortion. Thirdly, even for scenes without absorptive or reflective materials, the depth image may still involve small gaps around object borders. In general, depth information obtained by cheap scanning devices is unreliable, and practical indoor scene modeling algorithms must take this fact into consideration.

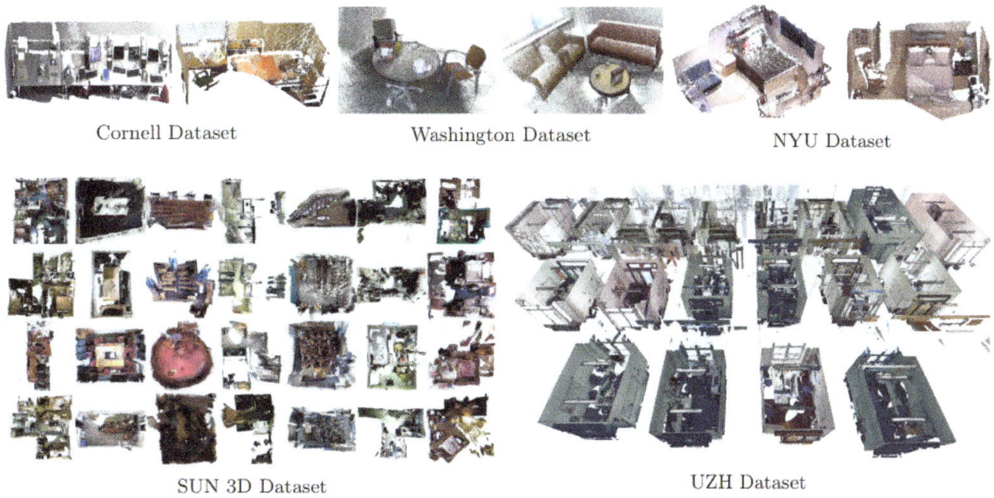

Figure 1: Example RGB-D data in each public dataset.

Public Datasets

A number of public RGB-D datasets containing indoor scenes have been introduced in recent years. Although most of these datasets were built and labeled for specific applications, such as scene reconstruction, object detection and recognition, scene understanding and segmentation, etc., as long as they provide full RGB-D image streams of indoor scenes, they can be used as input for indoor scene modeling. Here we briefly describe some popular ones (example scenes from each dataset are shown in Fig. 1).

Cornell RGB-D Dataset [9, 10]: this dataset contains RGB-D data of 24 office scenes and 28 home scenes, all of which were captured by Kinect. RGB-D images of each scene are stitched into scene point clouds using an RGB-D *SLAM algorithm*. Object-level labels are provided on the stitched scene point clouds.

Washington RGB-D Scenes Dataset [11]: this dataset consists of 14 indoor scenes containing objects in 9 categories (chair, coffee table, sofatable, bowl, cap, cereal box, coffee mug, and soda can). Each scene is a point cloud created by aligning a set of Kinect RGB-D image frames using patch volume mapping. Labels for the background and the 9 object classes are given on the stitched scene point clouds.

NYU Depth Dataset [12, 13]: this dataset contains 528 different indoor scenes (64 in the first version [12] and 464 in the second [13]) captured from large US cities, using Kinect. The scenes are mainly inside residential apartments, including living rooms, bedrooms, bathrooms, and kitchens. Dense labeling of objects at the class and instance level is provided for 1449 selected frames. This dataset does not contain camera pose information, because it was mainly built for singleframe segmentation and object recognition. To get full 3D scene point clouds, users may need to estimate camera poses from the original RGB-D streams.

SUN 3D Dataset [14]: this dataset contains 415 RGB-D image sequences captured by Kinect from 254 different indoor scenes, in 41 different buildings across North America, Europe, and Asia. Semantic class polygons and instance labels are given on frames and propagated through the whole sequences. Camera pose for each frame is also provided for registration. This is currently the largest and most comprehensive RGB-D dataset of indoor scenes.

UZH Dataset [15]: unlike other datasets mentioned above, this dataset was built specifically for modeling. It contains full point clouds of 40 academic offices scanned by a Faro LiDAR scanner, which has much higher precision than consumerlevel cameras like Kinect but is also much more expensive.

Open Source libraries

Since the release of the Kinect and other consumer-level RGB-D cameras, RGB-D data has become popular. Publicly available libraries that support effective processing of RGB-D data is thus in demand. The Point Cloud Library (PCL) [16] was introduced in 2011, which is an open source library for 2D/3D image and point cloud processing. The PCL framework contains numerous implementations of state-of-the-art algorithms including filtering, feature estimation, surface reconstruction, registration, model fitting and segmentation. Due to its powerful features and relaxed BSD license (Berkeley Software Distribution), it is probably the most popular library for RGB-D data processing for both commercial and research use.

Another useful library is the Mobile Robot Programming Toolkit (MRPT) [17] which comprises a set of C++ libraries and a number of ready-to-use robot-related applications. RGB-D sensors can be effectively used as "eyes" for robots: understanding real-world environments through perceived RGB-D data is one of the core functions of intelligent robotics. This library contains state-of-the-art algorithms for processing RGB-D data with a focus on robotic applications, including SLAM (simultaneous localization and mapping) and object detection.

MODELING TECHNIQUES

After introducing RGB-D data, we now discuss various techniques for modeling indoor scenes in this section. Based on modeling purpose, these methods can generally be classified into two main categories: geometric modeling (Section 3.1) and semantic modeling (Section 3.2) approaches. The former aims to recover the shapes of the 3D objects in the scene, whereas the latter focuses on recovering semantic meaning (e.g., object types).

Geometric Modeling

Geometric modeling from RGB-D data is a fundamental problem in computer graphics. Ever since the 1990s, researchers have investigated methods for digitizing the shapes of 3D objects using laser scanners, although 3D scanners were hardly accessible to ordinary people until recently. Early works typically start by registering a set of RGB-D images captured by laser sensors (i.e., transforming RGB-D images into a global coordinate system) and fuse the aligned RGB-D frames into a single point cloud or a volumetric representation which can be further converted into mesh-based 3D models. The use of the volumetric representation ensures the resulting geometry is a topologically correct manifold. Figure 2 is a typical geometric modeling result. Based on this pipeline, geometric modeling problems can be split into two phases: registration and fusion. Much research has been done and theoretically sound approaches have been established for both phases. For the registration phase, iterative closest point (ICP) registration [18, 19] and simultaneous localization and mapping (SLAM) [20] as well as their variants generally produce good solutions. For the fusion phase, the most widely adopted solution is the volumetric technique proposed by Curless and Levoy [21] which can robustly integrate each frame using signed distance functions (SDFs).

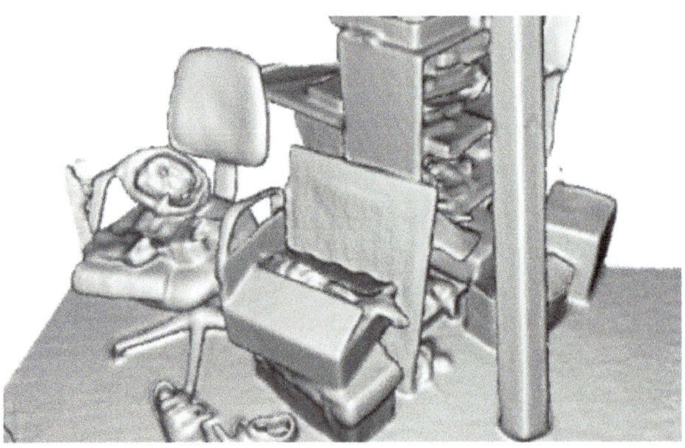

Figure 2: Geometric modeling result. Reproduced with permission from Ref. [5], c 2011 IEEE.

Geometric indoor scene modeling methods are extensions of traditional registration and fusion algorithms to indoor scenes. The major difference is that such techniques must take into account the properties of RGB-D data captured by consumerlevel RGB-D cameras, namely low-quality and real-time sequences. A well-known technique is the Kinect Fusion system [4, 5] which provides level-ofdetail (LoD) scanning and model creation using a moving Kinect camera. As in traditional schemes, Kinect Fusion adopts a volumetric representation of the acquired scene by maintaining a signed distance value for each voxel grid in the memory. However, unlike traditional frame-toframe registration, each frame is registered to the whole constructed scene model rather than the previous frames using a coarse-to-fine iterative ICP algorithm. This frame-to-model registration scheme has more resistance to noise and camera distortion, and is sufficiently efficient to allow realtime applications. The system has many desirable characteristics: ease of use, real-time performance, LoD reconstruction, etc. Recently, Heredia and Favier [22] have further extended the basic Kinect Fusion framework to larger scale environments by use of volume shifting. However, when used as a modeling system for indoor scene modeling, the volumetric representation based mechanism significantly limits its usage for large and complex scenes due to several reasons. Reconstructing large scale scenes even with a moderate resolution to depict necessary details requires a large amount of memory, easily exceeding the memory capacity of ordinary computers. Moreover, acquisition and registration errors inevitably exist, and can be significant for consumer-level scanning devices. Although frame-to-model registration is more robust than frame-to-frame registration, it is still not a global optimization technique. Scanning larger scenes requires longer moving trajectories. Error keeps accumulating over the long acquisition process and eventually breaks the reconstruction. A typical example is the loop closure problem which causes misalignment when reconstructing large rooms using Kinect Fusion when the camera trajectory forms a closed loop.

Kinect Fusion is designed for real-time online modeling and interaction within relatively small environments. A more general modeling framework is the RGB-D SLAM [23]. As mentioned before, the depth information obtained by cheap scanning devices is unreliable. However, the aligned RGB images can provide important additional information when estimating camera poses. The appearance features from the RGB image and shape features from the depth image can complement each other and together provide much more robust point correspondences between frames. In addition, in a practical scanning process, it is very common to have loop closures in the camera trajectories. Thus, overlaps may exist not only between consecutive frames. Loop closures can be detected and spatial relationship between the corresponding frames offers additional constraints when computing camera poses. The whole sequence ofRGB-D frames can be represented as a graph, where each node is a frame and each edge stores the spatial transform between two adjacent nodes. Such graphs are called pose graphs and can be efficiently optimized using SLAM algorithms [20] (see Ref. [24] for various state-of-the-art SLAM algorithms). The general pipeline of the RGB-D SLAM framework is shown in Fig. 3.

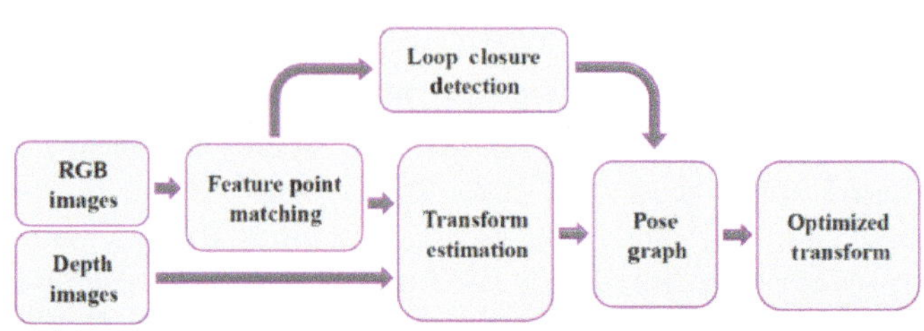

Figure 3: Pipeline of the RGB-D SLAM framework.

RGB-D SLAM approaches can be divided into two types: sparse mapping and dense mapping. For sparse mapping, only a few sparsely selected key frames are used for reconstruction which can quickly provide a rough structure of the target scene, while for dense mapping, the whole RGB-D stream is used, which can give detailed reconstruction as long as sufficient data is available. In both cases, the key technique is feature point matching, which is the basis for both transform estimation and loop closure detection. Due to the poor quality of depth images obtained by low-cost scanning devices, most sparse mapping systems mainly rely on distinctive feature descriptors detected in RGB images (e.g., SIFT [25], SURF [26], or ORB [27]) to find corresponding point pairs [23]. As real-world indoor scenes usually contain large textureless areas, e.g., painted walls, or repeated patterns, e.g., tiled floors, even state-of-the-art feature descriptors may easily generate falsely matched point correspondences. To reduce the impact of falsely detected point correspondences on reconstruction, the RANSAC (RANdom SAmple Consensus) algorithm [28] is often adopted to determine a subset of correspondences which conform to a consistent rigid transform. RANSAC is an iterative, randomized approach to estimate parameters of a mathematical model (in this case a rigid transform) that fits observed data (sample points) and is robust to outliers (which often occurs in low-quality RGB-D data) [29]. However, this may still fail in challenging cases as repetitive objects or large textureless areas may easily lead to many false correspondences. In practice, manual correction of some falsely estimated transforms is often needed in sparse mapping applications [7]. In contrast, with the help of dense depth streams, a frame-to-frame ICP registration algorithm can provide stronger cues for inferring camera poses. Thus, dense mapping RGB-D SLAM systems [23, 30–32] currently provide more automatic and robust solutions to modeling indoor scenes with consumer-level RGB-D sensors.

Semantic Modeling

The main objective of geometric modeling of indoor scenes is to fully recover 3D geometry. These methods take the target scene as a whole regardless of what it contains, and thus cannot provide a semantic representation of the modeled scene. However, semantic information is of vital importance in modeling for the following reasons. Firstly, semantic information can be used to improve modeling results. For example, in cluttered real-world indoor scenes, it is not practically possible to capture every single corner of the scene due to occlusion. Nevertheless, with simple semantic knowledge, e.g., that desk surfaces are horizontal planes, and chairs have mirror symmetry, we can easily infer the occluded structure. Secondly, semantic representation of the modeled scene is required by higher-level applications. For instance, to understand and interact with the modeled digital scenes, a semantic tag for each object or even part must be known. In fact, for many higher-level applications it can be preferable to lose some geometric precision in exchange for a semantically correct representation, as long as doing so does not lead to confusion in understanding the scene contents. In this spirit, growing attention has been paid recently to semantic modeling methods.

Semantic modeling algorithms focus on reconstructing scenes down to the level of specific objects. Typically, RGB-D data of each semantic region are separated from the surrounding environment and fitted using either existing object models, part models, or even geometric primitives (e.g., planes or cylinders). Semantic modeling has many advantages compared to geometric modeling. Apart from producing a semantically meaningful representation of the modeled scene (e.g., knowledge that the scene contains a table and four chairs) which is beneficial in many applications, the modeling process is much simpler compared to traditional geometric modeling which needs extensive effort for data acquisition, especially when capturing real-world indoor scenes with low-cost RGB-D sensors. In contrast, semantic modeling systems typically only require sparse RGB-D images because the basic shapes of most interior objects are already known a priori. Hence, semantic modeling techniques are particularly suited to modeling real-world indoor scenes from low-quality RGB-D data. The general pipeline of the semantic modeling framework is shown in Fig. 4.

Clearly, semantic modeling requires sound semantic segmentation of the input RGB-D data. Automatically separating an indoor scene into different kinds of semantic regions is a challenging problem. On one hand, to understand what objects are present in the scene, each object must be separated from its surroundings. On the other hand, recognizing the type and shape of an object is ultimately important for determining whether an adjacent region belongs to the object or not, for effective segmentation. This is an intricate chickenand-egg problem. To break the interdependency, human prior knowledge is often adopted in the form of semantic or contextual rules. Although many algorithms claim to take advantage of using semantic or contextual information, there are significant differences in terms of what they mean by semantic or contextual information. This is mainly because there is no universal definition of what degree of human prior knowledge can be considered as semantic. Therefore, based on the level of context being used, we classify semantic modeling methods into two categories: primitivebased methods (Section 3.2.1) and model-based methods (Section 3.2.2).

Primitive-Based Methods

An important observation concerning interior objects is that most of them can be decomposed into a set of geometric primitives (e.g., sphere, cone, plane, and cylinder). Figure 5 gives an example of a semantically modeled scene; note that objects in it are all constructed from basic geometric primitives.

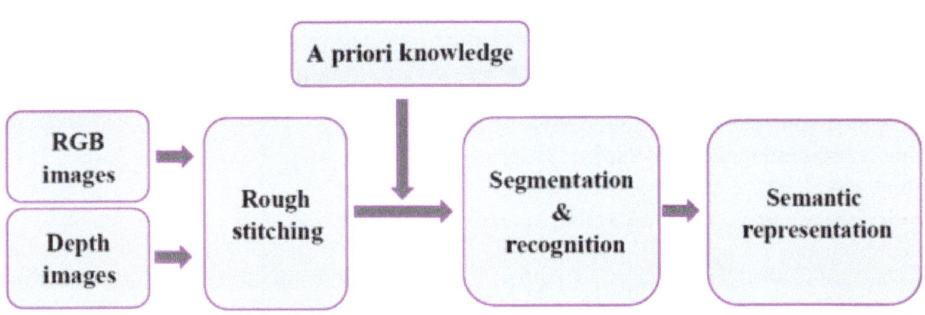

Figure 4: Pipeline of the semantic modeling framework.

Figure 5: Primitive-based semantic modeling result. Reproduced with permission from Ref. [39], c 2012 Association for Computing Machinery, Inc.

Finding proper primitives which best fit the unsegmented noisy input RGBD scan is the core of primitive-based methods. Thus, primitive fitting algorithms must be capable of reliably distinguishing between inliers and outliers. The state-of-the-art algorithm is based on RANSAC [28] due to its robustness to outliers. However, RANSAC can only estimate one model (i.e., a single primitive) for a particular data set. As for any one-model approach, when two (or more) instances exist, RANSAC may fail to find either one. As an alternative, the Hough transform [33] is often used for robust estimation of models when more than one model instance is present; it finds instances of objects within a certain class of shapes by voting in the parameter space. A major drawback of the Hough transform is that the time complexity increases at a rate of $O(A^{m-2})$ where A is the size of the input data and m is the number of parameters [34]. Thus, it is very time-consuming to detect complex models (large m) in large-scale input scans (large A). Furthermore, the Hough transform is generally more sensitive to noise than RANSAC. As a result, the Hough transform is most often used when we can convert the problem into a 2D parameter space to make the problem tractable [3, 35]. Otherwise, most approaches choose to detect multiple model instances one by one using RANSAC [36–38]. As the primitives are fitted locally from noisy and incomplete data, it is very common to see duplicated primitives where a single primitive is reported multiple times, or gaps in the set of fitted primitives. Thus global consolidation is also needed to get a consistent scene representation. Depending on the application, different types of global consolidation are used with different a priori assumptions (e.g., regarding typical primitives in the scene).

In large-scale interior architectural modeling, a box assumption is most commonly used. Specifically, walls can be fitted with vertical planar primitives, floors and ceilings can be fitted with horizontal planar primitives, and together they form a strict box. This assumption is the foundation of the state-of-the-art architectural modeling approach [3]. It first segments the scene point cloud into a set of horizontal 2D slices, and points in each slice are projected onto a 2D plane. Line segments are detected in the 2D space, which are then merged into 2D rectangles and combined with other slices to form 3D cuboids. In some cases, convex hull or alpha-shape algorithms are also needed to determine the spatial extent of each planar primitive [36], as they may form general polygonal shapes rather than the more common rectangles.

Many CAD and mechanical models are designed and manufactured by additive or subtractive combination of primitive shapes. Such types of objects can be naturally modeled by primitivebased methods with suitable assumptions. The state-of-the-art method for modeling such objects is proposed by Li et al. [37]. They consider three types of mutual relations (orientation, placement, and equality) and propose an iterative constrained optimization scheme to globally consolidate locally fitted primitives.

Recently, primitive-based methods have been extended to model large-scale indoor scenes, not only for walls or floors but for interior furniture as well. This is based on the observation that furniture items (e.g., chairs, tables, and cabinets) in a large-scale scene usually come from a small number of prototypes and are repeated multiple times. Kim et al. [39] proposed a supervised method which involves two stages. In the offline learning stage, each object of interest is prescanned and represented as a set of stable primitives along with necessary inter-part junction

attributes. In the online modeling stage, the whole scene is segmented and each segment is fitted with primitives. Then all repeated objects are detected and modeled through hierarchical matching. Variation between object parts can also be handled by specifying degree-of-freedom for each stable primitive in the pre-scanned object, which is the main advantage of this supervised method. Mattausch et al. [15] later introduced an unsupervised method for modeling with high-quality RGB-D data also by detecting repeated objects. They first convert the scene point cloud into a collection of nearly-planar patch primitives. Then, based on geometric similarity and spatial configurations of neighboring patches, patches are clustered in a Euclidean embedding space and repeated objects can thus be detected and modeled. Note that primitives used in these methods are not just meaningless geometric shapes but some kind of semantic abstraction of interior objects or parts, identified from repeated occurrences of instances in the training data, which helps to robustly recover repeated objects from incomplete and noisy data (e.g., chair backs, chair seats, monitors, etc.).

Model-Based Methods

Despite attempts with certain levels of success as described in the previous subsection, primitivebased methods have fundamental limitations in modeling interior objects. For example, both Refs. [39] and [15] only tackle large-scale public or office buildings with many repeated objects, but in typical home environments many objects only occur once (e.g., a television or a bed). Moreover, many interior objects (e.g., keyboards, desk lamps, and various types of chairs) are too complex to be depicted in detail using a set of simple primitives. Thus, primitive-based methods can only offer an approximation to the target scene.

What happens if we already have a database containing similar 3D models of objects to the ones that appear in the target scene? This is not unrealistic, as for example chairs frequently occur in indoor scenes and it is likely that a chair model similar to the one appearing in the target scene already exists in the database. In this case we no longer need to pre-scan the chair

[39] or cluster point cloud regions [15] to learn the underlying semantic structural knowledge of that chair. More importantly, 3D models are far more flexible and can provide more accurate depiction for chairs in the scene than a set of basic primitives. As long as we have sufficient 3D models in the database, it is much more feasible to get a visually plausible and semantically segmented digital scene by finding and placing correct models and parts, adapted to fit the input scans (see Fig. 6). This is the key spirit of model-based methods. The growing availability of free 3D models online (e.g., in the Trimble 3D Warehouse) has made it possible. Model-based methods thus represent a new trend in scene modeling.

Nan et al. [40] use a search-classify strategy and a region growing method to find independent point clouds from high-quality laser scans, and assign a semantic label for each meaningful object. They first train classifiers for individual pre-defined object categories. In the online stage, they first over-segment the input point cloud. Starting from a seed region in the over-segmentation, the point cloud of an individual object is detected and separated from the background by iteratively adding regions which help to increase classification confidence. After that, a deform-to-fit technique is used to adapt 3D models in the training set to fit the segmented and classified point cloud objects. Their method relies on high-quality scans, to make the problem more tractable.

Shao et al. [41] present an interactive approach to semantic modeling of indoor scenes from sparse sets of low-quality Kinect scans. To avoid problems brought by poor-quality depth images, they rely on user interaction to reliably segment RGB-D images into regions with semantic labels manually assigned. Then an automatic algorithm is used to find the best matched model for each object and arrange them to reconstruct the target scene.

Figure 6: Model-based semantic modeling result. Reproduced with permission from Ref. [7], c 2014 Association for Computing Machinery, Inc.

For complex scenes with many object instances, Shao et al.'s method [41] requires extensive user assistance for segmentation and labeling to resolve ambiguity due to noise and occlusion. Interior objects normally have strong contextual relationships (e.g., monitors are found on desks, and chairs are arranged around tables). Such relationships provide strong cues to determine semantic categories of each object, and has been used in a number of recognition and retrieval tasks, delivering significant improvements in precision. By utilizing such information, Chen et al. [7] propose an automatic solution to this problem. They exploit co-occurrence contextual information in a 3D scene database, and use this information to constrain modeling, ensuring semantic compatibility between matched models.

The performance of model-based methods relies heavily on the quality, diversity and the number of existing 3D models as well as scenes that represent plausible combinations of models. Novel scenes or scene items without representation in the existing 3D model database are likely to lead to poor results. This is currently the main bottleneck of model-based methods.

CONCLUSIONS

In this paper, we have presented an extensive survey of indoor scene modeling from RGB-D data. We first briefly introduced some public datasets and programming libraries in this area. We divided methods into two categories: geometric modeling and semantic modeling, and overviewed various indoor scene modeling techniques along with their advantages and limitations in each category. However, from the reviewed methods we can see that robust modeling of real-world complex, cluttered or large-scale indoor scenes remains an open problem because of numerous challenges. Generally, researchers in this area have reached a consensus that utilizing prior knowledge is the right direction to improve modeling algorithms, especially when the data is incomplete and noisy. In fact, with simple prior knowledge, even traditional geometric modeling methods can benefit significantly. Zhou et al. [42] use an observation that scene parts which have been scanned particularly thoroughly tend to be points of interest (POI). By detecting POI from the scanning trajectory and protecting local geometry in POI, they can significantly improve reconstruction results of complex scenes. Salas-Moreno et al. [43] extend the classic SLAM framework to object level using the prior knowledge that many scenes consist of repeated, domain-specific objects and structures. Therefore, obtaining more human prior knowledge and better using it have become a focus of current indoor scene modeling research. By summarizing a broad area of literature, we hope this survey will give valuable insights into this important topic and will encourage new research in this area.

ACKNOWLEDGEMENTS

This work was supported by the National Natural Science Foundation of China (Project No. 61120106007), Research Grant of Beijing Higher Institution Engineering Research Center, and Tsinghua University Initiative Scientific Research Program.

REFERENCES

1. Merrell, P.; Schkufza, E.; Li, Z.; Agrawala, M.; Koltun, V. Interactive furniture layout using interior design guidelines. *ACM Transactions on Graphics* Vol. 30, No. 4, Article No. 87, 2011.

2. Yu, L.-F.; Yeung, S.-K.; Tang, C.-K.; Terzopoulos, D.; Chan, T. F.; Osher, S. J. Make it home: Automatic optimization of furniture arrangement. *ACM Transactions on Graphics* Vol. 30, No. 4, Article No. 86, 2011.

3. Xiao, J.; Furukawa, Y. Reconstructing the world's museums. *International Journal of Computer Vision* Vol. 110, No. 3, 243–258, 2014.

4. Izadi, S.; Kim, D.; Hilliges, O.; Molyneaux, D.; Newcombe, R.; Kohli, P.; Shotton, J.; Hodges, S.; Freeman, D.; Davison, A.; Fitzgibbon, A. KinectFusion: Real-time 3D reconstruction and interaction using a moving depth camera. In: *Proceedings of the 24th Annual ACM Symposium on User Interface Software and Technology*, 559–568, 2011.

5. Newcombe, R. A.; Izadi, S.; Hilliges, O.; Molyneaux, D.; Kim, D.; Davison, A. J.; Kohi, P.; Shotton, J.; Hodges, S.; Fitzgibbon, A. KinectFusion: Real-time dense surface mapping and tracking. In: *Proceedings of 2011 10th IEEE International Symposium on Mixed and Augmented Reality*, 127–136, 2011.

6. Savva, M.; Chang, A. X.; Hanrahan, P.; Fisher, M.; Niener, M. SceneGrok: Inferring action maps in 3D environments. *ACM Transactions on Graphics* Vol. 33, No. 6, Article No. 212, 2014.

7. Chen, K.; Lai, Y.-K.; Wu, Y.-X.; Martin, R.; Hu, S.-M. Automatic semantic modeling of indoor scenes from low-quality RGB-D data using contextual information. *ACM Transactions on Graphics* Vol. 33, No. 6, Article No. 208, 2014.

8. Iddan, G. J.; Yahav, G. Three-dimensional imaging in the studio and elsewhere. *In: Proceedings of the International Society for Optics and Photonics,* Vol. 4289, No. 48, 48–55, 2001.

9. Anand, A.; Koppula, H. S.; Joachims, T.; Saxena, A. Contextually guided semantic labeling and search for three-dimensional point clouds. *International Journal of Robotics Research*Vol. 32, No. 1, 19–34, 2013.

10. Koppula, H. S.; Anand, A.; Joachims, T.; Saxena, A. Semantic labeling of 3D point clouds for indoor scenes. In: *Proceedings of the Conference on Neural Information Processing Systems*, 244–252, 2011.

11. Lai, K.; Bo, L.; Fox, D. Unsupervised feature learning for 3D scene labeling. In:*Proceedings of 2014 IEEE International Conference on Robotics and Automation*, 3050–3057, 2014.

12. Silberman, N.; Fergus, R. Indoor scene segmentation using a structured light sensor. In:*Proceedings of 2011 IEEE International Conference on Computer Vision Workshops*, 601–608, 2011.

13. Silberman, N.; Hoiem, D.; Kohli, P.; Fergus, R. Indoor segmentation and support inference from RGBD images. In: *Proceedings of the 12th European Conference on Computer Vision-Volume Part V*, 746–760, 2012.

14. Xiao, J.; Owens, A.; Torralba, A. SUN3D: A database of big spaces reconstructed using SfM and object labels. In: *Proceedings of 2013 IEEE International Conference on Computer Vision*, 1625–1632, 2013.

15. Mattausch, O.; Panozzo, D.; Mura, C.; Sorkine- Hornung, O.; Pajarola, R. Object detection and classification from large-scale cluttered indoor scans. *Computer Graphics Forum* Vol. 33, No. 2, 11–21, 2014.

16. Rusu, R. B.; Cousins, S. 3D is here: Point cloud library (PCL). In: Proceedings of 2011 IEEE International Conference on Robotics and Automation, 1–4, 2011.

17. Information on http://wwwmrptorg.

18. Besl, P. J.; McKay, N. D. A method for registration of 3-D shapes. *IEEE Transactions on Pattern Analysis and Machine Intelligence* Vol. 14, No. 2, 239–256, 1992.

19. Chen, Y.; Medioni, G. Object modeling by registration of multiple range images. *Image and Vision Computing* Vol. 10, No. 3, 145–155, 1992.

20. Durrant-Whyte, H.; Bailey, T. Simultaneous localization and mapping: Part I. *IEEE Robotics & Automation Magazine* Vol. 13, No. 2, 99–110, 2006.

21. Curless, B.; Levoy, M. A volumetric method for building complex models from range images. In: Proceedings of the 23rd Annual Conference on Computer Graphics and Interactive Techniques, 303–312, 1996.

22. Heredia, F.; Favier, R. Kinect Fusion extensions to large scale environments. Available at http://wwwpointcloudsorg/blog/srcs/fheredia.

23. Endres, F.; Hess, J.; Engelhard, N.; Sturm, J.; Burgard, W. An evaluation of the RGB-D SLAM system. In: Proceedings of 2012 IEEE International Conference on Robotics and Automation, 1691–1696, 2012.

24. Information on http://openslamorg.

25. Lowe, D. G. Object recognition from local scaleinvariant features. In: Proceedings of the 7th IEEE International Conference on Computer Vision, Vol. 2, 1150–1157, 1999.

26. Bay, H.; Ess, A.; Tuytelaars, T.; Van Gool, L. Speeded-up robust features (SURF).*Computer Vision and Image Understanding* Vol. 110, No. 3, 346–359, 2008.

27. Rublee, E.; Rabaud, V.; Konolige, K.; Bradski, G. ORB: An efficient alternative to SIFT or SURF. In: Proceedings of 2011 IEEE International Conference on Computer Vision, 2564–2571, 2011.

28. Fischler, M. A.; Bolles, R. C. Random sample consensus: A paradigm for model fitting with applications to image analysis and automated cartography. *Communications of the ACM*Vol. 24, No. 6, 381–395, 1981.

29. Tsai, C.-Y.; Wang, C.-W.; Wang, W.-Y. Design and implementation of a RANSAC RGB-D mapping algorithm for multi-view point cloud registration. In: Proceedings of 2013 International Automatic Control Conference, 367–370, 2013.

30. Henry, P.; Krainin, M.; Herbst, E.; Ren, X.; Fox, D. RGB-D mapping: Using depth cameras for dense 3D modeling of indoor environments. *International Journal of Robotics Research* Vol. 31, No. 5, 647–663, 2012.

31. Li, M.; Lin, R.; Wang H.; Xu, H. An efficient SLAM system only using RGBD sensors. In: Proceedings of 2013 IEEE International Conference on Robotics and Biomimetics, 1653–1658, 2013.

32. Lin, R.; Wang, Y.; Yang, S. RGBD SLAM for indoor environment. In: Proceedings of the 1st International Conference on Cognitive Systems and Information Processing, 161–175, 2014.

33. Duda, R. O.; Hart, P. E. Use of the Hough transformation to detect lines and curves in pictures. *Communications of the ACM* Vol. 15, No. 1, 11–15, 1972.

34. Stockman, G.; Shapiro, L. Computer Vision. Upper Saddle River, NJ, USA: Prentice Hall, 2001.

35. Oesau, S.; Lafarge, F.; Alliez, P. Indoor scene reconstruction using feature sensitive primitive extraction and graph-cut. *ISPRS Journal of Photogrammetry and Remote Sensing* Vol. 90, 68–82, 2014.

36. Sanchez, V.; Zakhor, A. Planar 3D modeling of building interiors from point cloud data. In: Proceedings of 2012 19th IEEE International Conference on Image Processing, 1777–1780, 2012.

37. Li, Y.; Wu, X.; Chrysathou, Y.; Sharf, A.; Cohen-Or, D.; Mitra, N. J. GlobFit: Consistently fitting primitives by discovering global relations. *ACM Transactions on Graphics* Vol. 30, No. 4, Article No. 52, 2011.

38. Arikan, M.; Schwärzler, M.; Flory, S.; Wimmer, M.; Maierhofer, S. O-snap: Optimization-based snapping for modeling architecture. *ACM Transactions on Graphics* Vol. 32, No. 1, Article No. 6, 2013.

39. Kim, Y. M.; Mitra, N. J.; Yan, D.-M.; Guibas, L. Acquiring 3D indoor environments with variability and repetition. *ACM Transactions on Graphics* Vol. 31, No. 6, Article No. 138, 2012.

40. Nan, L.; Xie, K.; Sharf, A. A search-classify approach for cluttered indoor scene understanding. *ACM Transactions on Graphics* Vol. 31, No. 6, Article No. 137, 2012.

41. Shao, T.; Xu, W.; Zhou, K.; Wang, J.; Li, D.; Guo, B. An interactive approach to semantic modeling of indoor scenes with an RGBD camera. *ACM Transactions on Graphics* Vol. 31, No. 6, Article No. 136, 2012.

42. Zhou, Q.-Y.; Koltun, V. Dense scene reconstruction with points of interest. *ACM Transactions on Graphics* Vol. 32, No. 4, Article No. 112, 2013.

43. Salas-Moreno, R. F.; Newcombe, R. A.; Strasdat, H.; Kelly, P. H. J.; Davison, A. J. SLAM++: Simultaneous localisation and mapping at the level of objects. In: Proceedings of 2013 IEEE Conference on Computer Vision and Pattern Recognition, 1352–1359, 2013.

CHAPTER 8

THE ACQUISITION AND MEASUREMENT OF SURFACE WAVES OF HIGH-SPEED LIQUID JETS

Chen Gong[1], Minguan Yang[1], Can Kang[1], and Yuli Wang[1,2]

[1]School of Energy and Power Engineering, Jiangsu University, Zhenjiang 212013, China
[2]Department of Mechanics, KTH-Royal Institute of Technology, 10044 Stockholm, Sweden

ABSTRACT

The instability analysis of the liquid jet issuing into ambient air was conducted with an emphasis placed upon the evolution of surface waves of the jet. An experiment was designed to visualize the microscopic morphology on the surface of a liquid jet. A spectral method was proposed to measure wavelength from the obtained jet images. We also discuss key setup parameters that significantly affect the resolution of desired jet features and the accuracy of the spectral measurement. The results show that the liquid jet near the nozzle exit can be divided into a laminar section, a transition section, an instability section, and a turbulence section. Surface wave scales range from 0.06 to 0.11 times of the nozzle diameter with the atomization breakup regime. For the atomization breakup regime, the growth ratio of the surface waves of the instability section is 0.06 which is 1.5 times the value of the second wind-introduced breakup regime and 3 times the value of the first wind-introduced breakup regime.

INTRODUCTION

Break up of liquid jet is a common phenomenon and it has been widely used in many fields. For example, the atomization process plays a critical role in combustion systems since most power generation processes necessitate liquid fuel. The purpose of injector design is to produce droplets of given size, distribution, and velocity under certain environment. The combustion efficiency and pollutant emission depend greatly on spray characteristics. However, our understanding on jet breakup process is still not adequate.

After a liquid jet discharges from a nozzle, surface waves are anticipated on the jet surface due to the boundary condition as the jet surface shifts from a non-slip boundary condition to a free surface boundary condition. These surface waves will be strengthened by the interaction between the jet and the ambient fluid. The development of these surface waves causes liquid jet breakup and droplets are finally produced (Lefebvre 1989). Based on Ohnesorge number and Reynolds number, the breakup of the liquid jet can be divided into four different regimes: Rayleigh breakup, first wind-induced breakup, second wind-induced breakup and atomization (Chigier and Reitz 1996). Lin and Reitz (1998) have proposed the expressions of the four regimes based on the Weber number. Atomization regime occurs at Weber numbers larger than 40.3. The jets with this regime break up near the nozzle exit and the diameters of the droplets which pinch off from the jets' surface are much smaller than the diameters of the jets. Some research suggested that the formation of the droplets was the result of the development of the jet surface waves.

Citation: Chen Gong, Minguan Yang, Can Kang, and Yuli Wang, The acquisition and measurement of surface waves of high-speed liquid jets, DOI: 10.1007/s12650-015-0307-9.

To explore the physical essence of jet breakup, the development of the surface waves should be granted a priority. Some researchers studied surface waves via numerical simulation. Representatively, Shinjo and Umemura (2010, 2011), Ménard et al. (2007), and Fuster et al. (2009) had depicted the development of surface waves that lead to atomization and captured the ligaments and droplets from the disturbed liquid core surface. Numerical simulation requires initial and boundary conditions which are pre-determined by either stability analysis of different degrees of complexity or experimental measurements. The existing stability analysis cannot explain all the physical mechanisms of the high-speed liquid jet.

Many researchers endeavored to study the development of the surface waves using experimental methods. Some of them are dedicated to small jets of diameters less than 1 mm. Yon et al. (2003) and Li and Collicott (2006) performed visualizations of the liquid jets using coupling shadowgraph and laser sheet techniques. Paciaroni et al. (2006) developed the ballistic imaging technique which makes use of the ultra-short laser pulse to image the near-field liquid core. The coupling of ballistic imaging and X-ray absorption imaging was used by Briggs et al. (2006) to investigate high-speed jet primary breakup. The high rate imaging technique and the very high spatial resolution imaging technique were developed by Delacourt et al. (2005) and Nakagawa et al. (2006), respectively. In Aliseda's experiment (Aliseda et al. 2008), the camera was focused through a microlens on a small region located at the outlet of the liquid nozzle, thereby, the micro-structures of capillary jet could be obtained. Blaisot and Yon (2005) used image-based techniques to describe the shape of liquid particles that are not fully atomized or relaxed.

The others consider the behavior of large jets with diameters exceeding 1 mm. Osta et al. (2012) investigated the surface topography of liquid jets using X-ray diagnostics. With the help of Shadowgraph, Mayer (1994) and Mayer and Branam (2004) captured the surface waves and measured the wavelengths using traditional approaches. The pulsed photograph and holograph were used by Faeth et al. (1995), Wu and Faeth (1993, 1995), and Wu et al. (1992, 1995) to observe breakup characteristics at jet surface, Sallam et al. (2002) completed the works of Wu and Faeth, and examined the breakup of the entire liquid column for turbulent liquid flows. In Hoyt and Taylor's experiments (Hoyt and Taylor 1977a, b), a relatively large nozzle was used and the backlight was employed. Jets with bright surface waves were produced. Moreover, surface wavelength measurement based on nine still images of their jet was provided and various stability analyses (Yoon and Heister 2003; Park 2005) validated by this wavelength. The aforementioned works provided several useful methods for further research works.

In this paper, a visualization experimental method is designed to capture the surface waves of high-speed liquid jet. The important parameters of the visualization experimental method are discussed. The velocities of the liquid jet range from 12 to 38 m/s. Spectral methods were used to process the captured jet images. Two commonly used spectral methods and their key parameters were discussed. Furthermore, the relationship between jet surface waves and Reynolds numbers is investigated based on quantitative information extracted from jet images. The vigorousness of the new method devised here to capture small-scale morphological information is highlighted and such a method is expected to be extended to other applications.

EXPERIMENTAL APPROACH

Setup

The experimental setup is presented in Fig. 1. Water is pumped from a container, the flow rate of the pump is controlled by gearing a variable-frequency drive, and the jet velocity is changed accordingly. The flow condition is produced with a straight stainless steel pipe of lengthH = 0.5 m and inner diameter d = 8 mm. The length-to-diameter ratio of the straight stainless steel pipe exceeds 40, ensuring fully developed inner turbulent flex (Wu et al. 1995). The pump and the straight stainless steel pipe are connected with a rubber hose. The nozzle is made of copper and consists of two parts, contraction section and straight section. The inlet diameter of the contraction section match the upstream pipe's inner diameter and the angle of the contraction section is 14°. The contraction section is followed by a straight section with diameter D = 3.0 mm and stretches to a length of L = 6.0 mm.

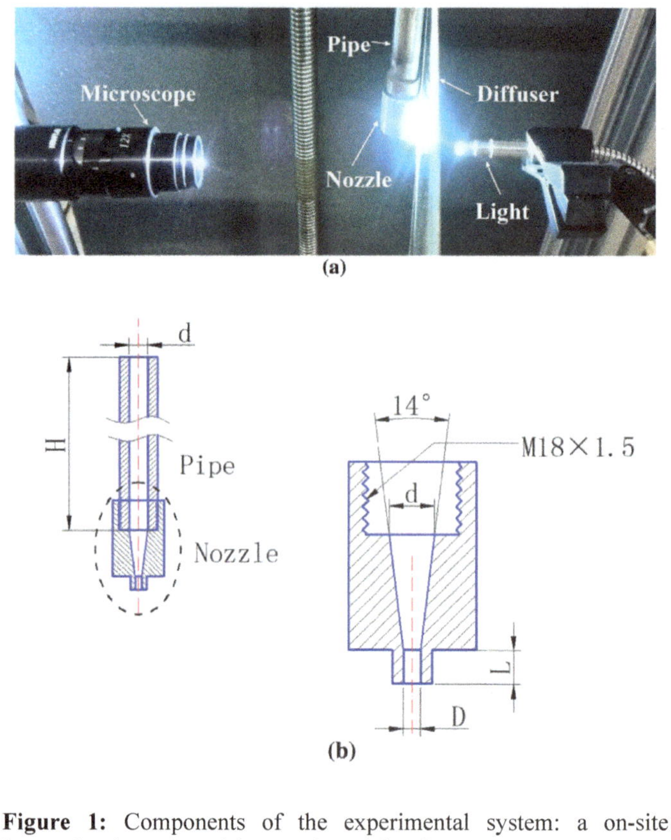

Figure 1: Components of the experimental system: a on-site image; b schematics of the nozzle and the pipe.

Jet images were captured with an OLYMPUS I-SPEED 3 camera and a microscope. The exposure time and the frame rate of the camera were set as 1 μs and 100 fps, respectively. For each experimental condition, 100 images were captured to constitute a complete sampling group. The image size of the camera is 1280 × 1024 pixels. The amplification of the microscope is set as 2.8 which provides typical resolution around 6 μm/pixel. The light is produced by OLYMPUS ILP-2 and transmitted through an optical fiber with a diameter of 6 mm. The light beam passes through a 5-mm-thick acrylic diffuser plate before touching the jet surface. The acrylic diffuser plate is used to produce a uniform light distribution. The light, liquid jet, and microscope are collinear.

The jet velocity near the exit of nozzle is measured by particle image velocimetry (PIV). The PIV system consists mainly of a YAG200-NWL pulsed laser, a POWER-VIEW 4MP CCD camera, and a macro lens. Water temperature is measured using a WS-T11PRO digital thermometer; density and kinematic viscosity are determined accordingly.

The flow in the straight section of the nozzle is treated as a flat plate flow (Hoyt and Taylor1977a). The momentum thickness δ_2 at the exit of the nozzle can be calculated by the laminar Blasius solution for a flat plate:

$$\delta_2 = 0.664\sqrt{\frac{\nu L}{U}}, \quad (1)$$

where ν is the kinematic viscosity, and U is the jet velocity.

The Reynolds number based on the momentum thickness can be calculated by

$$Re_{\delta_2} = \frac{U\delta_2}{\nu}. \quad (2)$$

The Weber number based on air density can be calculated by

$$We_g = \frac{\rho_g U^2 D}{\sigma}, \quad (3)$$

where ρ_g is air density, σ denotes surface tension.

The flow parameters and physical properties in our experiment are presented in Table 1.

Table 1: Flow conditions

Parameter	**Value**
Nozzle diameter (D)	3.0 mm
Liquid temperature (T)	293 K
Kinematic viscosity (ν)	1.007 m²/s
Liquid density (ρ_L)	998 kg/m³
Ambient pressure (P)	0.1 MPa
Air density (ρ_g)	1.21 kg/m³
Jet velocity (U)	12.0–38.2 m/s
Momentum thickness (δ_2)	8.35–14.9 μm
$Re_{\delta 2}$	177.7–316.7
Surface tension (σ)	0.07275 N/m
Weber number based on air density (We_g)	7.21–72.77

The accuracy of the digital thermometer (WS-T11PRO) used in our research is ±0.5 °C. Therefore, the uncertainty of the measured liquid temperature is 2.5 %. The liquid density, kinematic viscosity, and surface tension are estimated based on the liquid temperature. Based upon literatures (Bian et al. 2010; Syuto et al. 2010; Hori and Sakakibara 2004), the uncertainty of velocity measurement is less than 3 % with a confidence level of 95 %. The quantities of Reynolds number $Re_{\delta 2}$ and Weber number We_g can be calculated from their relationship with the above quantities. Taking account of error propagation, the accuracy of the $Re_{\delta 2}$ and We_g is less than 4.5 and 6 %, respectively.

To capture the micro-structures of the high-speed liquid jet, experiment must provide sufficient temporal resolution. The exposure time of the camera must be short enough to capture the instantaneous jet profile, otherwise motion blur will take place, as shown in Fig. 2a. Motion blur can be briefly explained by Fig. 2b; the jet is denoted by the square inside the rectangular windows. And the exposure time (Δt) is equally divided into three smaller moments (1/3 Δt). If the jet moves in an appreciable distance during the exposure time, namely, the position of the square varies within exposure time, which can result in motion blur. As can be seen in Fig. 2b, the three squares will not overlap in the last image, and that is the so-called motion blur. In this case, the exposure time should be reduced to 1/3 Δt to avoid motion blur. In principle, for continuous motions, the exposure time should be infinitely small. However, the distance that the camera can discern is limited. Therefore, if the distance covered by the jet within the exposure period is smaller than the distance that the camera can distinguish, the motion can be ignored and motion blur can be avoided accordingly. The minimum distance that can be distinguished by the camera used is 46 μm. Based on the maximum jet velocities exhibited in Table 1, the exposure time should be less than 1.1 μs. In this experiment, the exposure time is set to 1 μs.

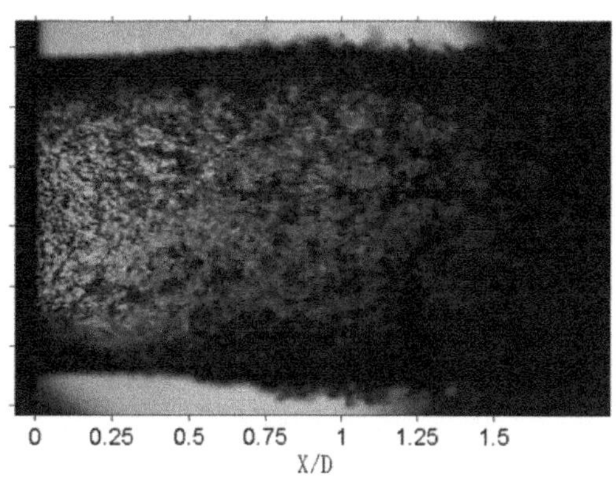

(a)

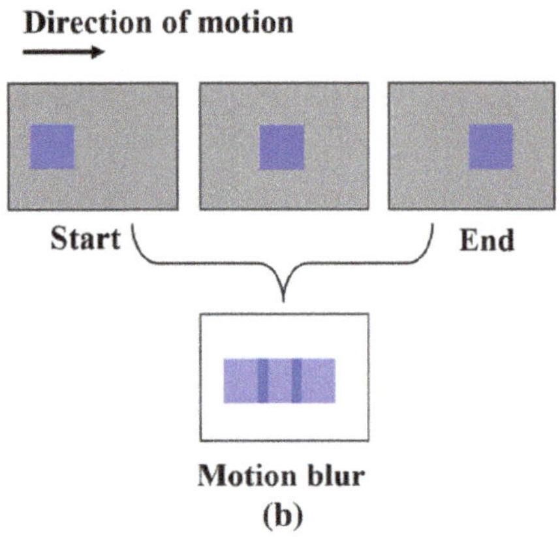

Figure 2: Motion blur. a A blurred jet image. b The schematic of motion blur.

Also there should be sufficient spatial resolution to resolve the surface waves. Based on the theory of Portillo, surface wave size scales with the momentum thickness (Portillo 2008). The momentum thicknesses vary from 8.1 to 14.9 µm; therefore, the spatial resolution of the jet images should be no less than 8.1 µm/pixel.

Jet images with different spatial resolutions are presented in Fig. 3. The two jets are produced under the same experimental condition. However, compared with Fig. 3a, the image in Fig. 3b is focused through a microscope on a smaller rectangular region (about 6 mm × 7 mm). In Fig. 3b, distinct structures, such as "fish skin"-like structures can be observed. Moreover, it can be seen that the surface waves are distributed along the streamwise periodically. But in the left picture, the surface waves appear to be blurry and the degree of order is rather low.

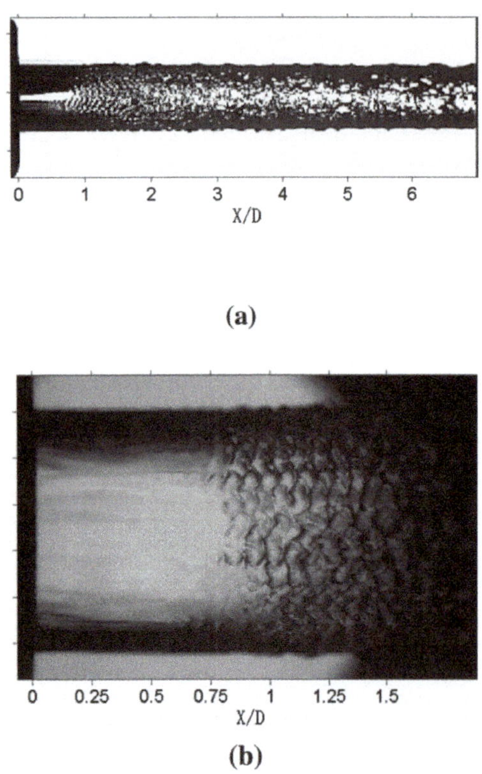

Figure 3: Jet images of different spatial resolutions. The spatial resolutions of a and b are 50 and 6 µm/pixel, respectively.

Image Processing

Detailed information of the jet surface waves can be measured by processing the image intensities of the pixels of the jet images. As shown in Fig. 4a, a red line extends from the nozzle in the streamwise direction. The corresponding image intensity distribution along this line is presented in Fig. 4b. Firstly, in the X/D range of 0–1.0, the curve of the image intensities fluctuates violently and it has small amplitude. Normally, such small difference of image intensities can hardly be perceived with naked eyes. Compared with Fig. 4a, it is easy to find that this part is corresponding to the smooth part of the jet. Then the curve has significant change near X/D = 1.0. The curve of this part has obvious periodicity. It has significantly bigger amplitude and lower frequency compared to the former part. The streamwise lengths between adjacent wave crests are about 0.09 D which is equal to the distance of adjacent surface waves in Fig. 4a. The development of the surface waves along the streamwise direction can be well represented by the image intensities. That is to say, the jet surface waves can be well measured by processing the digital signals extracted from the jet images.

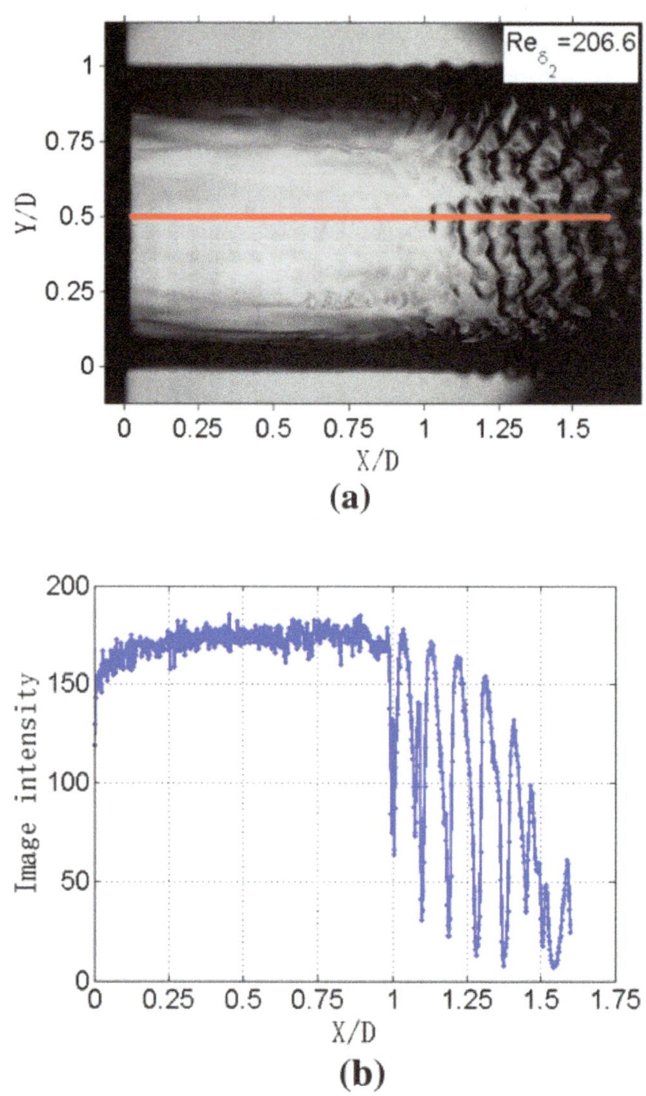

Figure 4: Jet image with $Re_{\delta 2}$ of 206.6. X is the streamwise direction; X = 0 is the orifice of the nozzle exit. Y is the spanwise direction, Y = 0 and Y = 1 are the upper periphery and lower periphery, respectively.

Jet images are constructed based upon digital information representing image intensities. The digital information essentially reflects morphological characteristics of the free surface. Two spots on the surface that have similar morphological structures will have similar values of image intensities. Therefore, we can use power spectral density (PSD) estimation to analyze the periodicity of image intensities variation and then calculate the wavelength.

Welch method is one of the commonly used digital signal processing methods (Mulgrew et al.2002). The computational formula of the Welch method is expressed as follows:

$$\bar{P}(w) = \frac{1}{MUL}\sum_{i=1}^{L}\left|\sum_{n=0}^{M-1} x_N^i(n)d(n)e^{-jwn}\right|^2, \qquad (4)$$

where N is the length of the sample, L is the number of the segments, and M is the length of each segment. $x_N^i(n)$ is the individual dataset. d(n)d(n) is the window function. $U = \frac{1}{M}\sum_{n=0}^{M-1} d^2$ is a normalizing factor used to achieve an asymptotic and unbiased estimation. $e^{jwn} = \cos(wn) + j\sin(wn)$ is the complex sinusoidal; w is the circular frequency. $\sum_{n=0}^{M-1} x_N^i(n)d(n)e^{-jwn}$ is the Fourier transform of random sequence of segment i, $1 \leq i \leq L$.

According to the principle of the Welch method, the result of the Welch method depends on the selection of window function. The measurement of jet surface waves is conducted to obtain the main wavelength. So the main lobe signal should be highlighted and the side lobe signal should be suppressed. The Blackmann window is one of the trigonometric function windows. It has relatively high side lobe attenuation rate boosting the concentration of spectrum energy on the main lobe. Therefore, the Blackmann window is selected.

Along the streamwise direction, a series of measurements are performed. The first sample is taken from the exit of the nozzle and the length of the sample is set equal to the window length. The measured result is set as the wavelength of the middle point of this sample. Then the second sample was taken from the position of 0.06 D, approximately 33 pixels, downstream of the nozzle exit. The length of the second sample is equal to the first sample. The procedure was repeated until the end of the data set.

In order to get appropriate length of the window, jet images are processed with different lengths of windows. Take the image intensities of Fig. 4b for example. The results are presented in Fig. 5. These curves can be generally divided into two parts along the streamwise direction. In the forepart, the wavelengths are all the same and smaller than 0.01 D. In the back part, the wavelengths are considerably bigger than forepart. Particularly, in Fig. 5a where the window length is smaller than 1/3 D, the wavelengths fluctuate violently. However, in Fig. 5b where the window length is larger than 1/3D, the wavelengths are nearly coincided and are around 0.09 Dwhich is equal to the value of the streamwise lengths between two adjacent wave crests in Fig. 4b. Clearly the window length should be larger than 1/3 D. However, as window length increases, the streamwise range of wavelength measurement decreases. As seen in Fig. 5b, for the window length of D, the streamwise range is only limited within X/D = 0.5–1.1. So the window length is set as 0.5 D.

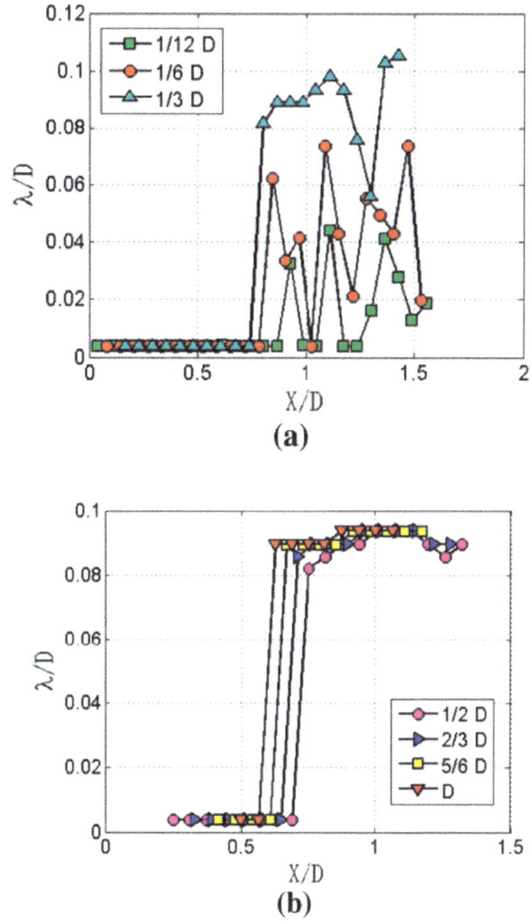

Figure 5: Wavelengths measurement with different lengths of window function. a Window lengths range from 1/12 D to 1/3 D. b Window lengths varies from 1/2 D to D.

Take a further look at Fig. 5b, when the length of window is equal to 1/2 D, the measured wavelength suddenly increases at the position near the X/D = 0.75. The corresponding sample was taken from X/D = 0.5–1. The measurement shows that the transition position from the smooth part to the part incorporating surface waves is located at about X/D = 1, as is in agreement with the results in Fig. 4.

Another typically digital signal processing method, Burg method, is also considered. This method does not require window function. The computational formula of the Burg method is

$$P_x(e^{jw}) = \frac{\sigma^2}{\left|1 + \sum_{k-1}^{P} a_k e^{-jwk}\right|^2}, \qquad (5)$$

where P is the degree of model k=1,2,...p, the reference value of P is N/3<P<N/2, N is the length of the sample. σ^2 is white noise. a_k is a coefficient. $e^{-jwk} = \cos(wn) - j\sin(wn)$ is the complex sinusoidal, and ω is circular frequency.

The key parameter of Burg method is the degree of model P (Portillo 2008). Using Burg method with different P values to process the same image intensity data of Fig. 4a, the results are presented in Fig. 6. Within the X/D range of 0.2–0.6, the wavelengths are nearly the same and are less than 0.01 D. The wavelengths fluctuate around 0.09 D within the X/D range of 0.6–1.4. The position at which wavelength significantly increases is about X/D=0.6, and the corresponding transition position is located at about X/D = 0.85. Clearly, the transition position measured by Welch method is more accurate, so the Welch method is selected for jet image processing in the presented study.

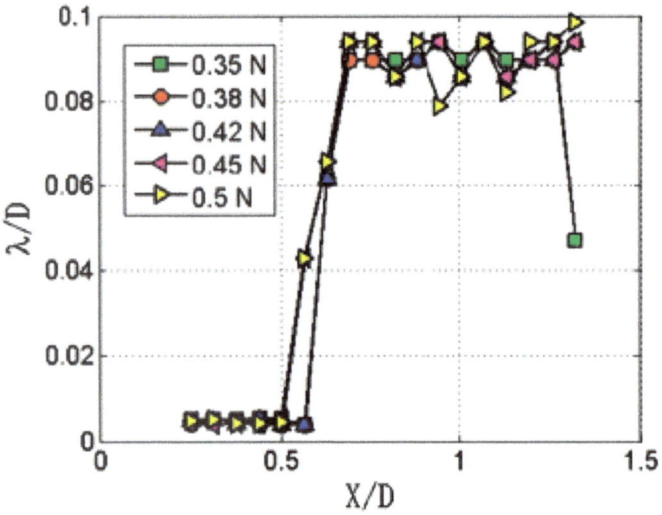

Figure 6: Wavelength measurement with Burg method of different P. The length of N is 1/2 D.

Based on the analysis above, the Welch method and Blackmann window were selected to process the jet images. The length of the window function was set as 0.5 D which corresponds to 260 pixels. To reduce the random error, spanwise positions between Y = 0.25 and Y = 0.75 were measured, and then, all the other 99 jet images which were captured under the same experimental condition were processed by the same method. Take the average value of these 100 images as the final wavelengths.

The average wavelengths of the jet with $Re_{\delta 2}$ equal to 206.6 are presented in Fig. 7. The results can be divided into three parts. Firstly, within the range of X/D = 0.25–0.6, the wavelengths are all the same and equal to 0.004 D. Secondly, within the X/D range of 0.6–1, wavelength increases with a slope of 0.23. Thirdly, the slope of the curve drops to 0.04 in the X/D range of 1–1.45.

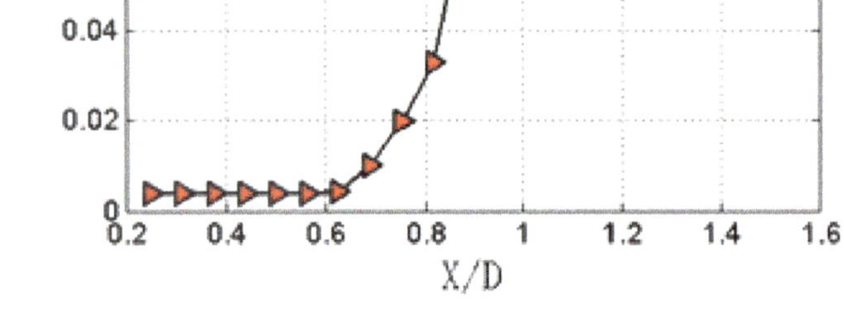

Figure 7: Average wavelengths of $Re_{\delta 2} = 206.6$.

In Fig. 7, wavelength increases with a slope of 0.23 in the streamwise range of X/D = 0.6–1. However, wavelength goes up vertically at the streamwise position of X/D = 0.75, as shown in Fig. 5. The obvious disparity between the two measured results can be explained, as shown in Fig. 8.

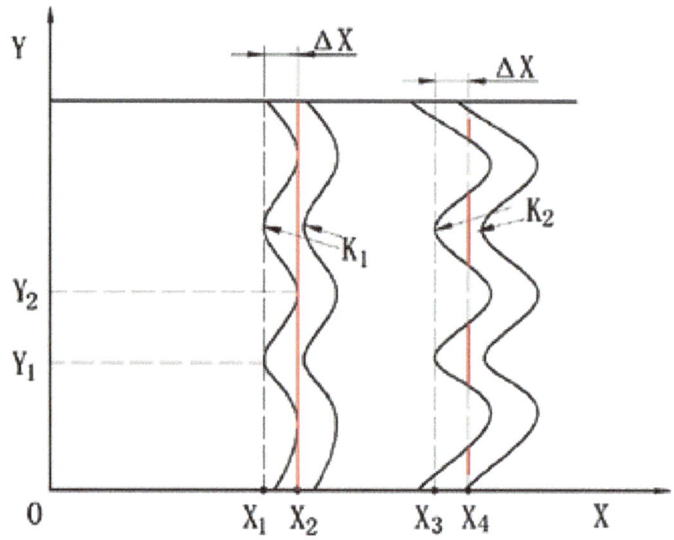

Figure 8: Analysis of difference between single measurement and multiple measurements. Xrepresents the streamwise direction; Y represents spanwise direction.

As depicted in Fig. 4a, along the spanwise direction, the surface waves of the jet are not straight lines but a group of curves with various curvatures. In Fig. 8, the arc segments are used to represent surface waves. Clearly, surface waves are different at different spanwise positions. For example, the sample taken from the spanwise position of Y_1 first reaches the surface waves at the streamwise position of X_1. However, for the spanwise position of Y_2, the sample first reaches the surface wave at the streamwise position of X_2. From X_1 to X_2, the length through which sample can reach the surface waves is increased. That is to say, average wavelength is increased along the streamwise direction. This explains why there is a difference between the averaged result and the single result.

Take a further look at Fig. 8; it is apparent that surface wave curvature has a great influence on the growth ratio of wavelength. There are two groups of surface waves in Fig. 8 with equivalent wavelengths but different curvatures. The surface waves relatively close to the origin have smaller curvature of K_1. The length between X_1 and X_2 is equal to ΔX which is the same as the horizontal distance between X_3 and X_4. The red line segments represent the increment of the spanwise range that sampling can reach the surface waves as the sample moves in streamwise direction with a distance of ΔX. Clearly, the surface wave with smaller curvature has an increased length. In other words, the surface wave with smaller curvature has a larger wavelength growth ratio.

Validation

In this section, the accuracy of the Welch method in image processing was validated. The validation was carried out based upon the examination of two parameters: wavelength and transition position.

Figure 9a exhibits an image of a ruler, the image intensities of the pixels located on the red line in Fig. 9a were processed.

These image intensities were divided into two parts. In the range ofX = 0–640 pixels, the image intensities were extracted from the background which has no explicit order. The image intensities of X = 640–1090 pixels were based on the ruler image, and the distance between the two adjacent calibrations is equal to 1 mm which corresponds to 11.6 pixels. The length of the window was set as 118 pixels which was decided with the aforementioned method. The distance between every two neighboring samples was set as 33 pixels.

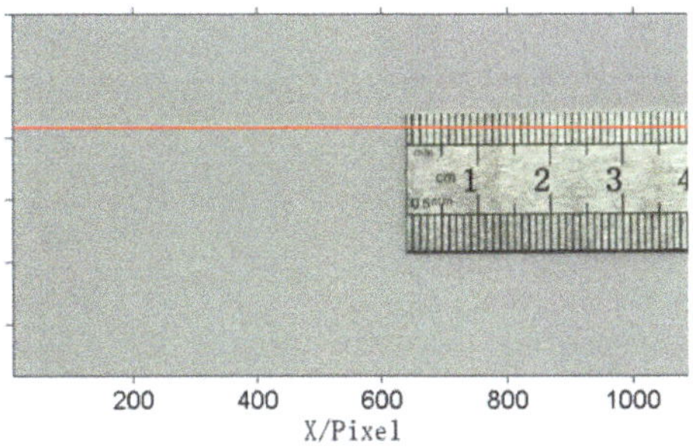

(a)

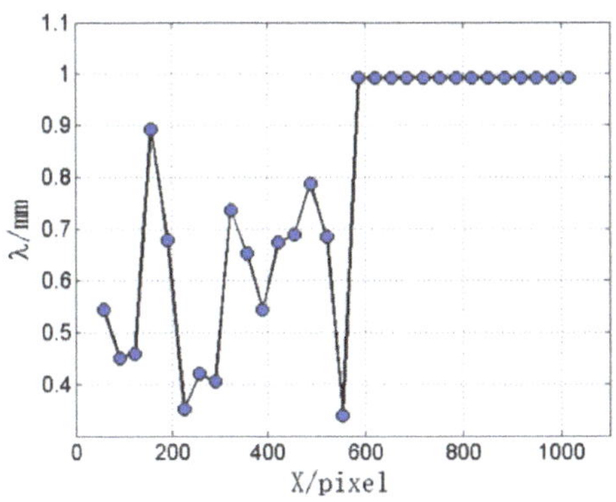

(b)

Figure 9: Validation with a ruler image. a Rule image. b Processing result.

The processing result was presented in Fig. 9b. In the range of X = 0–590 pixels, the wavelengths have no order and fluctuate from 0.3 to 0.9 mm. However, in the range ofX = 590–1090 pixels, the wavelengths are all the same and equal to 0.99 mm. The error of the wavelength measurement is 1 %. At the position of X= 590, wavelength significantly increases and corresponding samples were taken from X = 531–649 pixels. That is to say, the measured transition position is located at X = 649 pixels. The error of transition position measurement is about 1.4 %.

RESULTS AND DISCUSSION

Structures of Liquid Jets

The surface waves of the liquid jets with different Re $_{\delta 2}$ values are presented in Fig. 10. Re $_{\delta 2}$values in Fig. 10 vary from 177.7 to 316.7 and We $_g$ changes from 7.21 to 72.77 accordingly. Based on Lin's theory (Lin and Reitz 1998), the breakup regimes of these jets cover first wind-induced breakup regime, second wind-induced breakup regime, and atomization regime.

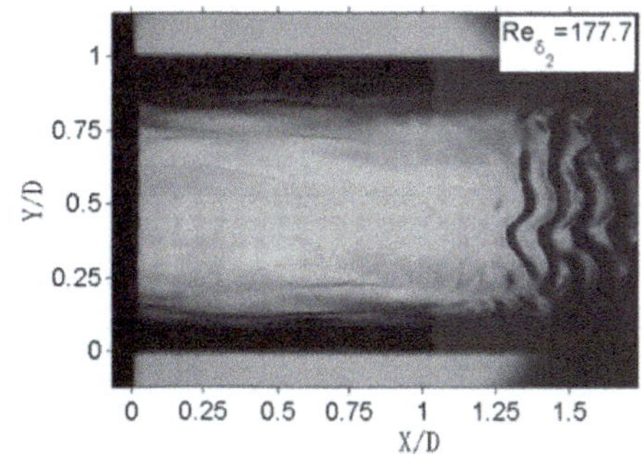

(a)

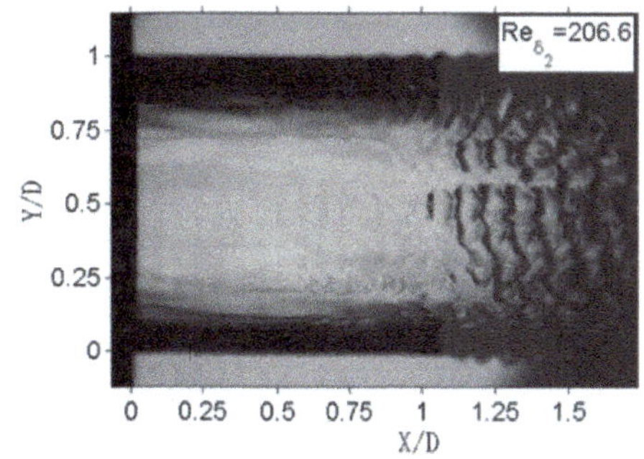

(b)

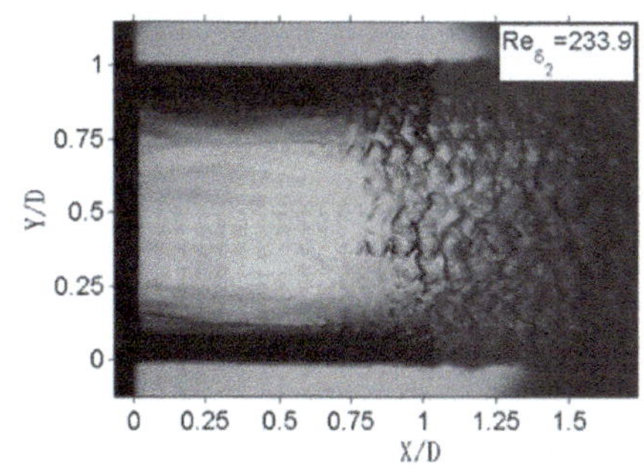

(c)

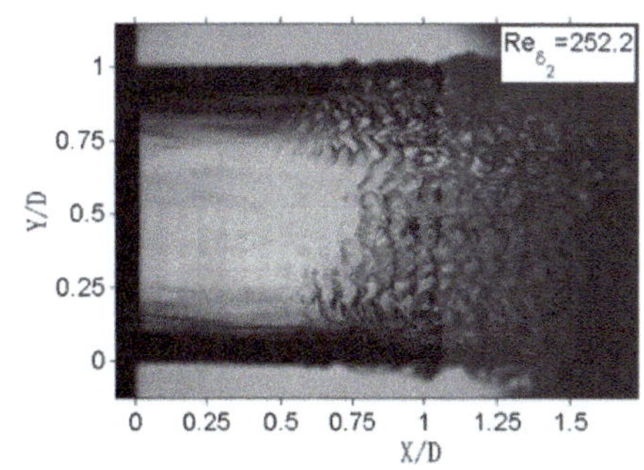

(d)

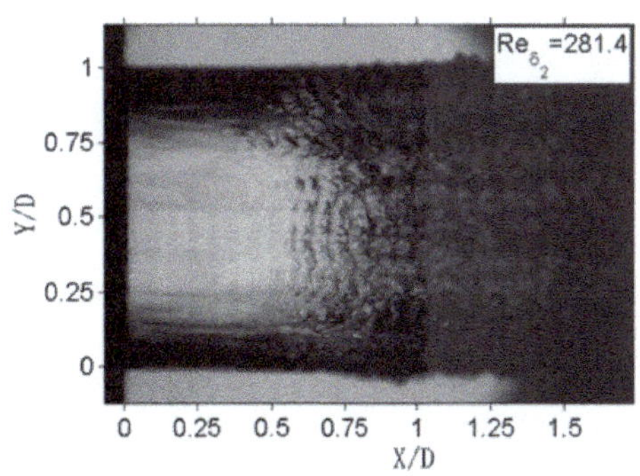

(e)

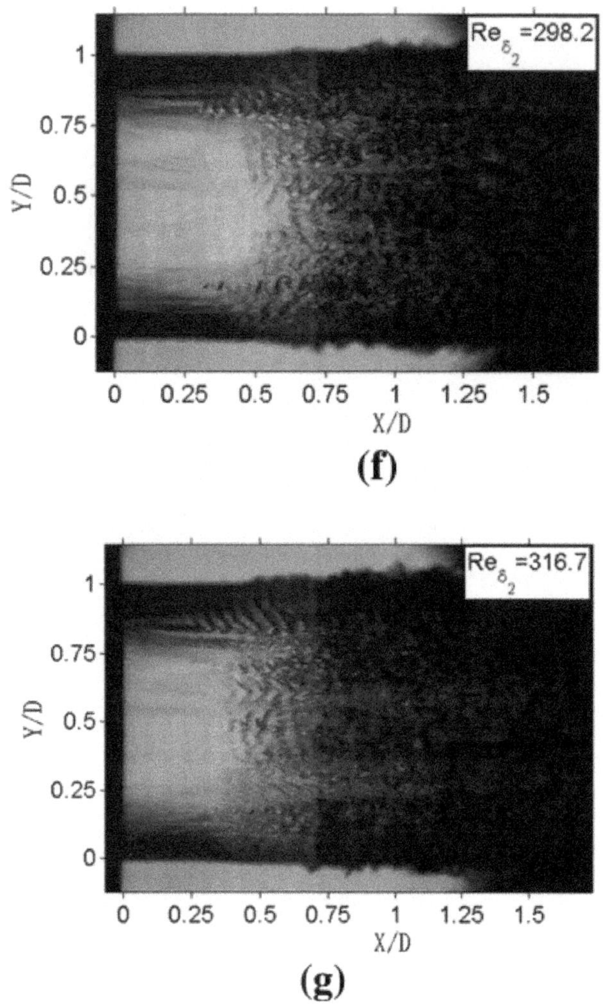

Figure 10: Surface waves of jets with different Re $_{δ2.}$

The jet in Fig. 10a falls into the first wind-induced breakup regime. The jet can be briefly divided into two parts. Firstly, within the streamwise range of X/D = 0–1.25, it has a nearly smooth surface. The upper periphery and lower periphery of the jet are straight lines. The diameter of the jet has no change in this part. Here the parts with smooth surface are defined as the laminar section. Secondly, at the streamwise position of X/D = 1.25, there is a group of structures featured by distinct waves. Along the spanwise direction, the configuration of these surface waves is apparently of sine-curve type, and the distance between crests and troughs is about a quarter of the diameter of the jet stream. Along the streamwise direction, these surface waves have remarkable periodicity: (1) the surface waves have the same configuration; (2) the distances between two adjacent surface waves are nearly all the same and equal to 0.12 D. The parts that have periodic surface waves are defined as the instability section.

The jets in Fig. 10b–d are compatible with the second wind-induced breakup regime. Similar to Fig. 10a, the jet of Fig. 10b can also be divided into laminar and instability sections. However, the instability section in Fig. 10b is different from that shown in Fig. 10a. Firstly, the surface waves in Fig. 10b arrive at the streamwise position of X/D = 1 approaching further to the nozzle exit. Secondly, the distance between adjacent surface waves is about 0.1 D, which is smaller than that shown in Fig. 10a. Thirdly, along the spanwise direction, surface waves in Fig. 10b are also in the shape of the sine curves, but the scales of these sine curves are smaller than its counterpart in Fig. 10a.

The surface waves in Fig. 10c are significantly different from the surface waves in Fig. 10a, b. On one hand, in the spanwise direction, the surface waves in Fig. 10c look like fish skin instead of sine curves. On the other hand, for different spanwise positions, the distances between two adjacent surface waves are different. For example, at the spanwise position of Y = 0.4, the distance is about 0.1 D, however, at the spanwise position of Y/D = 0.6, the distance is 0.07 D. In addition, only within the streamwise range of X/D = 0.75–1.25,the surface waves have periodicity. In the part downstream of X/D = 1.25, the interaction of the surface waves with different scales makes the structure of the surface waves more complex and unordered. The parts that only have unordered surface waves are defined as the turbulence section.

As for Fig. 10d, the streamwise positions at which surface waves appear are different at different spanwise positions. At the spanwise position of Y/D = 0.5, the surface waves arise at the streamwise position of X/D = 0.75. However, at the spanwise positions of Y/D = 0.25 andY/D = 0.75, the surface waves come out at the streamwise position of X/D = 0.6.

The jets in Fig. 10e–g are in the atomization regime. For this regime, transition from laminar to turbulence is accelerated. First of all, the distance between adjacent surface waves in Fig. 10e is about 0.06 D, which is only the half of the corresponding value for the jet of the first wind-induced breakup regime. Secondly, the lengths of the laminar sections of the jets in Fig. 10e–g are less than 0.5 D, which are also smaller than those of the first wind-induced breakup regime. Moreover, for Fig. 10f–g, no instability sections are perceived and the jet surface transforms from the laminar section to turbulence section directly.

Wavelengths

The measured wavelengths of different breakup regimes are presented in Fig. 11.

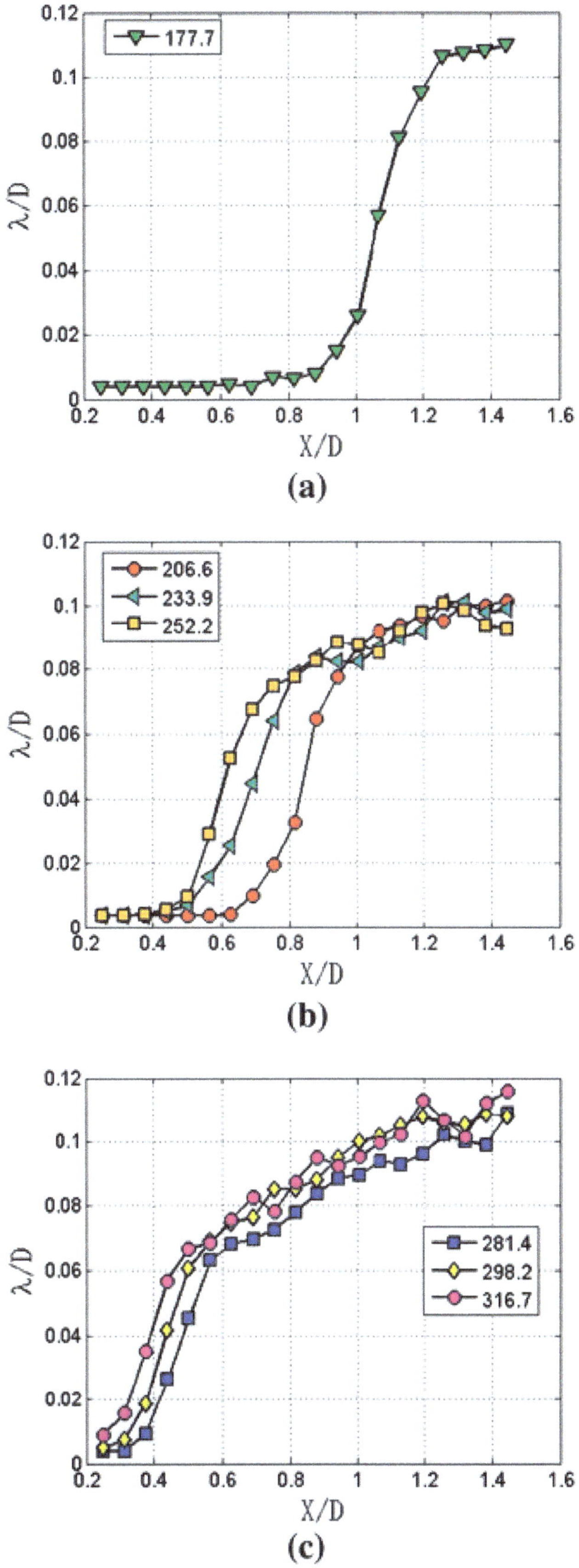

Figure 11: Wavelengths of different breakup regimes: a first wind-induced breakup regime, bsecond wind-induced breakup regime, c atomization regime.

The laminar section of the jet under the first wind-introduced breakup regime has the longest length of 0.75 D. In the transition section, the wavelengths went up from 0.004 D to 0.106 Dwith a slope of 0.23. The length of the transition section is 0.5 D. The instability section starts at the streamwise position of X/D = 1.2. The wavelengths of this section have a slight increase from 0.106 D to 0.11 D with a relatively small slope of 0.02. The wavelengths of this breakup regime are comparable to the diameter of the nozzle.

In the second wind-induced breakup regime, the jets have short lengths of laminar section. With the increase of Reynolds number, the lengths of laminar sections decrease from 0.628 D to 0.376 D. The transition sections of these three jets have similar trends; the length and the slope of these transition sections are 0.4 D and 0.23, respectively. The instability sections of these jets are nearly overlapped, and the slope of these instability sections is 0.04 which is twice the value of the slope of first wind-introduced breakup regime. The wavelengths of the instability sections range from 0.08 D to 0.1 D. At the streamwise position of X/D = 1.3, the wavelengths begin to decline. According to this, it is concluded that the inception of turbulence sections occurs at this position.

Under the atomization regime, the lengths of the laminar sections are further reduced. Particularly, with $Re_{\delta 2}$ of 316.7, the jet has no laminar section within the measurement range, which means the length of the laminar section is less than 0.5 D. The length of the transition section drops to 0.3 D, but the slope is still equal to 0.23. The instability sections range fromX/D = 0.6–1.2, and the wavelengths of instability sections rise from 0.06 D to 0.08 D with a slope of 0.06. Clearly, the growth rate of wavelength of the instability section is the largest under the atomization regime.

CONCLUSIONS

A visualization experimental method is designed to capture the surface waves of high-speed liquid jet. Two spectral methods were discussed and the Welch method was used to process the captured jet images. The main conclusions are as follows.

- Based on surface morphology and the obtained wavelengths, the jet stream near nozzle exit is divided into four sections: laminar, transition, instability, and turbulence sections. The jet under the atomization breakup regime has the shortest lengths of laminar section and transition section of 0.4 D and 0.3 D, respectively, but the longest length of instability section of 0.6 D. All the transition section slopes of the three breakup regimes are 0.23.
- In the first wind-introduced breakup regime, the lengths of surface waves of the jet are about 0.11 D. However, the wavelengths of the jet range from 0.08 D to 0.1 Dunder the second wind-introduced breakup regime. Moreover, the jet has a larger scale of wavelengths ranging from 0.06 D to 0.11 D under the atomization breakup regime.
- The slope of instability section depends on breakup regime. Under the atomization breakup regime, the slope is 0.06 which is 1.5 times that of the second wind-introduced breakup regime and three times that of the first wind-introduced breakup regime.

ACKNOWLEDGMENTS

The authors gratefully acknowledge the financial support of National Natural Science Foundation of China (51176065 and 51380246).

REFERENCES

1. Aliseda A, Hopfinger EJ, Lasheras JC, Kremer DM, Berchielli A, Connolly EK (2008) Atomization of viscous and non-newtonian liquids by a coaxial, high-speed gas jet. Experiments and droplet size modeling [J]. Int J Multiph Flow 34(2):161–175
2. Bian Shiyao, Ceccio Steven L, Driscoll James F (2010) A dual-camera cinematographic PIV measurement system at kilohertz frame rate for high-speed, unsteady flows [J]. Exp Fluids 48(3):487–495
3. Blaisot JB, Yon J (2005) Droplet size and morphology characterization for dense sprays by image processing: application to diesel spray. Exp Fluids 39:977–994
4. Briggs TE, Malave A, Farrell PV (2006) Dual-wavelength absorption imaging of diesel sprays. In: Proceedings of ICLASS 2006, Kyoto, Japan
5. Chigier N, Reitz RD (1996) Regimes of jet breakup and breakup mechanisms (physical aspects)[J]. In: Kuo KK (ed) Recent advances in spray combustion: spray atomization and drop burning phenomena, vol 1. AIAA, Reston, pp 109–135
6. Delacourt E, Desmet B, Besson B (2005) Characterisation of very high pressure diesel sprays using digital imaging techniques. Fuel 84:859–867
7. Faeth GM, Hsiang LP, Wu PK (1995) Structure and breakup properties of sprays. Int J Multiph Flow 21:99–127
8. Fuster D, Bagué A, Boeck T (2009) Simulation of primary atomization with an octree adaptive mesh refinement and VOF method[J]. Int J Multiph Flow 35(6):550–565
9. Hori Toshio, Sakakibara Jun (2004) High-speed scanning stereoscopic PIV for 3D vorticity measurement in liquids [J]. Meas Sci Technol 15(6):1067–1078
10. Hoyt JW, Taylor JJ (1977a) Turbulence structure in a water jet discharging in air [J]. Phys Fluids 20(10):253–257
11. Hoyt JW, Taylor JJ (1977b) Waves on water jets [J]. J Fluid Mech 83(1):119–127
12. Lefebvre AH (1989) Atomization and sprays [M]. Hemisphere Publishing Corporation, New York
13. Li H, Collicott SH (2006) Visualisation of cavitation in high-pressure diesel fuel injector orifices. At Sprays 16:875–886
14. Lin SP, Reitz RD (1998) Drop and spray formation from a liquid jet [J]. Annu Rev Fluid Mech 30:85–105
15. Mayer WOH (1994) Coaxial atomization of a round liquid jet in a high speed gas stream: a phenomenological study [J]. Exp Fluids 16(6):401–410
16. Mayer WOH, Branam R (2004) Atomization characteristics on the surface of a round liquid jet [J]. Exp Fluids 36(4):528–539
17. Ménard T, Tanguy S, Berlemont A (2007) Coupling level set/VOF/ghost fluid methods: validation and application to 3D simulation of the primary break-up of a liquid jet[J]. Int J Multiph Flow 33(5):510–524
18. Mulgrew B, Grant P, Thompson J (2002) Digital signal processing—concepts and applications [M], Palgrave Macmillan, vol 9, 2nd revised edn
19. Nakagawa H, Kamata S, Hori T, Okumura N, Senda J, Fujimoto HG (2006) Novel photographic imaging method for diesel spray structure with new lens and large sized film system. In: Proceedings of ICLASS 2006, Kyoto, Japan
20. Osta AR, Lee J, Sallam KA (2012) Study of the effects of the injector length/diameter ratio on the surface properties of turbulent liquid jets in still air using X-ray imaging [J]. Int J Multiph Flow 38(1):87–98
21. Paciaroni M, Linne M, Hall T, Delplanque JP, Praker T (2006) Single-shot two-dimensional ballistic imaging of the liquid core in an atomizing spray. At Sprays 16:51–69
22. Park H (2005) Flow characteristics of viscous high-speed jets in axial/swirl injectors, Ph.D. dissertation (Purdue University)
23. Portillo JE (2008) Nonparallel analysis and measurement of instability waves in a high speed liquid jet, Ph.D. dissertation (Purdue University)
24. Sallam KA, Dai Z, Faeth GM (2002) Liquid breakup at the surface of turbulent round liquid jets in still gases [J]. Int J Multiph Flow 28(3):427–449
25. Shinjo J, Umemura A (2010) Simulation of liquid jet primary breakup: dynamics of ligament and droplet formation[J]. Int J Multiph Flow 36(7):513–532
26. Shinjo J, Umemura A (2011) Surface instability and primary atomization characteristics of straight liquid jet sprays[J]. Int J Multiph Flow 37(10):1294–1304
27. Syuto T, Fujisawa N, Takasugi T, Yamagata T (2010) Flow visualization and scanning PIV measurement of three-dimensional structure in near field of strongly buoyant jet [J]. J Vis 13(3):203–211
28. Wu PK, Faeth GM (1993) Aerodynamic effects on primary breakup of turbulent liquids. At Sprays 3:265–289
29. Wu PK, Faeth GM (1995) Onset and end of drop formation along the surface of turbulent liquid jets in still gases. Phys Fluids 7:2915–2917
30. Wu PK, Tseng LK, Faeth GM (1992) Primary breakup in gas/liquid mixing layers for turbulent liquids. At Sprays 2:295–317
31. Wu PK, Mirandat RF, Faeth GM (1995) Effects of initial flow conditions on primary breakup of nonturbulent and turbulent liquid jets [J]. AIAA 5(2):175–196
32. Yon J, Blaisot JB, Ledoux M (2003) Unusual laser-sheet tomography coupled with backlight imaging configurations to study the diesel jet structure at the nozzle outlet for high injection pressures. J Flow Vis Image Process 9:1–20
33. Yoon SS, Heister SD (2003) Categorizing linear theories for atomizing round jets [J]. At Sprays 13(5):499–516

CHAPTER 9

PRESSURE-SENSITIVE PAINT TECHNIQUE FOR SURFACE PRESSURE MEASUREMENTS IN A LOW-DENSITY WIND TUNNEL

M. Anyoji[1], D. Numata[2], H. Nagai[2], and K. Asai[2]

[1]Institute of Space and Astronautical Science, Japan Aerospace Exploration Agency, 6-1-1 Yoshinodai, Chuo-Ku, Sagamihara 252-5210, Japan

[2]Department of Aerospace Engineering, Tohoku University, 6-6-1 Aoba, Aoba-Ku, Sendai, Japan

ABSTRACT

A low-density wind tunnel called the Mars wind tunnel, has been developed at Tohoku University that can produce a high subsonic flow at low pressures for aerodynamic measurements of low-Reynolds-number aircraft wings aimed at developing aircraft applicable to the atmosphere on the planet Mars. Accurate surface pressure measurements on the wing are essential for analysis of not only aerodynamic performance, including lift and drag, but also the flow fields around the wing. This paper presents a surface pressure measurement technique using pressure-sensitive paint (PSP) applicable for Mars wind tunnel tests under low-pressure conditions. The results show that a PSP composed of palladium tetra(pentafluorophenyl) porphyrin (PdTFPP) and poly[1-(trimethylsilyl)-propyne] [poly(TMSP)] exhibits a high-pressure sensitivity at pressures as low as 1 kPa, and the absolute values of the static pressures measured by the PSP accorded well with the values derived from static pressure sensors used as a reference. A calibration methodology for the non-uniform pressure sensitivity on the test model, including a temperature calibration, is also established. The PSP technique clearly demonstrated pressure sensitivity over a distinctive low-pressure region inside a leading edge separation bubble on a flat plate at low Reynolds numbers.

INTRODUCTION

Aircraft applicable to the atmosphere on the planet Mars, or Mars airplanes, have been proposed and studied as a refreshing approach to explore the surface of the planet Mars (Guynn et al. 2003; Tanaka et al. 2005). Aircraft on Mars could cover a wide observation area and obtain unique scientific data from a few kilometers above the surface. However, conventional aircraft design criteria cannot be directly applied to the design of a Mars airplane because the Martian atmosphere is extremely different from that on the Earth. The atmospheric mean pressure is approximately only 0.7 kPa. Consequently, the flight condition of a Mars airplane is characterized by a low-Reynolds-number flow ($Re = 10^3 - 10^4$). The flow around the wings at such low Reynolds numbers easily separates, and a separation bubble forms after the separated shear layer reattaches to the wing surface. These separation characteristics cause nonlinear aerodynamic performance and disrupt the design of airfoils. Additionally, it is conceivable that a Mars airplane would fly at relatively high speed to produce sufficient lift to sustain its weight. Hence the effect of compressibility at low Reynolds number is also a critical element for the optimal design of the Mars airplane wing.

We have developed a low-density wind tunnel known as the Mars wind tunnel (MWT) at Tohoku University, as shown in Fig. 1, which is capable of simulating Martian atmospheric

Citation: M. Anyoji, D. Numata, H. Nagai, and K. Asai, Pressure-sensitive paint technique for surface pressure measurements in a low-density wind tunnel, DOI 10.1007/s12650-014-0239-9.

flight conditions, where a Reynolds number in the range from 10^3 to 10^5 and a Mach number higher than 0.7 can be attained (Anyoji et al. 2010, 2011). The most significant characteristic of this tunnel is that the Reynolds number effect and the Mach number effect on the aerodynamic performance can be analyzed independently.

Figure 1: Mars wind tunnel (MWT) at Tohoku University.

Measuring the pressure distribution on airfoils under low-pressure conditions to understand the flow fields around airfoils is crucial because the separation characteristics, i.e., separation, transition, and reattachment, appear as a distinctive pressure-distribution pattern (Tani 1964; O'Meara and Mueller 1987; Gerakopulos 2010). However, it is well understood that under low-pressure conditions, a thin airfoil, which is difficult to equip with a conventional pressure sensor due to limitations of model construction, demonstrates higher aerodynamic performance than that of a thick airfoil (Oyama and Fujii 2006; Okamoto et al. 1996). In contrast, the pressure-sensitive paint (PSP) technique, which is a coated optical sensor, is applicable to thin airfoil models (Liu and Sullivan 2004).

The purpose of this study is to develop the PSP technique for quantitative surface-pressure distribution measurements in the MWT. The pressure distribution measurement using PSP is based on oxygen quenching of luminescent molecules. A typical PSP is composed of a luminescent molecule and a polymer binder which is permeable to oxygen. Poly[1-(trimethylsilyl)-propyne] [poly(TMSP)], which was first synthesized by Masuda et al. (1983), is a glassy material with a large free volume and has an extremely high oxygen permeability relative to all existing polymers. Mori et al. (2004) investigated the fundamental properties of three typical types of PSPs [platinum octaethylporphyrin (PtOEP), palladium tetra(pentafluorophenyl) porphyrin (PdTFPP), and platinumtetrakis (pentafluorophenyl) porphyrin (PtTFPP)] bound by poly(TMSP) in a pressure range below 14 kPa. The investigation results showed that PdTFPP exhibits high oxygen quenching and has the highest pressure sensitivity among the three PSPs. In this study, samples of PSP composed of PdTFPP and poly(TMSP) were tested using a calibration chamber and the fundamental properties of the PSP such as pressure sensitivity and photodegradation were evaluated at pressures less than 10 kPa. Furthermore, to demonstrate the applicability of the PSP for pressure measurements in the MWT, the pressure distribution on a blunt (flat-headed), flat-plate airfoil was measured in the Reynolds number range from 3.4×10^3 to 3.2×10^4, and the flow field around the airfoil was evaluated.

PRESSURE-SENSITIVE PAINT (PSP)

Stern–Volmer Equation

PSP is a coating-type sensor consisting of luminescent molecules and a binder. When illuminated with light of an appropriate wavelength, the luminescent molecules in the PSP are elevated to an excited state. The excited molecules return to the ground state through several photochemical mechanisms: luminescence, thermal deactivation, and oxygen quenching. The principle of PSP is based on oxygen quenching. In the presence of oxygen molecules, the energy of the excited molecules is transferred to the oxygen molecules and no luminescence is emitted. As a result, the luminescence intensity decreases with increasing oxygen concentration.

The luminescence quantum yield φ of PSP is expressed as the ratio of the luminescence intensityI to the absorption intensity I_a in accordance with the following equation (Liu 1997):

$$\phi = \frac{I}{I_a} = \frac{k_L}{k_L + k_D + k_q[O_2]}, \quad (1)$$

where k_L is the rate constant for the luminescence and k_D is the rate constant for the radiationless deactivation. The rate constant for oxygen quenching and the concentration of oxygen are expressed by k_q and $[O_2]$, respectively. The ratio of the luminescence intensity I to that in the absence of oxygen I_0 is given by

$$\frac{I_0}{I} = \frac{k_L + k_D + k_q[O_2]}{k_L + k_D} = 1 + \frac{k_q[O_2]}{k_L + k_D} = 1 + k_q[O_2]\tau_0, \quad (2)$$

where $\tau_0 = 1/(k_L + k_D)$ is the luminescent lifetime in the absence of oxygen molecules. According to Henry's law, the concentration of oxygen in a polymer binder is proportional to the partial pressure of oxygen P_{O_2} or air pressure P:

$$[O_2] = S(T) \cdot P_{O_2} = S(T) \cdot \phi_{O_2} \cdot P. \quad (3)$$

Here, T is the temperature, S is the oxygen solubility in the polymer binder layer, and ϕ_{O_2} is the mole fraction of oxygen in the test gas. For the present study, the mole fraction of oxygen ϕ_{O_2} is 21 %, and the oxygen solubility in the polymer binder layer S is a function of temperature. Hence, Eq. (2) can be put in the following form, known as the Stern–Volmer relation:

$$\frac{I_0}{I} = 1 + K_{SV}(T) \cdot P, \quad (4)$$

where $K_{SV}(T)$ is the Stern–Volmer constant.

As a practical issue, it is difficult to obtain I_0 in the zero-oxygen condition. Instead of I_0, a reference luminescent-intensity I_{ref} at a known reference pressure P_{ref} is typically used. As such, Eq. (4) is modified as

$$\frac{I_{ref}}{I} = A(T) + B(T)\frac{P}{P_{ref}}, \tag{5}$$

where A (T) and B (T) are temperature-dependent calibration coefficients.

Temperature Dependence of Luminescence Intensity

The temperature dependence of the coefficients in Eq. (5) is attributed to the rate constant for the luminescence k_L, the rate constant for the radiationless deactivation k_D, and the rate constant for oxygen quenching k_q. The luminescence intensity is significantly influenced by k_D and k_q. The rate constant for radiationless deactivation k_D is expressed as the sum of a temperature-independent term k_0 and a temperature-dependent term k_1, as given in Eq. (6) below:

$$k_D = k_0 + k_1 \tag{6}$$

The rate constant k_1 is given by the Arrhenius equation (Liu 1997) in Eq. (7).

$$k_1 = C\exp(-E_A/R_0T) \tag{7}$$

Here, E_A is the Arrhenius activation energy, R_0 is the universal gas constant, and C is a pre-exponential factor. Equation (7) indicates that k_1 increases with increasing temperature, and, thereby, k_D also increases with increasing temperature.

When a polymer is used as a binder, the rate for oxygen quenching k_q is dominated by the diffusion coefficient of the oxygen molecules D_Q in the polymer and given by the Smoluchowski relation (Liu 1997):

$$k_q = 4\pi N_m q D_Q, \tag{8}$$

where N_m is the number of the molecules per millimole, and q is a factor that depends on the quenching mechanism.

The dependence of the diffusion coefficient of the oxygen molecules on temperature is also given by the Arrhenius relation (Liu 1997):

$$D_Q \propto \exp(-E_Q/R_0T), \tag{9}$$

where E_Q is the activation energy for the diffusion of oxygen molecules in the polymer. Equation (9) indicates that D_Q increases with increasing temperature, indicating that k_q increases with increasing temperature, as shown in Eq. (8). Hence, it is apparent from Eq. (1) that the luminescence intensity I decreases with increasing temperature. Although the diffusion coefficient D_Q depends on the polymer employed as a binder, a larger D_Q results in a PSP with a higher pressure sensitivity. Therefore, it is considered that a binder with a larger D_Q will provide for better pressure sensitivity, particularly under low-pressure conditions (Niimi 2005).

Temperature Calibration

In typical wind-tunnel tests, the surface pressure can be calculated from the ratio of luminescence intensity images obtained at the wind-on and wind-off (reference) conditions. The temperature of the working fluid in the wind-on condition increases with time, and this temperature change causes a surface temperature-change on a test model. Because the luminescence intensity of the PSP changes with temperature, it is necessary to compensate for the effect of temperature change during the test. Brown (2000), Bell (2004), and Mitsuo et al. (2005) suggested that a raw image taken immediately after a tunnel shutdown be used as a wind-off image to minimize errors due to the temperature change. In addition, Yamashita (2007) proposed a temperature correction method based on a temperature-correction factor α(T). Using α (T), Eq. (5) can be transformed to the following expression:

$$\frac{I(P_{ref}, T_{ref})}{I(P,T)} = \alpha(T)\cdot\left(A(T) + B(T)\frac{P}{P_{ref}}\right), \tag{10}$$

$$\text{where } \alpha(T) = I(P_{ref}, T_{ref})/I(P_{ref}, T) \tag{11}$$

and T_{ref} is the reference temperature.

In this method, the wind-off data obtained just after wind-tunnel shutdown are used so that the error caused by a spatial distribution of the model temperature can be minimized. In addition, α(T) is calculated using a single-point measurement of the model surface temperature under the following two specific conditions.

- A_{ref}(T) and B_{ref}(T) which are Stern–Volmer coefficients for the case of $T = T_{ref}$ are independent of temperature.
- α (T) is uniform over the test model surface.

The PSP satisfying the first condition is denoted as the ideal PSP (Bell 2004; Gouterman et al.2004), and, under these conditions, the Stern–Volmer relation [Eq. (4)] can be expressed by the following equation.

$$\frac{I(P_{ref}, T_{ref})}{I(P,T)} = \alpha(T)\cdot\left[A_{ref} + B_{ref}\frac{P}{P_{ref}}\right] \tag{12}$$

Equation (12) clarifies that only α (T) is dependent on the temperature of the model surface. This indicates that the effect of temperature change can be corrected even if the temperature is not uniform over the model. The resulting change in pressure ΔP owing to a temperature distribution based on a change in the temperature-correction factor Δα(T) can be evaluated by the following equation.

$$\frac{\Delta\alpha(T)}{\alpha(T)} = B_{ref}\cdot\frac{\Delta P}{P} \tag{13}$$

EXPERIMENTAL SETUP AND CONDITIONS

PSP Formulation

We chose PdTFPP as the sensor molecule and poly(TMSP) as the binder. A PSP composed of PdTFPP and poly(TMSP) is known to have good pressure sensitivity under low-pressure conditions (Niimi et al. 2005; Mori et al. 2006), and thereby, is considered to be applicable to the low-pressure experiment in the MWT (Ono et al. 2010). The composition of the PSP is PdTFPP (4.8 mg), poly(TMSP) (0.16 g), and toluene (20 ml). The absorption and emission peaks are approximately 407 and 670 nm, respectively.

Experimental Setup for Sample Tests

The experimental setup for sample tests is illustrated in Fig. 2. A PSP-coated sample plate made of aluminum was placed in a calibration vacuum chamber where the inner pressure and temperature could be controlled from 0.1 to 105 kPa and from ambient temperature to 213 K, respectively. The PSP was excited by a UV-emitting LED unit with a peak wavelength of 395 nm. A band-pass filter (transmission wavelength 400 ± 50 nm) was placed in front of the light source to remove undesirable near-infrared radiation. The luminescence from the PSP sample was captured by a thermoelectrically cooled 12-bit CCD camera (Hamamatsu C4742-95-12ER) with an optical band-pass filter (transmission wavelength 670 ± 20 nm). The film thicknesses of the PSP membranes used for the temperature dependence, photodegradation, and pressure-sensitivity calibration tests were approximately 1.2, 2.2, and 1.2 μm, respectively.

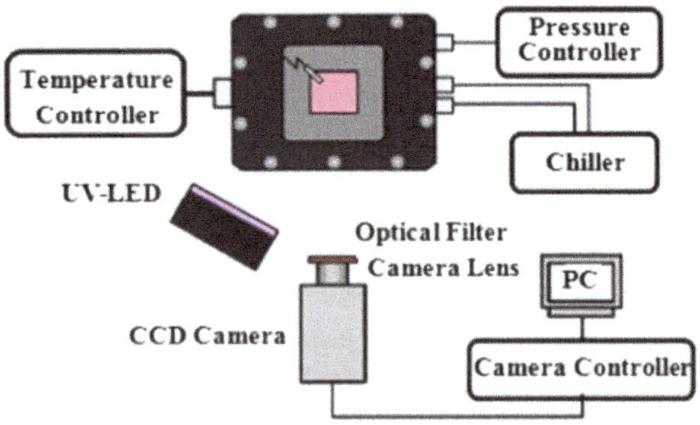

Figure 2: Setup for the calibration tests.

Wind Tunnel and Test Models

The MWT consists of a vacuum chamber, an induction wind tunnel, and a buffer tank. The induction-type wind tunnel is located inside the vacuum chamber where the pressure of the Martian atmosphere can be simulated. The test gas used typically is dry air, but it can be replaced with carbon dioxide. The wind tunnel is driven by multiple-nozzle supersonic ejectors located downstream of the test section. The gas inside the vacuum chamber is exhausted to the buffer tank through a connecting flexible pipe. The pressure in the vacuum chamber is kept constant by controlling a butterfly valve placed in the connecting pipe. For air-mode operation, the MWT can cover a Reynolds number range from 10^3 to 10^5 for airfoil models with the chord length of 50 mm. A Mach number higher than 0.7 can be achieved at a total pressure of 1 kPa. Currently, the MWT is being operated at ambient temperature only.

The test section of the MWT is 100 mm wide and 150 mm high. The upper and lower walls diverge downstream to compensate for the evolution of wall boundary layers. As shown in Fig. 3, an aluminum flat plate with a blunt leading edge was used as a test model. The chord length of the plate was 50 mm, the thickness 2.5 mm, and the span length 100 mm. One thermocouple and five pressure taps were provided on the centerline of the model. The pressure taps were connected to an electric pressure scanner (PSI Model 9116), which has a sufficient response time, through Teflon tubes of 1 mm diameter and about 400 mm length.

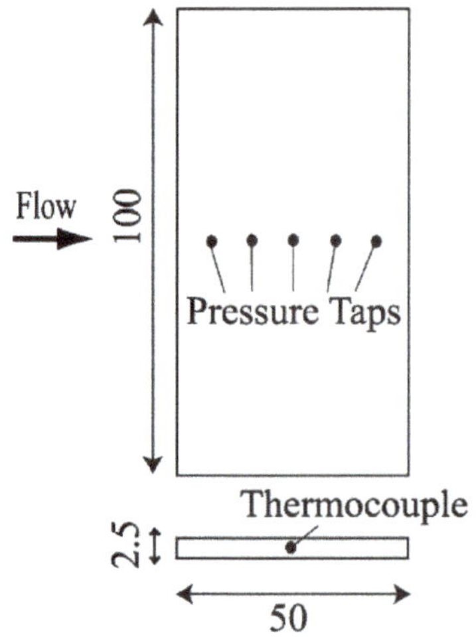

Figure 3: Model coated with the PSP.

Optical Setup for Wind Tunnel Tests

The setup for PSP measurements is shown in Fig. 4. The optical equipment was placed outside the vacuum chamber and measurements were made through an optical window on the top of the vacuum chamber. We used the same LED units and CCD camera as used for the calibration tests. The exposure time and frame rate were set to 359 ms and 3 frames per second, respectively. A F/5.6 camera lens (TAMRON SP23A) and a 560 nm long-pass filter (HOYA O-56) were attached to the camera. The spatial resolution of the PSP measurements was approximately 140 μm. To filter out the background noise, we preliminarily obtained a dark-current image in the wind-off condition, and this image was subtracted from the reference images and the wind-on images.

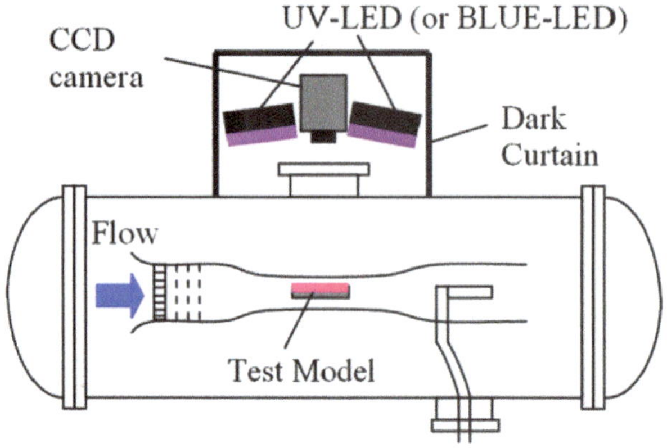

Figure 4: Optical setup for PSP measurements in the MWT.

Experimental Conditions and Method

The pressure sensitivity of the sample used for the calibration tests in the calibration chamber was evaluated in the pressure range from 0.4 to 1 kPa and from 1 to 10 kPa using air as a test gas. The temperature was adjusted from 278 to 293 K.

The total pressure in the wind tunnel was varied from 1 to 10 kPa, and the corresponding chord Reynolds number was from 3.2×10^4 to 3.4×10^4. The Mach number was set at around 0.3 (from 0.29 to 0.31) by changing the supply pressure of the ejectors from 0.2 to 0.65 MPa. The angle of attack was fixed at 0 degrees.

RESULTS AND DISCUSSIONS

Sample Calibration Tests

Sample Tests

The temperature dependence of the pressure sensitivity of PdTFPP/poly(TMSP) is shown in Fig. 5a for the pressure range 0.4 to 1 kPa and Fig. 5b for 1 to 10 kPa, and the reference pressure (P_{ref}) of each range considered was 1 and 10 kPa, respectively. The luminescence intensity was obtained by spatially averaging the intensity over all areas of the sample plate. The pressure sensitivity defined from the slope of I_{ref}/I versus P/P_{ref}, assuming a linear relation, indicates that the pressure sensitivity decreases with decreasing temperature in both Fig. 5a and b, i.e., the luminescence intensity I decreases with increasing temperature. This is attributed to an increase in k_I and D_Q given by Eqs. (7) and (9), respectively, where both k_I and D_Q increase with increasing temperature. Consequently, k_D and k_q increases, and the luminescence intensity thereby decreases [see Eq. (1)]. However, Takada et al. (1985) and Masuda (1988) revealed some unique features of poly(TMSP). Their results show that the activation energy for diffusion is nearly zero, and the gas permeability of poly(TMSP) has negligible temperature dependence. Therefore, we deduce that the dominant factor causing the observed decrease in the luminescence intensity is k_I. In addition, the temperature dependence of the pressure sensitivity in the pressure range 1.0 to 10 kPa is large compared with that from 0.4 to 1 kPa. It is considered that this is due to the rate constant k_q, which depends on both the oxygen pressure and the surface temperature (Niimi et al. 2005).

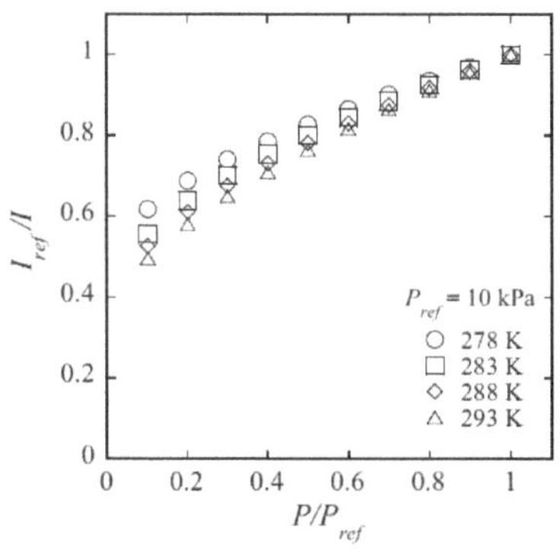

(a) 1.0–10 kPa (P_{ref} = 10 kPa)

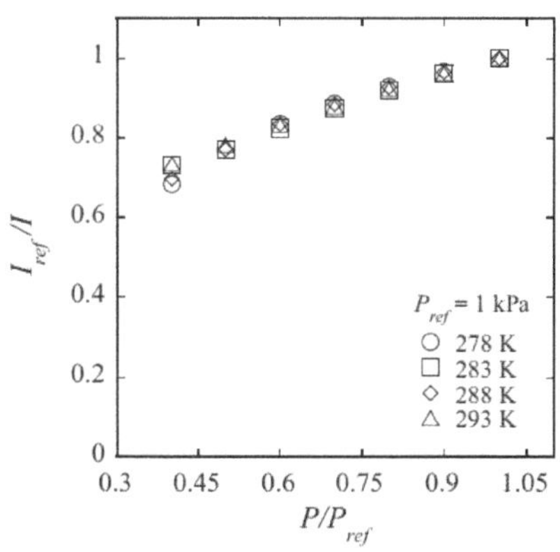

(b) 0.4–1 kPa (P_{ref} = 1 kPa)

Figure 5: Dependence of pressure sensitivity on temperature.

Figure 6 shows the effect of photodegradation due to continuous UV light irradiation. This test was repeated three times and each dot indicates an averaged value. Error bars are shown in Fig. 6, although they are negligibly small. The luminescent intensity decreases approximately 3 % over 30 min. Therefore, the effect of photodegradation is considered negligible in MWT tests because the test time is usually no more than 1 min.

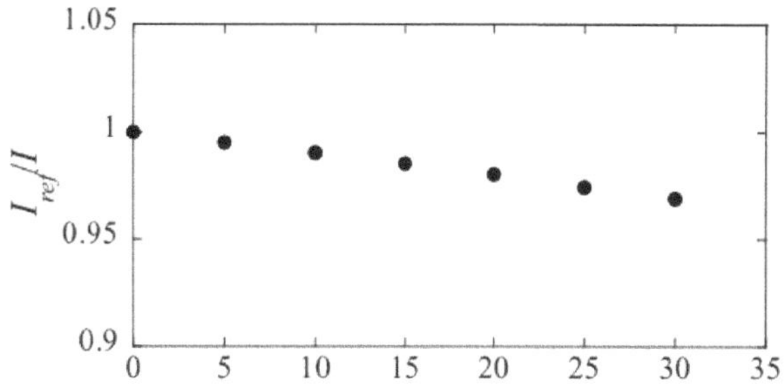

(a) 105 kPa

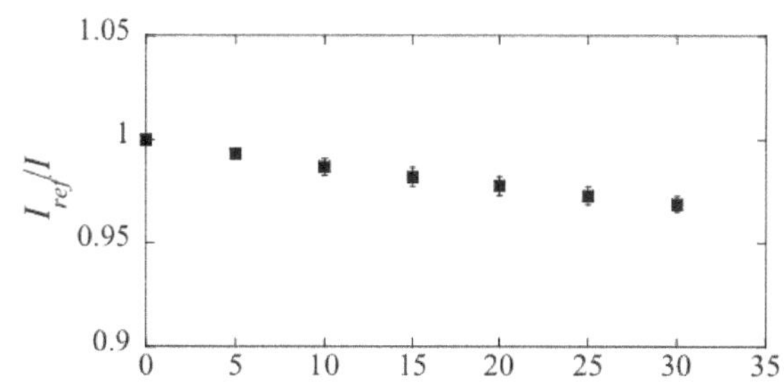

(b) 1kPa

Figure 6: Results of the photodegradation test.

Figure 7 shows the daily variation of the luminescence intensity. The day when the PSP was applied to the model is regarded as the standard. Little change is observed in the slope of I_{ref}/Iversus P/P_{ref}, corresponding to the pressure sensitivity, in the pressure range 1–10 kPa. However, the pressure sensitivity deteriorates in the pressure range 0.4–1 kPa. The variation over 4 days is notable, whereas little change is observed from the fifth day and later. It should be noted that the reference luminescence intensity I_{ref} at the reference pressure P_{ref} is different between Fig. 7a and b. Although the pressure sensitivity shown in Fig. 7b decreases 34 % over 7 days, the degradation of the pressure sensitivity becomes relatively large because the luminescence intensity is compared over the narrow pressure range of 0.4–1 kPa. The decrease in the pressure sensitivity with time is due to the variation of the oxygen permeability of poly(TMSP). Masuda et al. (2013) investigated the time dependence of the gas permeability of poly(TMSP). They concluded that the decrease in the gas permeability of poly(TMSP) is caused by both the decrease of microvoids due to structural relaxation and the adsorption of organic vapors. Reduction of the gas permeability of poly(TMSP) was also investigated by Nagai et al. (2001). Their results revealed the effect of physical aging under vacuum conditions using an oil diffusion pump compared with the vacuum conditions using a molecular turbopump. When poly(TMSP) is stored under vacuum using an oil diffusion pump, it absorbs pump oil vapors. Consequently, the decline in oxygen permeability is caused by contamination of the polymer with the hydrocarbon oil. In our calibration test, we did not use an oil diffusion pump but an oil-sealed rotary pump. Hence, we consider that the effect of contamination by pump oil vapors on the oxygen permeability of poly(TMSP) is negligible in the present study. The luminescence-intensity distribution on the sample plate is shown in Fig. 8. The luminescence intensity on the sample plate is nearly uniform, and a spatial nonuniformity due to the absorption of organic vapors is not observed. From these results, we deduce that the observed decrease in the pressure sensitivity shown in Fig. 7b is primarily caused by structural relaxation with time.

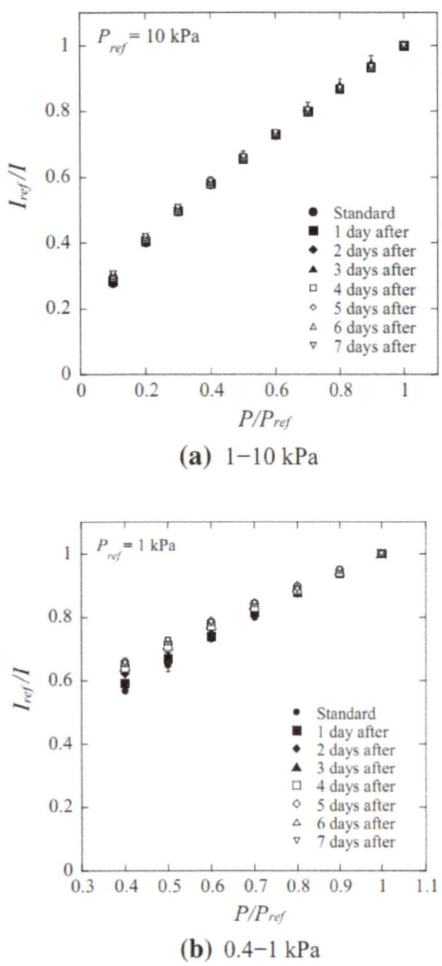

Figure 7: Pressure-sensitivity variation as a factor of time after PSP application to the model.

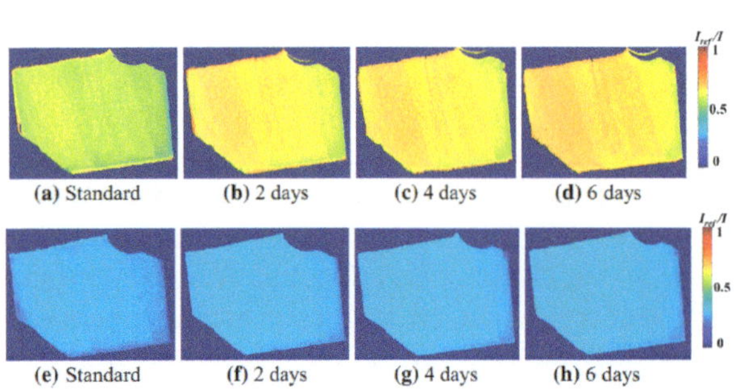

Figure 8: Luminescence-intensity distribution of sample image (a–d: P_{ref} = 1 kPa, with a chamber pressure of 0.4 kPa; e–h: P_{ref} = 10 kPa, with a chamber pressure of 1 kPa).

Calibration in the Wind Tunnel

Figure 9 shows the pressure sensitivity of the PSP on the flat plate in the pressure range 0.4–1 kPa in the wind-tunnel tests compared with the sample test result. The luminescence intensity in the wind-tunnel tests was obtained by locally averaging the intensity over a 100 × 100 pixel area around the center of the test plate. The calibration tests were repeated 10 times in the wind-off condition by evacuating the air from the wind tunnel chamber and operating the ejector to ventilate the test model in each run, with the exception of Run 0 shown in Fig. 9, which indicates the test before the first ventilation. The pressure sensitivity of PdTFPP/poly(TMSP) in the wind tunnel tests is lower in comparison to the pressure sensitivity in these sample tests. The pressure sensitivity in the wind tunnel is nearly half of the pressure sensitivity in the sample test. An oil-sealed rotary pump was used for the sample tests, whereas an oil diffusion pump was utilized for the wind-tunnel tests. When poly(TMSP) is stored under vacuum conditions using an oil diffusion pump, the pressure sensitivity of the PSP decreases due to the contamination of the polymer with oil vapors (Nagai et al. 2001), as described in "Sample tests". Hence, the decline in the pressure sensitivity is attributed to contamination of the polymer by oil vapors that derive from the oil diffusion pump. Figure 10 shows the distribution of the luminescence-intensity ratio calculated from the wind-off images taken before and after the tunnel run. The spatially non-uniform distribution, which is not observed in the sample test using the oil-sealed rotary pump, is also due to oil contamination. Dust included in the test gas may also contribute to contamination of the polymer. However, dust contamination had little effect as almost no variation is observed between Run 0 and Run 10, as shown in Fig. 9. From these results, a calibration method that applies the calibration coefficients in the Stern–Volmer relation to the entire image, the typical a priori calibration, cannot be applicable to the MWT tests.

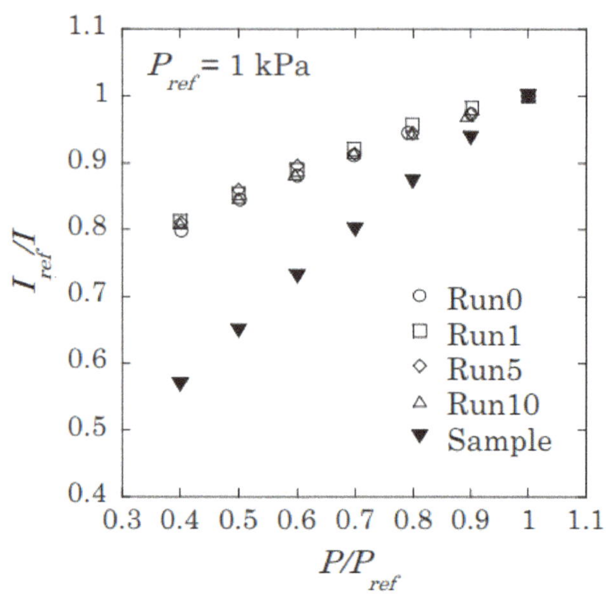

Figure 9: Pressure sensitivity of the sample test and for each wind tunnel test run.

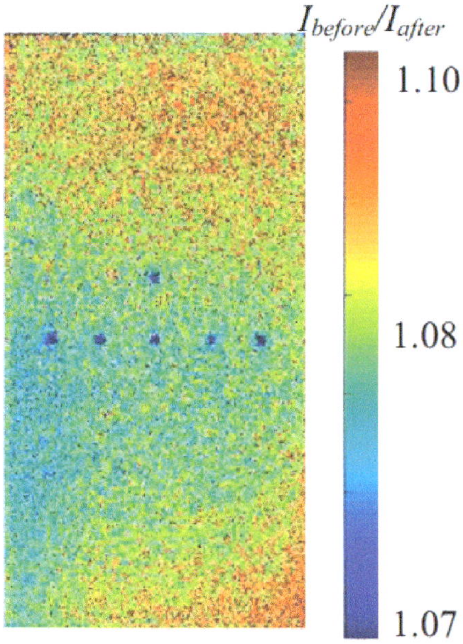

Figure 10: Luminescence intensity distribution without calibration at 1 kPa.

To obtain calibration coefficients using the Stern–Volmer relation, we employed the a priori (direct) model calibration: the PSP-coated model was installed in the test section, and the relation between the luminescence intensity ratio I_{ref}/I and the pressure ratio P/P_{ref} was obtained by varying the pressure inside the wind-tunnel chamber. The temperature change on the test model during the calibration was about 0.18 K at maximum over the entire pressure range from 1 to 10 kPa. As shown in Fig. 5a, the effect of this temperature change on the pressure sensitivity can be considered negligible.

In this method, the calibration coefficients are obtained for each pixel of the image of the model using the direct model calibration method. If a common calibration equation is applied to all pixels, the nonuniformity in the pressure ratio P_{after}/P_{before} distribution calculated from the wind-off images taken before and after the tunnel run is observed, as shown in Fig. 11a. In contrast, the nonuniformity can be considerably canceled when the calibration equation obtained at each 3 × 3 pixel area is applied to the appropriate pixel area. Hence, we consider that pixel-based calibration is an appropriate method for the MWT tests. The following results are discussed based on the pixel calibration method.

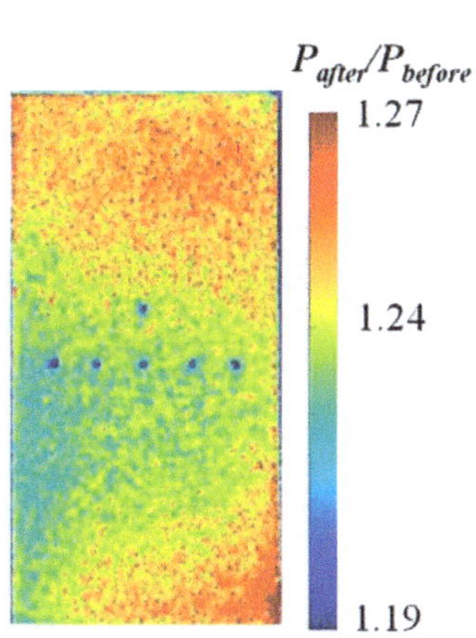

(a) A single common calibration equation

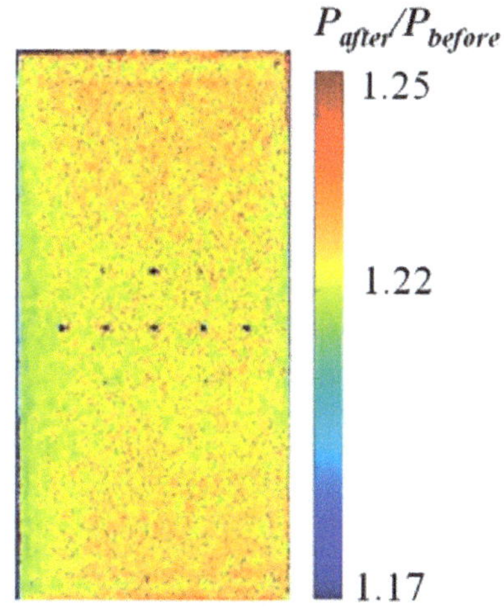

(b) 3 × 3 pixel calibration equation

Figure 11: Pressure/ratio distribution in wind-off condition at 1 kPa.

The temperature change on the test plate during the test time is 0.02 and 1.04 K at chamber pressures of 1 and 10 kPa, respectively. The effects of the temperature changes on the pressure sensitivity are 0.482 and 2.15 %/K at 1 and 10 kPa, respectively, indicating that the variation of the pressure coefficient C_p due to the temperature change is $\Delta C_p = 0.0045$ at 1 kPa and $\Delta C_p = 0.67$ at 10 kPa. The pressure coefficient is defined as the following equation:

$$C_p = \frac{p - p_\infty}{\frac{1}{2}\rho U^2}, \tag{14}$$

where p is the local static pressure, p_∞ is the main-stream static pressure, ρ is the density of the main stream, and U is the main-stream velocity. The variation ΔC_p can be minimized to within 0.12 at the most using the temperature calibration involving α (T) and the reference images taken immediately after the tunnel shutdown. Furthermore, ΔC_p eventually reduces to within 0.05 by shifting the PSP pressure level to the pressure measured by the static pressure tube, which is called in situ calibration.

Figure 12 shows wind-on images at the angle of attack of 0° and the C_p distributions along the centerline of the panel for total pressures of 10 kPa (Re = 3.2 × 10^4) in (a) and 1 kPa (Re = 3.4 × 10^3) in (b). The wind-on image was obtained by averaging eight images and was normalized by the wind-off image. The pressure distribution results with and without both temperature correction and in situ calibration are compared in the right-hand graphs of Fig. 12a, b, for total pressures of 10 kPa (Re = 3.2 × 10^4) and 1 kPa (Re = 3.4 × 10^3), respectively.

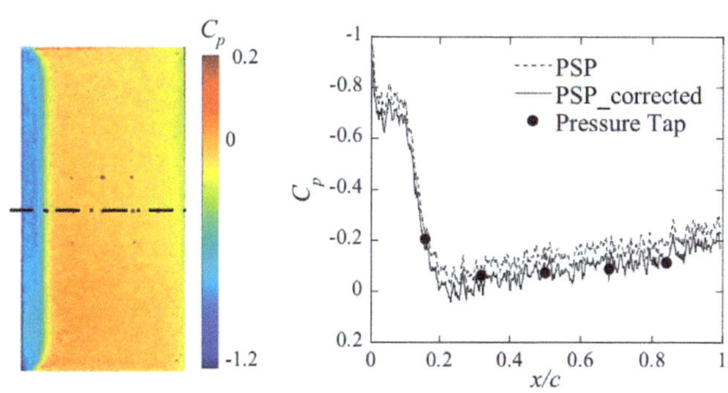

(a) Re =3.2 × 10^4

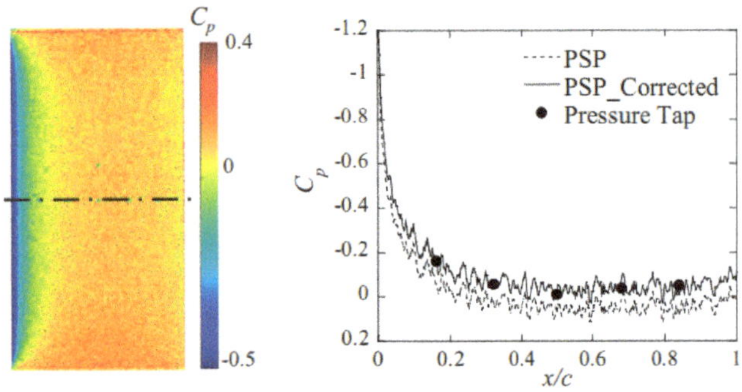

(b) $Re = 3.4 \times 10^3$

Figure 12: C_p distribution on the centerline of the test model at an angle of attack of 0° in the wind-on condition.

In such a low-Reynolds-number flow around a flat plate with a blunt leading edge, flow separates at the leading edge and reattaches to the surface after transition. Then, a laminar separation bubble forms between the separation and reattachment locations (Ota 1976). The negative pressure regions around the leading edge observed in Fig. 12 indicate the presence of the laminar separation bubble. The transition location can be identified as the point where the surface pressure begins to rapidly recover (Tani 1964). O'Meara and Mueller (1987) suggested that the reattachment location can be defined as the location downstream of the transition point where a rapid decrease in the rate of the pressure recovery is observed. On the basis of this approach, Gerakopulos et al. (2010) proposed that the reattachment point was estimated as the location of the local minimum in the second derivative of the polynomial fit. In accordance with these criteria, the transition point can be estimated at around $x/c = 0.1$ at $Re = 3.2 \times 10^4$. However, no rapid increase in the C_p distribution at $Re = 3.4 \times 10^2$ is observed in Fig. 12b, indicating that the separated shear layer does not undergo a laminar-to-turbulent transition. The reattachment locations are estimated at approximately $x/c = 0.22$ at $Re = 3.2 \times 10^4$ and$x/c = 0.21$ at $Re = 3.4 \times 10^3$.

Tani et al. (1961) conducted surface pressure measurements for the flow over a backward-facing step. Their results showed that the separated flow at the corner does not undertake a transition and reattach in a laminar state when the step height is very small, and that the pressure on the surface slowly recovers without a steep pressure recovery due to a laminar-to-turbulent transition. The C_p distribution shown in Fig. 12b reveals a feature very similar to the moderate pressure recovery in the step flow observed by Tani et al. Sasaki and Kiya (1991) investigated a separation bubble on a flat plate using a water tunnel and concluded that the separated shear layer is still laminar at the reattachment point based on visualization results over $2.0 \times 10^3 < Re < 6.0 \times 10^3$. These past results support our results and explanation, and it can be said that this PSP measurement technique can quantitatively and qualitatively capture fluid physics phenomena at low Reynolds numbers under low-pressure conditions.

CONCLUSION

A pressure-sensitive paint technique has been developed for surface pressure measurements at low Reynolds number in the Mars wind tunnel at Tohoku University. Sample tests were conducted to evaluate the characteristics of the PSP. A blunt, flat-plate model was tested in the MWT to assess the effectiveness of the PSP technique. A PSP consisting of PdTFPP and poly(TMSP) exhibits high-pressure sensitivity at low pressures and is suitable for use in low Reynolds number testing in the MWT. It was determined that the pressure sensitivity of the PSP is not uniform over the model surface and decreases gradually with time. These factors can be canceled by conducting a pixel-by-pixel calibration in the tunnel. The accuracy of PSP measurements can be improved by using the wind-off image obtained just after the tunnel run and by applying a temperature correction. The PSP data arc in good quantitative agreement with pressure tap data, and we succeeded in quantitatively and qualitatively measuring characteristic fluid phenomena at low Reynolds numbers such as a leading edge separation bubble.

ACKNOWLEDGMENTS

This work was partially supported by KAKENHI (2056081). We would like to express our sincere thanks to Tadashi Ono, who graduated from Tohoku University, and Daisuke Sasaki, who is a current student at Tohoku University, for this research.

REFERENCES

1. Anyoji M, Ida S, Nose K, Numata D, Nagai H, and Asai K (2010) Characteristics of the Mars wind tunnel at Tohoku University in CO_2 operation mode. The 49th AIAA Aerospace Sciences Meeting, Orlando, Florida. AIAA 2010-1490
2. Anyoji M, Nose K, Ida S, Numata D, Nagai H, Asai K (2011) Development of a low-density wind tunnel for simulating martian atmospheric flight. Trans Jpn Soc Sp Sci 9:21–27
3. Bell J H (2004) Applications of pressure-sensitive paint to testing at very low flow speeds. 42nd AIAA Aerospace Sciences Meeting and Exhibit, Reno, Nevada AIAA 2004-878
4. Brown O (2000) Low-speed pressure measurements using a luminescent coating system. Ph.D. thesis, Stanford University
5. Gerakopulos R, Boutilier M S H, and Yarusevych S (2010) Aerodynamic characterization of a NACA 0018 airfoil at low Reynolds numbers. The 40th Fluid Dynamics Conference and Exhibit, Chicago, Illinois. AIAA 2010-4629
6. Gouterman M, Callis J, Dalton L, Khalil G, Mebarki Y, Cooper KR, Grenier M (2004) Dual luminophore pressure-sensitive paint: III. application to automotive model testing. Meas Sci Tech 15:1986–1994
7. Guynn M D, Croom M A, Smith S C, Parks R W, and Gelhausen P A (2003) Evolution of a Mars airplane concept for the ARES Mars scout mission. The 2nd AIAA Unmanned Unlimited Systems, Technologies, and Operation. AIAA 2003–6578
8. Liu T, Sullivan JP (2004) Pressure and temperature sensitive paints. Springer, New York
9. Liu T, Campbell BT, Burns SP, Sullivan JP (1997) Temperature- and pressure-sensitive luminescent paints in aerodynamics. Appl Mech Rev 50(4):227–246

10. Masuda T, Isobe E, Higashimura T (1983) Poly[1-(trimethylsilyl)-1-propyne]: a new high polymer synthesized with transition-metal catalysts and characterized by extremely high gas permeability. J Am Chem Soci 105(25):7473–7474
11. Masuda T, Iguchi Y, Tang BZ, Higashimura T (1988) Diffusion and solution of gases in substituted polyacetylene membranes. Polymer 29:2041–2049
12. Masuda T, Okamoto K, Sone T, Sakaguchi T, Hashimoto T, Amaya N, and Mibae S (2013) Studies on time dependence of the gas permeability of poly(1-trimethylsilyl-1-propyne). Memoirs of the Fukui Institute of Technology. 43:293–302 (in Japanease)
13. Mitsuo K, Kurita M, Nakakita K, and Watanabe S (2005) Temperature correction of PSP measurement for low-speed flow using infrared camera. In: Proceeding of International Congress on Instrumentation in Aerospace simulation facilities, pp 207–213
14. Mori H, Niimi T, Oshima Y, Hirako M (2004) Development of pressure sensitive paint suitable to surface pressure measurement in high-Knudsen number flow. Trans Jpn Soci Mech Eng 70(699):2721–2728 (in Japanese)
15. Mori H, Niimi T, Hirako M, Uenishi H (2006) Pressure sensitive paint suitable to high Knudsen number regime. Meas Sci Tech 17:1242–1246
16. Nagai K, Masuda T, Nakagawa T, Freeman BD, Pinnau I (2001) Poly [1-(trimethylsilyl)-1-propyne] and related polymers: synthesis, properties and functions. Prog Polym Sci 26:721–798
17. Niimi T, Yoshida M, Kondo M, Oshima Y, Mori H (2005) Application of pressure-sensitive paint to low-pressure range. J Thermophys Heat Trans 19(1):9–16
18. O'Meara MM, Mueller TJ (1987) Laminar separation bubble characteristics on an airfoil at low reynolds numbers. AIAA J 25(8):1033–1041
19. Okamoto M, Yasuda K, Azuma A (1996) Aerodynamic characteristics of the wings and body of a dragonfly. J Exp Biology 199:281–294
20. Ono T, Anyoji M, Ida S, Nose K, Numata D, Nagai H, and Asai K (2010) Development of pressure-sensitive paint technique for surface pressure measurement in a Mars wind tunnel. In: Proceedings of the 14th ISFV, ISFV14-4D-5
21. Ota T (1976) A separated and reattached flow on a blunt flat plate. J Fluids Eng 98(1):79–84
22. Oyama A, Fuji K (2006) A study on airfoil design for future Mars airplane. The 44th AIAA Aerospace Sciences Meeting and Exhibit, Reno, Nevada. AIAA 2006-1484
23. Sasaki K, Kiya M (1991) Three-dimensional vortex structure in a leading-edge separation bubble at moderate Reynolds number. J Fluids Eng 113(9):405–410
24. Takada K, Matsuya H, Masuda T, Higashimura T (1985) Gas permeability of polyacetylenes carrying substituents. J Appl Polym Sci 30(4):1605–1616
25. Tanaka Y, Okabe Y, Suzuki H, Nakamura K, Kubo D, Tokuhiro M, Rinoie K (2005) Conceptual design of Mars airplane for geographical exploration. J Jpn Soc Aeronaut Sp Sci 54(624):24–26
26. Tani I (1964) Low speed flows involving bubble separations. Prog Aerosp Sciences 10:70–103
27. Tani I, Luchi M, Komoda H (1961) Experimental investigation of flow separation associated with a step or a groove. Aeronautical Research Institute, University of Tokyo, Report No. 364
28. Yamashita T et al (2007) Pressure-sensitive paint measurement of the flow around a simplified car Model. J Vis 10(3):289–298

CHAPTER 10

RESOLUTION ENHANCEMENT OF ELECTRICAL RESISTANCE TOMOGRAPHY BY ITERATIVE BACK PROJECTION METHOD

Noriaki Ichijo[1], Shinsuke Matsuno[1], Taiji Sakai[1], Yoshikatsu Tochigi[1], Meguru Kaminoyama[2], Kazuhiko Nishi[2], Ryuta Misumi[2], and So Nishiyama[2]

[1]IHI Corporation, 1 Shin-nakahara-cho, Isogo-ku, Yokohama 235-8501, Japan

[2]Division of Materials Science and Chemical Engineering, Faculty of Engineering, Yokohama National University, 79-5 Tokiwadai, Hodogaya-ku, Yokohama 240-8501, Japan

ABSTRACT

An iterative back projection method (i-BP) has been developed to improve the resolution of reconstructed images produced by electrical resistance tomography (ERT). This solution is based on an iterative calculation of the electrical fields and it is possible to reconstruct clearer images than those reconstructed by the conventional back projection method without divergence. However, it does take several minutes to finish the iteration process, and therefore this solution can be applied to flow fields that require high spatial resolution rather than short processing times, such as the accumulation of noble metals in glass melters. Numerical simulations and experiments using a simple model are performed in this study. The numerical simulations show that clear images are reconstructed both near the wall and at the center by i-BP. The conductivity correlation coefficient between the genuine distribution and the reconstructed image is improved from 0.4 to 0.9. The validity of the i-BP method is also confirmed by the experimental results. As a result, it is confirmed that ERT and i-BP are capable of reconstructing acceptable images and have potential for use in the visualization of the accumulation of noble metals in a glass melter.

INTRODUCTION

Joule-heated glass melters are used for vitrification processing of the high-level radioactive liquid waste (HLW) generated during the nuclear fuel cycle. The outline of a glass melter is shown in Fig. 1. The width and the height of the vessel are both approximately 1.5 m. In this process, the HLW and the glass material (glass beads) are melted by Joule heating and mixed inside the melter. The molten glass is then drained into a metal canister for the next stage of the storage process.

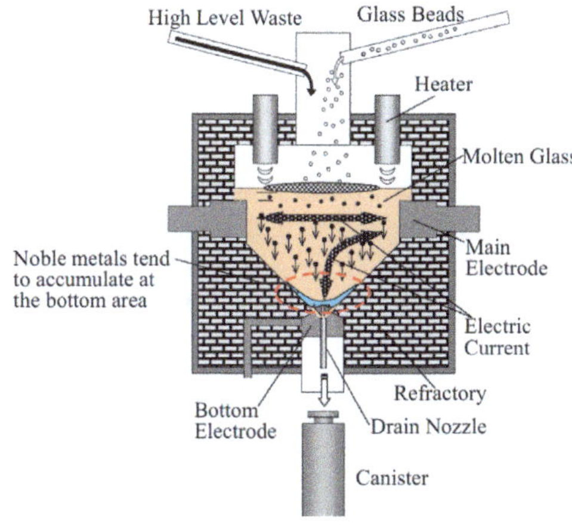

Figure 1: High-level radioactive liquid waste glass melter.

Citation: Noriaki Ichijo, Shinsuke Matsuno, Taiji Sakai, Yoshikatsu Tochigi, Meguru Kaminoyama, Kazuhiko Nishi, Ryuta Misumi, and So Nishiyama, Resolution enhancement of electrical resistance tomography by iterative back projection method, DOI 10.1007/s12650-015-0308-8.

Throughout the process, the behavior of the noble metals is very important for stable operation of the melter, because Joule heating is strongly influenced by the high electrical conductivity of these noble metals. To clarify the behavior and accumulation of the noble metals, many simulation studies have been performed (Matsuno et al. 2008; Iso et al. 2008). The numerical results agreed well with the experimental data in terms of the temperature distributions and electrical resistance values. However, in-situ observation of the behavior of the noble metals in the glass melter is strongly required to ensure an efficient melting process.

Electrical resistance tomography (ERT) has previously been applied to many industrial processes, including a suspension polymerization reactor (Kaminoyama et al. 2005, 2010), a gas–liquid two-phase flow in a pipe (Ma et al. 2001), and a stirred tank (Mann et al. 1997). Other electrical tomographic techniques use capacitance (Corlett 1999) and electrostatic charge (Machida and Kaminoyama 2008). These conventional methods are exclusively applied to cylindrical sections and electrodes that are installed on a wall. In contrast, the glass melter has a non-circular section and it is possible to insert the electrodes from the top of the melter to inspect the local accumulation. Furthermore, the information of the inside the melter is temperatures and resistivity of some limited points. Therefore, requirements of ERT are not only the resolution but also the reliability of the reconstructed image with fewer errors. When considering these measurement conditions, the following problems must be solved:

- application to a rectangular section
- clarification of a suitable image reconstruction algorithm.

A previous study (Ichijo et al. 2012) has shown that conventional methods (data acquisition methods; the adjacent method, image reconstruction algorithms; the back projection method) can be applied to a rectangular section and better images were obtained when the electrode arrangement was circular. However, the clarity of the images was not sufficient to detect the accumulation of the noble metals, especially at the center of the vessel. Therefore, developing a high resolutional image reconstruction algorithm is required.

In this study, a suitable image reconstruction algorithm for application to a glass melter is proposed. Many image reconstruction algorithms have been proposed previously, including the back projection method (Kotre 1989), the Tiknohov regularization method (Vauhkonen et al.1998), and the modified Newton–Raphson method (MNR method) (Yorkey et al. 1987), among others. When focusing on the application to glass melters, the spatial resolution takes priority over a high sampling rate because of the low flow velocity (less than 10^{-3} m/s) inside the glass melter. In addition, erroneous images must not be reconstructed to prevent misoperation of the glass melter. When these requirements are considered, the conventional back projection method (CBP) does not have sufficient resolution and the MNR method has a risk of divergence in its iterative calculations. Therefore, this study describes the development of a new iterative image reconstruction algorithm, the iterative back projection method (i-BP), with particular focus on high-resolution imaging and the stability of the iterative calculations.

ERT THEORY AND METHOD

Image Reconstruction Algorithm

The ERT technique is used to visualize the distribution of a multiphase flow based on the electrical conductivity difference between two substances. In a glass melter, ERT visualizes the distribution of the noble metals that are contained in the molten glass.

CBP and i-BP are used as the reconstruction algorithms. The measurement flow is shown in Fig. 2. I-BP is Algebraic Reconstruction Technique same as CBP. The measurement flow of the back projection method is shown on the right side of Fig. 2, while the left side shows the additional calculation flow for i-BP. $V_{(n)\mathrm{fir}}$ is the measured voltage when the entire area is filled with a lower resistance substance, $V_{(n)\mathrm{obj}}$ is the measured voltage when the entire area is filled with a higher resistance substance, $V_{(e,n)}$ is the measured voltage when the eth element is filled with the higher resistance substance and the other elements are filled with the lower resistance substance, $^{(e)}$ is the fractional area of the eth element, $P_{(e)}$ is the equivalent resistance value, and $V_{(k)}$ is the measured voltage obtained experimentally. Before the voltage is measured, the sensitivity matrix $S_{(e,n)}$ is calculated by the finite element method (FEM). After the calculation is performed, the resistance distribution is reconstructed based on the sensitivity matrix and the measured voltage. $\overline{V}_{(k)\mathrm{measured}}$ measured is the normalized voltage calculated using Eq. (1):

$$\overline{V}_{(k)\mathrm{measured}} = \frac{V_{(k)\mathrm{measured}} - V_{(k)\mathrm{fir}}}{V_{(k)\mathrm{obj}} - V_{(k)\mathrm{fir}}} \tag{1}$$

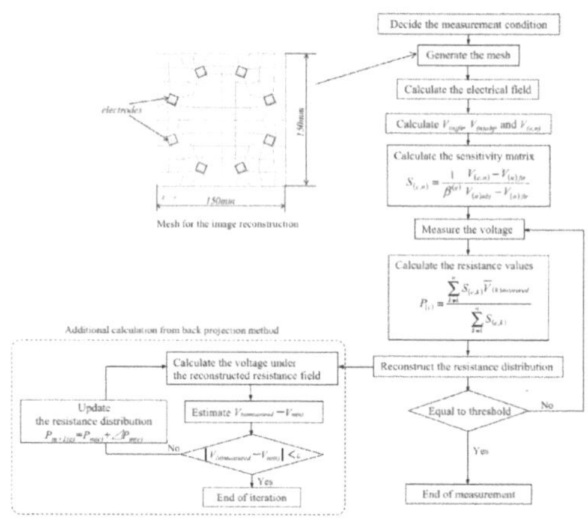

Figure 2: Measurement flows of ERT and i-BP.

The measurement is terminated by using a measurement time or a measurement count. For the iterative algorithm, an electrical calculation is implemented for the resistance field that was estimated by the back projection method. The boundary condition for one of the current injecting electrodes is $+I$, while the other is $-I$; the voltage is then calculated under the same conditions as those used in the experiment and 20 voltage measurement values are obtained. If the difference between the calculated and experimental values is below the threshold value "ε", then the iteration is complete. If not, the iteration continues and updates the resistance distribution. The updated value is calculated based on the sensitivity coefficient and the difference between the voltage measurement value from the experiments and that from the calculations. The updated resistance value $P_{m+1(e)}$ is defined as

$$P_{m+1(e)} = P_{m(e)} + \Delta P_{m(e)} \tag{2}$$

where $\Delta P_{m(e)}$ is given by

$$\Delta P_{m(e)} = \sum_{k=1}^{n} \left(V_{(k)\text{measured}} - V_{m(k)}\right) \cdot S_{(e,k)} \tag{3}$$

where $V_{(k)\text{measured}}$ is the kth voltage value measured experimentally and $V_{m(k)}$ is the kth voltage value estimated by the mth iteration. The iteration process only uses electric field calculations based on Poisson's equation, and does not use an ill-conditioned matrix like Hessian matrix. In addition, the resistivity distribution obtained by back projection is used as an initial condition of the iterative calculation, therefore, the number of iteration can be reduced and i-BP can obtain a stable solution.

DATA ACQUISITION METHOD

The data acquisition method used here is the adjacent method (Dickin and Wang 1996; Williams and Beck 1995), which is shown in Fig. 3. A current is injected through two neighboring electrodes and the voltages are measured by other pairs of neighboring electrodes. After the voltages are measured, a current is then injected through the next pair of electrodes and the voltage measurement process is repeated until all independent measurements have been completed. In the adjacent method, the total number of independent measurements is calculated using Eq. (4).

$$M = N(N-3)/2 \tag{4}$$

where M is the total number of independent measurement values and N is the number of electrodes. In the case where $N = 8$, M is calculated to be 20.

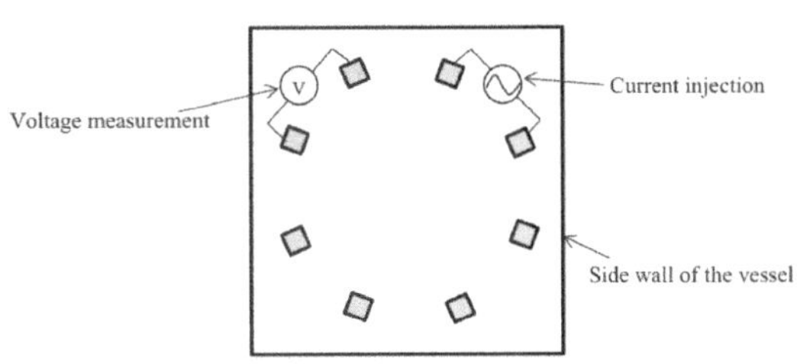

Figure 3: Adjacent data acquisition method.

NUMERICAL SIMULATION

Calculation Method

The numerical simulation model has the same section size as the experimental vessel that was described in Sect. 4.1. A steady-state 2D calculation is implemented to reduce the calculation time. A 2D calculation can ignore the effects of the bottom wall and the liquid surface, and thus this simulation focuses on evaluation of the image reconstruction algorithm. The electrode arrangement is circular, as shown in Fig. 3. The electrical field is calculated using the general-purpose simulation code ANSYS Fluent ver. 12.1.4. The electrical field is solved using a user-defined function, and the basic equation for the electrical potential is defined as

$$\nabla(\sigma \cdot \nabla\varphi) = 0 \tag{5}$$

where σ (S/m) is the electrical conductivity and φ (V) is the electrical potential. The current is injected between neighboring electrodes as the boundary condition, and the electrical potentials between the other neighboring electrodes are calculated. The numerical conditions are summarized in Table 1. The electrical conductivity and the temperature are almost in the same range as those quantities in the actual glass melter.

Table 1: Numerical conditions

Calculational parameter	
Temperature (°C)	1000
Electrical conductivity (molten glass) (S/m)	8.6
Electrical conductivity (molten glass containing noble metals) (S/m)	36.4
Conductivity ratio (with/without noble metals) (–)	4.2
Electric current (mA)	85

Results and Discussion

Conductivity images showing genuine distributions and images that were reconstructed by CBP and i-BP are shown in Fig. 4. When compared with the genuine distributions, the images that were reconstructed by CBP are blurred and the resolution is low, especially when the high conductivity substance is located at the center of the vessel. In contrast, images that were reconstructed by i-BP become clearer at both the corner and the central region, and the more that the iteration is repeated, then the clearer the reconstructed image becomes. To confirm the effect of i-BP quantitatively, the reconstructed images and the voltage measurement values are evaluated using Pearson's correlation coefficient (Pearson, 1895). The conductivity correlation coefficient (CCC) and the voltage correlation coefficient (VCC) are given by

$$\text{CCC} = \frac{\sum_{e=1}^{n}\left(C_{r(e)} - \overline{C_r}\right)\left(C_{i(e)} - \overline{C_i}\right)}{\sqrt{\sum_{e=1}^{n}\left(C_{r(e)} - \overline{C_r}\right)^2}\sqrt{\sum_{e=1}^{n}\left(C_{i(e)} - \overline{C_i}\right)^2}} \tag{6}$$

$$\text{VCC} = \frac{\sum_{k=1}^{n}\left(V_{r(k)} - \overline{V_r}\right)\left(V_{i(k)} - \overline{V_i}\right)}{\sqrt{\sum_{k=1}^{n}\left(V_{r(k)} - \overline{V_r}\right)^2}\sqrt{\sum_{k=1}^{n}\left(V_{i(k)} - \overline{V_i}\right)^2}} \tag{7}$$

where $C_{r(e)}$ is the electrical conductivity of the eth element of the genuine distribution, $C_{i(e)}$ is the electrical conductivity of the eth element at the ith iteration of the reconstructed image, $V_{r(k)}$ is the kth experimental voltage value, $V_{i(k)}$ is the kth voltage value at the ith iteration, and $\overline{C_r}$, $\overline{C_i}$, $\overline{V_r}$ and $\overline{V_i}$ are arithmetic mean values. The correlation coefficient can be interpreted thus: 1 is perfect, 0.7–0.9 is strong, 0.4–0.6 is moderate, 0.1–0.3 is weak and 0 represents no correlation (Dancey and Reidy 2004). The CCC is improved significantly by i-BP, as shown in Fig. 5, to 0.9 after 15 iterations, while the CCC is rather low at 0.4 when using CBP, which is equivalent to the case where iteration = 0. Similarly, the VCC increases with repeated iterations. The correlation coefficient is effectively improved, especially at the early stage of the iterations, but the calculation time is proportional to the number of iterations, as shown in Fig. 5a. The calculation time depends on the performance of the computer, and it takes within 2 min to complete one iteration by a typical desktop computer with 2 GB of RAM. Although 20–30 min are required to complete 15 iterations, clear images can be obtained after even a few iterations. Therefore, the actual calculation time to obtain the acceptable reconstructed image is normally within 10 min.

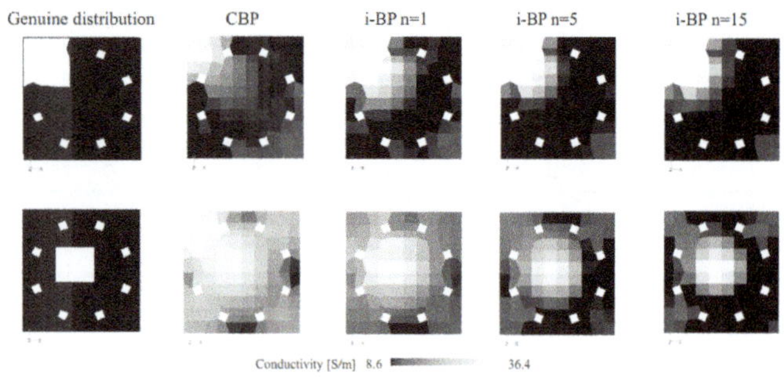

Figure 4: Reconstructed images (effect of iterative method).

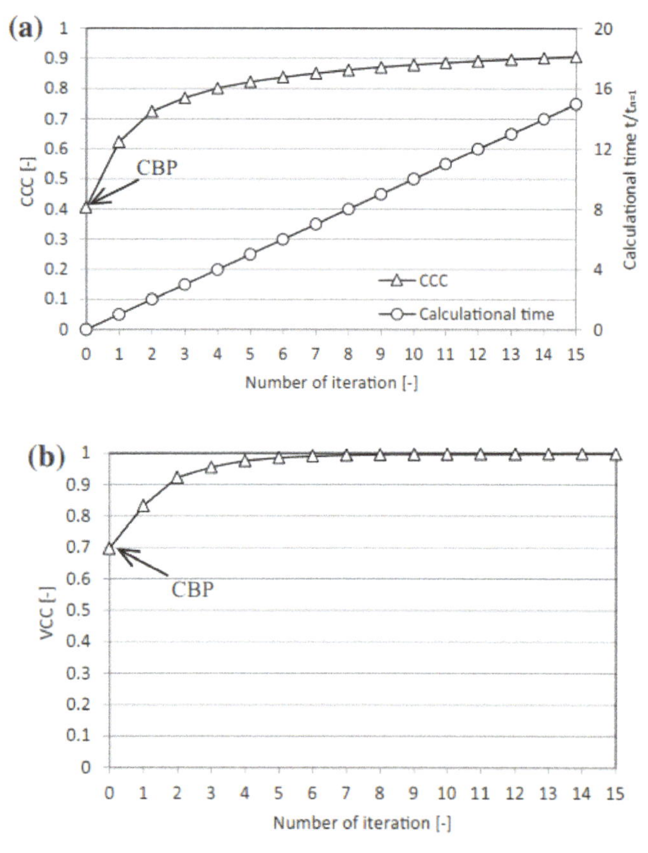

Figure 5: Improvement in a CCC and b VCC by using i-BP when the high conductivity substance is at the corner $t_{n=1}$ on the vertical axis is the calculation time for the 1st iteration.

Other image reconstruction algorithms requires less calculation time, for example, CBP requires within one second and MNR requires within 1 min (Yorkey et al. 1987). However, when the flow in the glass melter is considered, the calculation time of i-BP is acceptable.

EXPERIMENTAL

Experimental Method

The experimental apparatus is shown in Fig. 6. The vessel is 150 mm wide, 150 mm long and 200 mm high. The electrodes are 3 mm in diameter and these electrodes are covered with a sheath pipe made from aluminum oxide, except at the lower sections. This sheath pipe insulates the upper parts of the electrodes. At the lower section of the electrode, a 10 mm × 10 mm stainless steel piece is welded to increase the surface area. The electrode arrangement is circular, which is the same as the arrangement in the numerical simulation. The image reconstruction methods used are CBP and i-BP.

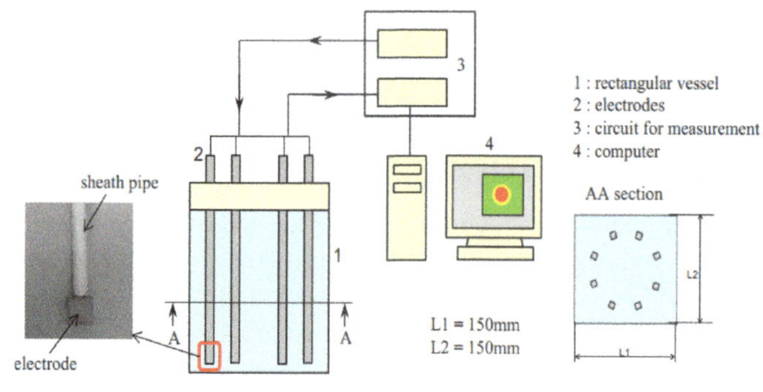

Figure 6: Experimental apparatus.

The experimental conditions are summarized in Table 2. In this experiment, a sodium chloride solution made from a higher concentration sodium chloride solution and agar are used as the background fluid and as a simulant of the noble metal accumulation, respectively. However, the electrical conductivity of molten glass contained the noble metals of 1000° is much higher than that of a saturated sodium chloride solution of normal temperature, therefore, only the electrical conductivity ratio is adjusted based on the calculational conditions, as shown in Table 1, and the actual electrical conductivity value of background fluid is 3.0 S/m, which is three times lower than that of molten glass. Instead, the injecting electrical current is 20 mA, therefore, voltage levels of the numerical simulation and the experiments are almost the same. Figure 7 shows an example of the measurement setup.

Table 2: Experimental conditions

Experimental parameter	
Electrical conductivity (sodium chloride solution) (S/m)	3.0
Electrical conductivity (agar made of sodium chloride solution) (S/m)	12.6
Conductivity ratio (with/without noble metals) (–)	4.2
Electric current (mA)	20

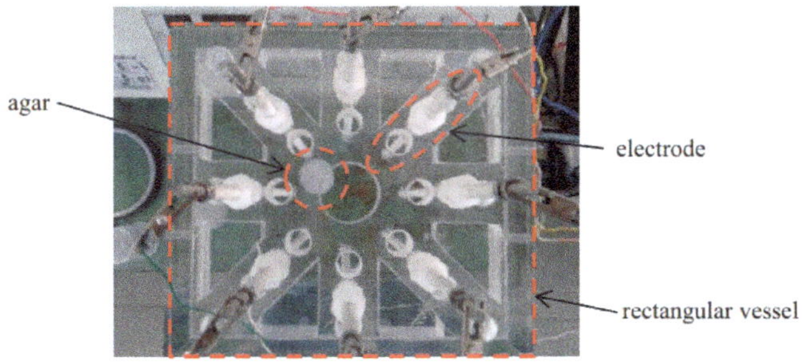

Figure 7:Experimental setup (*top view*).

Results and Discussion

The agar positions and the images reconstructed by CBP are shown in Fig. 8. Agar, which has high conductivity, can be detected in the case where it is located near the electrodes (agar positions B and C). In contrast, when agar is at the corner of the vessel (agar position A), the reconstructed image misrecognizes the presence of agar between two electrodes. Also, when agar is at the center (agar position D), the reconstructed image recognizes the correct position, but the contrast becomes too low. This shows similar tendencies to the numerical simulation results. To analyze the reasons for such low resolution, the non-dimensional voltage $V_{(n)}$ and the average of absolute values of non-dimensional voltages $\overline{V}$ are defined as

$$V_{(n)} = \frac{v_{(n)\text{agar}} - v_{(n)\text{NaCl}}}{v_{(n)\text{NaCl}}} \tag{8}$$

$$\overline{V} = \sum_{n=1}^{20} \left| V_{(n)} \right| \tag{9}$$

where $v_{(n)\text{agar}}$ is the experimental voltage when agar is in the sodium chloride solution and $v_{(n)\text{NaCl}}$ is the experimental voltage when no agar is in the sodium chloride solution. A larger absolute value for the non-dimensional voltage indicates high sensitivity towards the agar position. The numbers from 1 to 20 along the horizontal axis match the measurement numbers in Fig. 9b. Table 3 shows the average and maximum values of the absolute non-dimensional voltages in each agar position. The absolute values of the non-dimensional voltages of agar positions B and C are much larger than those of agar positions A and D. The average of the absolute values of the non-dimensional voltages in agar position C is five times larger than that in agar position A as shown in Table 3. This means that the distance between the agar and the electrodes has an effect on the sensitivity of the voltage measurement values. In agar position D, the absolute maximum value is smaller than that of agar position B and C, however every measurement pattern has a little sensitivity. Therefore, the average is larger than that in agar position A. As a result, the reconstructed image of agar position D is blurred.

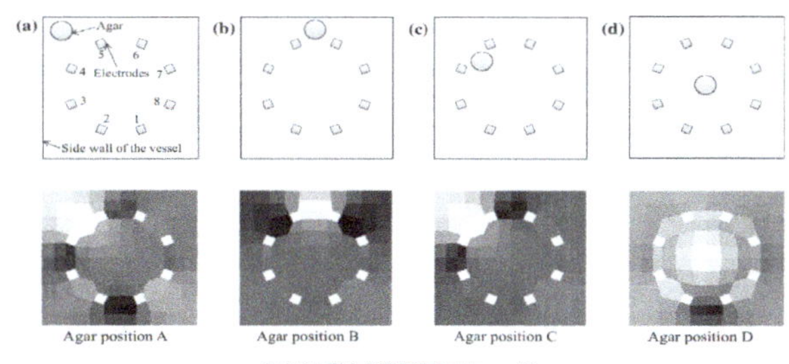

Figure 8: Reconstructed images of experiments using CBP, a agar position A, b agar position B, c agar position C, d agar position D.

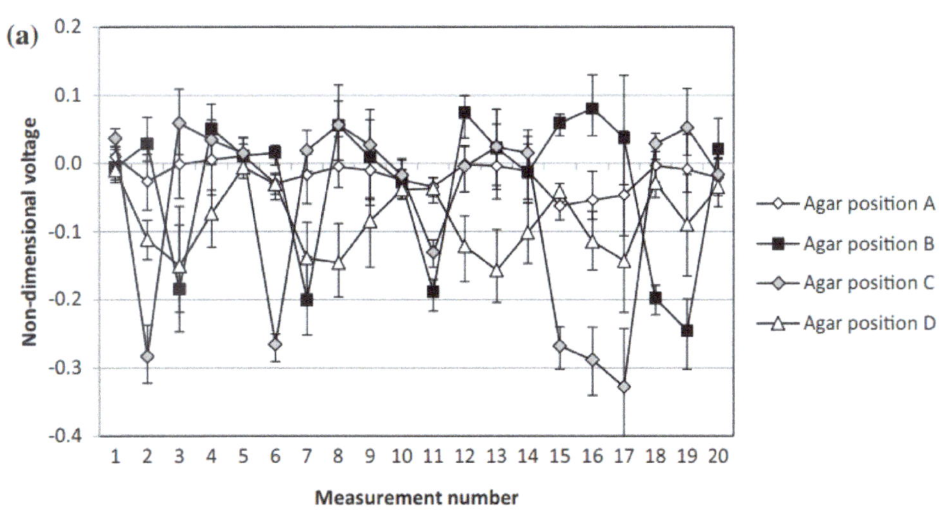

(b)

Measurement number	1	2	3	4	5	6	7	8	9	10	11	12	13	14	15	16	17	18	19	20
Pair of current injecting electrodes	1-2	1-2	1-2	1-2	1-2	2-3	2-3	2-3	2-3	2-3	3-4	3-4	3-4	3-4	4-5	4-5	4-5	5-6	5-6	6-7
Pair of voltage measuring electrodes	3-4	4-5	5-6	6-7	7-8	4-5	5-6	6-7	7-8	8-1	5-6	6-7	7-8	8-1	6-7	7-8	8-1	7-8	8-1	8-1

Figure 9: a Voltage measurement values at each agar position; b current injection electrodes and voltage measurement electrodes for each measurement number.

Table 3: The average and maximum values of the absolute non-dimensional voltages in each agar position

Agar position	A	B	C	D
Maximum |V(in)|	0.06	0.25	0.33	0.16
$\overline{V_{(in)}}$	0.02	0.08	0.10	0.08

To improve the resolution for agar positions A and D, i-BP is applied. The agar positions and the images that were reconstructed by the CBP and i-BP are shown in Fig. 10. Thc rcconstructed images produced by i-BP are much clearer than those produced by the CBP at both agar positions A and D. When the agar is at the center, the contrast of the reconstructed image is effectively improved. VCC becomes closer to 1.0 as the iterative calculation is repeated, as shown in Fig. 11. However, there is an error element near the electrode in the case of agar position A. This error may be caused not only by measurement errors but also by the sensitivity matrix. In this experiment, the sensitivity matrix is estimated by a 2D model and not by a 3D model to shorten time required for the whole process. Therefore, the effects of the bottom wall of the vessel and the liquid surface cannot be considered. The sensitivity matrix calculated by 3D model has a potential to minimize both the error and the noise. In addition, increasing the value of the electrical current is also effective in enlarging both the voltage value and the signal-to-noise ratio.

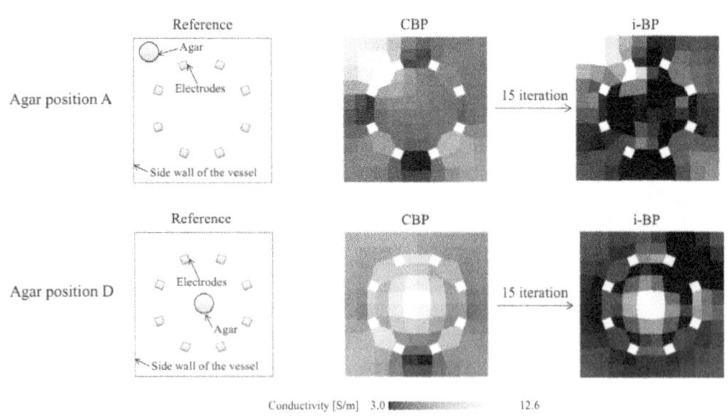

Figure 10: Reconstructed images of experiments produced by i-BP.

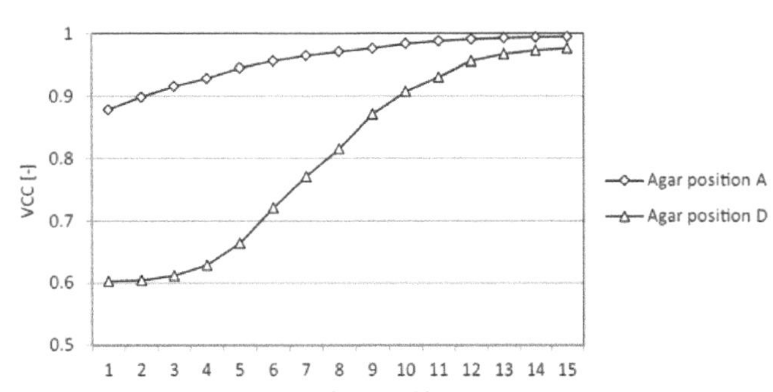

Figure 11: VCC from i-BP in agar position A and D.

CONCLUSION

In this study, numerical simulations and experiments are performed to demonstrate a new reconstruction algorithm called i-BP. The numerical simulations focus on development of the image reconstruction algorithm, and i-BP can obtain better reconstructed images than the CBP. The experiments also reveal the validity of i-BP. Consideration of these results shows that ERT and i-BP have the potential to be used to visualize the distribution of the noble metals and molten glass inside of a glass melter.

REFERENCES

1. Corlett AE (1999) Three-phase flow pattern recognition in horizontal pipelines using electrical capacitance tomography. J Vis 2(1):31–36
2. Dancey C, Reidy J (2004) Statistics without maths for psychology: using SPSS for windows. Prentice Hall, London
3. Dickin FJ, Wang M (1996) Electrical resistance tomography for process applications. Meas Sci Technol 7:247–260
4. Ichijo N, Matsuno S, Tokura S, Tochigi Y, Kaminoyama M, Nishi K, Misumi R, Higashi K (2012) Applicability of electrical resistance tomography to monitoring noble metal accumulation in glass melter. In: 6th International symposium on process tomography (ISPT6), Cape Town PO16
5. Iso Y, Matsuno S, Uchida H, Oono I, Fukui T, Ooba T (2008) Numerical simulation of platinum group metal particles behaviour in a Joule-heated glass melter. J Power Energy Syst 2(2):815–825
6. Kaminoyama M, Taguchi S, Misumi R, Nishi K (2005) Monitoring stability of reaction and dispersion states in a suspension polymerization reactor using electrical resistance tomography measurement. Chem Eng Sci 60:5513–5518
7. Kaminoyama M, Kato K, Misumi R, Nishi K (2010) Measurements of the phase inversion phenomenon in a suspension polymerization reactor with an electrical resistance tomography system. J Chem Eng Jpn 43(1):52–55
8. Kotre CJ (1989) A sensitivity coefficient method for the reconstruction of electrical impedance tomograms. Clin Phys Physiol Meas 10(3):275–281
9. Ma Y, Zheng Z, Xu L, Liu X, Wu Y (2001) Application of electrical resistance tomography system to monitor gas/liquid two-phase flow in a horizontal pipe. Flow Meas Instrum 12:259–265
10. Machida M, Kaminoyama M (2008) Sensor design for development of tribo-electric tomography system with increased number of sensors. J Vis 11(4):375–385
11. Mann R, Dickin FJ, Wang M, Dyakowski T, Williams RA, Edwards RB, Forrest AE, Holden PJ (1997) Application of electrical resistance tomography to inter-

rogate mixing process at plant scale. Chem Eng Sci 52(13):2087–2097

12. Matsuno S, Iso Y, Uchida H, Oono I, Fukui T, Ooba T (2008) CFD Modeling Coupled with Electric Field Analysis for Joule-Heated Glass Melters. J Power Energy Syst 2(1):447–455

13. Pearson K (1895) Notes on regression and inheritance in the case of two parents. Proc R Soc Lond 58:240–242

14. Vauhkonen M, Vadasz D, Kaipio JP, Somersalo E, Karjalainen PA (1998) Tikhonov regularization and prior information in electrical impedance tomography. IEEE Trans Med Imaging 17:285–293

15. Williams RA, Beck MS (1995) Process tomography: principles techniques and applications. Butterworth-Heinemann, Oxford. ISBN 0750607440

16. Yorkey TJ, Webster JG, Tompkins WJ (1987) Comparing Reconstruction Algorithms for Electrical Impedance Tomography. IEEE Trans Biomed Eng 34(11):843–852

CHAPTER 11

3D MODELING AND MOTION PARALLAX FOR IMPROVED VIDEOCONFERENCING

Zhe Zhu[1], Ralph R. Martin[2], Robert Pepperell[3], and Alistair Burleigh[3]

[1]TNList, Tsinghua University, Beijing 100084, China.

[2]School of Computer Science & Informatics, Cardiff University, UK

[3]Cardiff School of Art & Design, Cardiff Metropolitan University, UK

ABSTRACT

We consider a face-to-face videoconferencing system that uses a Kinect camera at each end of the link for 3D modeling and an ordinary 2D display for output. The Kinect camera allows a 3D model of each participant to be transmitted; the (assumed static) background is sent separately. Furthermore, the Kinect tracks the receiver's head, allowing our system to render a view of the sender depending on the receiver's viewpoint. The resulting motion parallax gives the receivers a strong impression of 3D viewing as they move, yet the system only needs an ordinary 2D display. This is cheaper than a full 3D system, and avoids disadvantages such as the need to wear shutter glasses, VR headsets, or to sit in a particular position required by an autostereo display. Perceptual studies show that users experience a greater sensation of depth with our system compared to a typical 2D videoconferencing system.

INTRODUCTION

The way people communicate remotely has evolved as technology has developed. The telegraph and later the telephone allowed information to be transmitted electronically instead of by a physical written letter; it also allowed remote communication in real time. Modern tools such as Microsoft Skype and Apple FaceTime further improve telepresence for remote communication, allowing both voice and video so that remote participants can hear and see each other.

The history of videoconferencing dates back to the 1930s when the German Reich Postzentralamt video telephone network connected Berlin and several other German cities via coaxial cables. Rosenthal's very early work [1] already considered the issue of transmission of eye contact during video broadcast. Various works have also described multiparty videoconferencing [2–6], in which it is important to preserve gaze directional cues to see who is speaking.

Humans have long attempted to record their visual experience of three-dimensional space on a flat pictorial plane, from early cave art, through centuries of painting and drawing, to photography and highdefinition digital media. Although most pictures are presented on a two-dimensional surface, they are full of differing visual cues that allow us to infer depth [7]. Occlusion, lighting, object shading, stereopsis, and parallax are all used by the visual system to perceive depth in the real world, and many of these can be replicated in pictures to create the illusion of spatial depth on a flat surface [8].

Artists at Cardiff School of Art & Design have been exploring new methods of generating depth cues within the context of digital media, some of which are based on discoveries made by earlier artists about the nature of visual

Citation: Zhe Zhu, Ralph R. Martin, Robert Pepperell, and Alistair Burleigh, 3D modeling and motion parallax for improved videoconferencing, DOI 10.1007/s41095-016-0038-4.

perception and how to depict it [9]. By observing fundamental features of visual experience, such as the size, shape, and distribution of objects in the visual field, they have established that pictures generated by artistic methods can outperform ones generated by conventional geometric techniques in terms of representational accuracy [10].

Since the development of linear perspective in the 15th century, artists have sought ways to create greater depth in their work [11]. Most imaging technology today uses standard principles of linear perspective to represent space on a flat picture surface [12]. Videoconferencing solutions are no exception, with images of the participants normally presented on flat monitors in geometrical perspective. However, linear perspective images are normally generated from a fixed, monocular viewpoint, while natural vision is normally experienced with two mobile eyes [13]. The development of new sensing technologies presents an opportunity to enhance the sense of space in flat images by integrating more naturalistic cues into the images. This paper concerns the use of real-time, user-responsive motion parallax for videoconferencing, combined with simple 3D modeling, with the goal of improving the sense of immersion and quality of the user experience. Other work has also considered using motion parallax cues, and we will discuss them further in Section 2.

An alternative way of providing 3D cues for the user on a flat 2D display is stereopsis. However, many stereopsis systems require users to wear shutter glasses, which may be acceptable when watching 3D movies, but not in videoconferencing, as participants rely on seeing each other's faces unobstructed for full communication. Alternatively, autostereo displays may be used, but these require the user to sit in a fairly precisely controlled location. While this may be achievable for videoconferencing, as head motion is usually limited, such systems are still costly.

Our system is intended for two-person face-toface videoconferencing, so we need not consider the gaze direction problem present in multiparticipant systems [3, 5]. Each end of the link uses a Kinect camera for data acquisition, an ordinary 2D display for output, and a commodity PC. The Kinect camera allows a 3D model of each sender's head and shoulders to be transmitted; the background is sent separately. Furthermore, the Kinect tracks each receiver's head, allowing the system to render a view of the sender according to the receiver's viewpoint.

We assume that users only make small movements during videoconferencing, such as slight swaying of body and shaking of head. We are only interested in transmitting the head and shoulders, and do not consider any hand or other body movements. We also assume that the background is static, allowing us to model foreground and background separately, and to ignore any changes to the background after the initial setup.

A key idea is that we do not aim to model the foreground and background in 3D accurately, which would lead to high computational costs in both time and space, and is also unlikely to be robust. Instead we aim to model the foreground and background with sufficient realism to convey a more convincing sense of depth. We do not just layer the foreground and background like Refs. [14, 15], as such models are too flat. Neither do we use KinectFusion [16, 17] to do the modeling, even though at first it might seem suitable, for two reasons. Firstly, models generated by KinectFusion are noisy, with gaps in the surface and edges that are not smooth (see the top row of Fig. 1). Secondly, the resulting models are large and would place a heavy burden on the network— the amount of data to be transmitted should be kept as reasonably small as possible. Instead, we use a robust, realistic, but lightweight parameterized model customized to each participant. Our model typically has fewer than 1000 vertices. Compared to Ref. [18] which transmits whole depth frames, our model requires much less network bandwidth.

The main technical contribution of our work, other than a demonstration of the advantages of using motion parallax for videoconferencing, is a practical system for doing so. It is based on a parametric model of the head and shoulders and allows videoconferencing based on commodity hardware. The model can cope with the high levels of noise in Kinect data, and is lightweight yet sufficiently realistic. Our approach allows our system to be more robust to noise than other generic models, while providing more realistic results than simply layering the foreground and background.

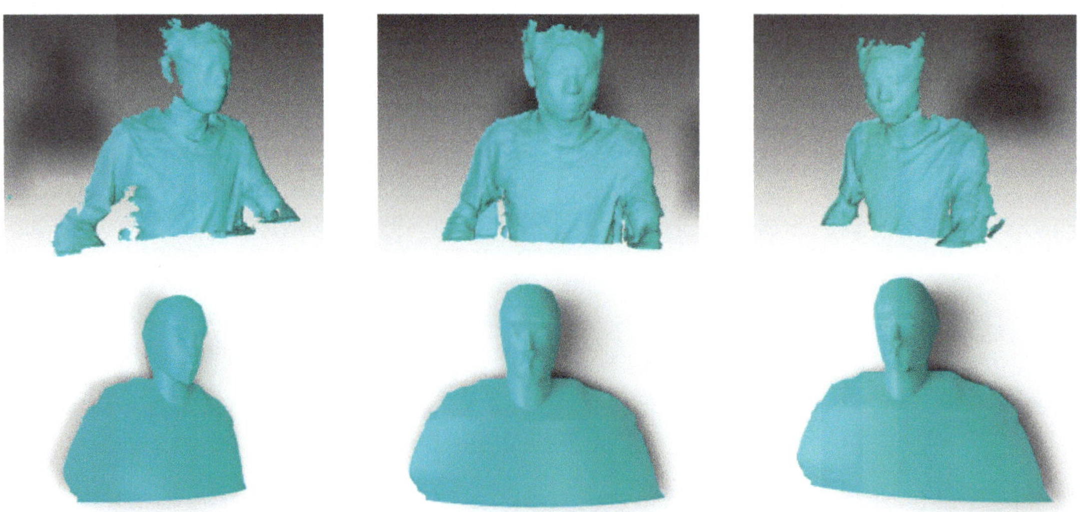

Figure 1: Top: KinectFusion modeling result, from various viewpoints. The model is very noisy and is unsuited to videoconferencing. Bottom: our modeling result. Our smoother parametric model is better suited to videoconferencing.

RELATED WORK

Motion Parallax and its Application in Videoconferencing

Motion parallax is an important kinetic monocular depth cue that provides the visual system with information about the configuration of space and objects in the surrounding physical environment [8]. Motion parallax works by comparing the relative movement of objects in space; e.g., as a viewer's head rotates or moves through space, objects further away move quicker in relation to objects that are closer. This allows the viewer to form accurate judgements about both their current position in the world, and also the relative location of objects around them.

Lee [19] devised a system which tracked user's head position with a Nintendo Wii remote to determine a suitable camera position for a 3D scene in real time. The resulting shift of the digital space in response to user's head position produces a powerful depth illusion for the viewer, which in Lee's words "effectively transforms your display into a portal to a virtual environment".

Apple's iOS 7 and later operating systems include a motion parallax effect that moves the icons and tabs on the screen very slightly in response to phone or tablet motion from the user [20]. This synthetic motion parallax again creates an enhanced feeling of digital space as the layers move separately.

Applying the same kind of depth separation and 3D modeling approach to a videoconferencing application is potentially promising. However, the complexity of modeling objects in depth in a realtime application, and with sufficient quality to be visually believable (including moving facial features), raises complex technical issues.

Harrison and Hudson [14] proposed a pseudo-3D videoconferencing system based on a commodity webcam. They initially capture a background image and then extract the foreground sender in real time during conferencing. The sender and background are layered at different depths, and a virtual camera is put at a 2D position corresponding to the x–y tracked position of the receiver's head. To overcome imperfections in the edges of the foreground, simple Gaussian bluring is used along the composition boundary. The system provides some motion parallax but is not particularly realistic as it gives the appearance of two planes in relative motion.

Zhang et al. [15] proposed a similar system, using a feature-based face-tracking algorithm to robustly estimate the position and scale of the face. A time-of-flight camera is used to improve the segmentation of background and foreground, and a matting strategy [21] is used to improve the composition result. Although this provides improved accuracy face tracking and higher quality foreground/background composition, there is still a lack of realism due to the planar modeling of the foreground.

Kim et al. [18] described TeleHuman, a cylindrical 3D display portal for life-size human telepresence. Their system relies on 10 Kinects to capture 360° 3D video; each frame contains an image and a depth map. Their system supports both motion parallax and stereoscopy. Nevertheless, as the Kinect depth stream is noisy, the 3D images are of low quality. The cylindrical display and the need for 10 Kinect devices also make it unsuitable for general use in home and office.

Our system provides a 3D model of the sender's head, and tracks the 3D position of the receiver's head, and so can generate more realistic motion parallax than these earlier systems. At the same time, it only needs an ordinary 2D display and a single low-cost Kinect camera.

Modeling

Parameterized Facial Models

Many works have considered parameterized face models; CANDIDE-type models are widely used for modeling the human face. These are predefined triangle meshes whose shape can be adjusted by animation units and shape units. The animation unit parameters represent facial expression, while the shape units tailor the proportions of the face to a particular individual. The initial version of CANDIDE [22] contained 75 vertices and 100 triangles. Since the mouth and eyes are crudely represented, this version of the model is unrealistic and so is rarely used. Welsh [23] produced an improved CANDIDE model with 160 vertices and 238 triangles, covering the entire frontal head and shoulders. However, using a fixed number of vertices to model the shoulders does not lead to good results. The most popular version, CANDIDE- 3 [24], provides more details for mouth, cheeks, nose, and eyes, using 113 vertices and 168 triangles. This version is much improved and is used in the Microsoft Kinect SDK. The most obvious drawback of such models is that they only represent the frontal face so look like a mask when rendered. In videoconferencing, this presents problems if the sender turns their head too far to one side.

Real-Time 3D Modeling

Making 3D models from data is a fundamental problem in computer graphics and computer vision, with much research. Balancing speed and accuracy is a key issue. Rusinkiewicz et al. [25] pioneered the real-time modeling of objects from depth data. Their approach uses a 60 Hz structured-light rangefinder; the user rotates an object in front of it to get a continuously-updated model. However this procedure is unsuited to human body capture since any non-rigid movement of the body leads to inaccurate modeling results. While commercial systems exist for dynamic face and body capture, such as those produced by 3dMD [26], they are far too expensive for home and office use. Based on the much lower-priced Kinect, KinectFusion [16, 17] provides a real-time, robust, room scale GPU-based modeling technique, as part of the Microsoft Kinect SDK. It uses a volume representation in which each voxel contains color information. Models can be updated at an interactive rate. By providing a human body detection module in the Microsoft Kinect SDK, KinectFusion can reconstruct the body even in the presence of non-rigid movement. However KinectFusion has two obvious drawbacks. Firstly, it is memory intensive. Chen et al. [27] showed how to use a fast and compact hierarchical GPU data structure instead of a regular 3D voxel grid to save an order of magnitude of memory. Secondly, the modeling result is noisy, mainly due to the noisy depth data provided by the Kinect itself. This could be overcome to some extent by hardware improvements.

In our low-cost system, we use a parameterized approach to model the body, which is robust, fast, and provides good quality. It can model more of the body than CANDIDE-type approaches, but with much lower noise than approaches that directly use KinectFusion.

SYSTEM OVERVIEW

Our system is intended for one-to-one videoconferencing. We assume the users are indoors and the background is static. The hardware needed by our system is cheap and readily available, comprising a Kinect, a commodity PC, and a standard 2D display for each participant. When our system is started, it initially models the background (at each end) while the sender stands to one side, outside the view of the Kinect. A 2D background image is captured, and is texture mapped to a plane whose depth is set to the average distance of the depth image. Our justification for using such a simple model for the background is that the users of a videoconferencing system spend nearly all of their time looking at the other person, and only peripherally observe the background. An alternative approach to prior background capture would be to use an image completion approach [28] to fill background gaps resulting from foreground movement. Apart from the extra computational effort needed, a further disadvantage is that such completed backgrounds always have undesirable artifacts in practice. Since the background is static, it only needs to be transmitted once at the start of the session.

After background capture, the user then sits in front of the system, which builds a model of the front of his or her head, neck, and shoulders in real time; at this stage the user should also turn his head to the left and right to allow modeling of the sides of the head. Since the Kinect is located above the top of the display, it can also capture much of the top of the head. We assume that the bottom part of the head (under the chin) always remains unseen, and that users do not significantly tilt their heads up and down. The user is given feedback in real time to allow verification that the constructed model is satisfactory. The model we produce is a 3D mesh model with a corresponding image texture: the color image provided by the Kinect is mapped via texture coordinates to the 3D vertices of the mesh model.

After model acquisition is finished, the two users are then connected to each other. The background model is transmitted first. After that, real-time transmission of the foreground model is sent for each frame. In particular, the location of each mesh vertex and its texture coordinates are sent, together with the current texture image. While the connection is active, each receiver sees the sender as a rendered 3D model, rendered according to the receiver's viewpoint. Thus, as the receiver's head moves, the viewpoint used for rendering changes, and the resulting motion parallax and 3D modeling give the receiver a sense of 3D. We illustrate our system in Fig. 2.

Subsequent sections now give further details: Section 4 discusses our parameterized model of the upper part of the human body, while Section 5 explains how we construct the virtual scene. We evaluate our system in Section 6 and conclude our work in Section 7.

Real-Time Modeling of the Upper Part of the Body

For videoconferencing, we wish to model the upper part of the body, including the head, neck, and the shoulders. During videoconferencing, the front of the head always faces the camera, so this is modeled separately in greater detail. Looking down from above, this frontal model encompasses 180° as seen from the front. Horizontal movement and rotation of the head may occur. Thus, we must also model the sides and back of the head, which we do using separate low-detail models for the left-back and right-back. These left and right back parts each provide a further 90° to provide a 360° head model. The top of different parts of the head is modeled along with each of these three parts (we assume vertical movement does not in practice occur).

For the front of the head, we use the CANDIDE-3 model based on parameters representing individual shape and facial expression. A mesh model based on a quarter ellipsoid, but which does not allow for changes in expression, is used for each of the left-back and right-back of the head. These are joined with appropriate continuity to the front of the head and each other to complete the head. Further similar expressionless models are used for the neck and shoulders. Each model is based on a standard template, appropriately deformed to suit a particular individual, with further transformations that may represent rotation and translation. The position and orientation of the model are continuously updated to capture the movement of the user.

The model parameters are of two types, those that are constant for an individual, and those that vary from frame to frame (e.g., representing facial expression). Thus our model building process extracts individual body features in an initial step before the conversation begins, to determine the parameters describing the body shape of a particular person. The textures of the left-back and right-back head are also captured at this stage, and are transmitted with the texture coordinates of the corresponding vertices just once at the start of the session—these are assumed to be relatively unimportant and can be considered to be unchanging. Then as the conversation occurs, feature tracking is used to acquire the dynamic parameters. The textures for the front of the head, neck, and shoulders are also captured for each frame to allow for changes in expression and hence facial appearance, as well as for minor body movements. The vertex positions of the head, neck, and shoulders, their texture coordinates, and the current image are transmitted for each frame.

The Parameterized Model

We now consider the models in more detail. The front, left-back, and right-back of the head are modeled separately and seamlessly joined together. The upper end of the neck is inserted into the head while the lower end of the neck is inserted into the shoulders, connecting the three parts as a whole.

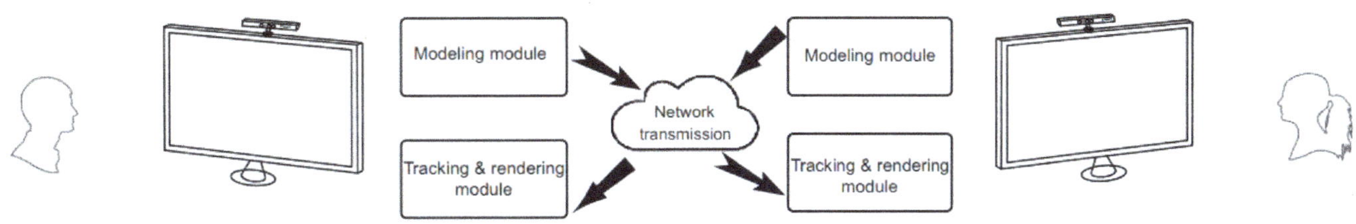

Figure 2: System overview.

The Head

The head model comprises three parts: front, leftback, and right-back. The frontal head uses the CANDIDE-3 model [24], which can be written as

$$M_{\mathrm{h}}^{\mathrm{f}} = R(\sigma S_{\mathrm{f}} + A) + t \tag{1}$$

where $M_{\mathrm{h}}^{\mathrm{f}}$ represents the 3D model of the frontal face in terms of a 3N-dimensional vector containing the (x, y, z) coordinates of the vertices (h denotes head, f denotes front). S_f is a predefined standard face model, representing standard positions on a standard face, connected into a triangulation with known topology. σ deforms the standard face to match a specific face, and is derived from the shape units describing a particular individual's face, e.g., the height of the head and the width of the chin. A encapsulates animation units (AUs), which describe expression changes from a neutral facial expression. Note that σ is invariant over time but A varies. R is a rotation matrix and t is a translation to allow for head movements.

The left-back of the head is defined as

$$M_{\mathrm{h}}^{\mathrm{l}} = R(\omega S_{\mathrm{l}}) + t \tag{2}$$

where S_l is a predefined left-back of the head model, containing 3 triangle strips making an arched shape; each strip has 9 vertices in total. We do not model the shape of the ears as they typically occupy a tiny area in videoconferencing, and furthermore their geometry is complicated and hard to model robustly. Texture mapping to a curved surface suffices for our application. ω deforms the template to a specific head. We illustrate the left-back of the head model in Fig. 3(a). The right-back of the head model is symmetrically defined as

$$M_{\mathrm{h}}^{\mathrm{r}} = R(\omega S_{\mathrm{r}}) + t \tag{3}$$

To seamlessly connect the different parts of the head model we ensure that appropriate triangles in each part share vertices. In reality, these parts of the head undergo only very limited deformation due to changes in expression, and for simplicity in this application we assume they are rigid.

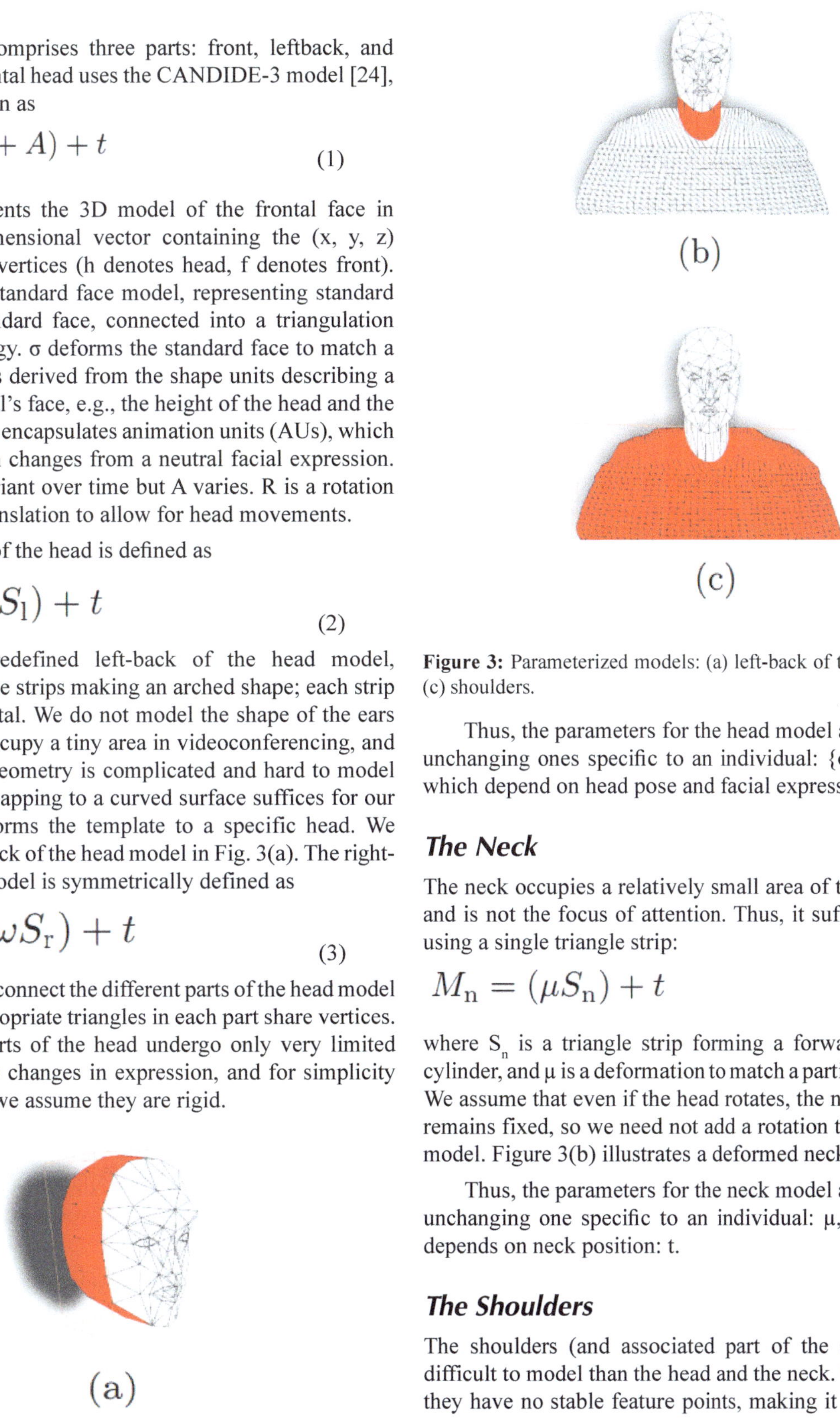

Figure 3: Parameterized models: (a) left-back of the head, (b) neck, (c) shoulders.

Thus, the parameters for the head model are of two kinds, unchanging ones specific to an individual: {σ, ω}, and those which depend on head pose and facial expression: {A, R, t}.

The Neck

The neck occupies a relatively small area of the field of view, and is not the focus of attention. Thus, it suffices to model it using a single triangle strip:

$$M_{\mathrm{n}} = (\mu S_{\mathrm{n}}) + t \tag{4}$$

where S_n is a triangle strip forming a forward facing semi-cylinder, and μ is a deformation to match a particular individual. We assume that even if the head rotates, the neck more or less remains fixed, so we need not add a rotation term for the neck model. Figure 3(b) illustrates a deformed neck model.

Thus, the parameters for the neck model are of two kinds, unchanging one specific to an individual: μ, and that which depends on neck position: t.

The Shoulders

The shoulders (and associated part of the chest) are more difficult to model than the head and the neck. Unlike the head, they have no stable feature points, making it harder to define a template based on feature points. The shoulders occupy a much larger part of the image than the neck, and their shape varies significantly between different individuals. We also note that human observers are more sensitive to the shape of the shoulders than to their texture or appearance. Our main goal in modeling the shoulders is to smoothly approximate their silhouette. We thus define them as

$$M_s = [\alpha, \beta]S_s + t_s \quad (5)$$

where S_s is a standard shoulder template.

To form the shoulder template, we first define edge vertices. These are divided into two sets, those lying on the more or less vertical sides of the shoulders (i.e., the arms), and those lying on the more or less horizontal top of the shoulders. See Fig. 4: "vertical" edge vertices are marked with triangles and "horizontal" points are marked with stars. The vertical edge vertices are used to separate the shoulder model into layers; left and right vertical vertices sharing the same y value are connected by a curve. To define this curve, we add another auxiliary vertex with the same y value and whose x coordinate is the average of their x coordinates. Its z coordinate is closer to the viewer by a distance of 1.2 times the radius of the neck. These three vertices determine a circular arc, which is uniformly sampled by N_v vertices (N_v = 40 in our implementation). Horizontal vertices share the same z values as the vertical edge vertices, and are connected to the first layer of vertical edge vertices, as illustrated in Fig. 3(c). α and β are deformations in vertical and horizontal directions respectively which we explain later. t_s is the translation of the shoulders. Thus, the parameters for the shoulder model are of two kinds, unchanging ones specific to an individual: {α, β}, and that which depends on shoulder position: t_s.

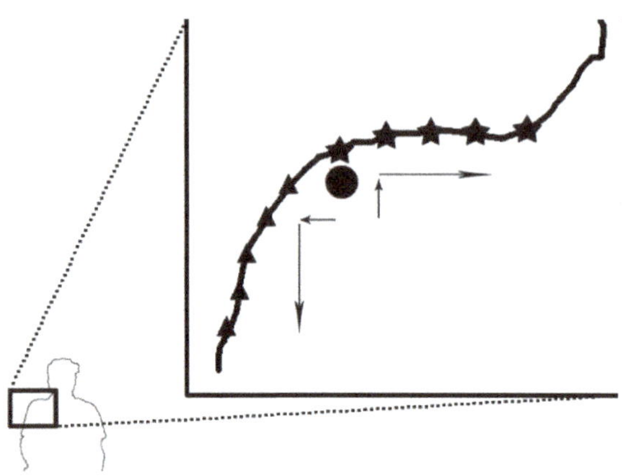

Figure 4: Shoulder edge point detection. The black circle is the corner point found after several iterations. It is then snapped to the vertical edge and vertical edge points (triangles) are detected by downwards search. After horizontal snapping, horizontal edge points (stars) are detected by horizontal search.

Parameter Determination

We now explain how we determine the various parameters. The overall set of parameters describing the model is

$$p = \{R, t, \sigma, A, \omega, \mu, \alpha, \beta, t_s\} \quad (6)$$

These parameters fall into two categories: {σ, ω, α, β, μ} are unchanging in time and describe the body shape of an individual, while {R, t, t_s, A} change over time, describing expression, position, and orientation.

Offline Parameter Calculation

We initially determine each of the unchanging parameters. σ can be calculated from the 11 shape units as explained in Ref. [24], while ω can be calculated from the distance between the cheek bone and the ear; the necessary information in both cases can be obtained using the Kinect SDK. μ can be calculated from the width and height of the neck.

We approximate the width of the neck as the x distance between the left/right jawbone points of the face provided by the Kinect SDK: such feature points of the face provide a more stable solution than determining the neck location from the 2D image. The length of the neck is determined as the y distance between the skeleton joint of the head and the center of the shoulders, provided by the Kinect skeleton stream. α and β can be calculated from the vertical and horizontal edge points on the shoulders, respectively. α comes from corresponding pairs of vertical edge vertices, which define a deformation for each horizontal strip. β defines how horizontal edge vertices are translated from an initial position to their current position.

Online Parameter Calculation

During real-time transmission, the changing parameters must be determined. A can be calculated using the MPEG-4 face animation parameters, again provided by the Kinect SDK. R and t can be straightforwardly calculated from the face tracking output also provided by the Kinect SDK. To determine t_s, we average all x centers of vertical edge vertex pairs, and the y centers of all horizontal edge vertex pairs. Finding these edge vertices depends on fast and robust edge point extraction. Our approach is based on edge point detection and edge point filtering, which are further explained.

Edge Point Detection

First, we must search for the shoulder edge points. The Kinect provides three different data streams: a color stream, a depth stream, and a skeleton stream. The skeleton stream provides robust tracking information for twenty joints of the user's body. We use the left and right shoulder joints as initial shoulder corner points at which we switch from horizontal to vertical edge points.

Since the Kinect depth stream is noisy, we do not perform the search on the depth image. Instead, we make use of player ID information also contained in the depth stream. Each pixel is allocated a positive number indicating the player ID if this pixel belongs to a person, or 0 if this pixel is outside any person. As the player ID image is less noisy than the depth image (see Fig. 5), we use the player ID information to determine which pixels belong to the sender.

Starting from the initial corner points, we first search for more accurate shoulder corner points, located on the person's outline, and then find vertical and horizontal edge points. An iterative approach is used to find the accurate corner points. Starting from the initial left corner point, we find the first pixel going vertically upwards that is outside the person; we also perform a similar horizontal search from right to left. The midpoint of the 2 pixels found gives a more accurate corner point. This process is repeated until the distance between the two points is under than 2 pixels.

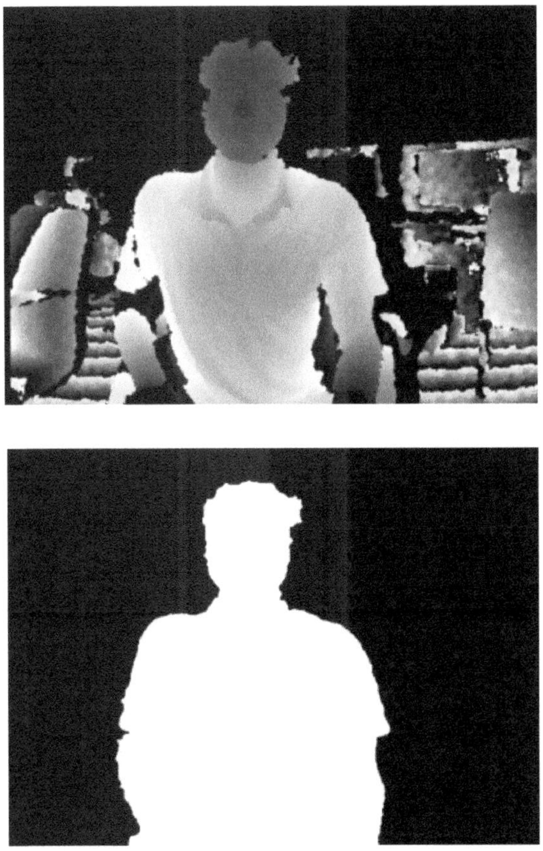

Figure 5: Raw depth data and player ID data.

Using this accurate corner point we follow the edge downwards to find successive vertical edge points until reaching the bottom of the frame. For horizontal edge points, we search from the corner rightwards until reaching the neck. We consider the neck to start when the edge slope exceeds 45°. Edge points are sampled 5 pixels apart.

Edge Point Filtering

We next stabilize this edge point data. We have two sets of vertical and horizontal edge points (one on either side of the body). As these have been determined from player ID data that still has a somewhat noisy boundary, we need to smooth them both within each individual frame, and in between frames. Within each frame, each row and column of points is filtered using a Gaussian filter with radius 4 pixels. To help alleviate jitter in the player ID image, we calculate the average position for each row and column of points, and if the change between frame i + 1 and frame i is more than 5 times the change between frames i and i−1, we regard the frame i+ 1 as having significant jitter, and keep the positions of the points unchanged from frame i. Within a frame, if the change in any one row (or column) is more than twice as big as that of its neighbours, we again assume this is due to jitter and keep the positions of these two rows the same as in the previous frame.

Model Part Connection

The parameter values and standard models provide a description for each part. We next need to consider how to connect them into a whole.

It is common to add geometric constrains when assembling parts to make a model [29– 32]. These approaches usually optimize an energy function which satisfies connectivity constraints, while ensuring the positions of the vertices after optimization have texture coordinates as close as possible to the correct ones. Concentricity, coplanarity, parallelism, etc. are commonly used constraints, and are useful for such things as mechanical parts, but are not particularly useful for organic objects such as the human body. This has many non-rigidly deformable parts whose connections can be hard to precisely define.

Instead, we opt for a simpler approach, and add softer geometric constraints. We only adjust the z values of the head and shoulders, and z and y values for the neck. Three principles are used to provide a simple modeling approach:

- Boundary vertices of the shoulders all share the same z value, and are located on the same plane as the edges of the semi-cylindrical neck.
- The (vertical) axis of the neck semi-cylinder has the same z value as the midpoint of the left and right jawbones.
- Since the neck is thinner than the head and shoulders, and behind them, it can be made a little longer (at both ends) than it is in reality, as a way of ensuring connectivity.

To meet these requirements, we determine the z depth of the head first, based on the depth values. Then we adjust the depths of the neck and shoulders, according to the first two principles above. Next, we connect the top two vertices on the back of the neck to two key points on the head located under the ears. No special steps are needed to join the neck and the shoulders due to the extra length of the neck; the shoulders cover its end. This simple approach avoids solving any optimization problem and is very fast.

SCENE RENDERING

We now consider how the scene is rendered on the receiver's side.

At setup time, the background texture image, the background model and its texture, and texture images of the left-back and right-back head are transmitted to the receiver just once.

During videoconferencing, the color image of each frame is sent as a texture image together with the foreground model as triangle meshes and vertex texture coordinates. The resolution of the color image is 640×480, with 8 bits per channel. The frame rate of our system is 30 fps. The color information is sent using a video codec, while typically the foreground model has fewer than 1000 vertices, which requires little extra bandwidth over that needed by the color stream. On the receiver's side, the head of the receiver is tracked during model building and the received scene models are rendered taking into account the position and orientation of the tracked head. Our goal is to give the receiver a realistic impression of parallax. Our basis for rendering is that the receiver's attention is assumed to be fixed on the sender's face, at the midpoint of sender's eyes. Thus, we render the scene so that the sender appears at a fixed location on the screen.

Most of the parallax is seen in the relative motion of the background; slight changes to the sender's appearance are also seen as the receiver moves the head relative to the position of the sender's head—as the receiver moves more to one side, more that side of the sender's head will be seen. Detailed rendering parameters are determined according to the position of the receiver's head, using a predetermined scene layout which simulates real face-to-face communication. We now give the details.

Scene Layout

We must consider two problems when arranging the scene to be rendered. The first is that positions of models transmitted to the receiver's side are determined by the relative positions of the sender's Kinect and the sender. Suppose the distance between the Kinect and the foreground and background on the sender's side are Df and Db respectively. Since the simulated distance between the receiver and the sender is arbitrary, we simply assume that the receiver sits at the position of the Kinect on the sender's side. Suppose the rendering distance between the receiver and the sender is df, and that between the receiver and the sender's background is db, we thus have:

$$d_f = D_f, \quad d_b = D_b \tag{7}$$

However, the receiver may move backwards and forwards to a limited extent. Moving backwards would cause the receiver to see unmodeled parts of the sender's scene, losing realism. To prevent this problem arising, we slightly reduce the angle of view relative to the sender's side. If the angle of view at the sender's side is ψ_s and is ψ_r at the receiver's side, we set ψ_r to

$$\psi_r = \rho\,\psi_s \tag{8}$$

In our implementation we set ψ_s to 45° and ρ to 0.9.

Camera Position

We assume that the receiver's gaze is fixed at the midpoint of the sender's eyes. If the receiver always accordingly rotated his head in compensation while moving it, it would be straightforward to perform rendering based on this new viewing position and direction, using the head tracking information. In practice, however, the receiver may often just rotate his eyes as he moves his head, and such eye movement cannot be readily determined. Thus, rather than using the measured rotation of the head as a basis for rendering, for simplicity we model the situation as if his eyes were fixed in his head to look forwards, and work out how much he would have to rotate his head to keep looking at the same point.

Thus, we separate the movement of the receiver's head into two parts: translation, and consequent head rotation. The tracked midpoint of the receiver's eyes provides changes in position. For each frame, the change in position relative to the previous frame, is used to update the camera position. Camera rotation based on modeled head rotation is assumed to occur in two orthogonal directions, through small angles θ about the y axis and φ about the x axis. If the distance between the camera and the sender along the z axis is Ds, and the offsets relative to the original locations in x and y directions are D_x and D_y respectively, the changes in rotation angles are simply given by

$$\theta = D_x/D_s,\ \varphi = \arctan D_y/D_s \approx D_y/D_s \tag{9}$$

The camera position and orientation are accordingly updated in each frame.

EXPERIMENTS AND EVALUATION

Our system has been implemented in C# using the Microsoft Kinect SDK v1.8, on a PC with an Intel Core i7 3770 3.40 GHz CPU, an Nvidia GTX780 GPU, and a first generation Kinect. We illustrate the results of our system in Fig. 6.

We have performed an initial user study; a much fuller and more carefully designed perceptual study is also planned. We invited 10 participants to take part in the user study; they were Ph.D. students in computer graphics and computer vision, whose background might perhaps make them more critical than the general public. Each participant took part in videoconferencing using our system, and using Microsoft Skype as a typical 2D videoconferencing system as a basis for comparison.

We were interested in particular in how much our system gave an enhanced impression of depth during videoconferencing. We thus specifically asked them to evaluate their experience of depth when using our system compared to the typical 2D videoconferencing system. Five subjective scores could be chosen, ranging from −2 to +2, where −2 meant our system gave much less sensation of depth, −1 meant somewhat less sensation of depth, 0 meant both systems gave more or less equal sensations of depth, +1 meant our system gave somewhat more sensation of depth, and +2 meant much more sensation of depth. Furthermore, to achieve further insight, we asked participants to give a short written comment justifying their evaluation.

Eight out of the ten participants gave our system a score of 2, while two of them gave a score of 1. These initial results clearly show that our approach leads to a greater sensation of depth during videoconferencing. Of the two participants who gave a score of 1, one of them justified his score on the basis that the background seemed like a flat plane, when the subject could see it was actually composed of two orthogonal walls. The other participant who gave a lower score said the edge of the head did not seem sufficiently smooth, and the lack of realism caused him to keep looking at the edge, distracting him. Since we made the assumption that the receiver would fixate at the midpoint of the sender's eyes, staring at the edge of the sender violates the assumption, perhaps leading to the lessthan-perfect satisfaction with the depth realism.

Scene 1, frame 1

Scene 1, frame 100

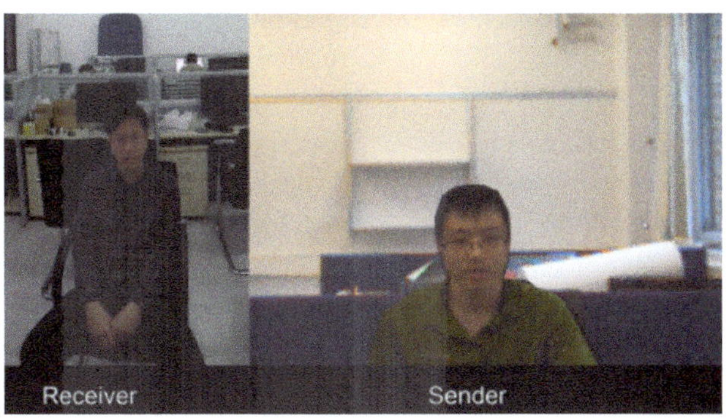

Scene 2, frame 1

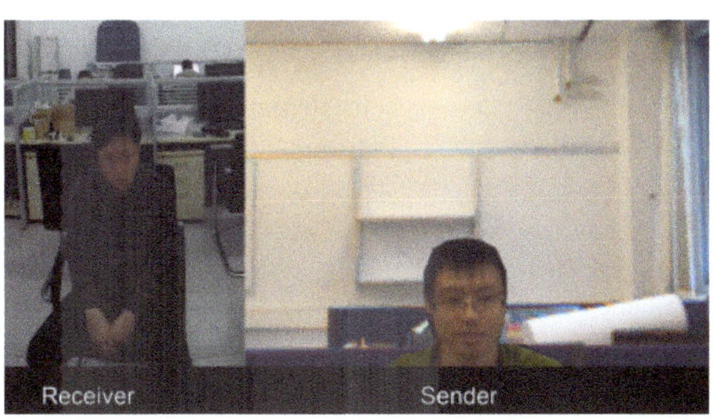

Scene 2, frame 100

Figure 6: Four frames were selected from 2 scenes. In scene 1, the receiver tilted his head to the left in frame 1 while in frame 100 he tilted his head to the right. The viewpoints for rendering the sender's scene were changed with respect to the head's position. In scene 2, the receiver sat straightly in frame 1 while in frame 100 he leaned forward.

These comments will be used to inform future improvements of our system, along with those for the eight participants who gave the highest score. Their most frequent comments can be summarized as "I observed the motion parallax between the foreground and background" and "the perspective of the scene is very consistent with my viewpoint".

CONCLUSIONS

In this paper, we proposed a videoconferencing system based on 3D modeling and motion parallax to give an improved sensation of depth. We use a parameterized model of the sender, and position a synthetic camera based on tracking the receiver's head position. Initial experimental results show that users feel that our system gives a greater sensation of depth perception than a typical 2D videoconferencing system. Further, fuller perceptual testing is planned for the future.

Our system has some limitations. Our system does not support hand gestures or large movements, e.g., standing up or large shoulder rotations, as these are harder to track and would need more complete models. Our system assumes there is only one person in the field of view—the Kinect depth stream is noisier when there are multiple persons, and this makes it hard to give a visual-pleasing modeling result.

We hope to improve our system in the future by using a more detailed model of the sender based on more vertices; newer Kinect-like devices will also help to make improved models. We will also make more complex models of the background; this can be done readily, even if a little slow, as part of the offline modeling before videoconferencing begins.

ACKNOWLEDGEMENTS

This work was supported by the National Hightech R&D Program of China (Project No. 2013AA013903), the National Natural Science Foundation of China (Project Nos. 61133008 and 61272226), Research Grant of Beijing Higher Institution Engineering Research Center, an EPSRC Travel Grant, and the Research and Enterprise Investment Fund of Cardiff Metropolitan University.

REFERENCES

1. Rosenthal, A. H. Two-way television communication unit. US Patent 2420198, 1947
2. Okada, K.-I.; Maeda, F.; Ichikawaa, Y.; Matsushita, Y. Multiparty videoconferencing at virtual social distance: MAJIC design. In: Proceedings of ACM Conference on Computer Supported Cooperative Work, 385–393, 1994
3. Sellen, A.; Buxton, B.; Arnott, J. Using spatial cues to improve videoconferencing. In: Proceedings of the SIGCHI Conference on Human Factors in Computing Systems, 651–652, 1992
4. Tang, J. C.; Minneman, S. Video Whiteboard: Video shadows to support remote collaboration. In: Proceedings of the SIGCHI Conference on Human Factors in Computing Systems, 315–322, 1991
5. Vertegaal, R. The GAZE groupware system: Mediating joint attention in multiparty communication and collaboration. In: Proceedings of the SIGCHI Conference on Human Factors in Computing Systems, 294–301, 1999

6. Vertegaal, R.; Ding, Y. Explaining effects of eye gaze on mediated group conversations: Amount or synchronization? In: Proceedings of ACM Conference on Computer Supported Cooperative Work, 41–48, 2002
7. Pirenne, M. H. Optics, Painting and Photography. Cambridge, UK: Cambridge University Press, 1970
8. Solso, R. L. Cognition and the Visual Arts. Cambridge, MA, USA: MIT Press, 1996
9. Pepperell, R.; Haertel, M. Do artists use linear perspective to depict visual space? Perception Vol. 43, No. 5, 395–416, 2014
10. Baldwin, J.; Burleigh, A.; Pepperell, R. Comparing artistic and geometrical perspective depictions of space in the visual field. i-Perception Vol. 5, No. 6, 536–547, 2014
11. Kemp, M. The Science of Art: Optical Themes in Western Art from Brunelleschi to Seurat. New Haven, CT, USA: Yale University Press, 1990
12. Kingslake, R. Optics in Photography. Bellingham, WA, USA: SPIE Publications, 1992
13. Ogle, K. N. Research in Binocular Vision, 2nd edn. New York: Hafner Publishing Company, 1964
14. Harrison, C.; Hudson, S. E. Pseudo-3D video conferencing with a generic webcam. In: Proceedings of the 10th IEEE International Symposium on Multimedia, 236–241, 2008
15. Zhang, C.; Yin, Z.; Florencio, D. Improving depth perception with motion parallax and its application in teleconferencing. In: Proceedings of IEEE International Workshop on Multimedia Signal Processing, 1–6, 2009
16. Izadi, S.; Kim, D.; Hilliges, O.; Molyneaux, D.; Newcombe, R.; Kohli, P.; Shotton, J.; Hodges, S.; Freeman, D.; Davison, A.; Fitzgibbon, A. KinectFusion: Real-time 3D reconstruction and interaction using a moving depth camera. In: Proceedings of the 24th Annual ACM Symposium on User Interface Software and Technology, 559–568, 2011
17. Newcombe, R. A.; Izadi, S.; Hilliges, O.; Molyneaux, D.; Kim, D.; Davison, A. J.; Kohli, P.; Shotton, J.; Hodges, S.; Fitzgibbon, A. KinectFusion: Real-time dense surface mapping and tracking. In: Proceedings of the 10th IEEE International Symposium on Mixed and Augmented Reality, 127–136, 2011
18. Kim, K.; Bolton, J.; Girouard, A.; Cooperstock, J.; Vertegaal, R. TeleHuman: Effects of 3D perspective on gaze and pose estimation with a life-size cylindrical telepresence pod. In: Proceedings of the SIGCHI Conference on Human Factors in Computing Systems, 2531–2540, 2012
19. Lee, J. C. Head tracking for desktop VR displays using the Wii remote. Available at http://johnnylee.net/projects/wii/.
20. iPhone User Guide For iOS 8.1 Software. Apple Inc., 2014
21. Levin, A.; Lischinski, D.; Weiss, Y. A closed form solution to natural image matting. IEEE Transactions on Pattern Analysis and Machine Intelligence Vol. 30, No. 2, 228–242, 2008
22. Rydfalk, M. CANDIDE, a parameterized face. Technical Report LiTH-ISY-I-866. Link¨oping University, 1987.
23. Welsh, B. Model-based coding of images. Ph.D. Thesis. British Telecom Research Lab, 1991
24. Ahlberg, J. CANDIDE-3—An updated parameterised face. Technical Report LiTH-ISY-R-2326. Linköping University, 2001
25. Rusinkiewicz, S.; Hall-Holt, O.; Levoy, M. Real-time 3D model acquisition. ACM Transactions on Graphics Vol. 21, No. 3, 438–446, 2002
26. 3dMD Static Systems. Available at http://www.3dmd.com/3dMD-systems/.
27. Chen, J.; Bautembach, D.; Izadi, S. Scalable real-time volumetric surface reconstruction. ACM Transactions on Graphics Vol. 32, No. 4, Article No. 113, 2013
28. Wexler, Y.; Shechtman, E.; Irani, M. Space–time completion of video. IEEE Transactions on Pattern Analysis and Machine Intelligence Vol. 29, No. 3, 463–476, 2007
29. Chen, T.; Zhu, Z.; Shamir, A.; Hu, S.-M.; Cohen-Or, D. 3-Sweep: Extracting editable objects from a single photo. ACM Transactions on Graphics Vol. 32, No. 6, Article No. 195, 2013
30. Gal, R.; Sorkine, O.; Mitra, N. J.; Cohen-Or, D. iWIRES: An analyze-and-edit approach to shape manipulation. ACM Transactions on Graphics Vol. 28, No. 3, Article No. 33, 2009.
31. Schulz, A.; Shamir, A.; Levin, D. I. W.; Sitthi-amorn, P.; Matusik, W. Design and fabrication by example. ACM Transactions on Graphics Vol. 33, No. 4, Article No. 62, 2014.
32. Zheng, Y.; Fu, H.; Cohen-Or, D.; Au, O. K.-C.; Tai, C.-L. Component-wise controllers for structurepreserving shape manipulation. Computer Graphics Forum Vol. 30, No. 2, 563–572, 2011

CHAPTER 12 ACCURATE DISPARITY ESTIMATION IN LIGHT FIELD USING GROUND CONTROL POINTS

Hao Zhu and Qing Wang

School of Computer Science, Northwestern Polytechnic University, Xi'an 710072, China

ABSTRACT

The recent development of light field cameras has received growing interest, as their rich angular information has potential benefits for many computer vision tasks. In this paper, we introduce a novel method to obtain a dense disparity map by use of ground control points (GCPs) in the light field. Previous work optimizes the disparity map by local estimation which includes both reliable points and unreliable points. To reduce the negative effect of the unreliable points, we predict the disparity at non-GCPs from GCPs. Our method performs more robustly in shadow areas than previous methods based on GCP work, since we combine color information and local disparity. Experiments and comparisons on a public dataset demonstrate the effectiveness of our proposed method.

INTRODUCTION

With the rapid development of computational photography, many computational imaging devices have been invented, based on, e.g., coded apertures [1], focal sweep [2], and light fields [3, 4], examples of the latter being the Lytro (https://lytro.com) and Raytrix (http://www. raytrix.de) cameras. As a light field camera captures both spatial and angular information about the distribution of light rays in space, it provides a potential basis for many fundamental operations in computer vision [5–8]. In this paper, we focus on accurate disparity estimation using the light field.

Disparity estimation in stereo [9–11] is a longstanding problem in computer vision, and it plays an important role in many tasks. Given two or more images captured from different viewpoints, the fundamental problem is to find the optimal correspondence between these images. Unlike the point information captured by a traditional camera, a light field camera captures information about the light, providing a full description of the real world via a 4D function. We can obtain so-called subaperture images [12], and synthesize a multi-view representation of the real world. Unlike the wide baseline used in traditional multi-view stereo, the multi-view representation synthesized by the light field has a narrow baseline, which can provide more accurate sub-pixel disparity estimation.

Previous work [13, 14] has computed an optimized disparity map based on local estimation, which includes both reliable and unreliable information. Undoubtedly, reliable points will have a positive effect on the global disparity map, but the effect of unreliable points may be detrimental. To reduce the negative effects of unreliable points, we propose to obtain a dense disparity map from certain reliable estimation points in the light field called ground control points (GCPs)

Citation: Hao Zhu and Qing Wang, Accurate disparity estimation in light field using ground control points, DOI 10.1007/s41095-016-0052-6.

[15]. GCPs are sparse points which can be matched reliably in stereo, and are often obtained by stable matching or laser scanning. We determine GCPs by the reliability of the structure tensor, and construct the GCP spread function based on color similarity and local disparity similarity. By combining local disparities, the proposed method performs more robustly than the previous GCP method in shadow areas: experimental results on the LFBD dataset [16] show that our method performs more robustly than the original light field method [14] and the original GCP method [15].

The rest of this paper is organized as follows. In Section 2, we review the background and prior work on depth estimation from a light field and the GCP method. Section 3 describes our algorithm. We give the experimental results in Section 4, and our conclusions and suggestions for future work are provided in Section 5.

BACKGROUND AND RELATED WORK

A light field [17] is represented by a 4D function f(x, y, u, v), where the dimensions (x, y) describe the spatial distribution of light, and the dimensions (u, v) describe the angular distribution of light. When we fix one spatial dimension y^* and one angular dimension v^*, we get the epipolar plane image (EPI) [18] (see Fig. 1).

In a rectified EPI, the slope k of a line has a linear relationship with the depth d (see Fig. 2), the larger the depth, the larger the slope: d = fsk/c, where f is the focal length of the lens, s is the baseline between the two views, and c is the pixel size. Given the EPI structure, the depth estimation problem is converted into a slope detection problem. As light field cameras capture angular information, analyzing the EPI is a suitable way to estimate depth using the light field.

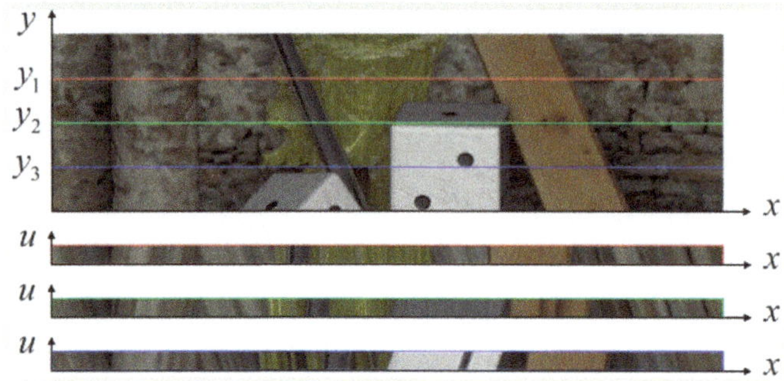

Figure 1: The epipolar plane image obtained by fixing one spatial dimension and one angular dimension.

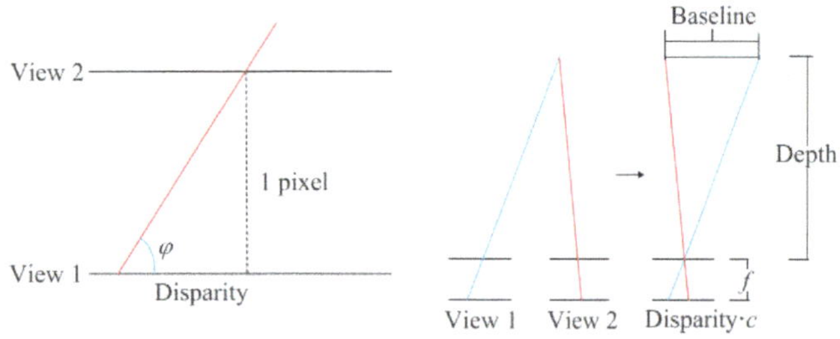

Figure 2: Left: epipolar plane image. Note that the slope is the reciprocal of the disparity. Right: the inverse relationship between disparity and depth. The relationship between slope and depth is linear.

Structure Tensor (ST)

Wanner and Goldluecke [14] proposed to analyze the EPI by the structure tensor, obtaining the local disparity and the corresponding reliability at the same time. They then optimized the local disparity map by a global energy function based on variational regularization. However, as they pointed out, the sampling of viewpoints must be dense enough to guarantee that the disparity between two views is less than 2 pixels, otherwise the straight line will become a broken line in the EPI, leading to inaccurate local estimation. This issue will be discussed in Section 3.1.

Lisad Transform

Tosic and Berkner [19] proposed the light field scale and depth transform. They initially detected the slope of the epitube [20] in Lisad-2 space, and then repaired depth discontinuous areas using the slope of the epistrip [20] detected in Lisad-1 space.

Multiple Cues

Tao et al. [21] proposed a method to estimate depth by combining multiple cues, including correspondence cues and defocus cues. The advantages of using different cues in different areas were exploited, and they obtained good results for real scenes.

RPCA (Robust Principle Component Analysis) Matching

Heber and Pock [22] considered the highly redundant nature of the light field, and proposed a new global matching term based on low rank minimization. Their method achieves the best results on synthetic datasets.

GCP Method

Ground control points are sparse points which can be matched reliably in stereo. Wang and Yang [15] proposed to predict the disparity of non-GCPs from GCPs, and optimized the initial disparity map using a Markov random field (MRF) energy function containing three terms: a data term, a smoothness term, and the GCP term. The top ranking results achieved on the Middlebury dataset prove that it is a good approach to stereo matching. However, it performs poorly in shadow (see Fig. 5) as it assumes that two points with similar colors should have similar disparities, but the colors may differ between a center point and its neighbors while their disparities are similar.

THEORY AND ALGORITHM

Algorithm Overview

Our approach is given in Algorithm 1. The input is the 4D light field L(x, y, u, v) and the reference view index r.

Algorithm 1: Our GCP algorithm

Input:
Multi-view images $I_1, \ldots, I_N$ generated from light field L; reference view index r.
Output:
Global optimal disparity map D.
Process:
$(D_0, R_0) = \text{StructureTensor}(I_1, \ldots, I_N)$; ▷ Section 3.2
$G = \text{GetGCPs}(R_0)$; ▷ Section 3.2
$\tilde{D} = \text{GCPSpread}(I_r, D_0, G)$; ▷ Section 3.3
$E = E_{\text{data}} + E_{\text{smooth}} + E_{\text{GCP}}(\tilde{D})$; ▷ Section 3.4
$D = \text{GraphCut}(E)$. ▷ Section 3.4

The output is the disparity map D. The algorithm consists of five steps:

1. *Local Estimation*: The local disparity map and its reliability map are obtained by using the structure tensor method (see Section 3.2).
2. *GCP detection*: The most credible points as determined by the reliability map are selected as the GCPs (see Section 3.2).
3. *GCP Optimization*: The GCP spread function is built using the local disparity map and the set of GCPs. By using this function, intermediate results are obtained (see Section 3.3).
4. *Building the Energy Function*: The intermediate results from GCP optimization are combined with traditional stereo matching function results (see Section 3.4).
5. *Final Optimization*: The energy function is found by optimization (see Section 3.4).

Local Disparity and GCPs

We use the structure tensor to detect the slopes of lines in the EPI:

$$\boldsymbol{J} = \begin{bmatrix} G_\sigma(S_x S_x) & G_\sigma(S_x S_y) \\ G_\sigma(S_x S_y) & G_\sigma(S_y S_y) \end{bmatrix} = \begin{bmatrix} J_{xx} & J_{xy} \\ J_{xy} & J_{yy} \end{bmatrix} \quad (1)$$

where G_σ represents a Gaussian smoothing operator, and S_x, S_y represent the gradients of the EPI in x and y directions respectively.

Then, the direction of the line is

$$\phi = \frac{1}{2}\arctan\left(\frac{J_{yy} - J_{xx}}{2J_{xy}}\right) \quad (2)$$

and its reliability is measured by the coherence of the structure tensor:

$$r = \frac{(J_{yy} - J_{xx})^2 + 4J_{xy}^2}{(J_{xx} + J_{yy})^2} \quad (3)$$

It is worth noting that the structure tensor performs poorly in the near field (see Fig. 4), which corresponds to the low-slope area in the EPI; in other words, the disparity between two views is larger than 2 pixels in these areas. We adopt the easiest method to solve this issue—by scaling up the EPI along the y axis in these areas to convert the low-slope area into a high-slope area. We use bicubic interpolation to scale up the EPI. After calculating the slope of the scaled EPI, we can recover the slope of the original EPI by dividing by the scaling factor. An original EPI and the scaled up EPI can be seen in Fig. 3. The improvement of our method can be seen in Fig. 4.

Having obtained the coarse disparity map D_0 and its reliability map R_0 from the structure tensor, it is unnecessary to do stable matching or laser scanning to obtaining GCPs; to do so would be timeconsuming and laborious. We obtain the set of GCPs G from the reliability map R_0.

Figure 3: Top: an original EPI. Bottom: the scaled up EPI. Clearly, the slopes of the lines are greater in the latter.

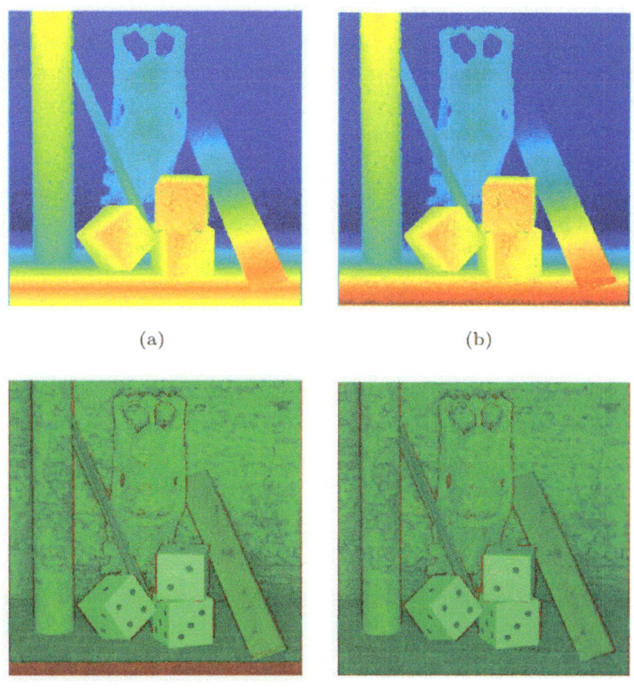

Figure 4: Disparity and error map obtained by the basic structure tensor method and our method for the Buddha dataset. (a) Disparity map obtained by the basic structure tensor method. (b) Disparity map obtained by our improved method. The basic structure tensor method performs poorly at close range. (c) and (d) Relative depth error maps for the above two methods. Relative depth errors of more than 1% are indicated in red. The error rates of these two methods are 7.87% and 3.97%, respectively.

GCP Spread Function

The inputs to our GCP spread function are the reference view image I_r, the local disparity map D_0, and the set of GCPs G.

Unlike Wang and Yang's method [15], which constrains similar colors to have similar disparities, we use the constraint that two neighboring pixels p and q should have similar disparities if not only their colors are similar but also their local disparities are similar. This constraint can be described by minimizing the difference between the disparity of p and a weighted combination of its neighbors' disparities. The global cost function is given by

$$J(\tilde{D}) = \left(\tilde{D}_p - \frac{\sum_{q \in N_8(p)} \omega_{pq} \tilde{D}_q}{\sum_{q \in N_8(p)} \omega_{pq}} \right)^2 \tag{4}$$

where $\tilde{D}$ is the optimal disparity map found by minimizing this global cost function. $N_8(p)$ comprises p's 8-connected neighbors; ω_{pq} are weights based on a color term and a disparity term:

$$\omega_{pq} = \max\left(\exp\left(\frac{-\Delta C_{pq}}{\gamma_c} + \frac{-\Delta D_{0,pq}}{\gamma_d}\right), \epsilon\right) \tag{5}$$

where ΔC_{pq} and $\Delta D_{0,pq}$ are respectively the Euclidean distances between pixels in RGB color space and local disparity (D_0) space. Parameters γ_c, γ_d, and ϵ control sharpness of the function. To ensure that the disparity term and the color term have the same order of magnitude, the parameter γ_d is not independent, and is calculated from the following equation:

$$\gamma_d = s_{\gamma_d} \frac{\gamma_c (d_{\max} - d_{\min})}{(C_{\max} - C_{\min})\sqrt{N_C}} \tag{6}$$

where C_{max} and C_{min} are the maximum and minimum values in color space, 255 and 0 respectively. N_C is the number of color channels, here 3. Parameters d_{max} and d_{min} are the maximum and minimum values in hypothetical disparity space, respectively. $s_{\gamma d}$ is a weight to control the strength of the disparity term. We suggest that the disparity term should be larger than the color term, so $s_{\gamma d} < 1$.

Equation (4) is a quadratic function. After taking its derivative to find the extremum, we find that the disparity of the center point p has a linear relationship with the disparities of its neighbors:

$$\tilde{D}_p = \frac{\sum_{q \in N_8(p)} \omega_{pq} \tilde{D}_q}{\sum_{q \in N_8(p)} \omega_{pq}} = \sum_{q \in N_8(p)} \alpha_{pq} \tilde{D}_q \tag{7}$$

$$\alpha_{pq} = \frac{\omega_{pq}}{\sum_{q \in N_8(p)} \omega_{pq}} \tag{8}$$

Given the linear relationship above, we can derive the disparity of non-GCPs from GCPs by solving a system of sparse linear equations (I−A)x = b, where I is an identity matrix, and A is an N ×N matrix (N is the number of points in the image). In each row of A, if the corresponding pixel p belongs to the GCPs, all elements are zero, otherwise only the 8-connected neighbor points q have non-zero values, equal to their weights α_{pq}. Similarly, for the elements in vector b, only the pixels belonging to GCPs have non-zero values, and are equal to their initial disparities. x is the optimal disparity map that we hope to obtain.

Energy Functions with the GCPs

Our energy function contains three terms: a data term, a smoothness term, and the GCP term. As the length of the baseline between two views in the light field camera is narrow, we combine the basic sum of squared differences (SSD) and sum of squared gradient differences (SSGD) as our data term to ensure good matching:

$$E_{\text{data}}(D) = E_{\text{basic}}(p, D(p)) + E_{\text{grad}}(p, D(p)) \tag{9}$$

where

$$E_{\text{basic}}(p, D(p)) = \sum_{i \in V} \sum_{q \in N(p)} \{I_i(q) - I_r[q + D(p)(i - r)]\}^2 \tag{10}$$

and

$$\begin{aligned} E_{\text{grad}}(p, D(p)) &= (1-\alpha) \cdot \sum_{i \in V} \sum_{q \in N(p)} \{I_{i,gx}(q) - I_{r,gx}[q + D(p)(i - r)]\}^2 \\ &+ \alpha \cdot \sum_{i \in V} \sum_{q \in N(p)} \{I_{i,gy}(q) - I_{r,gy}[q + D(p)(i - r)]\}^2 \end{aligned} \tag{11}$$

Here, D is the global optimal disparity map, D(p) is the disparity value of point p, V is the number of views in the light field, N(p) is an image patch centered at pixel p, I_r is the reference view in the light field, and $I_{i,gx}$ and $I_{i,gy}$ are the gradients of the i-th view image in x and y directions, respectively

We select the widely used linear model based on a 4-connected neighborhood system as our smoothness term, which is expressed as

$$E_{\text{smooth}}(D) = \lambda_s \sum_{p \in I_r} \sum_{q \in N_4(p)} \omega_{pq} \Delta D_{pq} \tag{12}$$

where ΔD_{pq} is the difference in disparity between pixels p and q, λ_s is a smoothness coefficient to control the strength smoothing, and ω_{pq} is a weight based on the distance between p and q in RGB color space:

$$\omega_{pq} = \max\left(\exp\left(\frac{-\Delta C_{pq}}{\gamma_c}\right), \epsilon\right) \tag{13}$$

Given the optimal disparity $\tilde{D}_p$ obtained by the GCP spread function in Eq. (7), we can now employ the robust penalty function [15]:

$$E_{GCP}(D) = \lambda_r \sum_{p \in I_r} \varphi(D_p, \tilde{D}_p)$$
$$= -\lambda_r \sum_{p \in I_r} \ln((1-\eta)\exp(\frac{-|D_p - \tilde{D}_p|}{\gamma_d}) + \eta) \quad (14)$$

where λ_r is a regularization coefficient that controls the strength of the GCP energy; γ_d and η control the sharpness and upper-bound of the penalty function.

EXPERIMENTAL RESULTS

Parameters and Dataset

In our experiments, we have found that the structure tensor method performs poorly for lines in the EPI with slope larger than 0.65. So, we first analyze the EPI by structure tensor, and then if the slope of 50% of points is larger than 0.65, we scale this EPI from 9 to 17 pixels in the y direction, and reanalyze the EPI.

We set two thresholds to select GCPs, using absolute reliability and relative reliability. The absolute reliability is set to 0.99 in our implementation. If the reliability of a point is larger than 0.99, it is classified as a GCP. If only this criterion is used, GCPs may be too sparse in some datasets to reliably determine the disparity map calculated from the GCPs. We thus also consider relative reliability. If the fraction of GCPs obtained by considering absolute reliability is smaller than a set percentage (20%), we select the 20% most relaible points as GCPs.

For the disparity map obtained from GCPs, the parameters γ_c and ϵ are set to 30 and 0, respectively. The weight parameter $s_{\gamma d}$ is set to 0.25. Note that if γ_c or γ_d is unsuitable, the sparse linear system may be singular.

In the data term, the parameter α is set to 0.5, and the size of image patches is 7 × 7. The parameters γ_c and ϵ in the smoothness term are set to 3.6 and 0.3, respectively. And the parameters η and γ_d are set to 0.005 and 2 according to Wang and Yang [15], respectively. In the final energy function, the smoothness coefficient λ_s and the GCP scaling coefficient λ_r are set to 1.67 and 4.67, respectively. We divide the disparity into 120 levels, and use linear interpolation to get floating point values for use in the data term. We use GCO-v3 [23–25] to optimize our energy function.

We tested our method using HCI LFBD [16], which contains synthetically generated light fields, each of which is represented by 9 × 9 sub-aperture images. The dataset was rendered by Blender (http://www.blender.org), and contains the ground truth.

Our algorithm was implemented in MATLAB, on MacOS X 10.11.1 with 8 GB RAM and a 2.7 GHz processor. The running time for a 9×9×768×768×3 light field is 60 minutes. Most of the cost is to build two large sparse matrices for the smoothness term and the GCP term, and could be greatly reduced by reimplementation in C.

Comparision with Previous Works

We compare our GCP propagation method with the basic structure tensor method and Wang and Yang's method [15] in Fig. 5. Our method performs more robustly than Wang and Yang's in shadows and in color discontinuous areas.

We also compare our results with Wanner and Goldluecke's [14] and Wang and Yang's [15] results, as shown in Fig. 6. Note that there is much noise in the initial map; there is reduced noise after the GCPs' spread. A quantitative comparison can be seen in Table 1. We select the relative depth error as our criterion (we used 0.2% here). Our method performs better than Wanner and Goldluecke's on 4 datasets, but worse on 3 datasets. On analyzing these 7 datasets we find that there are few transparent materials in the Buddha, StillLife, Horses, and Medieval datasets, but more transparent materials and shadows, lamps, and mirrors in the Buddha2, Mona, and Papillon datasets. Stereo matching outperforms the structure tensor method in a Lambertian environment, whilst the structure tensor performs better in nonLambertian environments.

Figure 6: Results of our method on Buddha, StillLife, Mona, and Horses datasets from LFBD. Top: initial disparity map D_0. 2nd row: results $\tilde{D}$ from the GCP spread function. 3rd row: final results of our method. 4th row: ground truth. Bottom: error map. Relative depth errors of more than 0.2% are shown in red.

Table 1: Percentage of pixels with depth error more than 0.2% for LFBD [16]. The results of Wanner and Goldluecke's method were obtained by running their public source code. The results of Wang and Yang's method were obtained by our implementation (Unit: %)

	Buddha	Buddha2	Mona	Papillon	StillLife	Horses	Medieval
Wanner and Goldluecke's [14]	7.28	26.55	15.08	16.64	4.50	16.44	24.33
Wang and Yang's [15]	5.50	35.31	25.80	18.39	4.55	14.25	24.75
Our method	5.50	34.81	25.86	17.56	3.61	13.29	23.24

Figure 5: Comparison. (a) Input dataset; there are two colors in the butterfly and a shadow on the leaves to the left of the butterfly. (b) Basic structure tensor result, showing many points with wrong values. (c) Wang and Yang's propagation strategy assigns wrong disparities to shadow areas and divides the butterfly into 2 parts along the color boundary in its tail. (d) Result of our GCP propagation method, with few wrong values and good performance in shadow areas.

Our method performs better than Wang and Yang's method, especially for the Papillon, StillLife, and Horses datasets. Note that there exist some shadows in these datasets; the disparities of shadow areas ought to be the same as those of their neighborhoods. As local disparity information is combined in our GCP spread function, our method outperforms Wang and Yang's.

CONCLUSIONS AND FUTURE WORK

In this paper, we have proposed the idea to determine GCPs by using the reliability of the structure tensor. We also give a more robust GCP spread function than Wang and Yang's [15] to propagate disparity from GCPs to non-GCPs. Experimental results on LFBD show that our method performs more robustly than Wanner and Goldluecke's and Wang and Yang's methods. However, our method performs less well in strong light and complicated shadow areas; this is a problem for most stereo methods. In the future, we will continue to investigate stereo in light fields, and take the advantages of more features of light field to solve these problems.

ACKNOWLEDGEMENTS

The work was supported by National Natural Science Foundation of China (Nos. 61272287, 61531014) and a research grant from the State Key Laboratory of Virtual Reality Technology and Systems (No. BUAA-VR-15KF-10).

REFERENCES

1. Levin, A. Analyzing depth from coded aperture sets. In: Lecture Notes in Computer Science, Vol. 6311. Daniilidis, K.; Maragos, P.; Paragios, N. Eds. Springer Berlin Heidelberg, 214–227, 2010.
2. Zhou, C.; Miau, D.; Nayar, S. K. Focal sweep camera for space-time refocusing. Columbia University Academic Commons, 2012. Available at http://hdl.handle.net/10022/AC:P:15386.
3. Lumsdaine, A.; Georgiev, T. The focused plenoptic camera. In: Proceedings of IEEE International Conference on Computational Photography, 1–8, 2009.
4. Ng, R.; Levoy, M.; Br´edif, M.; Duval, G.; Horowitz, M.; Hanrahan, P. Light field photography with a handheld plenoptic camera. Stanford Tech Report CTSR, 2005.
5. Birklbauer, C.; Bimber, O. Panorama light-field imaging. Computer Graphics Forum Vol. 33, No. 2, 43–52, 2014.
6. Dansereau, D. G.; Pizarro, O.; Williams, S. B. Linear volumetric focus for light field cameras. ACM Transactions on Graphics Vol. 34, No. 2, Article No. 15, 2015.
7. Li, N.; Ye, J.; Ji, Y.; Ling, H.; Yu, J. Saliency detection on light field. In: Proceedings of IEEE Conference on Computer Vision and Pattern Recognition, 2806–2813, 2014.
8. Raghavendra, R.; Raja, K. B.; Busch, C. Presentation attack detection for face recognition using light field camera. IEEE Transactions on Image Processing Vol. 24, No. 3, 1060–1075, 2015.
9. Scharstein, D.; Szeliski, R. A taxonomy and evaluation of dense two-frame stereo correspondence algorithms. International Journal of Computer Vision Vol. 47, No. 1, 7–42, 2002.
10. Du, S.-P.; Masia, B.; Hu, S.-M.; Gutierrez, D. A metric of visual comfort for stereoscopic motion. ACM Transactions on Graphics Vol. 32, No. 6, Article No. 222, 2013.
11. Wang, M.; Zhang, X.-J.; Liang, J.-B.; Zhang, S.-H.; Martin, R. R. Comfort-driven disparity adjustment for stereoscopic video. Computational Visual Media Vol. 2, No. 1, 3–17, 2016.
12. Wanner, S.; Fehr, J.; J¨ahne, B. Generating EPI representations of 4D light fields with a single lens focused plenoptic camera. In: Lecture Notes in Computer Science, Vol. 6938. Bebis, G.; Boyle, R.; Parvin, B. et al. Eds. Springer Berlin Heidelberg, 90– 101, 2011.
13. Wanner, S.; Goldluecke, B. Globally consistent depth labeling of 4D light fields. In: Proceedings of IEEE Conference on Computer Vision and Pattern Recognition, 41–48, 2012.
14. Wanner, S.; Goldluecke, B. Variational light field analysis for disparity estimation and super-resolution. IEEE Transactions on Pattern Analysis and Machine Intelligence Vol. 36, No. 3, 606–619, 2014.
15. Wang, L.; Yang, R. Global stereo matching leveraged by sparse ground control points. In: Proceedings of IEEE Conference on Computer Vision and Pattern Recognition, 3033–3040, 2011.
16. Wanner, S.; Meister, S.; Goldluecke, B. Datasets and benchmarks for densely sampled 4D light fields. In: Proceedings of Annual Workshop on Vision, Modeling

and Visualization, 225–226, 2013.

17. Levoy, M.; Hanrahan, P. Light field rendering. In: Proceedings of the 23rd Annual Conference on Computer Graphics and Interactive Techniques, 31– 42, 1996.
18. Bolles, R. C.; Baker, H. H.; Marimont, D. H. Epipolarplane image analysis: An approach to determining structure from motion. International Journal of Computer Vision Vol. 1, No. 1, 7–55, 1987.
19. Tosic, I.; Berkner, K. Light field scale-depth space transform for dense depth estimation. In: Proceedings of IEEE Conference on Computer Vision and Pattern Recognition Workshops, 441–448, 2014.
20. Criminisi, A.; Kang, S. B.; Swaminathan, R.; Szeliski, R.; Anandan, P. Extracting layers and analyzing their specular properties using epipolar-plane-image analysis. Computer Vision and Image Understanding Vol. 97, No. 1, 51–85, 2005.
21. Tao, M. W.; Hadap, S.; Malik, J.; Ramamoorthi, R. Depth from combining defocus and correspondence using light-field cameras. In: Proceedings of IEEE International Conference on Computer Vision, 673– 680, 2013.
22. Heber, S.; Pock, T. Shape from light field meets robust PCA. In: Lecture Notes in Computer Science, Vol. 8694. Fleet, D.; Pajdla, T.; Schiele, B.; Tuytelaars, T. Eds. Springer International Publishing, 751–767, 2014.
23. Boykov, Y.; Kolmogorov, V. An experimental comparison of min-cut/max-flow algorithms for energy minimization in vision. In: Lecture Notes in Computer Science, Vol. 2134. Figueiredo, M.; Zerubia, J.; Jain, A. K. Eds. Springer Berlin Heidelberg, 359–374, 2001.
24. Boykov, Y.; Veksler, O.; Zabih, R. Fast approximate energy minimization via graph cuts. IEEE Transactions on Pattern Analysis and Machine Intelligence Vol. 23, No. 11, 1222–1239, 2001.
25. Kolmogorov, V.; Zabin, R. What energy functions can be minimized via graph cuts? IEEE Transactions on Pattern Analysis and Machine Intelligence Vol. 26, No. 2, 147–159, 2004..

CHAPTER 13

SYNTHESIS OF A STROBOSCOPIC IMAGE FROM A HAND-HELD CAMERA SEQUENCE FOR A SPORTS ANALYSIS

Kunihiro Hasegawa and Hideo Saito

Keio University, Yokohama, 223-8522, Japan. E-mail: K. Hasegawa

ABSTRACT

This paper presents a method for synthesizing a stroboscopic image of a moving sports player from a hand-held camera sequence. This method has three steps: synthesis of background image, synthesis of stroboscopic image, and removal of player's shadow. In synthesis of background image step, all input frames masked a bounding box of the player are stitched together to generate a background image. The player is extracted by an HOG-based people detector. In synthesis of stroboscopic image step, the background image, the input frame, and a mask of the player synthesize a stroboscopic image. In removal of shadow step, we remove the player's shadow which negatively affects an analysis by using mean-shift. In our previous work, synthesis of background image has been timeconsuming. In this paper, by using the bounding box of the player detected by HOG and by subtracting the images for synthesizing a mask, computational speed and accuracy can be improved. These have contributed greatly to the improvement from the previous method. These are main improvements and novelty points from our previous method. In experiments, we confirmed the effectiveness of the proposed method, measured the player's speed and stride length, and made a footprint image. The image sequence was captured under a simple condition that no other people were in the background and the person controlling the video camera was standing still, such like a motion parallax was not occurred. In addition, we applied the synthesis method to various scenes to confirm its versatility.

INTRODUCTION AND MOTIVATION

Analyzing the performance of players has recently become popular in a variety of sports. Especially, using various technologies has become a major trend. A sensing technology is one of the examples. For example, the fatigue of athletic runners was evaluated using 12 wearable sensors to measure the displacement of the positions, angles, etc., of each joint and of the waist [1]. Data collected from sensors placed on a golf club and an athlete's body quantified a correctness of the performed golf swing [2]. Changes in ventricular rates when running have been visualized with heartbeat sensors [3]. Eskofier et al. [4] classified the motion of leg kicks during running by using an acceleration sensor. This classification could be used for fitting shoes, among other applications. Beetz et al. [5] proposed an analysing system for the football games using multiple sensors.

Using a video camera is also one solution for easy analysis. Various sports such as soccer [6], basketball [7, 8], and American football [9] are already using computer vision

Citation: Kunihiro Hasegawa, Hideo Saito, Synthesis of a stroboscopic image from a hand-held camera sequence for a sports analysis, DOI 10.1007/s41095-016-0053-5.

technologies. For example, an off-side line was visualized by tracking of multiple players in the soccer [6]. Lu et al. [7] and Per˘se et al. [8] proposed methods of identification, tracking, and motion analysis, etc. Atmosukarto et al. [9] proposed a method of recognition of a formation in American football.

Athletics is one of the targets of such analysis. For the analysis of athletic running, stride length and speed in each interval provide significant information for improving running performance. However, most conventional sensing technologies require special equipment such as a laser measuring instrument, multiple cameras, and/or motion sensors attached to the runners, which is expensive. Moreover, the interest of amateur runners in such analyses has been growing, and for these users, easy and on-site analysis of running performance is needed.

In our previous work, we proposed measuring stride length and speed with a video camera by manually moving a hand-held camera, so that it captured the entire running performance (e.g., completing a 100-m sprint) with sufficient resolution [10]. In that method, we measured the runner's landing position by using the homography between an image coordinate system and the real world coordinate system to estimate stride length and speed. We also tried to use a stroboscopic image that captured changes of a runner's poses in motion for automated measurement of speed and stride length. In our synthesis of a stroboscopic image, an image including only the background was synthesized first and then the runner was extracted from each frame and overlaid on the background image. The image in which only the runner was extracted could be synthesized by taking the difference between the background image and the image in which the runner was previously overlaid. We felt that the problem of landing timing determination could be solved by analyzing the stroboscopic image, but the background image synthesis we used was based on the mean-shift of each pixel, which was computationally expensive.

In the present work, we propose a method for synthesizing the stroboscopic image of a sports player from a hand-held camera sequence based on a computationally efficient algorithm that generates a stitched background image by using the bounding box of the player detected by HOG (histograms of oriented gradients). This algorithm can also extract accurately a player by using a mask synthesized by subtracting images. These series of processing using masks to improve computational speed and accuracy are main improvement and novelty points from our previous method. We also analyzed various other sports using video camera images and found that it should be possible to use the stroboscopic image synthesized by our method for sports other than running. Therefore, we consider our use of the stroboscopic image for runners to be a representative example.

This paper is organized as follows: Section 2 describes several related works. Section 3 shows an environment and a condition of capturing video for proposed method. Section 4 describes a detail of each step of the algorithm. Section 5 discusses experiments and results to confirm a superiority. Section 6 concludes this paper.

RELATED WORKS

As we are going to describe later, our proposed method can be divided into three parts: synthesis of background, synthesis of stroboscopic image, and removal of shadow. The first part also has a color alignment process and the second part is the same as foreground extraction and blending. Therefore, these four areas are related area.

Ebdelli et al. [11] have recently proposed an efficiently video inpainting method for synthesis of a background. They have used an energy function for object removal. There is a feature also of being less than the required number of images. In our method, we are taking advantage of the fact that a removal target is moving. By this fact, we can synthesis a background image using only an image transformation and a mask synthesis.

About color alignment, the method for reducing undesirable tonal fluctuations in video [12] and a color collection between multi-camera [13] have been proposed. Reference [12] designates one or more frames as anchors and executes a color alignment on basis of these frames. Reference [13] solves a difference in color between multiple cameras by an energy minimization. In this part, we utilize the process used in the based method [14], that is, a gain compensation and a multi-band blending.

Foreground extraction and blending in synthesis of background is one of the feature points of our proposed method. GrabCut [15] and an image cloning [16] are the representative methods of foreground extraction and blending. Our proposed method executes these processes by synthesizing and using a mask of a player.

Various methods have also been proposed about shadow removal. Guo et al. [17] have proposed a region based approach. They have used a relational graph of paired regions for detecting shadows. Miyazaki et al. [18] have proposed another method. This method has utilized MRF (Markov random field) and graph-cut for removal. In our method, we employ a method using mean-shift.

Further, there is a similarity with a motion object editing and representation in terms of output. For example, there are a generation of dynamic narratives from video [19], a production of objectlevel slow motion effects, etc., [20] and scene-space video processing [21]. Features of the proposed method in comparison with these techniques are synthesis of a stroboscopic image and using a handheld camera.

ENVIRONMENT AND CONDITIONS OF CAPTURING VIDEO

In this paper, we assume that video footage is captured using a hand-held camera operated by a person who controls the camera to capture the subject with a sufficient resolution in each frame, as shown in Fig. 1. We assume the operator takes a video in a scene where the player is practicing in a running track, on an athletic ground, etc. It is assumed that no other people are in the background under this condition. The person controlling the video camera is standing still and catches the player on the screen in all frames. The video camera is held in the operator's own hand and is moved freely.

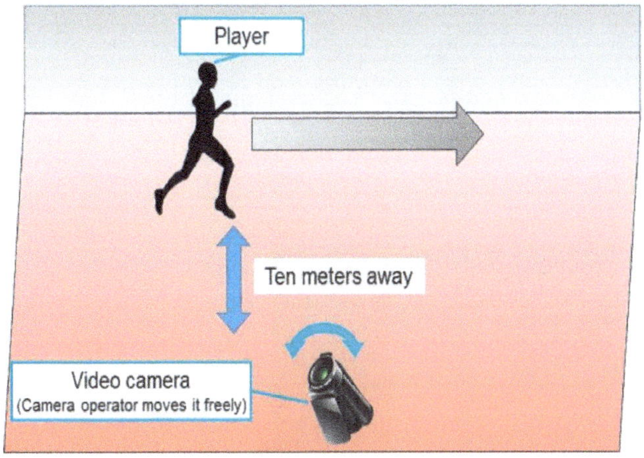

Figure 1: Image of capturing environment.

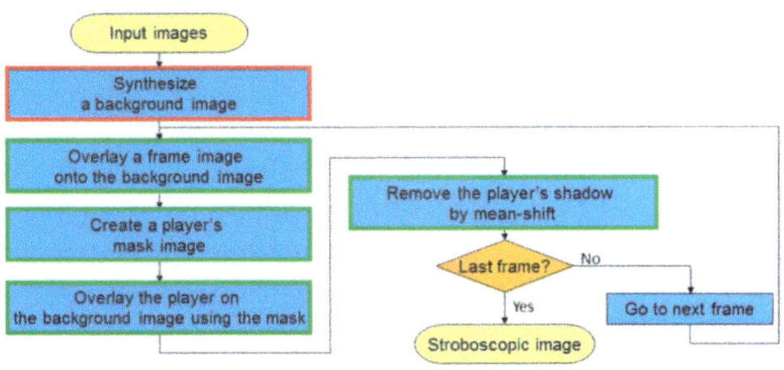

Figure 2: Flowchart of the proposed method.

The operator stands dozens of meters away from the center of the track to capture the player in the entire moving scene by using zoom. There are no restrictions on the player's clothes and background except that the color of the background and clothes should not be exactly the same.

PROPOSED METHOD

The goal of our previous method [10] was to synthesize a stroboscopic image for the automatic measurement of speed and stride length. In that method, a stitched image without a player has been synthesized and then the player has been overlaid on the stitched background image. As noted above, synthesizing the background image has been timeconsuming because mean-shift estimation [22, 23] has been executed on every pixel of the image. This has been the main drawback of the method [10]. Therefore, we need a way of synthesizing the image in a short amount of time.

In the method we propose in the present work, in order to reduce computation time, we mask only a region in which the player exists in the image of each frame used for the stitched image synthesis. As a result, any images containing only background are synthesized because the region where the player exists is excluded from the stitched image synthesis. We improve other parts of our previous method [10], as well. Specifically, we add methods for overlaying the player and removing the player's shadow. Figure 2 shows a flowchart including these improvement points, with the differences between our previous and present methods highlighted. Red frames indicate that a step for processing content is different and green frames indicate an added or interchanged step. In the proposed method, we use the bounding box of a player to synthesize a background image. We elaborate upon these points in Sections 4.1, 4.2, and 4.3.

Synthesis of Background Image

Here, we discuss the "synthesize a background image" process in Fig. 2. A background image shown in Fig. 3(c) is synthesized by stitching. As previously noted, we mask the area of the player as shown in Figs. 3(a) and 3(b) to reduce the computation time.

The area of this mask is the bounding box of a player detected by HOG-SVM [24]. The mask area of each frame is excluded in synthesizing a background image so that only a background pixel can be used for synthesizing the background image. HOG-SVM sometimes fails to detect the player in a motion sequence. Kalman filter [25] is applied for keeping track of the bounding box.

A stitching has two processing steps, calculating a homography and projection of images. The homography for this stitching uses feature points in each frame image. In order to extract feature points in complex environments such as the outdoors, SURF [26] is used as feature points and the stitch function of OpenCV is used for the synthesis, the same as in our previous method [10].

Our previous method [10] calculated each value of HSV for every pixel using mean-shift. In the proposed method, instead of mean-shift, we execute a stitching, as described above, which speeds up the synthesis of a background image.

Synthesis of Stroboscopic Image

Here, we describe the "overlay a frame image onto the background image", "create a player's mask image", and "overlay the player on the background image using the mask" processes in Fig. 2. In this step, we use the other mask synthesized by a subtraction of images, an example of which is shown in Fig. 3(e). This mask is the result of the "create a player's mask image" step and is used for overlaying the player on the background image in the "overlay the player on the background image using the mask" step. We elaborate upon these processes below.

Figure 3 except Fig. 3(b) shows images for each step of this subsection. In the "overlay a frame image on the background image" step, an input image of each frame, Fig. 3(a), is transformed and projected onto a coordinate system of the background image, Fig. 3(c). This background image is the result of Section 4.1. The homography for the transformation and projection of Fig. 3(a) is the same as in Section 4.1. As a result, a projected image, Fig. 3(d), is synthesized.

In the "create a player's mask image" step, the projected image, Fig. 3(d), and the background image, Fig. 3(c), are utilized again. A player's mask image, Fig. 3(e), is obtained by the subtraction and binarization of these two images. A part of the player area is occasionally lacking in the mask image if the color of the player's clothes is similar to that of the background, whereas we can compensate for this by a morphology process. Hence it is only a minor deficit.

(a) Input image (b) Mask for synthesizing a background (c) Background image

(d) Projected image (e) Mask for overlaying a player

Figure 3: Images for background and stroboscopic image synthesis.

To overlay an area of player onto the background image, a transformed input image of each frame as Fig. 3(a) is overlaid on the background image by using a player's mask image, such as Fig. 3(e). These steps are repeated to the last frame, at which point a stroboscopic image is synthesized. Of course, we change the background image to the stroboscopic image over making from the second frame. In our previous method, blending was needed to synthesize a stroboscopic image due to overlap of the bounding box of a player's area [10], and the difference between a player and a background might have become almost 0 in the worst case. In contrast, in our new method only the player is overlaid, so the player cannot disappear if the number of frames becomes enormous.

Removal of Player's Shadow

Here, we discuss the "remove the player's shadow by mean-shift" process in Fig. 2. The stroboscopic image synthesized in Section 4.2 results in the player's shadow being visible under certain capturing conditions such as a sunny day. An example is shown in Fig. 4, where some shadows remain in the red rectangles. In particular, shadows connected to the players expand the players' area. This negatively affects the calculation of the players' landing positions.

In order to remove these shadows, we use a synthesis method utilizing mean-shift, as explained in Ref. [27]. This method estimates each background pixel by mean-shift estimation. Input of this method is the pixels of input images which are projected onto each pixel of the background image. The number of frames having shadow is smaller than the number of frames having the background in views where the player is moving. Therefore, mean-shift can remove the shadows.

Figure 4: Stroboscopic image with shadow.

In mean-shift processing, the pixel value of each original image is assigned as the initial value. The bandwidth is 10. The kernel formula is Epanechnikovkernel the same as Ref. [27]. In addition, the weight for decision of the result is calculated for each candidate value. Finally, the value whose weight is the biggest is the background pixel value. In this calculation, the weight is the Gaussian to simplify the process. We select this removal area manually. The areas containing the shadow are quite small compared to the entire image. Processing time for this small area is a minor deficit.

EXPERIMENTS

We performed five experiments. In the first experiment, we compared our proposed method with our previous method in each step, and in the second, we measured player's landing position, speed, and stride length using the stroboscopic image. In this experiment, we also visualized the player's footprints. In the third experiment, we compared the results of our method with those of four existing methods: GrabCut [15], the image cloning [16], autostitch [14], and the frame subtraction. Then, we applied the synthesis method to various sports scenes to confirm its versatility. In the last experiment, we did some experiments in some complicated scenes to investigate limits of the proposed method. We used Microsoft Visual Studio 2010 as the IDE, C++ as the programming language, and OpenCV 2.4.11 as the image processing library for implementation. The PC we used had a 2.40 GHz CPU with 4 cores and 8.00 GB of memory. The HOG-SVM used to synthesize the mask was learned using about 20,000 player images for accurate detection. In some results, we show a subset of frames that have few intervals for visibility.

Synthesis of Runner's Stroboscopic Image

An input video for this experiment was captured by a hand-held camera. As described in Section 3, the camera was held in the operator's own hand to capture a runner in the center of the camera by manually tracking the runner. Figure 5 shows a part of the input image group used for the experiments. The size of the image was 640 × 480 pixels.

Synthesis of Background Image

Our previous method [10] utilizing mean-shift for synthesizing a background image was timeconsuming. In our new method, we use the bounding box of a player detected by HOG to reduce the computation time.

Figure 5: Example of input images.

A comparison of the processing time results is given in Table 1. We used only the three frames shown in Fig. 5 for this experiment to compare to our previous experiment. The processing time for the previous and proposed methods was measured 10 times each. As indicated in the table, the proposed method utilizing a mask to reduce processing time is even faster than our previous method [10].

Figures 6(a) and 6(d) show the background image synthesized by our previous method [10] and the proposed method. As shown, the two images are almost equivalent. These results indicate that the image synthesized by our proposed method can be applied to the following process.

Synthesis of Stroboscopic Image

Our previous method [10] needed to blend overlaying player's areas with a background image, which resulted in the difference between the player and the background becoming almost 0 in the worst case. In the proposed method, we use a mask synthesized by the input and background images to overlay the player on the background.

Table 1: Processing time of synthesizing a background image

	Previous [10]	Proposed
Average (s)	2.44×10^3	1.72×10^1
Maximum (s)	2.53×10^3	1.84×10^1
Minimum (s)	2.35×10^3	1.68×10^1

Figures 6(b) and 6(e) compare the results of our previous [10] and proposed methods. Players were blended in the image of our previous method, as shown in Fig. 6(e). In the previous method, it is believed to be as the player's legs clearly visible when the player is in contact with the ground. In practice, a timing at which the player does not ground, the background in the bounding box is shown in the same place. Thus, the player's legs become non clear because the background is also blended when the runner is grounding. In contrast, as shown in Fig. 6(b), the players in the stroboscopic image synthesized by the proposed method are not blended with the background.

In the result of the proposed method, the player's shadows are still not completely removed, as shown in Fig. 6(b). However, the shadow can be removed in the next step, as mentioned above in Section 4.3, so we conclude that our proposed method can synthesize a stroboscopic image.

Removal of Player's Shadow

Under some capturing conditions, a stroboscopic image contains the player's shadows. To remove these shadows, we use a synthesis method utilizing mean-shift, as explained in Ref. [27].

The result of removing the player's shadows from the image in Fig. 6(b) is visible in Fig. 6(c). A comparison of Figs. 6(b) and 6(c) clearly shows that our proposed method can remove shadows. We did not make the result of the previous method because it did not have this step. In addition, the processing time of this step was just 6.10 s on average, which was barely 0.003% of the time it took to apply mean-shift to the entire image. These results demonstrate that our proposed method can remove shadows without consuming a lot of time. They also indicate that our proposed method can synthesize a stroboscopic image to measure the player's speed and stride length more easily than the previous method.

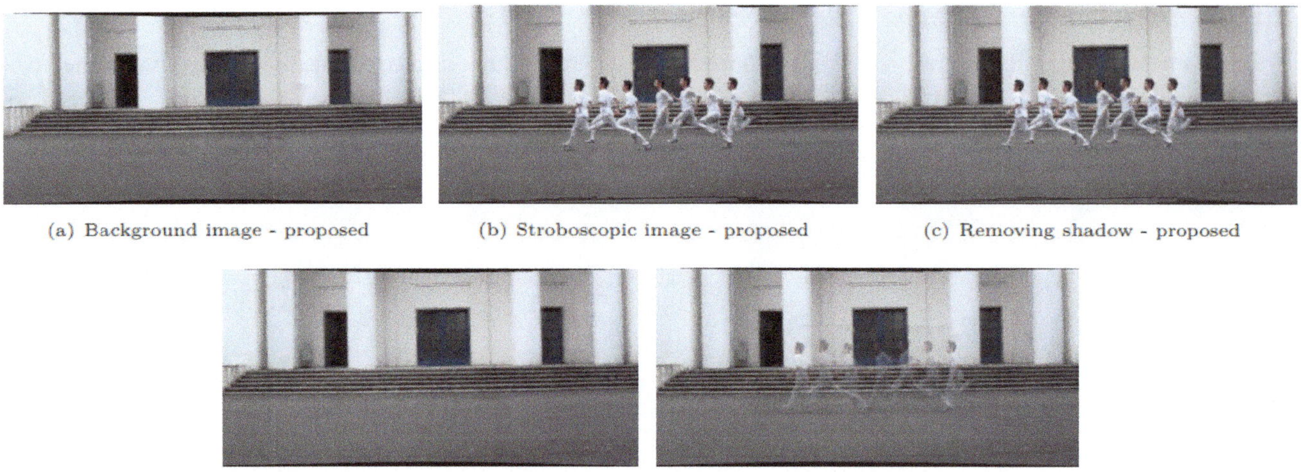

(a) Background image - proposed (b) Stroboscopic image - proposed (c) Removing shadow - proposed

(d) Background image - previous (e) Stroboscopic image - previous

Figure 6: Results of synthesizing a runner stroboscopic image.

Measurement of Player's Landing Position, Speed, and Stride Length

Our goal of this system is measurement of the player's speed and stride length. In this experiment, first, we measured the player's landing positions necessary to measure speed and stride length. Then, we measured the player's speed and stride length. In the last, we visualized the player's footprints in this scene by using stroboscopic images.

Table 2 shows measuring error of each player's landing positions after 50 m running. Error of each step is shown in Fig. 7. We measured the runner's landing position by using a homography between an image coordinate system and the real world coordinate system. Input of positions of foot was manually. We made actual footprints as a ground truth by spiked shoes. Mini corns were known points for calculating the homography. In previous work [10], it was considered that an error of less than 0.3 m did not adversely affect the analysis. About 90% of these measuring errors are less than 0.3 m in these results. Therefore, we think these results are almost useful.

Table 2: Error of measurement

Player	Average (m)	Maximum (m)	Minimum (m)	Variance
A	0.12	0.32	0.00	0.008
B	0.07	0.34	0.00	0.007
C	0.15	0.50	0.00	0.015

(a) Player A (b) Player B (c) Player C

Fig. 7 Measuring error.

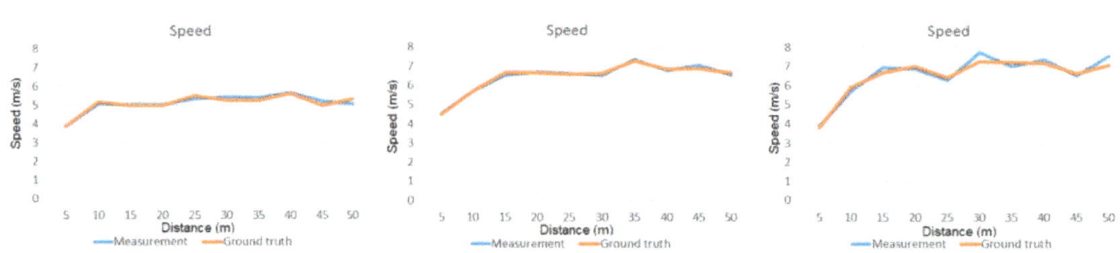

(a) Player A (b) Player B (c) Player C

Figure 8: Measurement of speed.

Figures 8 and 9 show results of measurement using the above landing positions. In the analysis of speed and stride length, an important point is to understand a trend, such as a timing of maximum stride length, speed up, slow down, etc. We can catch information from these figures. Therefore, we can confirm our method is useful. In a few points, for example, Player C's timing of maximum stride length is different. The reason is considered to be due to the large measuring error at the 25th and 27th steps which are near 45 m, as you can be seen from Fig. 7(c). Reduction of such a large error is a future study.

The result of the player's footprint visualization is shown in Fig. 10. We can also represent results as intuitively by this means.

As another example, we used a video sequence of an actual marathon race. Figure 11 shows a stroboscopic image and player's footprints. We took this video from a crowded walkway; therefore capturing range was shorter than other videos. The result of synthesis was successful. In this case, we used end of white lines on a road as known points. Ground truth could not be obtained in this situation, of course. Alternatively, we confirmed results of measuring using white lines as a guide. The results show that our proposed method can be used not only in one environment.

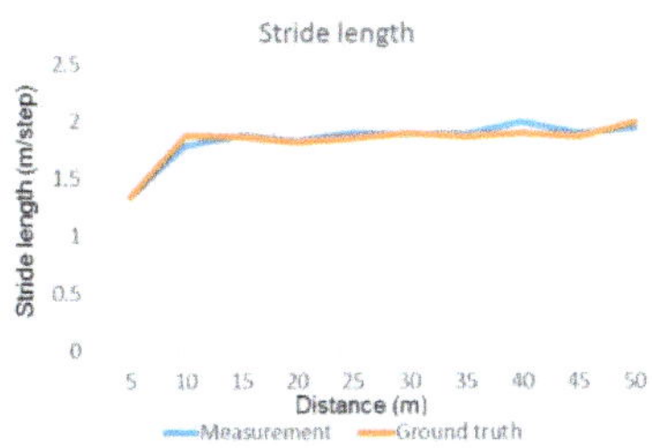

(a) Player A

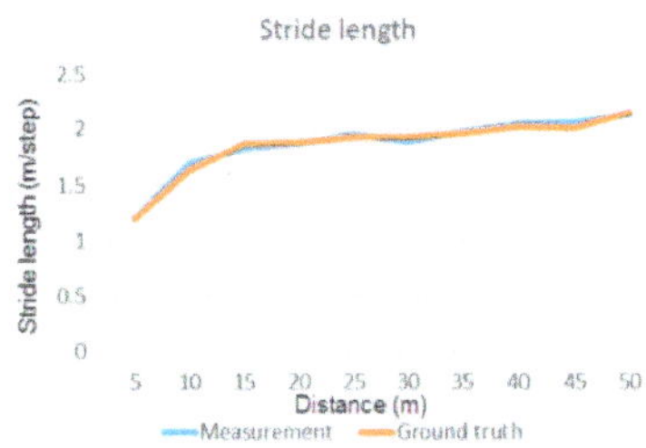

(b) Player B

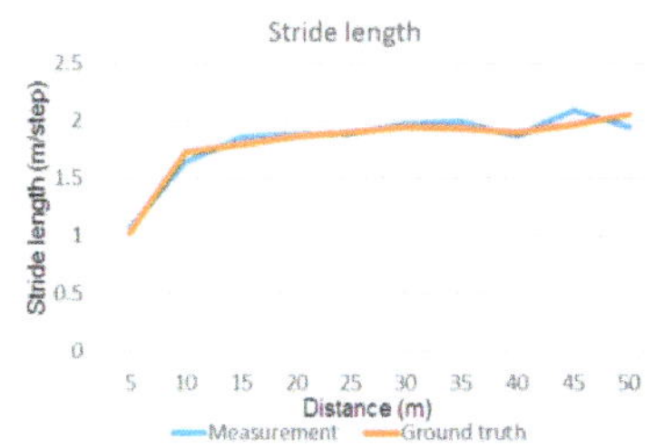

(c) Player C

Figure 9: Measurement of stride length.

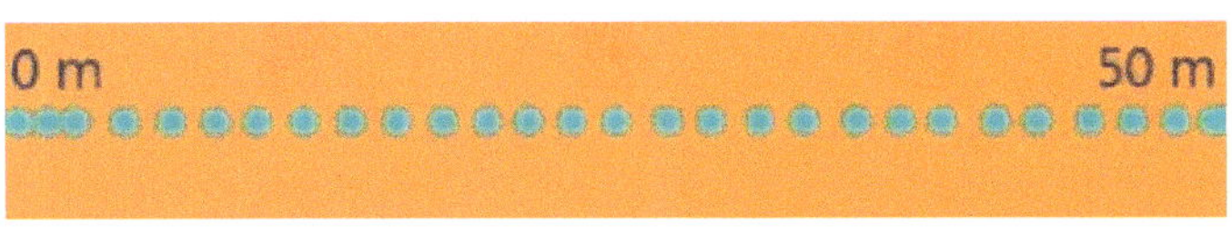

(a) Player A

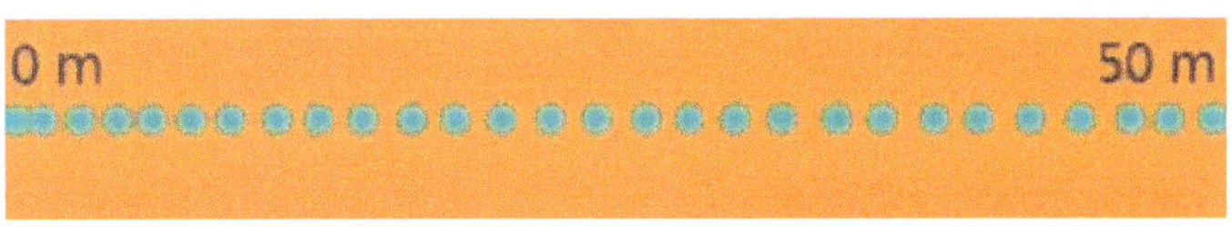

(b) Player B

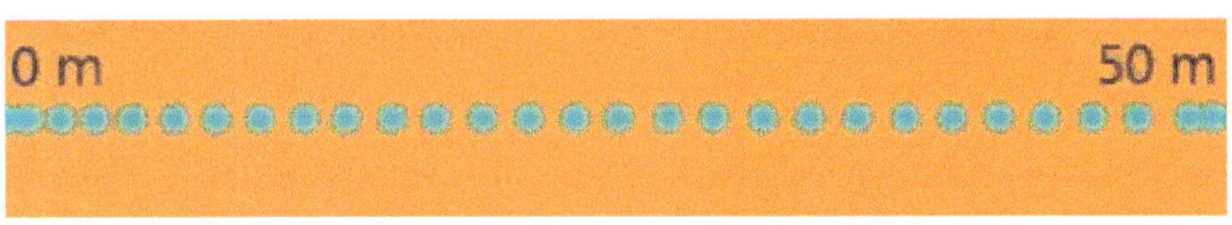

(c) Player C

Figure 10: Visualization of player's footprints.

Figure 11: Result of an actual marathon race.

Comparison with Existing Methods

First, we compared the performance of foreground extraction and image blending in our proposed method with GrabCut [15] and the image cloning [16].

Figure 12 shows the results of player extraction by our method and GrabCut. We input a target area of GrabCut manually. The green frame in each image is a target area. Our method could successfully extract a player clearly in all scenes, whereas GrabCut could not extract a player in some scenes. Especially, the part of foot or lower body was often lack. We estimate that a reason of this problem is a difference of color. For example, a color of a cloth is usually different from the upper and lower body or shoes. This difference makes an edge inside of a player area. GrabCut cannot extract a player clearly by this edge.

The images including these defects are not suitable for measurement of speed and stride length or checking forms because everyone cannot recognize a player clearly. In the case of using a cloth having a complex pattern such as figure skating (the third from the right in Fig. 12), GrabCut could not extract anything. Our proposed method subtracted the player region and the background area. Therefore, it does not occur the problem such as GrabCut.

Figure 13 shows the result of the image cloning. In this figure, we blended only two frames by the image cloning. We can find that the players blended with a background in some scenes. Since synthesizing a stroboscopic image by repeating the same process, we can understand it is difficult to synthesize a stroboscopic image using the image cloning from this result. This is because that the extracted image for cloning had a part of a background. The player in the other frame was blended with this background. To solve this problem, we need to extract only a player's area. Our proposed method executes the equivalent of it such as Fig. 6(b).

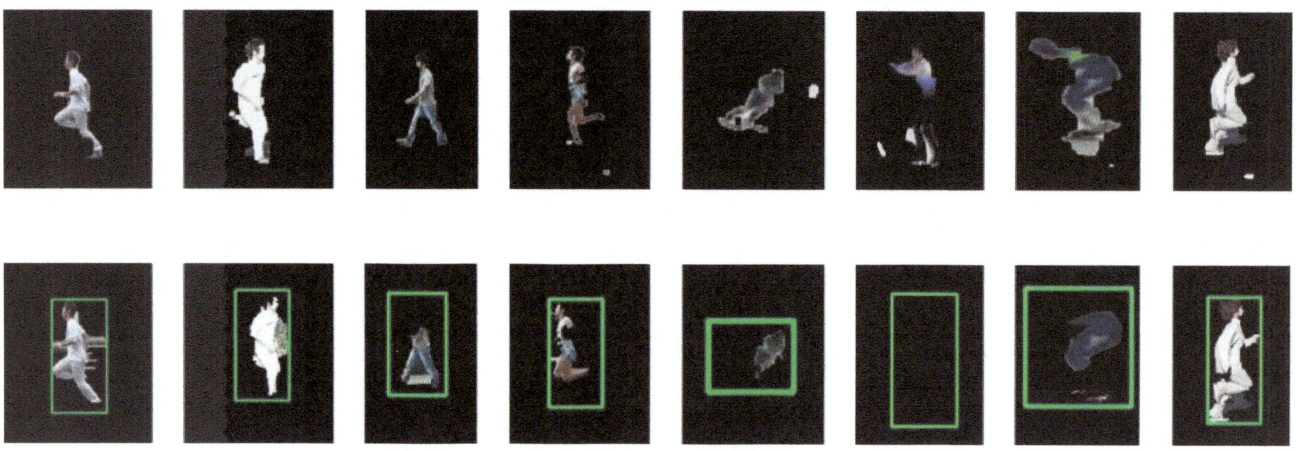

Figure 12: Comparison with GrabCut (top: proposed method, bottom: GrabCut).

Figure 13: Results of the image cloning.

Second, autostitch and frame subtraction were the targets to compare with synthesis of a stroboscopic image. Figure 14 shows the result of these methods. Autostitch does not concern itself with whether an image contains a person or not; therefore Fig. 14(a) has people in only a limited number of frames. The method using frame subtraction is originally for a fixed camera. As shown in Fig. 14(b), this method did not work on scenes captured by handheld camera.

Figure 15(a) shows the synthesis results of our proposed method in another scene in order to show that this method can be used in various environments. There are runners in all frames, the same as in Fig. 6(c). The results of the two existing methods are shown in Figs. 15(b) and 15(c). They are the same as the results in Figs. 14(a) and 14(b). These results clearly demonstrate the superiority of our proposed method.

(a) Autostitch (b) Frame subtraction

Figure 14: Results of existing methods.

Application to Other Scenes

As stated previously, we executed our method on other scenes, especially other sports in this experiment to confirm its versatility. Walking, downhill skiing, figure skating, and speed skating were the targets of this experiment. The walking scene was captured by us, the same as in other experiments. The other videos were captured by others. The results of this second experiment show that our proposed method can be used for various purposes such as checking player's form. This is because we have assumed the use of the image in addition to measuring.

The results are shown in Figs. 16, 17, 18, and 19. These results are the same as those in Figs. 6(c), 11, 14, and 15. Our proposed method overlaid players onto a background image; therefore players appear in all frames in Figs. 16(a), 17(a), 18(a), and 19(a). We made the footprints on walking scene. Skiing and skating do not have a concept of footprints, so we did not make the footprints on these scenes. Autostitch cannot always synthesize a stroboscopic image due to its not being able to extract the player from each frame. Figures 16(b), 17(b), 18(b), and 19(b) contain players in only part of the frames as a result. The method using the frame subtraction does not consider that the camera moves freely, so it cannot synthesize a stitched image and a stroboscopic image from a non-fixed camera sequence, as evident in Figs. 16(c), 17(c), 18(c), and 19(c).

These results confirm the versatility of our proposed method. If we change the object detection method, we can detect targets other than people, such as cars.

(a) Proposed method (b) Autostitch (c) Frame subtraction

Figure 15: Results of stroboscopic image synthesis in another scene.

(a) Proposed method (b) Autostitch (c) Frame subtraction

Figure 16: Examples of application to walking.

(a) Proposed method (b) Autostitch (c) Frame subtraction

Figure 17: Examples of application to downhill skiing.

(a) Proposed method (b) Autostitch (c) Frame subtraction

Figure 18: Examples of application to figure skating.

(a) Proposed method (b) Autostitch (c) Frame subtraction

Figure 19: Examples of application to speed skating.

Limitations

In the last experiment, we investigated limitations of our proposed method. First, we used a rollingshutter camera. A rolling-shutter camera is a weak to shoot a moving object. It is necessary to confirm whether or not our proposed method can use a smart phone which usually has a rolling-shutter camera.

We synthesized a stroboscopic image using a rolling-shutter camera and targeting a runner. The result in running scene is shown in Fig. 20. We can find that a synthesis of stroboscopic image using rolling-shutter camera by our proposed method was successfully in this case, such that a runner was a target. To synthesize a stroboscopic image using a rolling-shutter camera, it is necessary that all the pixels are captured at the same timing. In this scene, a video camera operator does not need to move a camera fast because the runner's speed is not so fast. Therefore, we estimate that the above condition was satisfied. Of course, if a target object moves faster, such as a car or a bike, the result may not be the same because it is difficult to satisfy this condition.

Second, we used the image sequence including a camera shake. A camera shake often occurs in using a hand-held camera. Figure 21 is the input image sequence of this experiment. As a result, our proposed method could not synthesize a stroboscopic image. We assume that our proposed method is used under a simple condition, as we described in Section 3. Therefore, complex conditions like this scene occurred a motion parallax or a complex background were out of scope. It is one of our future works to be able to use our proposed method under these conditions.

Figure 20: Result using rolling-shutter camera.

Figure 21: Input images in shaking scene.

s other candidate of a limitation, we examined the case that the colors between a video frame and the synthesized background are not perfectly matched. Because of an illumination variation, etc., in shooting, it is the color sometimes different between an input image and a background image. This difference makes noises in a mask image. In player extraction, these noises make an extra area of non-player. If this area exists near the player, it may connect with the player in the morphology processing. We execute the morphology processing so that this connection is not occurred. Of course, it is ideal that this noise does not occur. To realize this ideal condition, we should execute another processing in making a mask. For example, a slight difference in color is regarded as the same color or we perform a color reduction processing to match color easily.

CONCLUSIONS

In this paper, we have proposed the method of synthesizing a stroboscopic image to enable a measurement of a player's speed and stride length in an automated system. In particular, we have sped up the processing of background image synthesis by utilizing the bounding box of a player detected by HOG. We have also improved the overlaying of a player using mask and the removal of shadows. We have demonstrated the superiority of our proposed method through experiments and confirmed that it can be used in various scenes.

If we do not satisfy the condition listed in Section 3, our method cannot work well. For example, if the colors of the background and clothes are exactly the same, we cannot synthesize a stroboscopic image.

The conditions described in Section 5.5 are also representative examples. To solve this problem is one of our future works.

Our proposed method has a few of manual steps. For example, the morphology process in the synthesis stroboscopic image step and the selection of removal area in the removal of a shadow are manual. In addition to a measurement accuracy improvement of landing position, our future work will be to improve these steps for the realization of full automation. For example, in the shadow removal step, if the area of the shadow can be extracted automatically, the problem goes away. Therefore, tracking the shadow area with some sort of tracking method is one of the solutions. We will examine various solution candidates in our future work.

ACKNOWLEDGEMENTS

This work has been supported in part by JSPS Grant-in-Aid for Scientific Research(S) 24220004, and JST CREST "Intelligent Information Processing Systems Creating Co-Experience Knowledge and Wisdom with Human–Machine Harmonious Collaboration".

REFERENCES

1. Strohrmann, C.; Harms, H.; Kappeler-Setz, C.; Troster, G. Monitoring kinematic changes with fatigue in running using body-worn sensors. IEEE Transactions on Information Technology in Biomedicine Vol. 16, No. 5, 983–990, 2012.
2. Ghasemzadeh, H.; Loseu, V.; Guenterberg, E.; Jafari, R. Sport training using body sensor networks: A statistical approach to measure wrist rotation for golf swing. In: Proceedings of the 4th International Conference on Body Area Networks, Article No. 2, 2009.
3. Oliveira, G.; Comba, J.; Torchelsen, R.; Padilha, M.; Silva, C. Visualizing running races through the multivariate time-series of multiple runners. In: Proceedings of XXVI Conference on Graphics, Patterns and Images, 99–106, 2013.
4. Eskofier, B. M.; Musho, E.; Schlarb, H. Pattern classification of foot strike type using body worn accelerometers. In: Proceedings of IEEE International Conference on Body Sensor Networks, 1–4, 2013.
5. Beetz, M.; Kirchlechner, B.; Lames, M. Computerized real-time analysis of football games. IEEE Pervasive Computing Vol. 4, No. 3, 33–39, 2005.
6. Hamid, R.; Kumar, R. K.; Grundmann, M.; Kim, K.; Essa, I.; Hodgins, J. Player localization using multiple static cameras for sports visualization. In: Proceedings of IEEE Conference on Computer Vision and Pattern Recognition, 731–738, 2010.
7. Lu, W.-L.; Ting, J.-A.; Little, J. J.; Murphy, K. P. Learning to track and identify players from broadcast sports video. IEEE Transactions on Pattern Analysis and Machine Intelligence Vol. 35, No. 7, 1704–1716, 2013.
8. Perˇse, M.; Kristan, M.; Kovaˇciˇc S.; Vuˇckoviˇc, G.; Perˇs, J. A trajectory-based analysis of coordinated team activity in a basketball game. Computer Vision and Image Understanding Vol. 113, No. 5, 612–621, 2009.
9. Atmosukarto, I.; Ghanem, B.; Ahuja, S.; Muthuswamy, K.; Ahuja, N. Automatic recognition of offensive team formation in American football plays. In: Proceedings of IEEE Conference on Computer Vision and Pattern Recognition Workshops, 991–998, 2013.
10. Hasegawa, K.; Saito, H. Auto-generation of runner's stroboscopic image and measuring landing points using a handheld camera. In: Proceedings of the 16th Irish Machine Vision and Image Processing, 169–174, 2014.
11. Ebdelli, M.; Meur, O. L.; Guillemot, C. Video inpainting with short-term windows: Application to object removal and error concealment. IEEE Transactions on Image Processing Vol. 24, No. 10, 3034–3047, 2015.

12. Farbman, Z.; Lischinski, D. Tonal stabilization of video. ACM Transactions on Graphics Vol. 30, No. 4, Article No. 89, 2011.

13. Lu, S.-P.; Ceulemans, B.; Munteanu, A.; Schelkens, P. Spatio-temporally consistent color and structure optimization for multiview video color correction. IEEE Transactions on Multimedia Vol. 17, No. 5, 577– 590, 2015.

14. Brown, M.; Lowe, D. G. Automatic panoramic image stitching using invariant features. International Journal of Computer Vision Vol. 74, No. 1, 59–73, 2007.

15. Rother, C.; Kolmogorov, V.; Blake, A. "GrabCut": Interactive foreground extraction using iterated graph cuts. ACM Transactions on Graphics Vol. 23, No. 3, 309–314, 2004.

16. Farbman, Z.; Hoffer, G.; Lipman, Y.; Cohen-Or, D.; Lischinsk, D. Coordinates for instant image cloning. ACM Transactions on Graphics Vol. 28, No. 3, Article No. 67, 2009.

17. Guo, R.; Dai, Q.; Hoiem, D. Single-image shadow detection and removal using paired regions. In: Proceedings of IEEE Conference on Computer Vision and Pattern Recognition, 2033–2040, 2011.

18. Miyazaki, D.; Matsushita, Y.; Ikeuchi, K. Interactive shadow removal from a single image using hierarchical graph cut. In: Lecture Notes in Computer Science, Vol. 5994. Zha, H.; Taniguchi, R.; Maybank, S. Eds. Springer Berlin Heidelberg, 234–245, 2009.

19. Correa, C. D.; Ma, K.-L. Dynamic video narratives. ACM Transactions on Graphics Vol. 29, No. 4, Article No. 88, 2010.

20. Lu, S.-P.; Zhang, S.-H.; Wei, J.; Hu, S.-M.; Martin, R. R. Timeline editing of objects in video. IEEE Transactions on Visualization and Computer Graphics Vol. 19, No. 7, 1218–1227, 2013.

21. Klose, F.; Wang, O.; Bazin, J.-C.; Magnor, M.; Sorkine-Hornung, A. Sampling based scene-space video processing. ACM Transactions on Graphics Vol. 34, No. 4, Article No. 67, 2015.

22. Fukunaga, K.; Hostetler, L. The estimation of the gradient of a density function, with applications in pattern recognition. IEEE Transactions on Information Theory Vol. 21, No. 1, 32–40, 1975.

23. Comaniciu, D.; Meer, P. Mean shift: A robust approach toward feature space analysis. IEEE Transactions on Pattern Analysis and Machine Intelligence Vol. 24, No. 5, 603–619, 2002.

24. Dalal, N.; Triggs, B. Histograms of oriented gradients for human detection. In: Proceedings of IEEE Computer Society Conference on Computer Vision and Pattern Recognition, Vol. 1, 886–893, 2005.

25. Kalman, R. E. A new approach to linear filtering and prediction problems. Journal of Basic Engineering Vol. 82, No. 1, 35–45, 1960.

26. Bay, H.; Ess, A.; Tuytelaars, T.; Gool, L. V. Speededup robust features (SURF). Computer Vision and Image Understanding Vol. 110, No. 3, 346–359, 2008.

27. Cho, S.-H.; Kang, H.-B. Panoramic background generation using mean-shift in moving camera environment. In: Proceedings of the International Conference on Image Processing, Computer Vision and Pattern Recognition, 829–835, 2011.

CHAPTER 14

A SURGICAL SIMULATION SYSTEM FOR PREDICTING FACIAL SOFT TISSUE DEFORMATION

Xiaodong Tang[1], Jixiang Guo[1], Peng Li[2], and Jiancheng Lv[1]

[1]Machine Intelligence Lab, Sichuan University, Chengdu 610065, China

[2]West China College of Stomatology, Sichuan University, Chengdu 610065, China

ABSTRACT

In the field of cranio-maxillofacial (CMF) surgery, surgical simulation is becoming a very powerful tool to plan surgery and simulate surgical results before actually performing a CMF surgical procedure. Reliable prediction of facial soft tissue changes is in particular essential for better preparation and to shorten the time taken for the operation. This paper presents a surgical simulation system to predict facial soft tissue changes caused by the movement of bone segments during CMF surgery. Two experiments were designed to test the feasibility of this simulation system. The test results demonstrate the feasibility of fast and good prediction of post-operative facial appearance, with texture. Our surgical simulation system is applicable to computer-assisted CMF surgery.

INTRODUCTION

With the development of techniques in computerassisted orthognathic surgery, research into craniofacial morphology and models of bone and soft tissue have played an important role in maxillo-craniofacial therapy [1]. 3D reconstruction of bone and soft tissues, quantitative measurements, and virtual surgical simulation results provide significant underpinnings to optimize surgical programs. Prediction of new facial appearance is particularly important. Without any risk to patients, surgeons can operate on a patient virtually until an aesthetically satisfactory result is obtained. Therefore, building a precise prediction system for facial soft tissue deformation is very important and useful.

In this paper, we describe a simulation system for facial soft tissue prediction which is based on the linear finite element method. The simulation system can be used by surgeons to obtain an estimate of facial appearance. Our work utilizes individual patient data for both skull and skin surfaces to build the deformation model. The data needed can be acquired from 3D photography and 3D computed tomography (CT). To represent facial soft tissue deformation given the movement of bone structures, we build a correspondence between a face mesh and a bone mesh. Our facial models are composed of tetrahedral elements to permit finite element analysis. Facial tissue changes caused by bone movement can be well simulated.

The remainder of this paper is organized as follows. In Section 2, we present related research and underlying technologies related to our proposed method. We briefly review the principle of the linear elasticity finite element model (FEM) algorithm in Section 3. We then describe in detail in Section 4 our method for building the deformation

Citation: Xiaodong Tang, Jixiang Guo, Peng Li, and Jiancheng Lv, A surgical simulation system for predicting facial soft tissue deformation, DOI 10.1007/s41095-016-0046-4.

model and the functions of each module in the deformation prediction pipeline. In Section 5, we report test results obtained with our system, showing that our approach is feasible. Finally, in Section 6, we conclude our work and discuss possible future improvements.

RELATED WORK

In the early 1980s, the prediction of post-operative facial appearance was initiated. Some research [2] presented the idea of predicting soft tissue changes due to bone movement by combining bone structure models together with soft tissue models. Mass spring models (MSM) were originally used to predict the soft tissue behavior. They originated in computer animation and could achieve real-time effects, but are considered to be rather inaccurate when precise modeling of physiological behavior is required. Finite element models (FEM) provide another popular method to simulate facial soft tissue deformation. This is an accurate approach to simulating the mechanical and physiological characteristics of soft tissue, but it is more computationally expensive [3]. Keeve et al. [4] compared these two most popular soft tissue models for maxillofacial surgery. They concluded that FEM could be superior to MSM for biomechanically accuracy, but inferior in terms of speed and sample architecture.

Koch et al. [5] proposed an approach to simulate soft tissue changes arising because of realignment of underlying bone structure. However, their methods were not integrated into a surgical simulation system. Maciel et al. [6] designed a system for surgical simulation. However, their attempts focused on the interactions between the user and the computer. Due to the high efficiency requirements, most commercial software products for predicting facial soft tissue deformations for maxillofacial surgery planning are based on statistical strategies. However, the prediction accuracy depends on the number of patient samples involved. Among these strategies, physically based methods can simulate soft tissue deformation more accurately and realistically.

BASIC PRINCIPLES OF LINEAR FEM

In elasticity theory, the finite element method (FEM) is the most commonly used method to describe the continuous mechanical behavior of soft tissues [7]. This method is based on a volumetric discretization of the structure, using a 3D mesh. For 3D modeling, the most commonly used elements are hexahedra and tetrahedra. In our paper, we use tetrahedra as the mesh elements.

After the FEM discretization, the motion of a deformable tissue can be described by the Euler– Lagrange equation, which is a second order system of ordinary differential equations:

$$\boldsymbol{M}\ddot{\boldsymbol{U}} + \boldsymbol{D}(\boldsymbol{U}, \dot{\boldsymbol{U}}) + \boldsymbol{f}_{\text{in}} = \boldsymbol{f}_{\text{ext}} \tag{1}$$

where $M \in R^{3n\times 3n}$ denotes the mass matrix, $U \in R^{3n}$ denotes the displacement of the mesh points, $\dot{U}$ denotes the first derivative of the displacement vector, and $\ddot{U}$ denotes its second derivativer. f_{ext} denotes the external force (e.g., a user imposed force, or the force produced by the movement of bone). f_{in} denotes the internal force or volume force. The mass matrix M can be pre-computed from the object's mesh density distribution in the rest state. The damping forces $D(U, \dot{U})$ are independent of time, and can be represented as

$$\boldsymbol{D}(\boldsymbol{U}, \dot{\boldsymbol{U}}) = (\alpha\boldsymbol{M} + \beta\boldsymbol{K})\dot{\boldsymbol{U}} \tag{2}$$

where α and β are Rayleigh damping constants, which are the positive real-valued parameters, which are variable in this system. We use K to denote the tangent stiffness matrix, which can be represented by the Jacobian matrix of the internal forces f_{in}.

For each mesh element, f denotes the internal force acting on it. This satisfies the mechanical equilibrium equations:

$$\nabla\boldsymbol{\sigma} + \boldsymbol{f} = 0 \tag{3}$$

where σ is the stress tensor. We use u to describe the displacement of the element. From u we can calculate the strain tensor ε, which describes the deformation per unit area. There are two popular choices in the field of computer graphics, the Green– Lagrange nonlinear strain tensor ε_G: $\varepsilon_G = \frac{1}{2}(\nabla\boldsymbol{u} + \nabla\boldsymbol{u}^T + \nabla\boldsymbol{u} \times \nabla\boldsymbol{u}^T)$, and the Cauchy linear strain tensor ε_C: $\varepsilon_C = \frac{1}{2}(\nabla\boldsymbol{u} + \nabla\boldsymbol{u}^T)$, where ∇u denotes the gradient of the displacement vector u. In a large deformation setup, the Green–Lagrange strain tensor ε_G can provide a better result than the Cauchy strain tensor ε_C, while when the deformation displacements are relatively small, the Cauchy strain tensor ε_C suffices to calculate the result accurately. Using the Cauchy linear strain tensor can reduce the computation required. In this paper, we use the Cauchy strain tensor ε_C. Hooke's Law states that the stress–strain relationship is linear, σ = Dε, where:

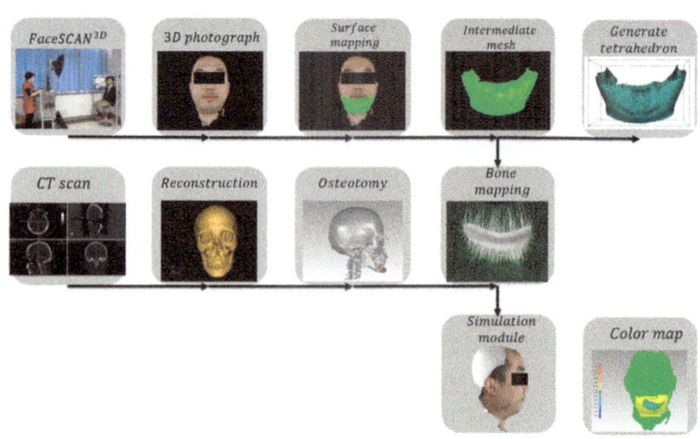

Figure 1: Pipeline of the facial soft tissue deformation prediction method.

$$\boldsymbol{D} = \begin{bmatrix} \lambda+2\mu & \lambda & \lambda & 0 & 0 & 0 \\ \lambda & \lambda+2\mu & \lambda & 0 & 0 & 0 \\ \lambda & \lambda & \lambda+2\mu & 0 & 0 & 0 \\ 0 & 0 & 0 & \mu & 0 & 0 \\ 0 & 0 & 0 & 0 & \mu & 0 \\ 0 & 0 & 0 & 0 & 0 & \mu \end{bmatrix}$$

Here λ and μ are Lam´e constants directly proportional to the well-known material properties of Young's modulus E and Poisson's ratio v:

$$\lambda = \frac{vE}{(1+v)(1-2v)}, \qquad \mu = \frac{E}{2(1+v)}$$

FRAMEWORK

Figure 1 shows our deformation prediction pipeline. It includes the following four parts.

Data preparation: The pre-operative CT scan taken to construct the model of bone structure and the pre-operative 3D photography taken to obtain a textured mesh model of facial surface are input. A mesh generator is used to construct a tetrahedral model for FEM.

Mapping: This part includes two kinds of meshmapping methods, a surface-mapping method and a bone-mapping method. The deformation result is directly expressed via the skin surface by the surface-mapping method. The bone-mapping method allows simulation of interaction between bone and soft tissue.

Simulation: The obtained forces are applied to the skin surface, according to the force-transfer principle, to simulate the deformation caused by bone movement. Using suitable boundary conditions for the biomechanical soft tissue model, the new facial appearance is computed using a linear elasticity FEM approach.

Control and Display: The overall control and display structure are based on the model-viewcontroller pattern.

Data Preparation

Data Acquisition

Prior to craniofacial surgery, a pre-operative 3D CT scan and 3D photographs are acquired. The commercial product F aceSCAN^{3D} is used to obtain a 3D facial mesh, which describes the structure of the surface of the face as well as giving texture information. 3D CT scans are widely used as a tool to observe diseased human tissue, and provide excellent visualization of craniofacial tissue. The marching cube algorithm [8] is employed to reconstruct dense, highly detailed bone surface mesh models. The high quality skin surface acquired from the 3D photography (see Fig. 2(a)) is registered together with the bone structure, ready for simulation.

Dividing the Intermediate Mesh

To simulate skin tissue deformation, we need to build a volume mesh data model containing all deforming skin tissues. As volume elements, we use tetrahedra; these permit a good expression of skin tissue properties. To save processing time and memory usage, we restrict the tetrahedral mesh to the surface region that will deform during surgery, near shifting bones. Our system allows the user to confirm the deformation region near such bones via an intermediate mesh. As shown in Fig. 2(b), the green region of the skin surface is chosen as the intermediate mesh. This intermediate mesh is then used to generate the tetrahedral mesh separately, to build the bone-mapping and surface-mapping models.

Generating Tetrahedral

Our "ST Generator" algorithm is shown in Algorithm 1; it generates a high quality tetrahedral mesh from the intermediate mesh. The algorithm establishes tetrahedral elements from the surface mesh based on the negative face normal and point normal directions. The algorithm creates new points in certain offset positions along the negative normal directions of the grid points. In the same way, new points can be generated at certain offset positions from the center of each triangle surface along the negative normal direction of the triangle. Then, the algorithm creates tetrahedral elements using the following principles:

- Each triangle determines a tetrahedral element using the offset point of its center, as shown in Fig. 3(a).
- Given two adjacent triangles, their common edges determine a tetrahedral element using the offset points of their centers, as shown in Fig. 3(b).

Algorithm 1: A ST Generator

Input: A fixed offset d; N initial connected triangles $(F_1, \ldots, F_N)$ with M junctions $(J_1, \ldots, J_M)$.
Output: A volumetric mesh $V := (P, E)$ composed of tetrahedral elements.

```
V ← ∅;
for i = 1 → M do
  P_i ← J_i;
  /* Move each junction J_i with a fixed offset d along the
  normal direction of J_i */
  P_{i+M} ← moved position of J_i;
end for
for i = 1 → N do
  P_{i+2M} ← center of F_i;
end for
/* Generate the tetrahedral elements of the volumetric
mesh */
l ← 1;
for i = 1 → N do
  E_l ← the tetrahedron comprising F_i and the center of
  F_i;
  l ← l + 1;
  /*Check the status of the adjacent faces around F_i */
  for j = 1 → 3 do
    if the index of adjacent face F_ij > i then
      E_l ← the tetrahedron comprising the center of F_i,
      center of F_ij and the shared points of F_i and F_ij;
      l ← l + 1;
      E_l ← the tetrahedron comprising the center of F_i,
      center of F_ij, one shared point b of F_i and F_ij, and
      the moved position of b;
      l ← l + 1;
      E_l ← the tetrahedron comprising the center of F_i,
      center of F_ij, another shared point c of F_i and F_ij,
      and the moved position of c;
      l ← l + 1;
    end if
  end for
end for
```

- Given two adjacent triangles, the two offset points of their centers separately determine a tetrahedral element using one of their shared points and its offset point, as shown in Fig. 3(c).

Mapping Methods

Surface-Mapping Method

For computational efficiency, the tetrahedral mesh used for simulation is restricted to the surface region near shifting bones. Thus, the tetrahedral mesh containing all facial tissues is unsuitable for clinical validation. Moreover, since the perception of the human face is mainly determined by the relationships between different parts of the face, it is important for surgeons to see the whole face when inspecting the effect of a maxillofacial procedure, not just a part of it. To combine the advantages of a smooth tetrahedral mesh for fast simulation and a realistic, highly detailed mesh with texture information for a good recognition, a surface-mapping method is used. The corresponding relationship between the intermediate mesh and the complete facial mesh is built by preserving the indices of vertices in the intermediate mesh in the surface-mapping method. In particular, the displacement vector of the intermediate mesh can be transformed to the facial grid by using the index information.

Bone-Mapping Method

As bone moves, facial deformation is inevitable in craniofacial surgery. Surgeons want to predict appearance changes caused by the movement of bone. Initially, we tried to build the relationship between the face mesh and bone mesh. However, we found that building a bone-related model directly is too time consuming if all the points are calculated in a time step. Our system restricts the tetrahedral mesh to the surface region near the shifting bones. For example, when the jawbone moves, tissue deformation near the upper skull bone can be ignored. We designed the relationship between the bone mesh and the intermediate mesh to take advantage of this approach.

The relationship between a bone and soft tissue is determined by point normals on the bone. As the ray along the point normal hits the soft tissue, the hit point is calculated, and the relationship is built. For efficiency, an object oriented binary space partitioning (BSP) tree is used to find the hit point quickly. Obviously, most points of the bone mesh will be connected to only a limited number of face meshes. A distance threshold value must be set to prevent hyperteloric points from being linked together. The effect is shown in Fig. 4(c), where the threshold value is set to 2 cm.

Simulation Method

Force-Transfer Principle

The displacement vector of the bone is regarded as the source of motion. We implement force-transfer method on the following principle:

$$\boldsymbol{F}_i = \boldsymbol{F} \cos\theta_i \tag{4}$$

where i donates the index of a vertex $(1 \leqslant i \leqslant N)$. We use the force vector F to represent the stress vector produced by the movement of the bone, which is a constant value for all points of the bone mesh. F_i denotes the force vector at the corresponding ith point P_i in the face mesh structure; θ_i denotes the angle between the normal at P_i and the direction of F.

Boundary Conditions

In the bone-mapping method, three types of points can be distinguished in the intermediate mesh: forced points, fixed points, and free points:

- *Forced points*: all points that join at a part of the skull.
- *Fixed points:* boundary points of the intermediate mesh are kept fixed.
- *Free points:* all other soft tissue points are free. During simulation their movement is completely determined by the elastic force at these points.

The boundary points restrict the deformation region and guarantee the stability of the model.

Simulation Principle

Before analyzing the finite element model based on the tetrahedral mesh, material property values which represent attributes of particular tissue types have to be assigned; these are Young's modulus and Poisson's ratio. Measuring precise human tissue material parameters is a difficult task, and many researchers are still working on this topic [9]. Here, we assumed the tissue to be isotropic, homogeneous, and linearly elastic. Based on research by Shlivko et al. [10], we set the value of Young's modulus to 1 MPa and the value of Poisson's ratio to 0.46 during all simulations.

The generated tetrahedral mesh and boundary conditions serve as inputs for our soft tissue simulator. When moving the lower jaw, the forced points are assigned according to the bone-mapping method and the force vectors at these points are calculated based on the force-transfer principle. The simulator calculates the displacements of these points in the tetrahedral mesh at each time step. At the same time, the steady-state situation of the free points near the forced points is broken. At each time step, the coordinate states of all points in the intermediate mesh are transferred back to the skin surface mesh and shown in real time.

Control and Display

Based on the model-view-controller pattern, our software framework is composed of several modules: the data model module, the view module, the simulation controller module, and the tetrahedron generation module. The data model module manages the pipeline of data and interaction between interfaces. The simulation controller applies physical rules to elements to modify their positions, velocities, accelerations, and other physical attributes. The tetrahedron generation module establishes the volume mesh composed of tetrahedral elements. The view module of our framework uses OpenGL to render meshes with appropriate structure, point coordinates, textures, and lighting information.

RESULTS AND DISCUSSION

We have tested the feasibility of the tetrahedral mesh. We also measured the accuracy of our simulation in terms of the differences between the effects of deformation, and data after operations.

Validation of ST Generator algorithm

To verify the operation of the ST Generator algorithm, we extracted the skin from CT image sequences using the marching cubes algorithm [11] and generated a tetrahedral mesh using TetGen [12]. To compare the quality of the two kinds of tetrahedral mesh, we used the aspect ratio, face angle, and dihedral angle of the data as evaluation criteria. As shown in Fig. 5, the tetrahedral meshes have similar peak values for aspect ratio, face angle, and dihedral angle. It indicates that they have the similar structural attributes and the mesh produced by the surface-based tetrahedral generator is suitable for building the tetrahedral volumetric FEM model.

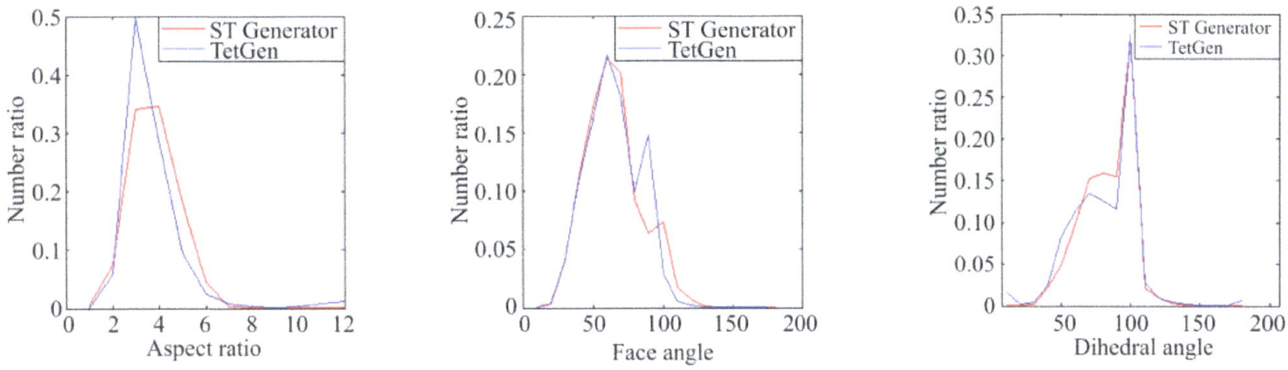

Figure 5: Statistics show the differences in aspect ratio, face angle, and dihedral angle of the tetrahedral meshes generated by TetGen and our ST Generator algorithm.

Prediction of Deformation

Proplanner is a commercial software product for operation design. It implements prediction of soft tissue deformation based on statistical strategies. In our experiment, we used our prediction system and this commercial system in turn to predict the shape of surface tissue when the mandible is moved to a fixed position. The difference between the results of these two systems is shown in Fig. 6.

In addition, we employed the color map method to represent the distance change between the two prediction results. As shown in Fig. 7(a), each color represents a difference value in millimetres as indicated by the color scale; hot colors such as red, orange, and yellow denote bulges in our simulation results, while cool colors such as indigo, blue, and violet denote concave parts relative to the simulation results of Proplanner.

In another experiment, a set data was collected from a patient undergoing jawbone plastic surgery. Figure 8 shows the shape of the face before and after osteotomy and advancement of the mandible. The surgical procedure greatly affected the facial appearance. Part of the mandible was moved into a position where the upper and lower teeth can clench normally. A further small part of the mandible moved to provide a good appearance.

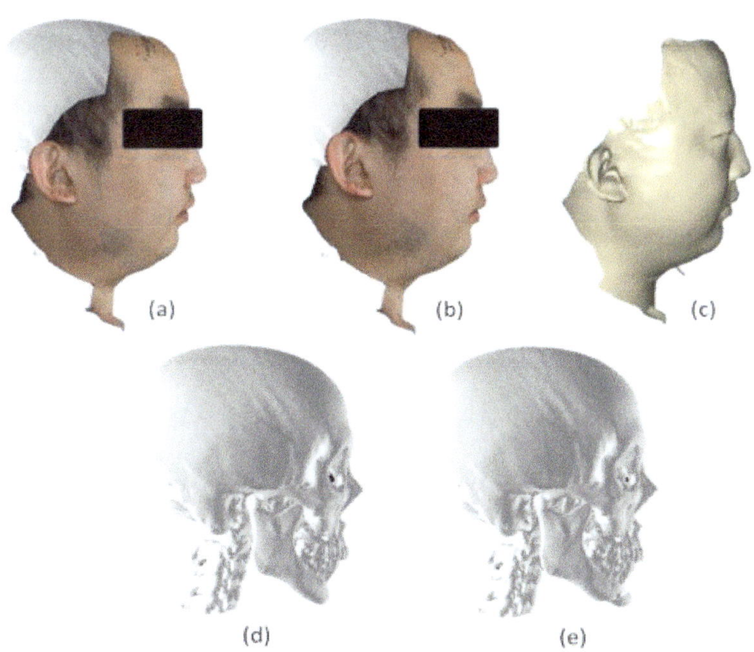

Figure 6: (a) Initial skin surface. (b) Deformed skin surface predicted by our system. (c) Deformed skin surface predicted by Proplanner. (d) Initial bone mesh. (e) Bone mesh with the mandible moved to a fixed position.

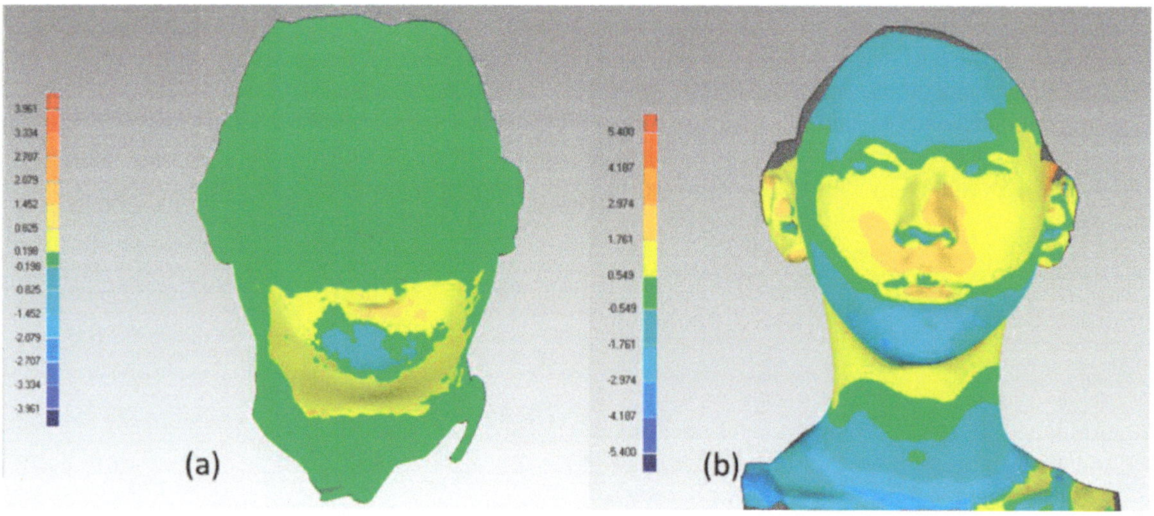

Figure 7: Error measurements of the simulated results.

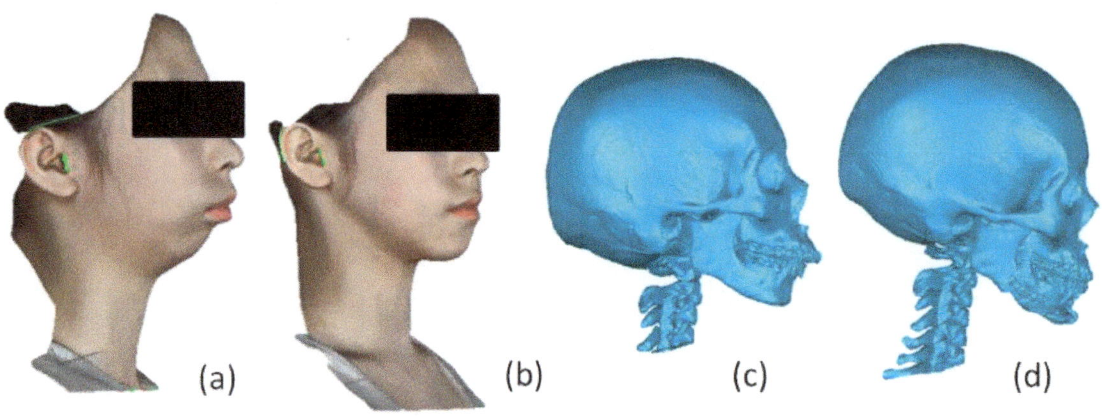

Figure 8: (a) 3D scan before surgery. (b) 3D scan after surgery. (c) Bone reconstruction model before surgery. (d) Bone reconstruction model after surgery.

We imitated the surgical procedure after capturing these parts of the mandible and measuring the displacement of these parts when moved into position after osteotomy as shown in Fig. 9. Figure 7(b) uses a color-map to indicate the distances between corresponding points of the predicted and actual postoperative facial skin surface. Keeping in mind the stability and predictability of maxillofacial surgery, these values show an acceptable accuracy. See Table 1: the first three columns show the number of vertices, faces, and elements used in the facial soft tissue model. The time needed to calculate the new facial appearance and to generate the tetrahedral mesh are summarized in the next two columns. In the last two columns, the mean and variance of errors are shown after simulation. The experiments ran on a standard personal computer with an Intel Core i7 CPU at 2.50 GHz and 4 GB memory.

DISCUSSION

The test results of these experiments demonstrated that our system can provide a good prediction of the post-operative facial appearance with texture. However, the prediction results inevitably have small differences from the post-operative data. Analysis reveals some drawbacks that lead to the inaccuracy of our simulated postoperative facial appearance:

- Due to the limitations of numerical calculations, our data model is based on skin surfaces and the mandible. The remaining materials such as fat tissue and muscular tissue are omitted as their presence would produce too great a density of elements. Better results would be obtained if these materials were incorporated.
- The model parameters such as Young's modulus and Poisson's ratio are recommended values; measuring precise human tissue material parameters is a difficult task.
- Some materials are inevitably needed to reconnect partially cut bone or to fix bone cuts in actual surgery, but these are not modelled in the simulated surgery.

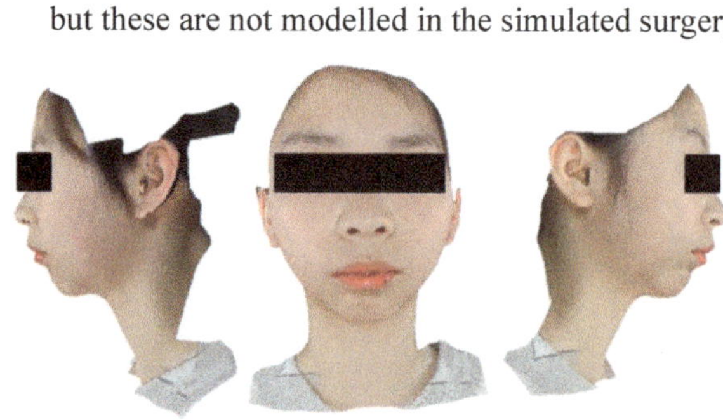

Figure 9: Deformation result for the second experiment.

Table 1: Statistics for two experiments

	Data information			Method efficiency (s)		Error analysis (mm)	
	N_{vertices}	N_{faces}	N_{elements}	$T_{\text{simulation}}$	$T_{\text{STGenerator}}$	E_{mean}	E_{variance}
Experiment 1	2192	4202	22841	27	63	0.111	0.174
Experiment 2	4817	9337	50911	139	241	1.227	1.189

CONCLUSIONS

The results of the first experiment show that our system can achieve similar effects to a commercial system called Proplanner. In addition, our system is able to show an appearance with texture and avoid an obvious fault at the edge of the deformation area. In the second experiment, we succeeded in imitating a surgical procedure with a complete set of actual patient data. In these experiments we achieved satisfactory results of CMF surgery simulation. The test results demonstrate that fast and good prediction of post-operative facial appearance with texture is feasible. Our surgical simulation system is applicable to computer-assisted CMF surgery.

In future, we plan to implement GPU support into the simulation system to improve performance. We will also consider how to include further soft tissue information such as muscle anatomy and fat tissue in our data models.

ACKNOWLEDGEMENTS

The authors would like to thank the anonymous reviewers for their comments, which helped to improve the quality of this paper. This work described in this paper was supported by a grant from the National Natural Science Foundation of China (Nos. 61402305, 61375065, 61432014, and 61432012), a grant from the National Hightech R&D Program of China (863 Program) (No. 2013AA013803), and a grant from the Department of Science and Technology of Sichuan Province (No. 2014JY0116).

REFERENCES

1. Chiang, P.; Zheng, J.; Yu, Y.; Mak, K. H.; Chui, C. K.; Cai, Y. A VR simulator for intracardiac intervention. IEEE Computer Graphics and Applications Vol. 33, No. 1, 44–57, 2013.
2. Vannier, M. W.; Gado, M. H.; Marsh, J. L. Three-dimensional display of intracranial soft-tissue structures. American Journal of Neuroradiology Vol. 4, No. 3, 520–521, 1983.
3. Pieper, S. D. CAPS: Computer-aided plastic surgery. Ph.D. Thesis. Massachusetts Institute of Technology, Cambridge, MA, USA, 1992.
4. Keeve, E.; Girod, S.; Kikinis, R.; Girod, B. Deformable modeling of facial tissue for craniofacial surgery simulation. Computer Aided Surgery Vol. 3, No. 5, 228–238, 1998.
5. Koch, R. M.; Gross, M. H.; Carls, F. R.; von B¨uren, D. F.; Fankhauser, G.; Parish, Y. I. Simulating facial surgery using finite element models. In: Proceedings of the 23rd Annual Conference on Computer Graphics and Interactive Techniques, 421–428, 1996.
6. Maciel, A.; Sankaranarayanan, G.; Halic, T.; Arikatla, V. S.; Lu, Z.; De, S. Surgical model-viewcontroller simulation software framework for local and collaborative applications. International Journal of Computer Assisted Radiology and Surgery Vol. 6, No. 4, 457–471, 2011.
7. Freutel, M.; Schmidt, H.; D¨urselen, L.; Ignatius, A.; Galbusera, F. Finite element modeling of soft tissues: Material models, tissue interaction and challenges. Clinical Biomechanics Vol. 29, No. 4, 363–372, 2014.
8. Guo, L.; Hu, M.; Li, Y.; Yan, W.; Zhao, L. Three dimension reconstruction of medical images based on an improved marching cubes algorithm. In: Proceedings of the 6th International Conference on Biomedical Engineering and Informatics, 64–68, 2013.
9. Ahmadian, M. T.; Nikooyan, A. A. Modeling and prediction of soft tissue directional stiffness using invitro force-displacement data. International Journal of Scientific Research Vol. 16, 385–389, 2006.
10. Shlivko, I. L.; Petrova, G. A.; Zor'kina, M. V.; Tchekalkina, O. E.; Firsova, M. S.; Ellinsky, D. O.; Agrba, P. D.; Kamensky, V. A.; Donchenko, E. V. Complex assessment of age-specific morphofunctional features of skin of different anatomic localizations. Skin Research and Technology Vol. 19, No. 1, e85–e92, 2013.
11. Newman, T. S.; Yi, H. A survey of the marching cubes algorithm. Computers & Graphics Vol. 30, No. 5, 854–879, 2006.
12. Si, H. TetGen, a delaunay-based quality tetrahedral mesh generator. ACM Transactions on Mathematical Software Vol. 41, No. 2, Article No. 11, 2015.

CHAPTER 15

EFFICIENT RENDERING OF VOLUMETRIC MOTION BLUR USING TEMPORALLY UNSTRUCTURED VOLUMES

Magnus Wrenninge

Pixar Animation Studios

ABSTRACT

We introduce temporally unstructured volumes (TUVs), a data structure for representing 4D volume data that is spatially structured but temporally unstructured, and Reves, an algorithm for constructing those volumes. The data structure supports efficient rendering of motion blur effects in volumes, including sub-frame motion. Reves is a volumetric extension to the classic Reyes algorithm, and produces TUV data sets through spatio-temporal stochastic sampling. Our method scales linearly and maximizes data locality and parallelism both during construction and rendering of volumes, making it suitable for ray tracing, and supports arbitrarily large input models. Compared to the current state-of-the-art in volumetric motion blur, our approach produces more accurate results using less memory and less time, and it can also provide high-quality re-timing of volumetric data sets, such as fluid simulations.

INTRODUCTION

In production rendering, motion blur is a crucial element. Without it, rendered frames appear to stutter when played back as an animation. The ability to handle motion blur effects accurately and efficiently, along with proper antialiasing, is a fundamental requirement for production rendering. Algorithms that produce correct motion blur for surface rendering are well known, but there are fewer available options for volume rendering.

Volumetric motion blur techniques generally have to balance correctness, speed, and memory use. The current state-of-the-art, microvoxel motion blur [Clinton and Elendt 2009] (see Figure 24 and Section A.2), achieves high visual quality and its memory overhead is low for coherent rays, but performance and memory use degrade as the amount of motion blur increases and as secondary rays require larger portions of the scene to reside in memory. With path tracing becoming a more common production rendering technique, it is desirable to find an approach that is both more robust in the face of heavy motion blur and also handles incoherent ray and screen sampling patterns.

Current techniques generally consider the temporal aspect of volumetric data as being due to motion within the volume, where the motion is defined by a separate volume containing motion vectors. We propose a new approach that shifts the viewpoint of volumetric motion blur from a geometric interpretation (an R 3 volume deformed by a vector field) into a purely Eulerian interpretation (a fixed R 4 volume). This change in perspective is fundamental, and it allows for new, more correct, and more efficient ways of rendering volumetric motion blur effects.

Citation: Magnus Wrenninge, Efficient Rendering of Volumetric Motion Blur Using Temporally Unstructured Volumes, http://jcgt.org/published/0005/01/01/Vol. 5, No. 1, 2016.

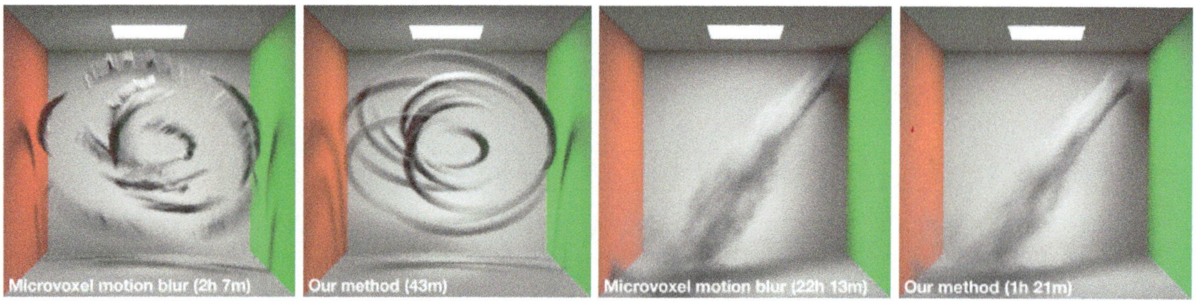

Figure 1: From left: A single volume generated procedurally using our Reves algorithm, rendered with vector-based motion blur (2h 7m); and rendered using our temporal volume method (43m). A smoke simulation using vector-based motion blur (22h 13m); and with our method (1h 21m). Our method improves the rendering speed by 3.0x and 16.4x, respectively, and shows correct blur with smooth, curved motion, while the current state-of-the-art approach exhibits linear overshoot throughout the volume.

The data structure that supports our method is called a temporally unstructured volume (TUV). Compared to three-dimensional volume data, our four-dimensional TUVs naturally support motion blur and can store arbitrarily complex motion while maintaining a small memory footprint, even for incoherent rays. In order to achieve high performance, we limit the scope of our work to fixed data sets; once created, there is no dynamic insertion or removal of data. This limitation suits the needs of motion blur in rendering, but is not intended for general storage of temporal volume data.

When volume-rendering complex production scenes, it is often more efficient to combine multiple volume primitives into a single volume, such that the sum of all contributing primitives can be queried with a single lookup. This step, known as volume modeling or volume construction, can also be used to pre-compute complex procedural volume primitives. Present solutions to the volume construction problem provide various ways of generating volume data, but none offer a robust, generalpurpose method that supports a wide variety of input model types, nor do they handle motion blur accurately.

Our algorithm for producing TUV data sets, Reves, is a novel solution to the volume construction problem that addresses all of the limitations of current methods: it supports a wide variety of modeling primitives along with SIMD programmable shaders; it has robust antialiasing and texture filtering support; it supports motion blur with an arbitrary number of motion samples; and it scales linearly (in terms of time and memory) with input-model quantity, concurrent execution threads, and outputmodel resolution.

The shift from seeing volumetric motion as "3D plus motion" to 4D functions also has implications for fluid simulation retiming. Because our method is able to store complex temporal changes in volumetric properties, it is able to capture subframe motion in simulation data and later replay the data at novel frame rates without artifacts.

BACKGROUND AND RELATED WORK

Motion blur was first introduced in computer graphics by Korein and Badler [1983] and Potmesil and Chakravarty [1983]. Both computed solutions that were continuous and analytic, where Korein and Badler used a method of parameterized motion, and Potmesil and Chakravarty used image-space convolution. Along with their analytic approach, Korein and Badler also mention a non-continuous method whereby images are repeatedly rendered at different time samples and accumulated into a buffer. Although this multi-sample approach works poorly when applied to entire images, it can be seen as a precursor to Cook et al. [1984], who effectively solved motion blur for production rendering, and whose method uses a multitude of point samples distributed in multiple dimensions in order to produce the appearance of motion blur and many other effects.

The types of scene primitives that could be motion-blurred using these early techniques were largely limited to geometry. Korein and Badler and Potmesil and Chakravarty do not mention the rendering of participating media, and although the method described in Cook et al. [1984] can achieve motion blur due to the temporal change in a volume, it does not mention this application.

In fact, when it comes to the context of realistic rendering of participating media, motion blur has often been ignored. Volumes are inherently Eulerian in nature, and the techniques used to describe motion for geometry generally do not apply. Fedkiw et al. [2001] computed the motion of a gaseous fluid and rendered it realistically, but without consideration for the motion of the fluid. Enright et al. [2002] simulated the motion of water using a two-phase fluid approach and signed distance volumes and mentions that sub-frame fluid states may be found by simple interpolation between two signed distance volumes. Zhu and Bridson [2005] later reported that this approach destroys details that are smaller than one simulation voxel.

Kim and Ko [2007] described a technique for computing the sub-frame state of signed distance volumes based on a fluid's velocity information, and, recently, Kulla and Fajardo [2012] mention the use of a similar approach in producing volumetric motion blur effects within a path tracing framework. The last two techniques are both referred to as Eulerian motion blur, in the sense that they produce motion blur of Eulerian volumes. We note, however, that both address a volume-plus-motion problem, rather than a true R 4 representation of volumes. Appendix A.1 provides an outline of these existing Eulerian motion blur techniques.

The field of sound rendering is also related to our method of constructing temporal data sets, and Funkhouser et al. [2003] gives a survey of current methods. In timeresolved imaging, recent work by Jarabo et al. [2014] provides a rendering framework using density estimation of transient signals.

Shader execution systems are a key component of production rendering systems. The Reyes algorithm, described by Cook et al. [1987], not only introduced an ef- ficient rendering system, but also showed how an intermediate rendering primitive (the micropolygon) could provide both efficient rasterization as well as opportunity for SIMD shading. Recently, Elendt [2005] provided implementation details of a production-grade shading system.

For production rendering, volumetric motion blur is handled differently in various types of renderers. Several of the systems described by Wrenninge et al. [2011] and Wrenninge and Bin Zafar [2011] use pre-integrated or smeared volume data. These produce inaccurate visual results, since shading and illumination are computed on already convolved data. More recently, the microvoxel technique described by Clinton and Elendt [2009] produces high-quality motion blur both due to transformation and deformation of volume data, but it requires a unique position differential at each sample location. Procedurally-generated volumes often include overlapping primitives with differing motion vectors, so storing only a single density and velocity sample per voxel limits its use to fluid simulation data. A general introduction to the production volume rendering subject can be found in Wrenninge's Production Volume Rendering [2012].

Related to production volume rendering is the procedural construction of volume data, often referred to as volume modeling. Several different methods exist, as described by Wrenninge [2011] and Bin Zafar [2011]. Most often, these methods are based on direct rasterization of simple primitives, such as spheres, with the addition of procedural, noise-based detail. Ideally, the process that produces TUV data sets should also address the limitations of those volume-modeling systems, such as the lack of support for wide ranges of input primitives and robust motion blur.

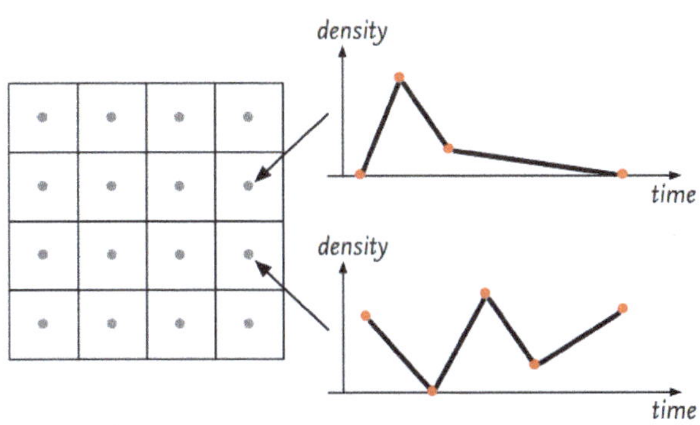

Figure 2: Each voxel in the data structure stores an independent set of sample points, specifying density as a function over time. The number of samples as well as their placement in time can vary from voxel to voxel.

VOLUME DATA STRUCTURE

Our approach to volumetric motion blur is based on the following observation: When rendering a volume using some form of ray-marching method, we answer queries of the type σ = f(P, t), i.e., the property of the medium is defined by some function that varies with both position and time. However, the rendering algorithm never directly queries the motion of the volume, i.e., $\partial P/\partial t$, and as such our method focuses on describing volumetric properties where time is simply another sampling dimension.

In order to efficiently sample four dimensions, our representation uses an independent function-over-time for each voxel in the data structure. That is, we preserve the spatial discretization of an ordinary, structured voxel buffer, but add a fourth, temporal dimension that is unstructured, storing an arbitrary number of htime, valuei pairs. By allowing both the sample count and spacing to vary, our data structure can capture arbitrarily fast or slow variations in volumetric properties. Figure 2 illustrates the configuration.

Lookups into our data structure take place in two steps: First, the enclosing 3D voxel coordinate is found, similar to an ordinary voxel buffer. Next, the temporal coordinate t is used to interpolate a value from the function curve stored in the voxel. The sample pairs are sorted, so finding the appropriate interval involves an O(logN) search; however the number of temporal samples is generally low, resulting in faster lookup performance than both Eulerian and microvoxel motion blur. Appendices A.1 and A.2 describe these differences in more detail.

Our TUV data structure has several implications for volume rendering. First, the temporal dimension is stored in an adaptive fashion that avoids excessive memory use. Second, it stores temporally continuous volumetric data, which can encode motion blur of all types, including material appearing or disappearing over time. Also, for fluid simulations, TUVs can be used to efficiently store every sub-frame simulation time-step, including material that appears and disappears.

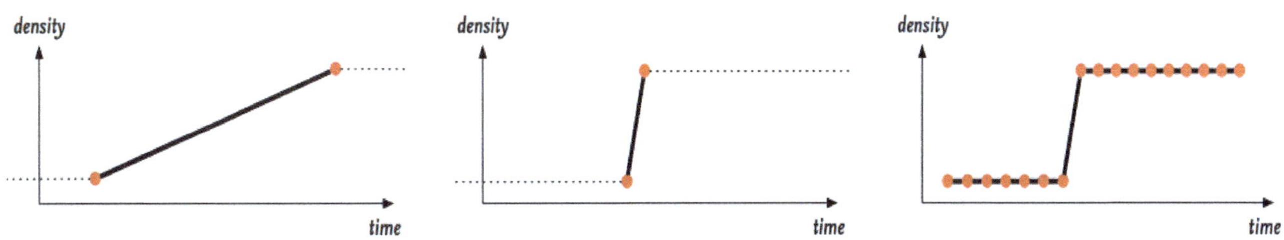

Figure 3: A slow-varying and fast-varying function (left and center) represented using the same number of sample points. Without the ability to specify a time value per-sample, a large number of fixed-time samples (right) would be required to capture the fast-varying function.

Representation of Data Structure

Our implementation structures the temporal data into N3 -sized blocks of voxels. The set of blocks can be organized into either a hash map or a 3D array, permitting both bounded and unbounded volumes to be handled. Blocks are only allocated when in use, so the overall structure is sparse. Using a block structure provides a good tradeoff between spatial adaptivity and fast access, and popular implementations exist in the open source projects Field3D [2009] and, more recently, OpenVDB [Museth 2013]. However, neither of these offer storage of temporally continuous volumes.

In order to accurately capture motion blur effects, a system must be able to process high temporal frequencies. Figure 3 shows that two samples may be sufficient for storing a linearly varying parameter, irrespective of its actual slope and implied frequency, as long as the samples can be placed arbitrarily in time. Without this adaptive placement, the sharp transition would require a large number of samples (and a large memory footprint). We also note that voxels with zero samples are valid (indicating zero value) and provide a good way to take advantage of sub-block sparsity.

Our data structure stores voxel data for a given block of voxels according to the following layout: We maintain one array of time values and a second array of density values, each of which varies in length-per-block from zero upwards. We also store an offset table of length $N^3 + 1$, which indicates the memory location at which the time and density values for a given voxel may be found. We avoid storing an explicit sample count for each voxel by computing it as the difference between consecutive offset values. Figure 4 illustrates this configuration.

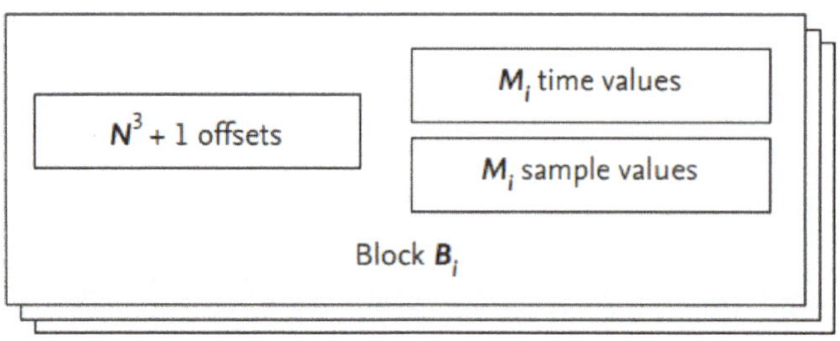

Figure 4: Memory layout for each block. Each block B_i stores a total of $N^3 + 1$ offset values, but each block contains a varying number of $M_i \geq 0$ time and sample values.

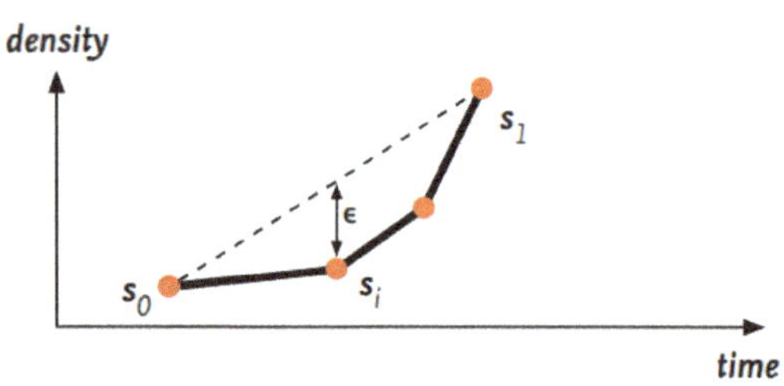

Figure 5: Line simplification step. The error ϵ is measured relative to the magnitude of the interval end points.

Compression of Temporal Functions

In order to further reduce the memory use of our data structure, we implement two compression steps. Since we assume linear interpolation between temporal samples, any repeated values are removed. As a second step, we apply line simplification to remove the least salient vertices. The data contained in each voxel is similar in structure to that of Lokovic and Veach [2000], but differs in that the functions are non-monotonic. As such, we implement a technique similar to Ramer [1972] and Douglas and Peucker [1973], in which vertices are removed in the order by which they cause the smallest error.

Our functions are one-dimensional, but we treat them as lines in 2D defined by the htime, valuei pairs as coordinates. Also, because our method must support volumetric properties in the range $(-\infty, \infty)$ (for example, motion vector fields), we compute an error threshold ϵ_r relative to the magnitude of each interval. That is, for a point $S_i = (t_i, v_i)$ which lies between end points S_0 and S_1, the error threshold is $\epsilon_r = \epsilon_u(v_1 - v_0)$, where ϵ_u is the user-specified threshold (see Figure 5). For zero-value vertices, we set $\epsilon_r = \infty$, as removal of such vertices leads to the introduction of material at a time where none should be present. Apart from these alternative error metrics, our implementation is standard, and the accompanying video (http://www.jcgt. org/published/0005/01/01/JCGT-TUV.mp4) illustrates the type of visual artifacts that an excessively large ϵ_u causes.

Interpolation Methods

We have explored two distinct methods for interpolating the 4D data in TUV data sets. The simplest is of quadrilinear type, where the eight voxels that surround a sample point are found, the temporal curve for each is linearly interpolated, and the results are combined using standard trilinear interpolation.

The second interpolation method is a 4D distance-weighted average. Similarly to the first method, we first find the eight surrounding voxels. Within each voxel, we then find the two nearest temporal samples and combine the resulting 16 values by weighting each by the 4D distance to the sample point:

$$v = \frac{\sum_{i=1}^{8} \dfrac{v_i}{\max(|(P - P_i)|, \epsilon)}}{\sum_{i=1}^{8} \dfrac{1}{\max(|(P - P_i)|, \epsilon)}}.$$

Higher-order schemes, such as cubic splines, could be implemented along the same lines. However, in our experience within the context of production volume rendering, it is more time-efficient to up-sample data sets using a smooth filter before rendering, and then linearly interpolate the result, since the number of point samples N taken by a path tracer from a voxel buffer of resolution R is generally $N \gg R^3$.

Overall, the cost of the weighted average is 40 ± 2% greater than the quadrilinear method, and the visual difference between the two approaches is small. In all of our examples we use the quadrilinear method.

THE REVES ALGORITHM

Before it is possible to leverage the benefits of TUVs for rendering, we must have a method for constructing them. Our approach, dubbed Reves, is inspired by the classic

Reyes algorithm [Cook et al. 1987]. Our approach allows for the input of both volumetric data (e.g., fluid simulations), as well as most common types of geometry (points, curves, and surfaces). A novel feature, compared to existing volume modeling techniques, is the introduction of an intermediate representation that decouples the input primitives from the process of rasterization into the output voxel buffer, much as micropolygons do in the Reyes framework. All inputs are handled uniformly in the shading and rasterization pipelines, and shaders may be run on all primitive types. The rasterization process itself uses spatiotemporal stochastic sampling rather than simple voxelization, and the separate shading and rasterization steps allow for orthogonal user controls of visual detail versus motion blur- and antialiasing quality.

Overall, the Reves modeling algorithm offers several benefits for volume modeling: The framework allows for a multitude of primitive types as inputs; multi-segment motion blur can be handled efficiently and allows for close approximation of curved motion paths; motion blur effects, being view-independent, are pre-computed and stored in our temporal data structure, which increases rendering efficiency; there is robust antialiasing and texture filtering; and finally, displacement shaders are fully supported. To our knowledge, no previous systems offer the union of all these features.

List of Terms

Input primitives are the models provided to the system. They may be geometric (e.g., a point cloud or a set of curves) or volumetric (e.g., fluid simulation densities). The primitives are accompanied by a set of uniform (constant for the entire model) or varying (unique per model vertex) properties, which are called primvars (primitive variables), following RenderMan's convention. The primvars drive the appearance of the model either directly or by binding to shader parameters. Elendt [2005] provides a good resource for how primvars are handled in a shading pipeline, and we follow a similar approach.

Output volumes are the discrete voxel data sets into which the final computed density values are stored. In our case, these are the TUVs described in the previous section. The number of output volumes can vary, from a single one (usually density), to multiple ones. Output volume names are matched by the rasterization engine against output primvars (see Shading vertices below).

Bucket. A bucket is a contiguous region of voxels in the output volume that is computed concurrently. Generally, the size is set to match the tile size of the output volume's sparse structure.

Voxel sample. Each voxel in a bucket is subdivided into multiple sub-voxels, from which a single point sample is drawn. The point sample has a unique time, t, assigned and is referred to as a voxel sample. During rasterization, a set of M3 voxel samples are used to construct the temporal function curve in each voxel. The value of M influences the quality of both antialiasing and motion blur. Voxel samples are conceptually similar to pixel samples in Reyes.

Multi-segment. A multi-segment is a property that has multiple temporal samples. This applies both to input primitives (where geometric primitives express motion by providing multiple time samples of the vertex positions) and to internal, computed properties (e.g., bounding boxes).

Volumetric primitives (vprims) are the internal representation of an input primitive. A vprim knows how to compute its own bounds, how to subdivide itself (splitting), and how to dice itself into a rasterizable representation. Vprims that are the result of splitting are referred to as sub-vprims. Geometric primitives such as point clouds and curves will generally include a radius property that define their three-dimensional extents. Vprims are not seen by the rasterization process, and, as such, do not need to provide a point sampling method. Figure 6 shows some examples of vprim types.

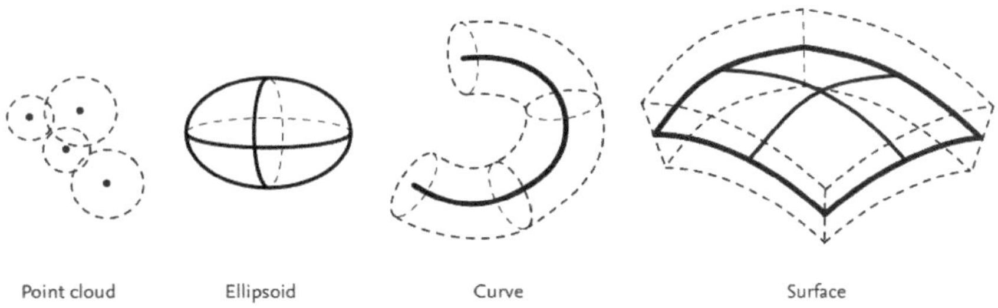

Figure 6: Examples of different types of volumetric primitives (vprims). The point cloud, the curve, and the surface use a radius property to define their volumetric extents (dashed lines), whereas the ellipsoid uses its natural volume.

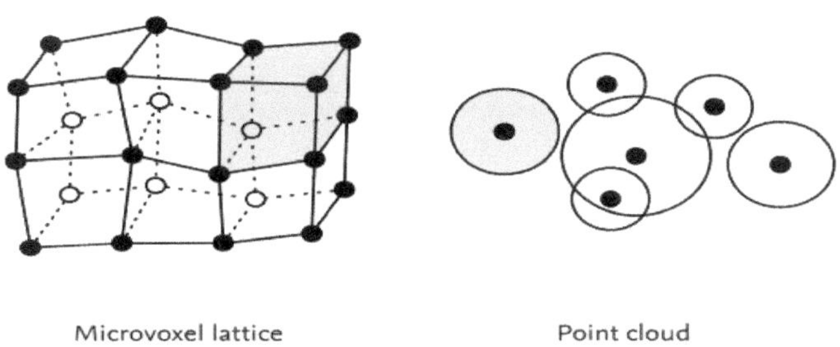

Figure 7: The two types of rasterization primitives (rprims). Each rprim type is made up of rasterization elements, which are shown shaded. The rasterization elements are in turn made up of individual shading vertices.

Rasterization primitives (rprims) are the intermediate representations that make rasterization of volumetric primitives efficient. They have the primary requirement of being fast compared to point sample, but do not need to perform any of the vprim's duties, such as splitting. Although Reves uses multiple types of rprims, they fall in the same conceptual category as micropolygons in the Reyes algorithm. In our implementation, there are two types of rprims: microvoxel lattices and point clouds, and each of the two is considered to be made up of rasterization elements: individual microvoxels and points, respectively. Figure 7 shows the two types.

Shader: A shader is a procedural description of a primitive's appearance. Shaders are generally used to provide detail at a finer level than is practical using geometric subdivision. They are assigned to individual vprims but are executed only after the vprim is diced into an rprim (see below). Shaders may affect the shading vertex's primvars and also its position, in which case they are referred to as a displacement shaders.

Microvoxel Lattices: are the most common form of rprim present in Reves and are analogous to micropolygon grids in Reyes. Most vprims can easily be broken down into a three-dimensional lattice, on which shaders can be executed, and which can efficiently be point-sampled. Because of its connected nature, the microvoxel lattice provides the shading engine with trivial SIMD opportunities and simple shading-derivative calculations.

Dicing: is the process of converting a vprim into its rasterizable form. This step is generally performed in the local space of the vprim and involves transformations from parametric to world space, but not vice versa. For this reason, it is inexpensive even for geometrically complex types. Without an intermediate rasterization primitive, vprims would need to be point-sampled directly, involving expensive inverse transformations.

Shading Vertices: are the vertices that make up an rprim. They carry information about each vertex's position and can also have an arbitrary number of output primvars. The output primvars are read by the rasterizer and are the actual values that are pointsampled and recorded in the temporal functions of each voxel. We note that Reves executes its shaders on rprims, not on vprims. We also note the difference between shading vertices (which relate to the shading sub-system) and rasterization elements (which interact with the rasterization sub-system, and are made up of individual shading vertices).

Overall Algorithm

The Reves algorithm works in a series of steps that turn an arbitrary number of input primitives into one or more output volumes. For acceleration purposes, we first insert the vprims into an octree. Then, the output volume is divided into buckets. A lookup in the octree provides a fast way to bounds-test the input vprims against the bucket's extents. These two steps efficiently partition the inputs and the outputs, such that only the minimal set of inputs that affect a given bucket is considered.

Vprims that intersect the bucket are given the opportunity to split into smaller subvprims as needed. Once sufficiently small sub-vprims are produced, each one is diced into an rprim, and its shader is executed, which produces and/or modifies an arbitrary number of output primvars at each shading vertex. The shaded rprims are then rasterized using spatiotemporal point sampling in order to construct the temporal function in each voxel of the bucket. Once rasterization is complete, the temporal function curves are compressed, and the whole bucket is stored into the block-based output volume. The pipeline is well-suited to threading, and our implementation parallelizes work at the granularity of individual buckets. Algorithm 1 shows a pseudocode implementation of the process, and the following sections outline the details of each step.

Bounding

Our scene database stores vprims in an ordinary octree structure. In order to handle motion blur efficiently, indexing is performed in raster space rather than world space coordinates, such that the leaf-level nodes of the octree perfectly align with each bucket in the output volume. Because the number of rprims that overlap any given bucket may be large, tight bounds-testing is needed in order to reduce memory use and rasterization time. In order to provide tight intersection tests during insertion, vprims use a multi-segment axis-aligned bounding box (MSAABB), with one sample per motion sample of the input primitive. The number of motion samples used affects how accurately curved motion can be approximated but does not affect the temporal quality of the final TUV. During octree insertion, vprims are added to any octree node that intersects the swept motion of the MSAABB, as illustrated in Figure 8. We use the moving bounding box test described by Ericson [2004] to test each segment of the MSAABB. Algorithm 2 outlines the insertion process. During lookups, candidate vprims are gathered trivially from the octree by testing each octree node's extents against the the current bucket.

Algorithm 1 The Reves algorithm.

Precondition: list of input vprims v, list of output buckets b

```
function REVES(v, b)
    s ← voxelSize(b)
    o ← ⟨empty octree⟩
    for each v_i in v do
        insert (o, v_i)
    for each b_i in b do
        r ← ⟨empty list⟩                                ▷ Storage of rprims
        for each p_i in lookup(o, b_i) do
            if shouldSplit(p_i, s) then
                n ← split(p_i)                          ▷ List of sub-vprims
                erase(o, p_i)
                insert (o, n)
            else
                insert(r, dice(p_i, s))                 ▷ Insert new rprim
        for each r_i in r do
            r_i ← shade(r_i)                            ▷ Shade each rprim in place
        for each i, j, k in b_i do
            c ← rasterize(r, i, j, k)                   ▷ Construct temporal curve
            b_i(i, j, k) ← compress(c)                  ▷ Apply compression
```

Figure 8: Intersection between an octree node and a multi-segment axis-aligned bounding box (MSAABB, green) for a vprim with multi-segment motion. Although the regular AABB (gray) encompassing the full motion intersects the octree node, the swept bounds of the MSAABB (dashed) provide a tighter and more accurate intersection test.

Algorithm 2 Insertion of a vprim into the octree.

Precondition: Octree node o, list of vprims v

```
function INSERT(o, v)
    for each v_j in v do
        for each i in [0, 8) do
            if intersect(o_i, v_j) then                 ▷ o_i denotes child node
                if size(v_j) < size(o_i) then
                    insert(o_i, v_j)                    ▷ Recurse if vprim is small
                else
                    addItem(o_i, v_j)
```

Splitting

Once a vprim is found in the octree, it is queried to see whether a reasonable-resolution rprim would be produced. We use several measures to determine when the appropriate size is found. Ideally, for minimizing cross-task dependencies, we want each shading lattice to intersect as few processing buckets as possible, which suggests small rprims with a small number of shading vertices per rprim. At the same time, splitting excessively results in more individual vprims to manage and insert into the octree and smaller batches for the SIMD shading system to process. Through testing, we have found lattices with 50–150 vertices to be optimal. Figure 9 shows the performance of the system with different average vertex counts per rprim, and Algorithm 3 shows the implementation. From the graph, we draw the conclusion that execution time suffers as vertex counts exceeds 200–300, but that shading and octree lookups become a bottleneck with small vertex counts, negating other gains. The data was captured from the data set in Figure 1, with motion blur disabled. For more complex shaders, the shading time would increase, making very small grids expensive. With motion blur enabled, the octree lookup and the acceleration structure dominate, but they are less influenced by the size of individual shading grids.

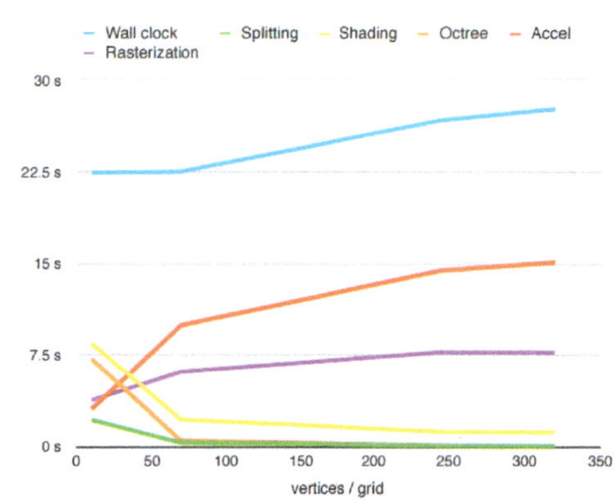

Figure 9: Plot of microvoxel lattice size versus run time for various parts of the Reves pipeline. (All times in seconds.).

Algorithm 3 Split criterion for ordinary vprim.

Precondition: Vprim or sub-vprim v, voxel size s

function SHOULDSPLIT(v, s)
  $d \leftarrow \text{extents}(v)$ ▷ World space isoparm lengths
  $r \leftarrow d/s$ ▷ Relative length
  return $r_x \cdot r_y \cdot r_z >$ ⟨split threshold⟩

Algorithm 4 Splitting an ordinary vprim.

Precondition: Vprim or sub-vprim v

function SPLIT(v)
  $d \leftarrow \text{extents}(v)$ ▷ World space isoparm lenghts
  $r \leftarrow d/s$ ▷ Relative length
  $v_1, v_2 \leftarrow v$ ▷ Clone v twice
  $i_1, i_2 \leftarrow \text{splitIsoparmBounds}(v, \text{longestAxis}(r))$
  $\text{assign}(v_1, i_1)$
  $\text{assign}(v_2, i_2)$
  return $\langle v_1, v_2 \rangle$

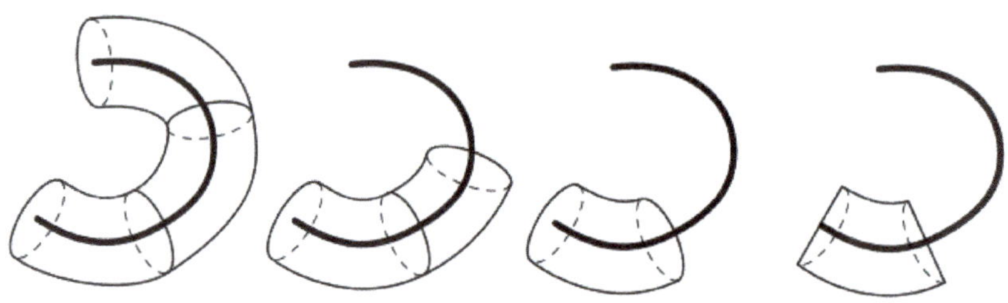

Figure 10: Three successive splitting steps. The first two split the vprim along the ∂P/∂u direction, whereas the third split happens along ∂P/∂v.

For ordinary vprim types (spheres, curves, surfaces, etc.), splitting is performed in parametric space along isoparametric lines. Each vprim stores a parametric bounding box, initially [0, 1] in each dimension, and each split event is binary, producing exactly two resulting primitives, which are then further split individually, as necessary. As illustrated in Algorithm 4, the axis to split is determined at each iteration by measuring the length of each dimension of the vprim or sub-vprim in world space. This ensures that the shading lattices produced are roughly isotropic. Our only exception to this rule is point clouds, which have no notion of parametric coordinates and which are bisected along the longest world space axis directly. Figure 10 shows three successive steps of splitting a curve vprim. Note that the last step's split direction is orthogonal to the first two. If a vprim is split, the resulting vprims are re-inserted into the octree.

Employing a splitting stage in the pipeline also allows for procedural primitives to perform detail amplification by emitting new geometry on-the-fly. This also allows for memory-efficient handling of input data sets that do not fit in primary memory, as primitives can be discarded from memory as soon a bucket is computed. The results (Section 6) show an example where a white-water element is generated from a point cloud by procedurally instancing line segments.

Dicing

The purpose of the dicing step is to convert a vprim or sub-vprim into an rprim, such that it's ready for shading to be applied and rasterization to take place. Spheres, ellipsoids, curves, and surfaces are all diced into $N_x \times N_y \times N_z$ resolution microvoxel lattices, such that the vertex spacing is roughly isotropic $(|\frac{\partial P}{du}| \approx |\frac{\partial P}{dv}| \approx |\frac{\partial P}{dw}|)$ and roughly equal in length to the output volume's voxel size S. The dicing happens along isoparametric lines within the vprim's parametric bounding box (as discussed previously). This yields a structure for which it is simple and efficient to transfer primvars from the vprim onto the lattice, which is required in order for the shading subsystem to work. Likewise, the connectivity of the lattice makes the calculation of shading derivatives straightforward, despite the fact that the shape of the lattice can be irregular. Our method uses simple finite differencing to compute these derivatives. Figure 11 shows a curve vprim diced into a microvoxel lattice rprim. During dicing, the vprim's primvars are transferred to the rprim, using linear interpolation in parametric space. Algorithm 5 outlines the process, which is the same for the aforementioned vprim types.

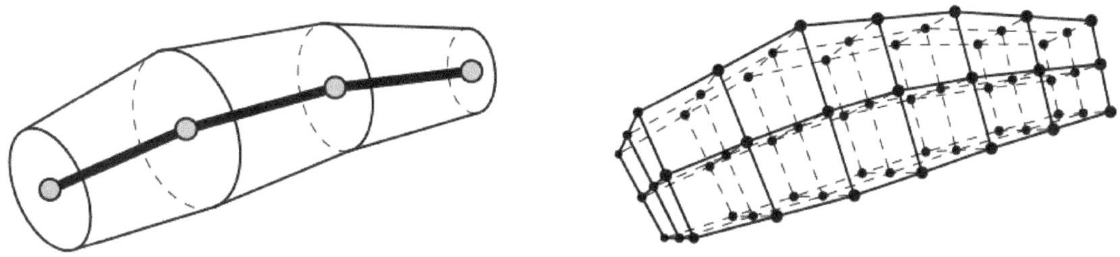

Figure 11: Left: A polygonal curve with varying radius. Right: The result of dicing the curve into a 3 × 3 × 7 microvoxel lattice.

The point cloud vprim is a special case of the dicing process, in that the vprim itself can be point sampled efficiently. Thus, the dicing step is a simple pass-through of the primvar data.

Algorithm 5 Dicing function.

Precondition: Vprim v, voxel size s

function DICE(v)
    $d \leftarrow$ extents(v) ▷ World space isoparm lengths
    $r \leftarrow d/s$ ▷ Relative length and resolution
    $M \leftarrow$ newMicrovoxelLattice(r)
    for each (i, j, k) in (r_x, r_y, r_z) **do**
        $P \leftarrow$ indexToParametric(i, j, k)
        $W \leftarrow$ parametricToWorld(P)
        setLatticePosition(M, i, j, k, W)
        for each x in primVars(v) **do**
            $x_v \leftarrow$ interpolatePrimVar(x, P)
            setPrimVar(M, x, i, j, k, x_v)
    return M

Shading

Once an rprim is diced, its vertices are passed to the shading system. The assigned shader reads uniform and/or varying values from input primvars and writes to an arbitrary number of output primvars, including new lattice point positions for displacement shading. The shading system takes advantage of the microvoxel lattice structure to compute accurate derivatives of position or any primvar, as needed. Derivatives can then be used in a shader's texture lookup to perform antialiasing and, in procedural routines, to properly filter out high frequency signals. Because of the vprim/rprim separation, this is supported uniformly for all vprim types, regardless of type.

Again, Cook et al. [1987] and Elendt [2005] provide very useful details on implementing a production-grade shading system, and our method follows their approaches closely. Algorithm 6 outlines the steps.

Algorithm 6 Shading function.

Precondition: Rasterization primitive r, shader s

function SHADE(r, s)
    $p \leftarrow$ interpolatePrimVars(r)
    $d \leftarrow$ computeDerivatives(r, p)
    bindPrimvars(p, s)
    executeShader(s, r, d)

Rasterization

Our rasterization process is a volumetric extension of the method introduced by Cook et al. [1987]. This is different from simple voxelization, which tends to compute a value per output voxel center. Our technique uses spatiotemporal stochastic sampling to select sub-voxel and temporal coordinates. Any well-behaved 4D blue noise function could be used; in our tests a 4D stratified random set of samples is employed. At its simplest, the process is as follows:

- For each voxel sample in each voxel, pick a position and time from the sampling distribution.
- Point sample each overlapping rasterization element at the given position and time, returning a set of output primvar values. We use additive composition for overlapping rprims, but other operations such as max are also valid.
- Insert each output primvar value into its corresponding temporal curve.

Interpolation of Microvoxels: Each microvoxel in a microvoxel lattice is effectively an eight-vertex cuboid, where each face is described by a bilinear patch. Any parametric interior point (u, v, w) ∈ $[0, 1]^3$ can be transformed into a position P using a linear combination of its control vertices, as illustrated in Figure 12. Thus, interpolation of a value V could be performed by finding (u, v, w) given P and then computing the value V (u, v, w) using the same linear combination. However, the inversion from P to (u, v, w) is difficult to solve exactly, and there are many vertex configurations that are non-invertible. Instead, we use a distance-weighted average for interpolating V within the voxel, which avoids having to find (u, v, w) explicitly:

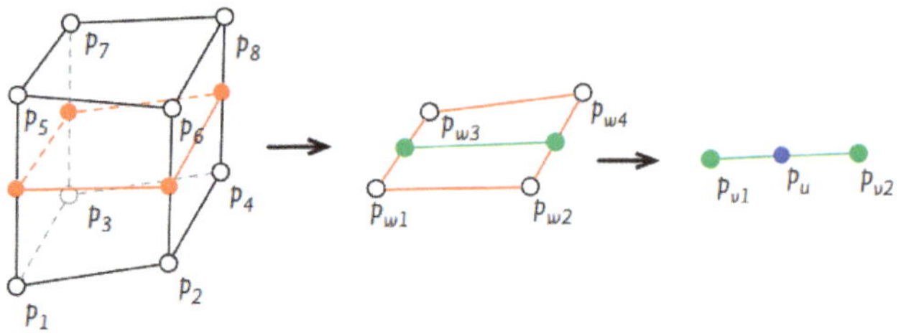

Figure 12: Finding a point P_U in a microvoxel based on (u, v, w) coordinates. Interpolating first along w yields a bilinear patch, then along v to yield a line, and finally along u to yield P.

$$V = \frac{\sum_{i=1}^{8} \frac{V_i}{\max(|(P - P_i)|, \epsilon)}}{\sum_{i=1}^{8} \frac{1}{\max(|(P - P_i)|, \epsilon)}}.$$

Before interpolating values, we must first determine whether a microvoxel overlaps a given sample point. The most accurate inside/outside test would check whether a point P is behind all of the bilinear patches of each microvoxel. For purposes of efficiency, we instead treat each bilinear patch face as two triangles, and test whether P is within the enclosing triangles of the cuboid. Because the size of individual microvoxels are similar to the output volume's voxels, we have not noticed any artifacts in our tests due to the approximation.

Interpolation of Point Clouds: Our interpolation method for point clouds is straightforward. The user selects one of several kernel functions k(P) (we have found box, triangle, and Gaussian to be sufficient), and the interpolated result is a sum according to

$$v = \sum_{i=1}^{N} v_i \cdot k(P - P_i).$$

In practice, there is no summation over the full set of points in the point cloud; an acceleration structure is built such that only the rasterization elements that overlap a given output voxel are considered. The structure is described below

Acceleration Structure: In order to achieve acceptable rasterization speeds, we employ an acceleration structure to quickly determine which rasterization elements overlap a given output voxel. For each output voxel in a bucket, we store a list of temporal slices, with each slice representing a fraction of the shutter interval. In effect, this forms a dense array of pointers to fixed-length lists of slices. Our goal is to use only one slice where the input scene is static, but to use progressively more slices as motion is introduced. Each slice stores a list of rasterization elements that need hit-testing for the time segment represented.

Each microvoxel lattice carries bounding information that is multi-segment, i.e. containing a set of htime, AABBi pairs. Given this bounding information, we first find the largest motion magnitude in the rasterization elements, M_{max}. With knowledge of the output voxel size S, we compute a heuristic for how many temporal slices to use according to

$$N = H\sqrt{\frac{M_{\max}}{S}}.$$

The square-root metric balances the amount of work required for acceleration structure construction against the actual efficiency of the acceleration structure. Through empirical testing, we have found that fewer slices allow too many entries for the acceleration structure to be effective, and a larger number of slices increases the construction time more than it decreases rasterization time. Figure 13 shows the performance of different multipliers on the square-root metric.

To fill the acceleration structure given N slices, we use the following steps: for each slice s, we consider the corresponding time interval T. We first perform an intersection test between the extents of output voxel (i, j, k) and m, which is the portion of the multi-segment bounds of each rasterization element over the interval T. If an intersection occurs, then the element is added to the acceleration structure for the given voxel.

This acceleration structure adapts well to both static and dynamic scenes and ensures that only relevant rasterization elements are tested against each output voxel. In the example shown in Figure 1, the acceleration structure improves performance by roughly 400x with motion blur disabled and 1300x with motion blur enabled. We have not found any failure cases in our testing, so the acceleration structure is generated and used at all times. Algorithm 7 illustrates our method for construction.

Algorithm 7 Constructing the acceleration structure.

Precondition: List of rprims r, acceleration structure a

```
function CONSTRUCTACCEL(r, a)
    M ← findMaxMotion(r)
    N ← H √(M/S)
    for each s in [0, N) do
        T ← [s/N, (s+1)/N]                          ▷ Time range
        for each r_i in r do
            for each e in rasterizationElems(r_i) do
                b ← discretebounds(e, T)             ▷ Voxel range
                m ← msaabb(e, T)
                for each (i, j, k) in b do
                    if movingBBoxIsect((i, j, k), m) then
                        append e to a(i, j, k, s)
```

Sampling: Once the list of potential rasterization elements has been determined, stochastic point sampling is used to construct the temporal function that describes how each output primvar evolves over time. By spatiotemporally sampling the microvoxels and point clouds, motion blur effects are captured both due to motion and due to change in the output primvars with time.

Figure 14 illustrates the sampling process in 2D, where a single microvoxel is sampled, and the resulting temporal curve is built. We note that the temporal function is noisy, due to the fact that samples are distributed both spatially and temporally. Ideally, in cases where the rasterization elements are static, no temporal stratification would be necessary, and the supersamples would be used only for spatial antialiasing, and vice versa in cases with fast motion.

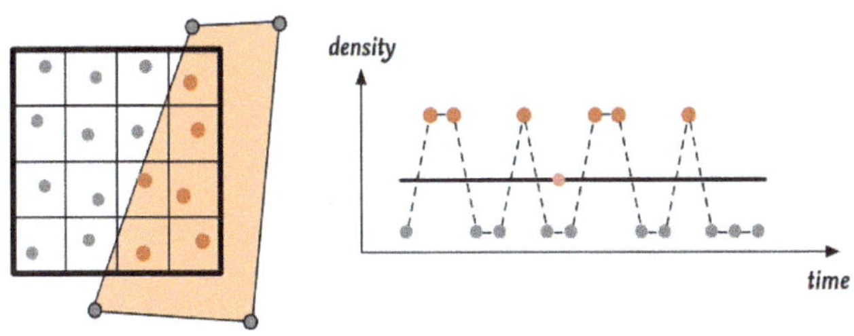

Figure 14: 2D illustration of sampling. A single, static microvoxel is sampled at 4 × 4 sub-voxel locations and the resulting temporal curve is constructed (dashed). Based on the measured motion, which is zero, the resulting values are filtered down to a single value (solid).

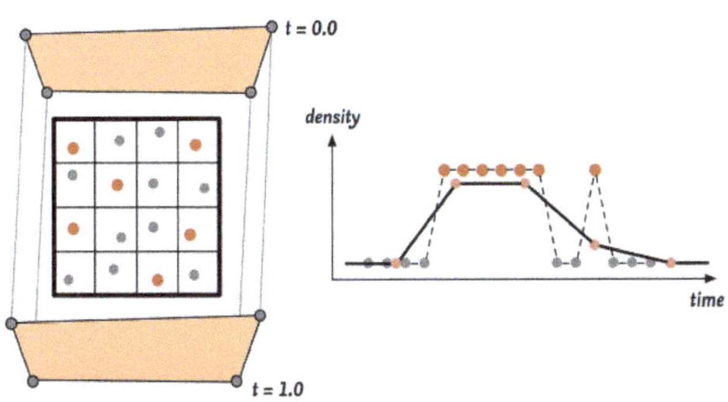

Figure 15: 2D illustration of a microvoxel moving a length of two voxels is sampled at 4 × 4 sub-voxel locations with the resulting temporal curve constructed (dashed). Based on the motion, five samples $(\frac{M_{max}}{S_r S_v} = 2)$ are used to reconstruct the output temporal curve (solid).

We solve this problem by post-processing the temporal curve using information from the acceleration structure. We place N new temporal samples over the shutter interval and re-sample the temporal curve using a $\frac{1}{N}$ -wide box filter. In selecting N, we note that the number of temporal samples, N, needed to capture the motion of a rasterization element is a Nyquist-like problem. Given a voxel of size S_v, a rasterization element size S_r, and the maximal motion length M_{max}, we can select the number N to ensure that the element is sampled before, during, and after entering the voxel:

$$N = 2\frac{M_{\max}}{S_r S_v} + 1.$$

Figure 15 shows the before-and-after result of post-processing the temporal function for a moving microvoxel. Compression of the curve, which was discussed in Section 3.2, is applied after the resampling stage.

APPLICATION TO FLUID SIMULATION RETIMING

We also apply our temporal volume data structure to the area of fluid simulation retiming. Here, the objective is to construct novel data sets based on existing fluid simulations such that a simulation may be played back at a slower or faster speed. The challenge lies in producing data that lies in-between the pre-computed animation frames. Common techniques for this include approaches such as direct interpolation, and forward-backward advection and blending of adjacent frames. However, even in the best case there is no way to accurately reconstruct the sub-frame state of the simulator, which may have used any number of time steps to compute one frame; the information is simply lost. In contrast to these techniques, TUVs are able to represent a continuously-varying temporal dimension, avoiding the need to synthesize in-between frames altogether.

In order to produce temporal volume data from fluid simulations, we maintain a cache of all computed sub-frame simulation fields for the duration of one animation frame. When completing a full simulation step, we construct a temporal curve per voxel by taking a number of time samples, determined by a CFL condition1 [Lewy et al. 1928], and for each time sample computing backward and forward advection of adjacent sub-frame simulation states, such that smooth motion is reproduced. Each sample is recorded into a temporal curve, which is then compressed using the algorithm described in Section 3.2. We note that the CFL condition can be computed per voxel, such that only areas with high velocities require a large number of samples. Algorithm 8 illustrates our method.

Algorithm 8 Constructing a temporal curve from fluid data.

Precondition: List of simulation states s, coordinate P

function RECONSTRUCT(s, P)
    $c \leftarrow \langle$empty temporal curve$\rangle$
    $v \leftarrow$ velocity(s_{first}, P) ▷ Velocity from first simulation state
    $d \leftarrow |v\Delta t|/\Delta x$ ▷ Length of motion in voxels; CFL
    for each n in $[0, d)$ **do**
        $t \leftarrow \frac{n+\xi}{d}$ ▷ Time offset
        $(s_0, s_1, f) \leftarrow$ findNeighborStates(s, t) ▷ f is fractional distance
        $V_0 \leftarrow$ density($s_0, P + v(t0 - t)$) ▷ Advect previous state forward
        $V_1 \leftarrow$ density($s_1, P + v(t1 - t)$) ▷ Advect next state backward
        record(c, t, lerp(V_0, V_1, f))
    return c

Using TUVs to store fluid simulation data has several benefits (see Figure 16):

- Motion effects are pre-computed and continuous time is recorded, increasing the speed of rendering.
- There is no need to store a velocity field, which is typically a dense data set that compresses poorly.

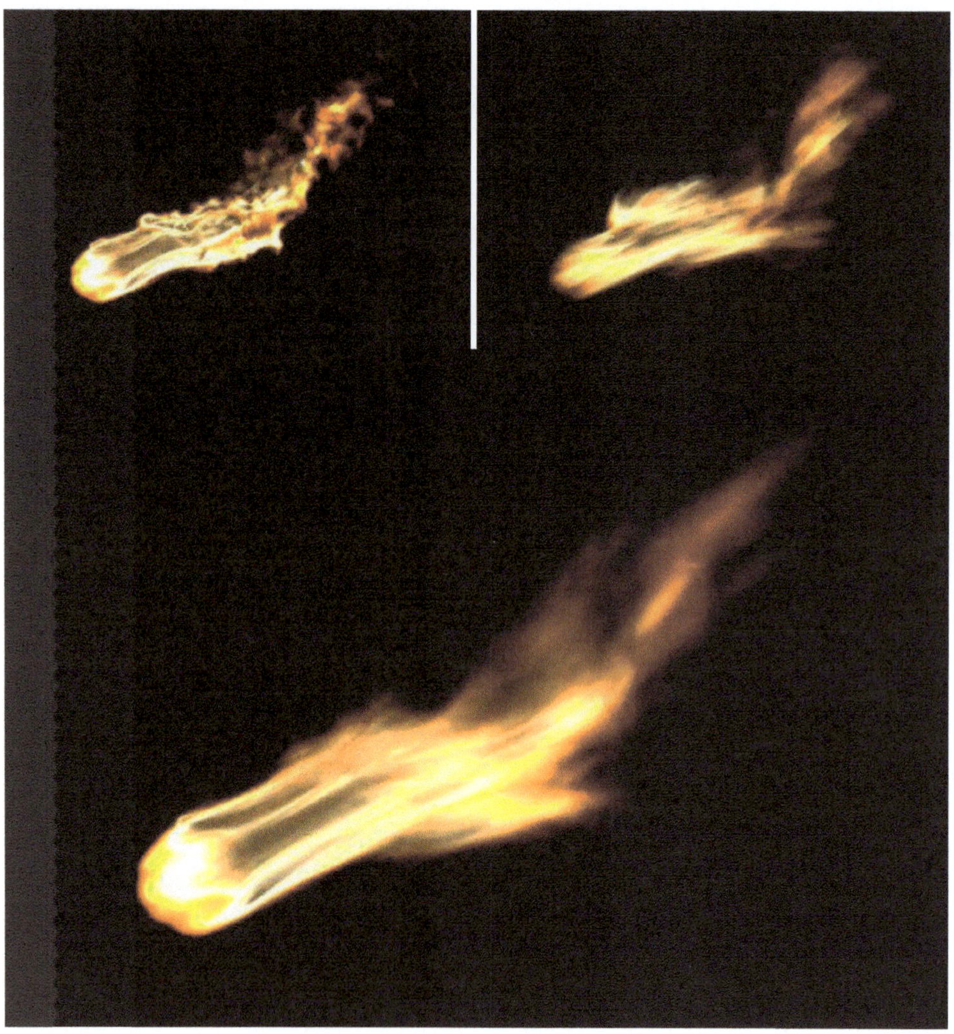

Figure 16: Fire simulation rendered without motion blur (top left, 6m 50s, 1.27GB), with microvoxel motion blur (top right, 20m 41s, 3.39GB), and with TUV data (bottom, 17m 22s, 2.29GB). Motion blur based on the fluid simulation motion vectors produces incorrect results, while our TUV approach captures both the steady state of the source, as well as complex nonlinear motion during the shutter open/close interval.

Re-timing the data is straightforward and produces high-quality results that incorporate the full motion of the original simulation. Because the data structure stores a continuous time dimension, rendering frame 4.5 is no different than rendering frame 4.0. Figure 17 shows how accurate sub-frame data can be extracted from a temporal data set by interpolating each temporal voxel at the chosen sub-frame time.

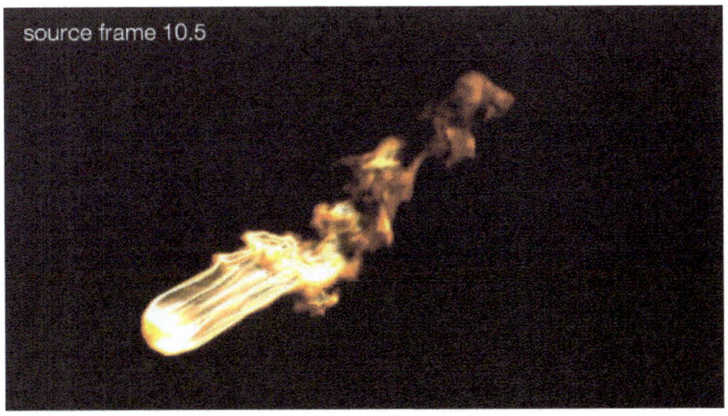

Figure 17: Extraction of sub-frame data from temporal volume. Note the lack of ghosting or other artifacts. The temporal adaptivity of our method allows for high-quality re-timing of fluid simulation data.

RESULTS

The images in Figure 18 show data sets generated by our Reves algorithm. The input primitives are eight curves, each with complex, rotational motion and a unique set of shader parameters. The curves are used to produce a 292×384×302 resolution voxel

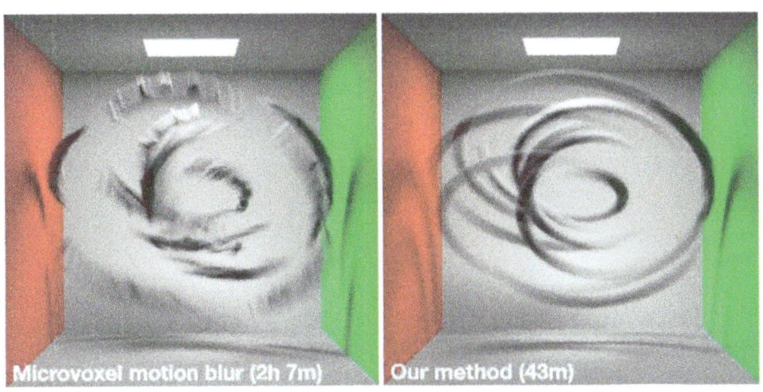

Figure 18: A single volume generated procedurally using our Reves algorithm, rendered with motion vector-based motion blur (left, 2h 7m); and rendered using our temporal volume method (right, 43m).

Figure 19: 8.5 million polygonal lines rasterized into a 8192×8192×4096 resolution volume.

buffer before rendering. In the first image, motion vectors are computed using central differencing, and the volume is motion-blurred using microvoxel-based motion blur. In the second image, a temporal volume is generated using 32 motion samples and 6^3 voxel samples. Reves constructs the volume data for the first image in 1m 20s. For the second image, the construction time is 14m 21s due to the extreme motion. Rendering of the data set using microvoxel motion blur takes 2h 7m, and using our method the render time is 43m. We note that although our method involves more precomputation for scenes with volumetric motion blur, the time spent generating the temporal volume data is small relative to the time saved during rendering. Although the processing time to produce this particular TUV data set may seem high, we stress that the example is extreme, in order to provide our algorithm with a very difficult motion blur case that the current state-of-the-art method fails to render correctly. The video supplement includes a 240-frame animation illustrating both test cases.

Figure 19 shows the test case we use to illustrate Reves' scaling properties. A point cloud with 4.3 million vertices is used to procedurally generate 8.5 million curve primitives, illustrating Reves' capacity for run-time detail amplification. We expect the Reves algorithm to scale no worse than linearly as we increase the resolution of the output volume (Figure 20(top)). In our experiments, we find super-linear scaling for scenes without motion blur and slightly sub-linear scaling with severe motion blur. The super-linear scaling is due to our various bounding optimizations—as the output volume is refined, intersection tests become more accurate and prune more irrelevant vprims and rprims in the various stages of the algorithm. The memory use shown does not include the storage of the input primitives, which is a constant 312MB (including primvars), nor the output volume, which increases linearly with the increase in voxel count. The increased memory use for the motion blur case is due to the high number of input primitives: at lower resolutions, many vprims overlap each processing bucket, but as the output volume resolution increases, bucket size decreases, and we are left with fewer vprims to process per bucket, which reduces the amount of data required to reside in memory concurrently.

We also expect Reves' performance to scale linearly with increasing numbers of input primitives. In our tests, we find slightly super-linear performance for increases where the primitive count is low, most likely due to general overhead. As the number of primitives increases, performance becomes more linear. The results in Figure 20 (bottom left) were generated using the same data as in the previous example, constructed at a resolution of 2048^3.

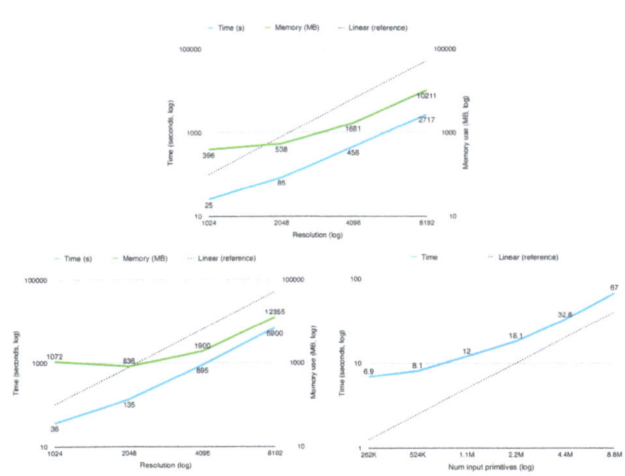

Figure 20: Reves' scaling behavior with increasing resolution without motion blur (top), increasing resolution with motion blur (bottom left), and increasing input primitive count (bottom right). The dashed line indicates linear increase.

The images in Figure 21 show a 512^3 resolution smoke simulation with fast motion, rendered first using motion vectors (22h 13m) and then using our temporal data structure (1h 21m). In this example, the extreme motion blur causes the microvoxel rendering described by Clinton and Elendt [2009] to consume more memory (4.12GB vs 2.25GB using temporal data) and take significantly longer (16.4x) to render than our method. Our method for producing temporal data from fluid simulations does add some overhead, on the same order of magnitude as performing advection. In this test, the simulation took an average of 39s per frame, and with temporal reconstruction the total time including simulation and reconstruction took 44s per frame. Compared to the time savings and increased correctness during rendering, the cost is small. The file size for the ordinary density and velocity volumes were an average of 1.47GB per frame, versus 1.37GB per frame for the density-only TUV using an error threshold of 0.05.

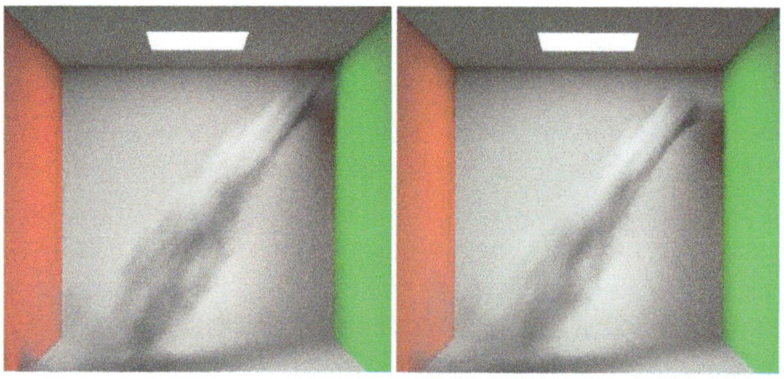

Figure 21: A smoke simulation using microvoxel motion blur (left, 22h 13m); and with our method (right, 1h 21m).

Figure 16 shows a fast-moving flame simulation simulated at 350^3 resolution. The first image (top left) is rendered without motion blur (6m 50s), the second (top right) shows microvoxel-based motion blur (20m 41s), and the third (bottom) shows our method (17m 22s). The motion vector technique shows several types of artifacts: the linear motion path of each microvoxel fails to capture the subtle and curved motion of the original simulation data; also the source itself is motion blurred, even though there is steady, continuous injection of fuel. Our method is able to correctly render the data set with smooth and curved motion and accurately preserving the static source. The video supplement includes a 48-frame animation of the tests. In this example, the speed advantage is smaller for temporal volume data, due to the large number of samples per voxel (30–40 in some voxels); however vastly more information is preserved. The resulting TUV files are larger: 158MB for two ordinary scalar and one vector field and 257MB for two scalar TUVs.

In Figure 17, we use the same data set as in Figure 16 to demonstrate our method's application to fluid re-timing. The fire simulation is slowed down by a factor of 10, and an ordinary voxel data set is extracted for each subframe time. Here, it is clear that our method is able to accurately capture the complex sub-frame motion of the fire. Included in the video supplement are examples of the simulation data rendered at full speed and slowed down using existing interpolation methods, as well as using our TUV structure.

Figure 22: Reves as applied to shots from The Good Dinosaur. 1000 polygonal curves were used to generate the storm funnel cloud in 2h/frame at 2000 × 2000 × 500 resolution with procedural detail added through shaders (top). 100M particles were rasterized in chunks to cover a 100m tall waterfall at 1cm resolution (middle). Temporal volumes were used to retime the snow simulation to give effects' artist exact control over evolution speed (bottom).

The potential failure case of our temporal data structure is over-compression: it is possible to specify a compression error threshold large enough that too much data is lost to produce accurate motion blur. The last example in the supplemental video shows how the quality of our temporal data degrades as the compression factor is increased from 0.05 to 0.5.

Our implementation of TUVs was done in Field3D, as it provides a flexible framework for adding novel data structures. Rendering was performed in Mantra using physically based shading with one diffuse and one volume bounce, with reference images produced using its native microvoxel method and with our temporal data structure implemented as a procedural volume type. All tests were performed on a 16-core 2.8GHz Xeon workstation and report wall clock time.

PRODUCTION USE

Our system is in active production use, most recently in The Good Dinosaur, where Reves was used extensively for volume modeling tasks and temporal volumes were used for re-timing of fluid simulation. Figure 22 shows some examples. On the upcoming Finding Dory, TUVs were used for volumetric motion blur, and as of version 21.0, Pixar's RenderMan natively uses TUVs to provide volumetric motion blur in the RIS framework.

CONCLUSION AND FUTURE WORK

Our work addresses efficient representation and construction of TUV data sets, most notably in the context of producing motion blur effects. The key idea is to abandon geometric interpretations of volume data when computing motion blur, and instead focus solely on the change that the volumetric properties undergo with time. We show that our technique provides a robust, general, and efficient way to generate and represent volume data with complex sub-frame motion, and that use of the temporal data leads to increased performance and correctness when rendering images with motion blur for film production. Because TUVs require no bounds padding to account for motion blur, they enable efficient path tracing, even for incoherent ray patterns. The fast random access times provided by TUVs also help in rendering of other visual effects that use path tracing, such as multiple scattering and depth of field. Finally, we also show that TUVs provide an attractive method for re-timing fluid simulation data.

Our Reves algorithm offers an efficient and robust way of constructing both TUV and ordinary volumetric data sets. It handles large input models and scales linearly with input and output model complexity. It also offers support for a wide variety of input primitives, multi-segment motion blur, shaders, displacement shaders, texture filtering, and anti-aliasing. The spatiotemporal reconstruction method provides orthogonal control over spatial resolution and the quality of motion blur and antialiasing.

In the future, we would like to explore compression techniques that leverage knowledge about the temporal nature of the function curves, as well as GPU methods for accelerating the performance of the stochastic rasterization step. Although our method uses a uniform voxel resolution, the temporal representation should translate well to adaptive-resolution volumes, which would be an interesting area to explore. Finally, we would also like to investigate the use of two-dimensional temporal data sets for image compositing.

APPENDIX

Eulerian Motion Blur

The most common motion blur scheme for ray-tracing and path-tracing renderers is Eulerian motion blur [Kulla and Fajardo 2012]. The scheme assumes that the volume properties are constant with time, and that the only change over time is due to advection within the volume. Given a volumetric property f, a point to sample P, a velocity field $\vec{v}$, , and a time offset t, Eulerian blur makes the approximation $f(P,t) \approx f(P - \vec{v} \cdot t, 0)$. That is to say, it is assumed that the field is known at

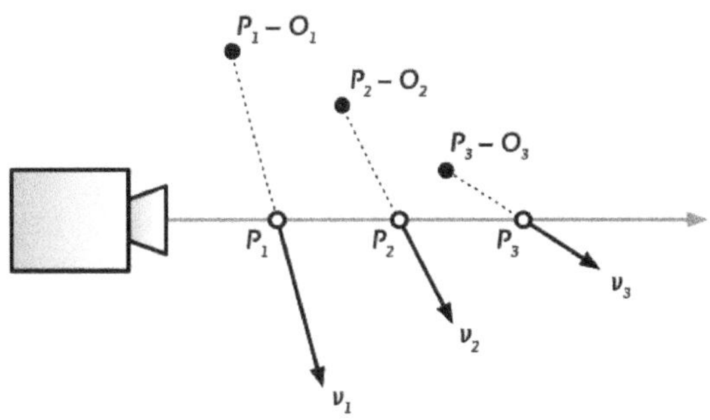

Figure 23: Eulerian motion blur. When querying the volume f at point P_i , we first find the motion vector $\vec{v}_i$, and then offset the query point by the time value t ∈ [0, 1] so that $f(P_i,t) \approx f(P_i - \vec{v}_i \cdot t, 0)$. This computation is similar to advection in fluid dynamics and could also use higher-order approximations.

t = 0, and it is gradually deformed by v as t increases. Figure 23 illustrates the process. The method is only approximate, because for any non-constant velocity field, $\vec{v}(P) \neq \vec{v}(P - \vec{v} \cdot t)$, and thus the material at $P' = P - \vec{v} \cdot t$ would never reach P.

When implementing Eulerian motion blur, we note that two lookups are required: First, one to query the vector field, then a second lookup to query the actual density. In extensive testing, we have found the cost of these two O(k)lookups to consistently be 30 ± 3% slower than a single lookup in a TUV, despite the O(logN) time complexity of the TUV lookup, since N is generally small.

We note that the process is almost exactly equivalent to the semi-Lagrangian advection used in fluid dynamics.

Microvoxel Motion Blur

In the microvoxel motion blur scheme [Clinton and Elendt 2009], the volume is subdivided into a connected lattice of points, with a spacing roughly equal to the projected pixel size. When tracing a ray against the lattice, a sub-frame state that depends on t is found by interpolating the lattice's animated vertex positions (see Figure 24). Although a single lookup into the free-form lattice would be expensive, the cost is amortized when traversing the lattice along a ray, as a DDA-like traversal can be used to decide through which face the ray leaves each microvoxel.

As opposed to Eulerian motion blur, there is not a fixed cost to the microvoxel scheme; it depends on the size and number of microvoxel lattices that each ray needs to traverse. The images in Figure 21 shows a 16.4x advantage for TUVs over microvoxels for an image with moderate motion blur.

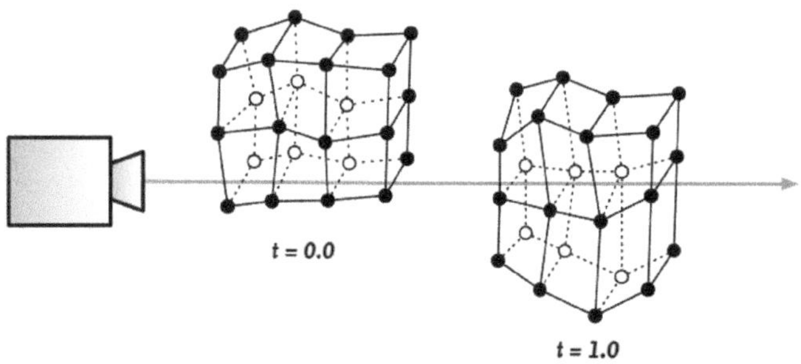

Figure 24: Microvoxel motion blur. At left, we see the lattice at t = 0.0, and on the right the lattice has moved and deformed at t = 1.0, as defined by the placement of each vertex. When tracing a ray through the volume, the sub-frame state of the volume can be found by interpolating each lattice vertex.

REFERENCES

1. CLINTON, A., AND ELENDT, M. 2009. Rendering volumes with microvoxels. In SIGGRAPH 2009: Talks, ACM, New York, NY, USA, SIGGRAPH '09, 47:1–47:1. URL: http:// doi.acm.org/10.1145/1597990.1598037, doi:10.1145/1597990.1598037. 2, 4, 26, 31
2. COOK, R. L., PORTER, T., AND CARPENTER, L. 1984. Distributed ray tracing. In Proceedings of the 11th annual conference on Computer graphics and interactive techniques, ACM, New York, NY, USA, SIGGRAPH '84, 137–145. URL: http://doi.acm. org/10.1145/800031.808590, doi:10.1145/800031.808590. 3
3. COOK, R. L., CARPENTER, L., AND CATMULL, E. 1987. The Reyes image rendering architecture. In Proceedings of the 14th annual conference on Computer graphics and interactive techniques, ACM, New York, NY, USA, SIGGRAPH '87, 95–102. URL: http://doi.acm. org/10.1145/37401.37414, doi:10.1145/37401.37414. 4, 8, 17
4. DOUGLAS, D. H., AND PEUCKER, T. K. 1973. Algorithms for the reduction of the number of points required to represent a digitized line or its caricature. Cartographica: The International Journal for Geographic Information and Geovisualization 10, 2, 112–122. 7
5. ELENDT, M. 2005. Shading. In Production rendering: Design and implementation, I. Stephenson, Ed. Springer, London, Berlin, Heidelberg, 105–136. 4, 9, 17
6. ENRIGHT, D., MARSCHNER, S., AND FEDKIW, R. 2002. Animation and rendering of complex water surfaces. In Proceedings of the 29th Annual Conference on Computer Graphics and Interactive Techniques, ACM, New York, NY, USA, SIGGRAPH '02, 736–744. URL: http://doi.acm.org/10.1145/566570.566645, doi:10.1145/566570.566645. 3
7. ERICSON, C. 2004. Real-Time Collision Detection. Morgan Kaufmann Publishers Inc., San Francisco, CA, USA. 13
8. FEDKIW, R., STAM, J., AND JENSEN, H. W. 2001. Visual simulation of smoke. In Proceedings of SIGGRAPH 2001, ACM Press / ACM SIGGRAPH, New York, E. Fiume, Ed., Computer Graphics Proceedings, Annual Conference Series, ACM, 15–22. 3
9. FIELD3D, 2009. v1.4.1. http://sites.google.com/site/ field3d. 6
10. FUNKHOUSER, T., TSINGOS, N., AND JOT, J.-M. 2003. Survey of methods for modeling sound propagation in interactive virtual environment systems. URL: http:// www.cs. princeton.edu/~funk/presence03.pdf. 4
11. JARABO, A., MARCO, J., MUNOZ ˜ , A., BUISAN, R., JAROSZ, W., AND GUTIERREZ, D. 2014. A framework for transient rendering. ACM Trans. Graph. 33, 6 (Nov.), 177:1–177:10. URL: http://doi.acm.org/10.1145/2661229. 2661251, doi:10.1145/2661229.2661251. 4
12. KIM, D., AND KO, H.-S. 2007. Eulerian motion blur. In Proceedings of the Third Eurographics conference on Natural Phenomena, Eurographics Association, Aire-la-Ville, Switzerland, NPH'07, 39–46. doi:10.2312/NPH/ NPH07/039-046. 4
13. KOREIN, J., AND BADLER, N. 1983. Temporal anti-aliasing in computer generated animation. In Proceedings of the 10th Annual Conference on Computer Graphics and Interactive Techniques, ACM, New York, NY, USA, SIGGRAPH '83, 377–388. URL: http://doi.acm.org/10.1145/800059.801168, doi:10.1145/800059.801168. 3
14. KULLA, C., AND FAJARDO, M. 2012. Importance sampling techniques for path tracing in participating media. Comp. Graph. Forum 31, 4 (June), 1519–1528. doi:10.1111/j.1467- 8659.2012.03148.x. 4, 30
15. LEWY, H., FRIEDRICHS, K., AND COURANT, R. 1928. Uber die partiellen Differenzen- ¨ gleichungen der mathematischen Physik. Mathematische Annalen 100, 32–74. URL: http://eudml.org/doc/159283. 22
16. LOKOVIC, T., AND VEACH, E. 2000. Deep shadow maps. In Proceedings of the 27th Annual Conference on Computer Graphics and Interactive Techniques, ACM Press/Addison-Wesley Publishing Co., New York, NY, USA, SIGGRAPH '00, 385–392. doi:10.1145/344779.344958. 7
17. MUSETH, K. 2013. VDB: High-resolution sparse volumes with dynamic topology. ACM Trans. Graph. 32, 3 (July), 27:1–27:22. URL: http://doi.acm.org/10.1145/ 2487228.2487235, doi:10.1145/2487228.2487235. 6
18. POTMESIL, M., AND CHAKRAVARTY, I. 1983. Modeling motion blur in computer-generated images. In Proceedings of the 10th Annual Conference on Computer Graphics and Interactive Techniques, ACM, New York, NY, USA, SIGGRAPH '83, 389–399. URL: http://doi.acm.org/10.1145/800059.801169, doi:10.1145/800059.801169. 3
19. RAMER, U. 1972. An iterative procedure for the polygonal approximation of plane curves. Computer Graphics and Image Processing 1, 3, 244 – 256. URL: http://www.sciencedirect.com/science/article/pii/

S0146664X72800170, doi:http://dx.doi.org/10.1016/S0146-664X(72)80017-0. 7

20. WRENNINGE, M., AND BIN ZAFAR, N. 2011. In Production Volume Rendering 1: Fundamentals, ACM, New York, NY, USA, ACM SIGGRAPH 2011 Courses. 4

21. WRENNINGE, M., BIN ZAFAR, N., HARDING, O., GRAHAM, G., TESSENDORF, J., GRANT, V., CLINTON, A., AND BOUTHORS, A. 2011. In Production Volume Rendering 2: Systems, ACM, New York, NY, USA, ACM SIGGRAPH 2011 Courses. 4

22. WRENNINGE, M. 2012. Production Volume Rendering: Design and Implementation. CRC Press, Boston, MA, USA. 4

23. ZHU, Y., AND BRIDSON, R. 2005. Animating sand as a fluid. In ACM SIGGRAPH 2005 Papers, ACM, New York, NY, USA, SIGGRAPH '05, 965–972. URL: http://doi. acm.org/10.1145/1186822.1073298, doi:10.1145/1186822.1073298. 3

CHAPTER 16

ADAPTIVE ADJUSTMENT FACTOR IN IMAGE ENHANCEMENT TECHNIQUE USING PARTICLE SWARM OPTIMIZATION WITH AGING LEADER AND CHALLENGERS (ALC-PSO)

Er. Avneet Kaur[1] and Er. Harman Preet Singh[2]

[1]Student, Computer Science Department, Guru Nanak Dev University, Regional Campus, Jalandhar, India

[2]Student, Electronics Department, Guru Nanak Dev University, Amritsar, India

ABSTRACT

The process of converting an image and performing some operations on it is known as image processing. The application of Image processing include: Image Enhancement. Image enhancement is a process of transforming an image and enhancing its quality in order to take out some important information from it. The image enhancement process can be done by an optimization technique like Particle Swarm Optimization method, which is a search technique used to find the best solutions out of several possible ones. The PSO technique can be efficiently used by taking the objective function for image enhancement as the fitness value for every particle image. This paper presents an overview of image enhancement techniques based on the use of Particle Swarm Optimization. The limitation of static adjustment factor is removed by using Particle Swarm Optimization with Aging Leader and Challengers (ALC-PSO). A new algorithm of image enhancement using ALC-PSO has been proposed, which will adaptively find the adjustment factor for the efficient performance of the process of image enhancement.

INTRODUCTION

Image Processing is a process of converting an image into digital form and performing some operations on it. The image can be enhanced in such a way that some useful information can be extracted from it. The process of image processing treats images as two dimensional signals and applies the already set signal processing methods on them. Image processing has many of its applications in the field of business, engineering and computer sciences.

Image Enhancement

Image enhancement is one of the important image processing techniques which can be treated as transforming an image into another to improve the perception of information or to provide a better input for some image processing techniques [1]. Image enhancement techniques are very important to image processing, which are used to improve image quality or extract the fine details in degraded images [7].

Citation: Er. Avneet Kaur and Er. Harman Preet Singh, Adaptive Adjustment factor in Image Enhancement Technique using Particle Swarm Optimization with Aging Leader and Challengers (ALC-PSO), doi.org/10.14257/ijcg.2015.6.2.02.

Original Image

Enhanced image

Types of Image Enhancement

The two types of image enhancement can be done- grayscale image enhancement and colored image enhancement.

Grayscale Image Enhancement

The black and white images are enhanced. Transformation steps for grayscale image Enhancement:

- Normalize the gray value of each pixel
- Transform the input image by the transformation function
- Calculate the gray value of the output image

Colored Image Enhancement

Image enhancement approaches applied directly to the three components (R, G, B) i.e., for Red, Green and Blue component, of a degraded color image may produce color artifacts which may make the enhanced image [7].

Adjustment Factor K

Adjustment factor K is used in image enhancement which decides the stretching intensity of computing the enhanced intensity value X_e for the two classes C1 and C2. Parameter K decides the stretching point to which the intensity values X should be stretched based on the membership values $u_{D1}$and u_{D2}. The value for K is usually computed empirically according to what extent the stretching is required (mostly fixed to be 128). The parameter M divides the histogram h(X) into two classes. The first class C1contains pixels values in the range [0,M − 1] and the second class C2 in the range [M, 255].

The mathematical representation of finding the membership value function for C1

$$u_{D1}(X) = 1 - (M - X)/\ M$$

where, u_{D1} is membership value of C1 and X€ C1.

Once the membership value for x is obtained, the intensified value X_e for the class C1can be computed as follows:

$$X_e = X + u_{D1}(X)K$$

$u_{D1}(X)$ decides what amount of adjustment factor K has to be added to X to get the enhanced value x_e .

Similarly, the mathematical representation of finding the membership value function for C2

$$u_{D2}(X) = 2 - (M - X)/\ M$$

where, u_{D2} is membership value of C2 and X € C2.

Once the membership value for X is obtained, the intensified value x_e for the class C2can be computed as follows:

$$X_e = X + u_{D2}(X)K$$

$u_{D2}(X)$ decides what amount of adjustment factor K has to be added to x to get the enhanced value X_e .

PREVIOUS WORK-IMAGE ENHANCEMENT USING PSO

PSO Algorithm

Particle swarm optimization (PSO) is a population-based stochastic approach for solving continuous and discrete optimization problems. PSO is an evolutionary computation technique[2]. In particle swarm optimization, particles move in the search space of an optimization problem. The position of a particle denotes a candidate solution to an optimization problem. Each particle searches for some better position in the search space by changing its velocity.

pbest- Each particle keeps track of its coordinates in the solution space. This position is associated with the best solution, called fitness, which has been achieved so far by that particle. This value is called the personal best (pbest).

gbest- It is the best value obtained by a particle so far in its neighborhood. This value is called global best (gbest).

During each iteration, every particle is accelerated towards the particle's previous best position (pbest) and the global best (gbest) position and a new velocity value for each particle is calculated. based on particle's current velocity, distance from its previous best position and distance from the global best position.

$$v_{it}+1 = w.v_{it}+c_1.r_1t*[pbest_{it}-X_{it}]+c_2.r_2t[gbest-X_{it}]$$

$$X_{it}+1 = X_{it}+ v_{it}+1$$

where v_{it} is velocity of ith particle at iteration t, w is weight inertia.

c_1, c_2 are acceleration Constants

r_1, r_2 are random number between 0 and 1

X_{it} is the current position of ith particle at iteration t, pbesti is personal best of ith particle, gbest is global best value of the group.

Functions used in Image Enhancement

For image enhancement, a transformation function is used which takes the intensity value of each pixel from the input image and generates a new intensity value for the corresponding pixel to produce the enhanced image. To evaluate the quality of the enhanced image, an evaluation function is required [9].

Transformation Function

Image enhancement uses a transform function which generates a new intensity value for each pixel of the original image, denoted as MN, to generate the enhanced image, where M is the number of columns and N is the number of rows. The enhancement process can be denoted by: g(i, j)= T [f(i,j)], where f(i,j) is the gray value of the pixel of the input image and (i,j) is the gray value of the pixel of the enhanced image. g(i,j) is the transformation function.

Local enhancement method is applied the transformation on a pixel, considering the intensity distribution among its neighboring pixels[3].

Evaluation Criterion

To evaluate the quality of an enhanced image, an objective function is required. Many objective functions are used [4-6]. The objective function may be formed by combining three performance measures:

- entropy value
- sum of edge intensities
- number of edge pixels. [9]

Proposed Work

There are some gaps in earlier work done in this field. The major gap in earlier research on image enhancement techniques is the Static adjustment factor, which means the existing k factor has been taken statically i.e., 128 by most of researchers.

We have seen that PSO has been used efficiently for enhancing the images. It was a challenging work to see if some variants of PSO can also be used in the image enhancement process. In order to fill these gaps, a variant of PSO called-ALC-PSO is used in this regard, which can take the k value used adjustment factor automatically and improves the results obtained for the process of image enhancement. The proposed method shows the PSO with Aging Leader and Challengers used to dynamically find the adjustment factor.

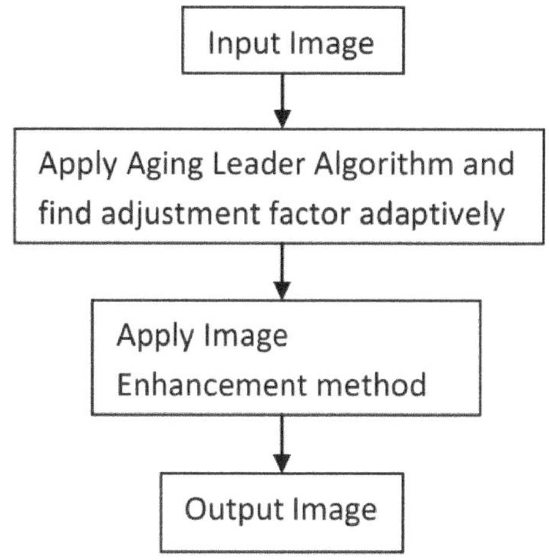

Particle Swarm Optimization with Aging Leader and Challengers (ALC-PSO) Technique

A new concept of leader is introduced in Particle Swarm Optimization Algorithm, in which the leader leads the whole swarm and brings all other particles to the best position efficiently. This algorithm is based on the aging mechanism, which says, after a certain time period the leader becomes unable to lead the swarm, so there is a need to replace this old leader with a new one. The challengers for challenging this position of the leader, comes up and the best one is selected as the new leader.

Each particle tries to modify its position by using its:

- current positions
- current velocities
- distance between the current position and pbest
- distance between the current position and the gbest

The velocity update rule of the classical PSO is updated to:

$$v_i^j = w.*\, v_i^j + c_1.r_1^j.\,(pBest_i^j - x_i^j) + c_2.\, r_2^j.\,(Leader^j - x_i^j)$$

where c1, c2 are acceleration Constants

r1, r2 are random number between 0 and 1

Xit is the current position of ith particle at iteration t,

pbesti is personal best of ith particle,

gbest is global best value of the group.

leader is the particle which is challenging to become the new leader of the swarm.

Table 1: Parameters of ALC-PSO

Parameter	Description
Particle	candidate solution to a problem
Velocity	rate of position change
Fitness	the best solution achieved
Leader	The particle challenging to become the new leader of swarm
Pbest	best value obtained in previous particle
Gbest	best value obtained so far by any particle in the population

Steps in ALC-PSO

Step 1: Initialization- Initialize the positions of particles to some predefined values.

Step 2: Updating velocity and position- Update the velocity and position of particle (leader) according to velocity and position update rules.

Step 3: Update pBest and Leader-Update pbest and leader positions and velocities according to rules.

Step 4: Generate challenger-Generate challengers for challenging leading position of leader of swarm.

Step 5: Evaluating challenger- Evaluate the best challenger for becoming the leader of swarm.

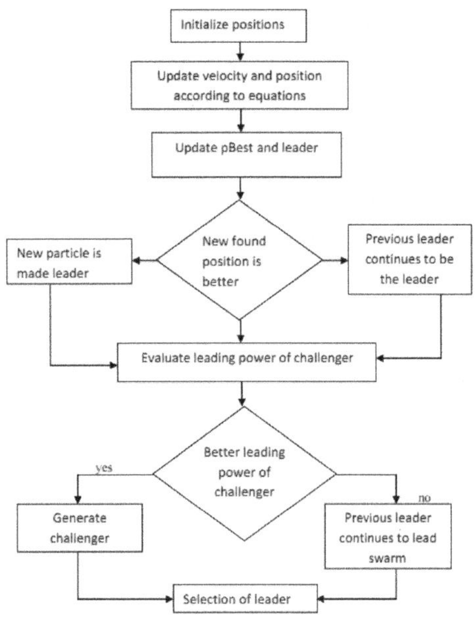

Flowchart: Aging Leader and Challengers.

Generating the Challengers in ALC-PSO

MATLAB tool is used for the process of generating challengers to improve the leading power of the swarm. Six generations of challengers is presented here, with their global values (gbest).

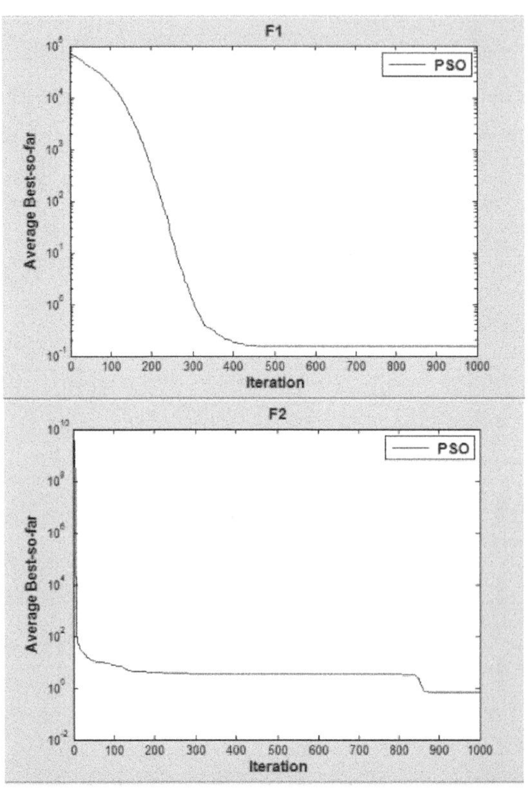

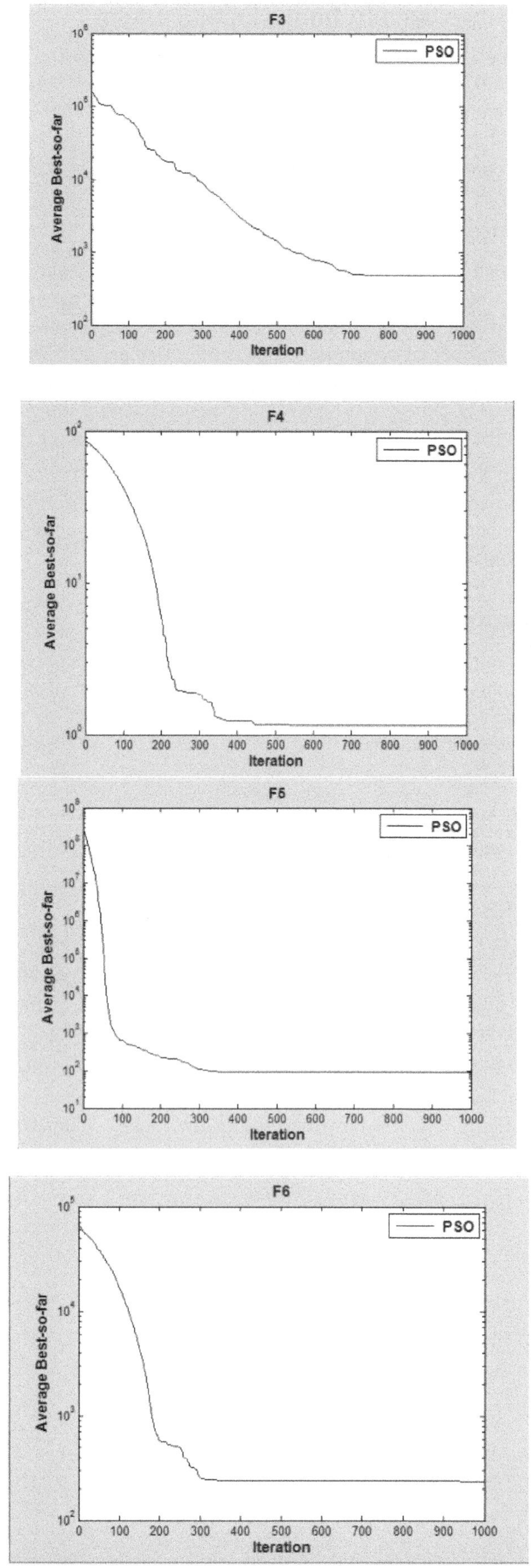

Figure: Generation of Challengers for Leading the Swarm.

Table 2: Results of Finding gbest Value

Sr. No.	Gbest Value
F1	0.0952
F2	0.1508
F3	0.7238
F4	1.1539
F5	91.6671
F6	234

After generating the challengers, the best-suited value for the adjustment factor is decided. Thus the concept of finding a leader using this algorithm, can be used to find out the best value from among the many best values. This best value is made to be the adjustment factor for the image enhancement method.

CONCLUSION AND FUTURE SCOPE

Image processing is an important process which can be used in applications like: image enhancement. The methodology used for image enhancement and has been proposed in this paper. The processing on an image to enhance its quality and to bring out some important information can be done using the optimization techniques. Here, one of the method to for image enhancement is reviewed i.e. Particle Swarm Optimization. One of the shortcoming of using this method is identified to be the fixed value of adjustment factor. This limitation can be removed by using a variant of PSO, called- Particle Swarm Optimization with Aging Leader and Challengers (ALC-PSO) is used. In this algorithm, the concept of finding a new leader for leading the swarm, every time the old leader becomes weak to lead the swarm is used. It can be used to dynamically find the adjustment factor for increasing the performance of Image Enhancement technique. Many other optimization techniques like: Genetic Algorithm can be used for this process in future and other shortcomings in the process of image enhancement can be studied as a future work.

REFERENCES

1. N. Singh, M. Kaur and K. V. P. Singh, "Parameter Optimization In Image Enhancement Using PSO", American Journal of Engineering Research (AJER), e-ISSN: 2320-0847 p-ISSN: 2320-0936, vol. 02, no. 05, pp. 84-90.
2. J. Kennedy and R. C. Eberhart, "Particle swarm optimization", Proc. IEEE Int. Conf. Neural Networks, November-December 15, pp. 152-158.
3. C. Munteanu and A. Rosa, "Gray-scale enhancement as an automatic process driven by evolution", IEEE Transaction on Systems, Man and Cybernatics-Part B:Cybernetics, vol. 34, no. 2, (2004), pp. 1292-1298.
4. S. Jingquan, F. Mengyin and Z. Chanjian, "An image enhancement algorithm based on chaotic optimization", Computer Engineering and Applications, vol. 27, (2003), pp. 4-6.
5. G. Runqiu, L. Junfeng and L. Xiaochun, "The infrared image enhancement and the correlative technique based on the parallel genetic algorithm", XIDIAN Univ. Journal, vol. 31, (2004), pp. 6-8.
6. T. Xiaodong and L. Zhong, "Compare and analysis of enhancement methods of sonar image", Ship Electronics Eng. Journal, vol. 26, (2006), pp. 154-157.
7. X. Su, W. Fang, Q. Shen and X. Hao, "An Image Enhancement Method Using the Quantum-Behaved Particle Swarm Optimization with an Adaptive Strategy", Mathematical Problems in Engineering, (2013).
8. A. Gorai and A. Ghosh, "Gray-level Image Enhancement by Particle Swarm Optimization", World Congress on Nature & Biologically Inspired Computing (NaBIC 2009).
9. A. Kaur and M. Kaur, "Review of Image Processing-Introduction to Image Enhancement Techniques using Particle Swarm Optimization", International Journal of Artificial Intelligence and Applications for Smart Devices, vol. 3, no. 1, (2015), pp. 15-20.

INDEX

O

P

R

S

T

V

W